THE BATTLE FOR BRITAIN

THE BATTLE FOR
BRITAIN

SCOTLAND AND THE INDEPENDENCE REFERENDUM

DAVID TORRANCE

Biteback Publishing

This publication ... published ... by
Westminster ...
... Edinburgh ...

Copyright © David Torrance 2013

David Torrance has asserted his right under the Copyright, Designs and Patents Act 1988 to be identified as the author of this work.

Material from *Arguing for Independence: Evidence, Risks and the Wicked Issues* by Stephen Maxwell (2012) quoted by permission of Luath Press.

Material from *The Break-Up of Britain: Crisis and Neo-Nationalism* by Tom Nairn (2003) quoted by permission of Common Ground Publishing.

Material from *Questioning Sovereignty: Law, State, and Practical Reason* by Neil MacCormick (1999) quoted by permission of Oxford University Press.

Material from *Scotland's Future: The Economics of Constitutional Change* by Andrew Goudie (2013) quoted by permission of Dundee University Press.

Every reasonable effort has been made to trace copyright holders of material reproduced in this book, but if any have been inadvertently overlooked the publishers would be glad to hear from them.

ISBN 978-1-84954-594-5

10 9 8 7 6 5 4 3 2 1

A CIP catalogue record for this book is available from the British Library.

Set in Sabon and Clarendon

Printed and bound in Great Britain by
CPI Group (UK) Ltd, Croydon CR0 4YY

MIX
Paper from
responsible sources
FSC® C020471
www.fsc.org

CONTENTS

Introduction: The Break-Up of Britain? ix

1. The Edinburgh Agreement 1
2. Whither the United Kingdom? 33
3. The Economics of Independence 71
4. Defence and Foreign Affairs 111
5. Welfare and Pensions 154
6. Culture and National Identity 178
7. 'Devo-Max' and Other Options 217
8. Better Together versus Yes Scotland 250
9. Looking Back: Scotland Votes 'No' 297
10. Looking Back: Scotland Votes 'Yes' 310
11. Conclusion: Stands Scotland 322
 Where It Did?

Endnotes 343
Bibliography 357
Index 363

To all sincere (and polite) advocates of either 'independence' or the 'Union' – you'll probably find the solution is somewhere in between.

INTRODUCTION: THE BREAK-UP OF BRITAIN?

To accuse those who support freedom of self-determination, i.e. freedom to secede, of encouraging separatism, is as foolish and hypocritical as accusing those who advocate freedom of divorce of encouraging the destruction of family ties.
Lenin, 'The Right of Nations to Self-Determination' (1914)

It [the UK] might or might not break up. Labour might or might not recover. What the Scots Tories and Liberals might or might not do is anyone's guess. The safest prophecy is that Scottish politics would be complex and unpredictable, and might be rather savage if the hope of universal prosperity as the Kuwait of the North, or as an industrial economy whose problems will miraculously disappear with independence (unlike those of, say, the English north-east), proves unreal. What is pretty certain is that it will be nothing like another Norway.
Eric Hobsbawm, 'Some Reflections on "The Break-Up of Britain"' (1977)

In 1977 – the year I was born – the left-wing writer Tom Nairn published a book (actually a collection of his writing for the *New Left Review*) called *The Break-Up of Britain: Crisis and Neo-Nationalism*. It proved to be an incredibly influential work, not least among a generation of Scottish Nationalists who, that same year, seemed on the cusp of gaining a devolved Scottish Assembly, if not outright independence. 'An independent voice,' gushed *The Observer* of the book's author, 'and an eloquent one.'

Nairn's central thesis was that the state of 'Britain' (or rather the United Kingdom) was in the process of breaking up. Although he was rather vague as to timescale, looking ahead to the 'next century' he concluded it was 'certain that at some point in this period the British regime will finally founder'. This, he argued, was a result of 'capitalist uneven development'; Welsh and Scottish Nationalism, in short, was viewed by the author as an 'escape from the final stages of a shipwreck'.

A lot of the analysis in *The Break-Up of Britain* concerns themes that remain familiar several decades on. Not exactly an out-and-out separatist (a word Nairn did not feel embarrassed to use), he instead advocated 'building up a new, fairer, more federal British order' as opposed to the 'dingy, fearful compromise' of 'devolution', and wrote approvingly of a Scottish National Party (SNP) advancing the 'concept of an Association of British States as the successor to the United Kingdom', preserving what was 'functional' or 'viable' in the Union via 'negotiated agreements among the constituent parts'.

Nairn was dismissive of again familiar-sounding counter-arguments such as 'You could never manage on your own … Surely we're better all together … It's irrelevant to people's real problems' while noting acerbically that the recent debate surrounding the UK's accession to the then European Economic Community demonstrated that 'nationalism' in the 'familiar disparaging sense' was 'by no means confined to the smaller nations'.[1] Nairn's analysis was Marxist, although in a review Eric Hobsbawm felt Nairn needed reminding 'of the basic fact that Marxists as such are not nationalists'.

But while engagingly written and frequently insightful (though Hobsbawm noted 'a tendency to anti-English invective'),[2] Nairn got much wrong. Self-evidently the UK was not about to break up, for when the third edition of *The Break-Up of Britain* appeared in 2003 'Britain' was still very much together, as it remains in the early twenty-first century.

Public support for Scottish independence remains stuck at around a third; in Wales secessionist momentum is virtually non-existent, while in Northern Ireland, where support for the status quo is rising even among its Catholic community, independence – or rather reunification with the South – is less in prospect than at any point since the height of the Troubles.

But then, the UK described by Nairn thirty-six years ago is in important respects very different from today. In 1997/98 the British state opted for the 'dingy, fearful compromise' of devolution to Scotland, Wales and London, and shortly after signed the Good Friday Agreement, demonstrating that even violent, seemingly intractable territorial disputes could be resolved. Nevertheless, Nairn's Britain is at the same time familiar: an electorally popular SNP, devolution and independence debated at length, an economy in crisis, anxiety over immigration, the Queen celebrating her Jubilee and a hung Parliament preoccupied with matters Continental.

All of which serves as a reminder, if one was needed, that in politics there is nothing new under the sun, and particularly so when it comes to the Scottish Question. Indeed, many of the issues discussed in this book have been raked over since the late 1960s, when the SNP first achieved its electoral breakthrough. But this is a new perspective with more up-to-date statistics, anecdotes and, inevitably, prejudices. Its purpose is to explore the greatest challenge facing the famously uncodified British constitution since the early 1920s. Naturally, readers will search for – and even identify – bias. About this there is little I can do. And although what follows may appear to point in one direction (or indeed the other), that was not my intention.

Rather, the starting point of this book is that anything is possible, which is not to say it would be either easy or desirable. At the time of writing it looks likely 'no' will trump 'yes' when Scots go to the polls on 18 September 2014, but I have tried hard not to assume that outcome in the analysis that follows. Too often the independence debate has thrown up large topics for discussion – the role of government, the limits of welfare, or how to square globalisation with aspirations of 'sovereignty' – only to argue about them in small ways. Too much stress has been placed on personalities and transient governments; too little on what used to be called the art of the possible.

So this, essentially a distillation (hopefully a fine-tasting one) of more than a decade writing, thinking and broadcasting about Scottish politics and the independence question, attempts to cut through the noise and get as close as possible to the essence of the current debate. Hopefully, it will also answer the question I often get asked – particularly in London – as to why a sizeable minority of Scots are so intent on pursuing independence. 'It is not at all obvious,' pondered the *Times* columnist Bill Emmott in May 2011,

> except to English nationalists happy to wave the Scots goodbye. Too few opportunities to fly the Saltire, or too weak a sense of national identity? Come off it. Too little autonomy over vital public-policy issues such as health, the law, or education? Hardly. Frustration at not sharing the delights of being a small, peripheral country in the Eurozone, or of not having had responsibility for Fred the Shred and the Royal Bank of Scotland? Er, well, no.[3]

The Scottish debate can be baffling to outsiders, so this book has also been written with non-Scots in mind, and naturally focuses on the SNP's vision of independence. As the former Scottish government minister Bruce Crawford observed in 2012:

> There are of course others with a legitimate view of how an independent Scotland would look. We should respect their views, give them the space to articulate them but make no

mistake. It will be the SNP view that will predominate, and it will be the SNP view that the vast majority of the people will hear.[4]

This book was also written against the backdrop of endless chatter about the UK's future relationship with Europe. At points it all seemed terribly familiar: speculation as to whether there would be a referendum, if so when it would be held, what question it would ask and what precisely its instigators hoped to achieve in constitutional terms. Most of the time – certainly viewed from Westminster – that European debate easily drowned out its Scottish analogue.

The Liberal Democrat MP Charles Kennedy summed it up well in a tweet: 'Amazing that the Conservative and Unionist party still obsesses over a euro ref when the UK itself is under threat from a real ref next year.' The former Tory grandee turned BBC chairman Lord Patten made a similar point at a Press Gallery lunch, expressing surprise that so much time was spent talking about Europe 'and not nearly as much time, indeed hardly any time, talking about the Scottish referendum'.

All the more curious when one remembers that while a Euro referendum is both hypothetical (dependent, among other things, on a Conservative majority in 2015) and some way off, that on Scottish independence is both tangible and fast approaching. Only the outgoing Cabinet Secretary Sir Gus O'Donnell recognised both as 'enormous challenges' in late 2011: 'whether to keep our kingdom united and how to make the EU operate in the best interests of its citizens'.

Both Europe and Scotland have been much discussed in Room 12 of the Parliamentary Press Gallery, where I have spent an enjoyable year masquerading as a lobby correspondent, kept company by Graeme Demianyk (born in Stirling) and Nick Lester (formerly of Falkirk), who listened to me banging on about Scottish politics with unfailing humour and even occasional interest. I should also record my thanks to Sean Bye for letting me bounce thoughts and ideas off him. His perspective as an intelligent outsider was invaluable, while Olivia Beattie at Biteback did a fine job of editing the original typescript.

This book will obviously appear in the midst of a debate that is constantly developing. Scarcely a day goes by without the publication of a report, a (UK or Scottish) government statement or an important piece of commentary. *The Battle for Britain* is not the first word on the subject, nor will it be the last, and therefore I have not been able to comment on anything that appeared after September 2013. Let me conclude with the usual line about any errors of fact or interpretation being my responsibility and mine alone. We all make mistakes, something that is certain not to change even if Scotland becomes independent.

David Torrance
London/Edinburgh
September 2013
www.davidtorrance.com
@davidtorrance

CHAPTER 1

THE EDINBURGH AGREEMENT

It was almost as if Scotland had already become an independent country. Sitting at an unremarkable table in Alex Salmond's equally unremarkable office at St Andrew's House in Edinburgh, David Cameron glanced at his Scottish counterpart before handing over his copy of what became known as the 'Edinburgh Agreement'. The First Minister of Scotland beamed as he added his signature to the document; the Prime Minister of the United Kingdom was more controlled, appearing businesslike rather than pleased. Salmond looked up for the benefit of photographers, Cameron did not. 'Right,' said the latter as both men got to their feet. 'The switch,' he added, almost as if talking himself through the agreed sequence of events. The two men then exchanged their copies – printed on neutral beige paper – of the Agreement. Finally, they shook hands as the Prime Minister murmured 'there we are', and photographers snapped away.

After more than a year of political shadow boxing they had agreed that Scots would vote on independence in a referendum to be held by the end of 2014. But the symbolism was obvious. 'Scotland is already looking and feeling like an independent nation,' noted one of Salmond's advisers. '[This] sets a template for the relationship that would exist after independence.' Constitutionally the more senior of the two, Cameron had travelled to Edinburgh rather than summon Salmond to London, while the exchange of signatures took place in front of a predominantly yellow map of Scotland. The yellow, although it was not immediately obvious, denoted constituencies won by the Scottish National Party in the Scottish Parliament elections of May 2011.[1]

It was that triumph, that overall SNP majority in a parliament designed to prevent one party dominating, which had brought the two politicians together on 15 October 2012, a crisp, clear autumn's day. It had begun with the First Minister at a school in Edinburgh (reading from the children's book *We're Going on a Bear Hunt*)[2] and the Prime Minister visiting the Rosyth dockyard with the none-too-subtle backdrop of a half-constructed aircraft carrier ('this is a success story that the whole of the United Kingdom can take great pride in'). Later they met, as two leaders within one kingdom, at the entrance to St Andrew's House, an imposing 1930s edifice which used to house the old Scottish Office. Aptly, one of the allegorical figures above its large brass doors is called 'State Craft', depicting a male figure holding open a scroll with both hands.

But the day did not feel statesmanlike, or particularly historic. As the Prime and First Ministers shook hands for the assembled media there were no demonstrations or banners, just barriers and police officers, while a lone voice yelled, slightly incoherently: 'Vote yes for independence, Mr Cameron.' Some of those present in Alex Salmond's fifth-floor office remembered him being uncharacteristically 'low-key', perhaps because his advisers had told him not to look triumphalist. 'We didn't regard this as a treaty, a summit or anything else; we were simply doing a deal to transfer power,' recalled a Whitehall adviser. 'The Prime Minister's role was also businesslike, he didn't stick around.'[3]

Although Salmond was deferential to inter-governmental protocol, this courtesy did not always extend to the Prime Minister ('So what drove the Camerons out of Scotland?' the First Minister once asked him nonchalantly, a barbed reference to Cameron's Scottish ancestry).[4] Nevertheless there was a degree of mutual respect. Both men were smart operators, shrewd tacticians who revelled in their political status if not the philosophy and nitty-gritty of politics. They had much in common, despite being separated by age and class, an Old (but at the same time younger) Etonian pitched against a product of Linlithgow High School. One of the first things Cameron had done on becoming Prime Minister in 2010 had been to visit Salmond in Edinburgh as part of his so-called 'respect agenda', while inside Downing Street the First Minister was generally held in high regard as a political operator.

Despite Westminster reluctance, the Scottish government had been keen to big up the significance of the event. Its website later referred to the signing as 'ratification' of the Agreement (Salmond called it an 'accord'), which imbued an essentially political agreement with a legal status it did not possess.[5] It did, of course, have legal and political ramifications, not least a commitment by the UK government to promote an Order in Council under Section 30 of the Scotland Act 1998, the legislation that had established the devolved Scottish Parliament. Although that parliament – housed in a controversial new building at Holyrood since 2004 – had wide-ranging powers, the ability to hold a referendum on independence was not among them.

But a Section 30 Order would temporarily grant the Scottish government that power, subject to a majority vote by Members of the Scottish Parliament (MSPs). Of course there were caveats: it was to be a single-question referendum, rather than the two-question ballot Salmond had often hinted at, and the question would have to be put by the end of 2014. (The UK government considered the temporary nature of these powers crucial, there existing a genuine fear that Holyrood might try to hold further referendums, for example following an election victory in May 2016). Constitutional lawyers had spent years speculating over what would happen were the Scottish government to hold an *ultra vires* poll, but a Section 30 Order, asserted the text of the Agreement, would put that 'beyond doubt'.

Otherwise, the UK and Scottish governments agreed the referendum should:

- have a clear base;
- be legislated for by the Scottish Parliament;
- be conducted so as to command the confidence of parliaments, government and people; and
- deliver a fair test and decisive expression of the views of people in Scotland and a result that everyone would respect.

It thus fell to the Scottish government to place a Referendum Bill before the Scottish Parliament, which the Agreement stipulated ought to 'meet the highest standards of fairness, transparency and propriety, informed by consultation and independent expert advice'. In particular, the legislation would set out:

- the date of the referendum;
- the franchise;
- the wording of the question;
- rules on campaign financing; and
- other rules for the conduct of the referendum.[6]

This, although it was not spelled out in the short text of the Agreement, meant the Scottish government could set the date of the referendum (provided it took place before the end of 2014), extend the franchise to sixteen- and seventeen-year-olds (a long-standing SNP, and indeed Liberal Democrat, pledge), decide the wording of the question (subject to Electoral Commission approval) and stipulate campaign financing (again, subject to EC oversight). Usefully, the fact that both governments had ceded some ground allowed both to claim victory; in reality, it was a political draw.

Nationalists later placed great emphasis on paragraph 30 of the Agreement, headed 'Co-operation', the final sentence of which read: 'The two governments are committed to continue to work together constructively in the light of the outcome, whatever it is, in the best interests of the people of Scotland and of the rest of the United Kingdom.'[7] Although the UK government considered this innocuous, their Scottish counterparts imbued it with greater significance, convinced it meant Westminster could neither 'scaremonger' against independence nor obstruct its progress should there be a 'yes' vote. Advisers at Westminster, meanwhile, dismissed this reading of paragraph 30 as 'absurd'.

Two other signatories to the Agreement had been notable players in the political drama thus far: the then Secretary of State for Scotland, Liberal Democrat MP Michael Moore, and Nicola Sturgeon, who, as Deputy First Minister of Scotland, had concluded the referendum negotiations just days before Salmond and David Cameron put pen to paper.[8] Once that was done, the Prime Minister gave brief television interviews on the roof of St Andrew's House before heading back to London without even acknowledging reporters gathered outside. His aides claimed this was to avoid hogging the limelight. 'The First Minister wants to attract as much attention as possible,' one UK government source said. 'We just want to bomb him with reasonableness.' Another official put it more cynically: 'We had given them just enough rope to hang themselves.'[9]

Reporters from all over the world had descended upon Edinburgh, no doubt intrigued by the novelty of the occasion. CNN referred to the referendum taking place 700 years after 'William Wallace died for Scottish independence', while the *Washington Post* said the vote 'sets up the possibility that Washington's closest strategic ally could be torn asunder'. Closer to home, the *Herald* newspaper dubbed it 'A DATE WITH DESTINY', while the *Scottish Sun* read simply: 'SHAKE OR BREAK TIME.'

'I want to be the Prime Minister that keeps the United Kingdom together,' Cameron told the BBC, betraying an understandable fear of becoming a 21st-century version of Lord North, who had lost the American colonies in 1776. 'The people of Scotland voted for a party that wanted to have a referendum on independence. I've made sure – showing respect – that we can have that referendum in a way that is decisive, that is legal, that is fair.' The Prime Minister even mimicked Salmond's populist rhetoric by claiming the deal had delivered 'the people's referendum'.

With that, he was off, leaving Salmond and his deputy, Nicola Sturgeon, to face the media in the bowels of St Andrew's House, where the Scottish government had been free to indulge itself with a couple of huge Saltires. The Agreement, Salmond told reporters, paved the way 'for the most important decision our country of Scotland has made in several hundred years'. When the BBC's political editor, Nick Robinson, asked why, after a summer in which Andy Murray and Sir Chris Hoy had wrapped themselves in the Union flag, he wanted to rip it up, Salmond replied with a smile: 'I don't want to rip anything, we're not in the business of ripping things up. We're in the business of developing a new relationship between the peoples of these islands; I think a more beneficial, independent and equal relationship – that's what we're about.'

Later, Salmond said the Agreement marked a 'significant step in Scotland's Home Rule journey', an interesting turn of phrase which summed up his gradualist approach to constitutional change. 'The Scottish government has an ambitious vision for Scotland,' he added, 'a prosperous and successful European country, reflecting Scottish values of fairness and opportunity, promoting equality and social cohesion. A Scotland with a new place in the world – as an independent nation.'

But despite the fine words, at this point – indeed, at every point in the process – Salmond was acutely aware independence was not the settled will of the Scottish people, only around a third of whom consistently told pollsters they would vote 'yes' in the autumn of 2014. Writing in *The Scotsman* the following day, Stephen Noon, the 'yes' campaign's chief strategist, cryptically remarked that 'detailed research' showed that opinion polls did 'not adequately reflect' where Scottish opinion was. 'For many who today say No,' he said, 'a more appropriate description would be not proven.'[10]

Nevertheless, the pan-Scottish jury was still out and smart political tactics required a recalibration of how independence was presented to the electorate. 'My passion has never been to cross some imaginary constitutional finishing line and think the race is won,' wrote Salmond, a little disingenuously, in *The Guardian* a few days later. 'My aim now, as it always has been, is to deliver a better and fairer society for the people of Scotland. *It happens that independence is the way to do this*' [my italics]. Key to this 'better and fairer society' was what the First Minister called Scotland's 'social contract', 'which has delivered universal benefits such as free university education and personal care for our elderly'; a contract he claimed was 'now threatened by both Labour and the Tories'. Only a 'yes' vote, therefore, could 'properly protect these gains'.

So welfare, then being reformed by the coalition government with partial support from the Labour Party, was – in the SNP's eyes – a key battleground in the independence debate. David Cameron, on the other hand, argued that UK-wide institutions like social security bound the nations and regions of the UK closely together. 'This marks the beginning of an important chapter in Scotland's story and allows the real debate to begin,' he said shortly before the Agreement was signed. 'It paves the way so that the biggest question of all can be settled: a separate Scotland or a United Kingdom? I will be making a very positive argument for our United Kingdom.'

Despite his relatively low-key presence in Edinburgh that day, the Prime Minister was quietly confident he had done the right thing by intervening in the Scottish debate and forcing – as the UK government saw it – Mr Salmond's hand, compelling him to stop dragging his feet and name the day. Until that point the SNP leader had appeared invincible. Despite the absence of any groundswell in support for independence, the First Minister's sheer force of personality and his unparalleled success in winning an overall majority at the 2011 Holyrood election had created the sense that anything was possible.

Still, while both leaders had handled the initial skirmishes well, this had only been the beginning. The phoney battle for Britain was over; now, with the completion of the Edinburgh Agreement, the real fight had begun – and the stakes could not be higher. 'The game's changing in this all the time,' Salmond told an interviewer that evening, 'and I think the game will change in favour of the "yes" campaign.'

'A change is coming, and the people are ready'

The game had begun more than a year earlier when, against all the odds, the SNP had won a remarkable 45.4 per cent of the constituency vote (to Labour's 31.7 per cent), and 44 per cent of the PR regional list (to Labour's 26.3 per cent) in the fourth elections to the Scottish Parliament in Edinburgh. This gave the SNP sixty-nine seats to Labour's thirty-seven, and thus an overall majority. Not only was this impressive, it was supposed to be electorally impossible.

It was an all-time high for the SNP in electoral terms, and therefore easy for Nationalists to interpret as indicating growing support for independence. As the playwright David Greig put it, 'If the Union between Scotland and England has been a marriage, then the Holyrood election was like the moment when the wife looks at her husband and realises – suddenly and clearly – that it's over.' The result, however, actually had relatively little to do with independence, the party's *raison d'être* since its formation in 1934. Historically, support for this among Scots voters had hovered around a third, and in 2011 remained at that level, perhaps even lower according to some opinion polls.

Rather, it was a perception of 'competence' (and indeed the incompetence of the possible alternatives) that had attracted voters to the SNP in record numbers. Alex Salmond had run an attractive, upbeat campaign on the basis of 'team, record, vision', and had been rewarded handsomely. But a post-election study revealed the 'vision' part of that vote-winning triumvirate was actually the least popular. It put support for independence at just 24 per cent, with the status quo and 'more powers' (of which more later) tied on 38 per cent.[11] Forty-five per cent of voting Scots might have backed the SNP to run a devolved government, but between a quarter and a third of those had no intention of supporting independence in a referendum.

Despite a high media profile during a six-week election campaign, turnout in the 2011 Holyrood election was just 50.4 per cent, which meant the SNP's overall majority was derived from just 22.5 per cent of the electorate. No one, of course, suggested Salmond did not have a mandate to govern, but it demonstrated that enthusiasm for political engagement in general, and independence in particular, was relatively low, and certainly no higher than it had been since the 1990s.

The gap between support for the SNP and support for its core aim was partly of the party's own making. Conscious that 'independence' might actually be preventing the party from increasing its representation within a devolved Scottish Parliament, in 2000 it adopted the then new policy of a referendum. Until that point the SNP had maintained that a majority of Scottish seats at Westminster or in the Edinburgh Parliament would be enough to begin independence negotiations; now it argued Scots should have a direct – and separate – say via the ballot box.

This was a conscious effort to neutralise the independence issue by indicating to members that the party still believed in independence (many believed Salmond was nothing more than a devolutionist), while sending a signal to voters that they could support the SNP without necessarily breaking up the UK. And although this strategy took time, it eventually produced results. By 2007 a Labour–Liberal Democrat coalition had governed Scotland (in what was known as the 'Scottish Executive') for eight years, but there were signs voters were bored with the status quo and believed Alex Salmond – who had been re-elected SNP leader in 2004 after a four-year hiatus – should have a chance at being First Minister. With one seat more than Labour, he formed a minority administration that appeared to capture the zeit-geist with a combination of upbeat rhetoric, populist policies and 'standing up for Scotland'. It also pursued independence by stealth, renaming the Scottish Executive the 'Scottish government' and generally conducting itself as if Scotland were already an independent nation.

Once the SNP had demonstrated it *could* govern responsibly, went Nationalist reasoning, then support for independence would increase. Only, that strategy did not work. If anything, Salmond and his party became victims of their own success: they pushed the devolution settlement to its limits and generally kept Scots happy. But having successfully 'stood up' for Scotland within the UK, it seemed as if most Scots saw no need to push that to its logical conclusion. More powers, perhaps, but not full independence. As the poet John Dryden put it, 'Even victors are by victories undone.'

And being in a minority, during the 2007–11 Scottish parliament the SNP had to rely upon other parties for backing; budgets and other legislation were able to pass with

Scottish Conservative support, something the SNP later chose to forget as it relentlessly attacked the Labour Party for campaigning 'in cahoots with' the Tories against independence. Meanwhile the SNP went through the motions of legislating for an independence referendum without ever actually introducing a Bill. Not only were there not enough votes in Parliament (the Liberal Democrats had refused to coalesce with the SNP if it insisted on holding a ballot), but there was still a very large question mark hanging over the legality of such a move, for the 1998 Scotland Act had specifically reserved responsibility for 'the constitution' to the Westminster Parliament.

Labour, still traumatised by the election result, detected the SNP's unease. In the spring of 2008 the then Scottish Labour leader, Wendy Alexander, a protégée of the late Donald Dewar, cried 'bring it on' during a television interview. The pitch was that if the SNP were serious about having a referendum then the main opposition party would back legislation allowing that to happen. At least, that was the plan. Although Labour MSPs generally held the line, when asked about it during Prime Minister's Questions at Westminster, Gordon Brown prevaricated. Already weakened by allegations over donations to her leadership campaign, Alexander quit as leader a few weeks later. But her instinct on this had been sound (indeed, the UK government's strategy after 2012 could be viewed as Wendy Alexander for slow learners). With the economy beginning to fray and the SNP still getting to grips with government, had she pulled it off then Alex Salmond would have been left arguing *against* holding an independence referendum.

Instead, the Scottish government held a 'national conversation' on its constitutional plans and published several papers defining, and indeed redefining, the meaning of 'independence'. The Referendum Bill had several relaunches – with the question 'I agree that the Scottish government should negotiate a settlement with the government of the United Kingdom so that Scotland becomes an independent state'[12] – but by late 2010 the date by which it had to be formally introduced in order to stand any chance of becoming law had come and gone. The First Minister argued that as it would not attract majority support he planned to take his case to the country rather than let it fall in the Scottish Parliament. This did not quite make sense, for even if the SNP once again became the largest party it would still lack the necessary votes. No one, not even the leader of the SNP, expected to win an overall majority.

But win one he did, and that – ironically – put the Nationalists in a bit of a bind. To an extent, the dynamic of a Unionist majority blocking an independence referendum had been a good one for the SNP, but now the electorate had removed it. Ever cautious, Salmond had shifted ground several times during the 2011 Holyrood election campaign, eventually pledging that a referendum would not be held until the 'second half' of the next, five-year-long, session, while just days before polling day he let it be known that it would be later still, 'well into' the second part of that term.

But now there existed no parliamentary barrier to a referendum, Salmond looked as if he was kicking it into the long grass. In other words, the party's position had moved from believing that when it did not have a majority (2007–11) there ought to have been a referendum, but now it did have overall control of Parliament, there was no rush. The First Minister claimed his immediate priorities were jobs and the economy, while reminding interviewers of the pledge he had made during the election campaign. This promise, however, had not actually appeared in the SNP's manifesto. Rather delphically, this promised a ballot on 'full economic powers' rather than independence, and made no mention of it being in the second half of that parliamentary session.[13] Meanwhile, in the wake of the election there was an internal debate as to whether to proceed with a referendum at all. Ducking the issue, however, was not a credible option: it was too far advanced, and there was a general expectation the SNP would deliver, not least among party activists.

Despite these reservations, just days after the election Salmond asserted that 'the destination of independence' was 'more or less inevitable',[14] but in reality – particularly given the distraction of government – little serious thinking had been done on the meaning of 'independence' in more than two decades. Delaying the referendum until 2014 or 2015, therefore, gave Salmond much-needed breathing space to do precisely that. Within a week of the election senior SNP figures floated the concept of 'independence-lite', whereby Scotland would assume full economic sovereignty but 'pool' areas such as defence and foreign affairs with the UK government. This 'thinking on independence', claimed a spokesman, was 'modern and forward looking', unlike 'old-fashioned and backward looking' Unionism.

'A change is coming, and the people are ready,' Alex Salmond told MSPs in his first speech after the May landslide.

> Whatever changes take place in our constitution, we will remain close to our neighbours. We will continue to share a landmass, a language and a wealth of experience and history with the other peoples of these islands. My dearest wish is to see the countries of Scotland and England stand together as equals.

'There is a difference between partnership and subordination,' he added with uncharacteristic touchiness. 'The first encourages mutual respect. The second breeds resentment.'

But any cursory reading of Salmond's speeches, and indeed Scottish government publications between 2007 and 2011, revealed that 'partnership' was no longer the same as independence. As well as floating concepts like 'independence-lite', Salmond and others repeatedly stressed how relaxed they would be with a referendum question on a scheme that fell short of full independence. 'Politics in stable democracies involves shadings rather than absolutes,' observed Professor James Mitchell, a close follower of SNP thinking. 'Shocking as it may be for some, we may be looking towards a future in which accommodation is found between union and independence.'[15]

The *ancien régime* at Westminster, meanwhile, had clearly been caught off guard by the scale of the SNP's election victory and its likely consequences. Days after the election the Prime Minister told MPs:

> Everyone in this House who believes in the future of the United Kingdom should join together and make sure that we fight off the threat of the idea of breaking up our United Kingdom. I believe the way that we'll make that argument is by saying being part of the United Kingdom is good for Scotland, and Scotland being part of the United Kingdom is good for the rest of the United Kingdom.

This was vague, to say the least, and it took until the autumn of 2011 before the coalition's 'Quad' (the Cabinet inner circle comprising Cameron, George Osborne, Nick Clegg and Danny Alexander) agreed a 'shift in gear' on the independence issue. A key figure in this respect was the red-haired Chief Secretary to the Treasury, whom one insider regarded as the 'de facto Secretary of State for Scotland'. '[Michael] Moore just doesn't have his link with Clegg,' he said. 'Nothing happens on Scotland without going past Danny.'[16] That dynamic, however, later changed, while the Advocate General, Lord Wallace (a former Deputy First Minister of Scotland), was also influential as the UK government planned its response. More generally, observed an adviser, No. 10 had at least 'finally sat up and noticed Scotland existed'.[17]

There were also Unionist voices – mainly the noble Lords Foulkes (a former Labour minister) and Forsyth (the last Conservative Scottish Secretary) – urging the UK government to 'call Salmond's bluff' by holding its own independence referendum. This proposal seemed to split the Scotland Office, part of what Westminster presented as one of Scotland's 'two governments', between Michael Moore (who was anti) and his Tory deputy David Mundell (who was broadly pro). As a Liberal Democrat adviser put it, 'We're much more cautious than the Tories; they're quite bloody minded about the whole thing and just want to get on with it.'[18] As for more powers, in October 2011 the Prime Minister said the Scotland Bill (see Chapter 7) – then making its way through Parliament – ought 'to settle the issue for a generation or longer. Scotland needs to move on from the constant constitutional debate.'

That was undoubtedly the Prime Minister's sincere belief as 2011 drew to a close, but with Alex Salmond still apparently unstoppable – whatever the reality of public opinion on independence – Cameron must have realised the status quo, even a status quo with more powers to come, was not an option. Although progressive elements within the Conservative Party had long ploughed a lonely furrow on 'fiscal autonomy', mainstream party opinion was hostile. Labour was also split internally, between those who wanted to devolve more powers and those who regarded that as 'appeasing' the Nationalists. Even the Liberal Democrats, ostensibly a federalist party, initially appeared reticent about advocating more devolution for Scotland.

Others naturally filled the vacuum: the Edinburgh-based think tank Reform Scotland gradually built the case for what it called 'devolution plus' (or devo+), which involved the devolution of income tax and certain aspects of welfare with the aim of making the Scottish Parliament 'responsible' for raising revenue as well as spending it. Curiously, Salmond became a more enthusiastic proponent of this 'third way' than any Unionist, even telling his 2011 party conference that 'fiscal responsibility, financial freedom, real economic powers is a legitimate proposal'. He repeatedly challenged the three Unionist parties to define a 'more powers' option that might form a second question on the referendum ballot paper.

They, of course, refused to be drawn, although the UK government had begun thinking seriously about enabling a referendum by legislative means. While Michael Moore had swiftly conceded the Scottish government's mandate to hold a ballot in the wake of 'Thistlenacht' (as one Westminster aide called the 2011 election result), the UK government had subsequently made clear that the constitutional power to do so lay in London rather than Edinburgh. Playing hardball on this point, however, would have achieved little, while a Westminster-backed poll would simply have been boycotted by the SNP and thus rendered useless.

This had happened during the first major referendum to be held in the UK, the Northern Ireland 'Border Poll' of 8 March 1973, a precedent much discussed at Downing Street during 2012 given that Ciaran Martin (lead official negotiator during the Edinburgh Agreement) hailed from the six counties. This had given voters a straight choice:

'Do you want Northern Ireland to remain part of the United Kingdom?'
    or
'Do you want Northern Ireland to be joined with the Republic of Ireland outside the United Kingdom?'

It was clearly contrived to consolidate the Union rather than settle the issue, something that led to a Nationalist boycott, while the Alliance Party expressed fears that it could become a 'sectarian head count'. This obstruction worked, contributing to a turnout of only 58.7 per cent of Northern Ireland's electorate, 98.9 per cent of whom opted to remain part of the UK (just 1.1 per cent voted to join the Republic).

However flawed the process, the Northern Ireland 'sovereignty referendum' had established the principle of 'self-determination' for distinct parts of the UK. It also represented a break with tradition in terms of British democracy, which had always regarded referendums as inappropriate given the 'sovereign' status of the Westminster parliament. But two years after voters in Northern Ireland were given a vote on leaving the UK, voters nationwide were given a vote on leaving what later became the European Union ('Do you think the UK should stay in the European Community (Common Market)?'). In 1979 voters in Scotland and Wales were consulted on plans for devolved assemblies,[19] as they were again – following a referendum-free period of nearly two decades – in 1997, along with London in 1998 and Northern Ireland (on the Good Friday peace agreement) the same year.

Thus the concept of a territorial referendum, even on the potential secession of one part of the UK, was nothing new, and it was certainly no longer regarded as 'foreign' to the Westminster system of government. Dr Matt Qvortrup calculated that since Texas, Tennessee and Virginia had voted on secession from the United States in 1861, forty-nine independence referendums had occurred around the world, generally coming in waves, for example in the wake of the Second World War and following the collapse of the Soviet Union.[20] In a UK context, referendums remained relatively novel, although a 2009 paper from the House of Lords Constitutional Committee regretted 'the ad hoc manner in which referendums have been used, often as a tactical device, by the government of the day'.[21] And so it proved with that on Scottish independence. When the Advocate General for Scotland, Lord Wallace of Tankerness, produced a list of possible options for the UK government, it included a Section 30 Order (under the 1998 Scotland Act), which he remembered being used to transfer responsibility for railways to the Scottish Parliament in 2005 when he had been Deputy First Minister of Scotland. The plan, however, took a while to fully germinate. The Constitution Unit at UCL, meanwhile, pushed the idea of holding two referendums – one on the principle of independence, another on a negotiated deal – although this struggled to gain traction despite the (fleeting) support of the Scottish Secretary. For its part, the Scottish government argued that the concept of a 'legally binding' referendum was a red herring, all such UK polls being advisory in nature. Otherwise, it dismissed reports of UK government plans as 'sabre rattling', which would – along with 'scaremongering' – become a favoured riposte to initiatives emanating from Westminster.

'It's now clear the referendum won't happen before the next general election unless we hold it ourselves or enable the Scottish government to do so with certain conditions,' a minister told me in November 2011. 'We can do that by amending the Scotland Bill [which was still making its way through Parliament] or under a Section 30 Order.'[22] Michael Moore had already opted for, and consistently advocated, the latter option, keen to finally close down Conservative attempts to hold a UK government-organised referendum. This was agreed and signed off by the Quad. 'It was considered the most reasonable way forward,' recalled a senior source, 'but we still didn't think they would accept it.'[23] The intention, meanwhile, was to announce the move in the second week of January 2012.

At least that was the plan. When journalists began to get wind of the UK government's intentions (both BBC Scotland and *The Herald* ran stories alluding to a Section 30 Order), advisers realised they 'had to move it on', and incredibly quickly at that. 'The time between the plan being agreed and announced,' recalled one official, 'was a matter of days.'[24] So on 7 January 2012, with Parliament still in recess, the Prime Minister took his place on the *Andrew Marr Show* sofa. 'We owe the Scottish people something that is fair, legal and decisive,' he told the show's presenter, 'so in the coming days we will be setting out clearly what the legal situation is.' He continued:

> The uncertainty about this issue is damaging to Scotland and Scotland's economy. And ... it is unfair on the Scottish people themselves, who don't really know when this question is going to be asked, what the question is going to be, who's responsible for asking it. I don't think we should just let this go on year after year. I think that's damaging for everyone concerned, so let's clear up the legal situation and then have a debate about how we bring this to a conclusion. My view is that sooner rather than later would be better.

The clear implication was that if Holyrood did not get a move on, then Westminster would, a position at odds with what coalition ministers had actually agreed. Coincidentally, senior SNP figures were holding a strategy meeting in Aberdeen as Cameron's interview went on air. 'Right slap bang in the middle of it David Cameron decided to telegraph his intentions,' recalled the SNP MP Angus Robertson. 'We were therefore in a position to plan our response immediately.'

The public line, however, sounded a little defensive. 'The Scottish government achieved an overwhelming mandate from the people of Scotland to hold the referendum in the second half of this parliamentary term,' protested Salmond's official spokesman, 'and that is exactly what we will do.' 'We're going to do what we said we'd do before the election,' quipped Deputy First Minister Nicola Sturgeon on the *Today* programme. 'I know that's a novel concept in England.'

Privately, however, the Scottish government was relieved. Although it had been ready to launch its own referendum consultation late the previous October, Salmond and Sturgeon had held back because they knew it would spark a prolonged legal row as to whether they had the power to stage a ballot at all. Officials had produced a form of words – which talked about transferring more powers to the Scottish Parliament rather than independence – they believed could get round the legal barrier, but it was so contrived it was likely to fall foul of any Electoral Commission scrutiny, which was why the Scottish government had proposed using its own *ad hoc* referendum commission to oversee the process. This was not, in short, a sustainable position.

But then there had been an exaggerated sense among UK ministers during the second half of 2011 that Salmond was wily and unpredictable, and a related suspicion that he was constantly on the verge of pulling a stunt. Westminster advisers thought the First Minister might announce something in a Hugo Young Memorial Lecture planned for late January, while a Tory minister confessed to a 'nervousness' that if Salmond got wind of the UK government's plans then 'he would trump it, as he's always been good at doing'.[25] This unease, however, was misplaced. At one meeting with David Cameron the First Minister even joked: 'If we can't agree on this then we'll see you in court.' But, as one of his advisers admitted, 'we didn't mean that, and it seemed obvious to us we couldn't win a court battle over the legality of the referendum'.[26]

The day after Cameron's *Marr* interview the Attorney General, Solicitor General and Scotland's Advocate General attended a special Cabinet meeting at London's Olympic Park at which they confirmed a Scottish Parliament-sponsored referendum would be unlawful, while on Tuesday 10 January Michael Moore announced a three-month consultation on a single-question referendum to the House of Commons. He insisted the move was designed to be 'helpful', using deliberately conciliatory language and explicitly ruling out any suggestion the UK government might hold its own referendum, which of course Cameron had hinted at in his *Marr* interview. 'The PM went off a bit half-cocked on Sunday,' confessed a Whitehall source with considerable understatement. 'There was some mopping up to be done.' Nevertheless, Moore made it clear that if Salmond tried to stage his own referendum (without a Section 30 Order) then the UK government, or a private citizen, could apply to have it struck down by the UK Supreme Court.

Initially, as was his habit, the First Minister went to ground, refusing to give interviews from his Aberdeenshire East constituency. And when Salmond did surface, he came out fighting. A Section 30 Order, he said, was nothing more than a 'smokescreen' for Westminster 'trying to pull the strings' of the referendum (although, confusingly, he also said he had 'no objection' to its possible use); the UK government were 'control freaks', while the Prime Minister ought to 'keep his nose out of Scottish business'. The general aim was to depict Cameron as the worst sort of patronising 'anti-Scottish' Tory. 'They think', blogged the SNP strategist Stephen Noon, 'they can treat us as though we were their Eton fag.'[27]

Then, on the evening of Tuesday 10 January 2012, Salmond dropped his own bombshell, informing Sky News as he left a Scottish government Cabinet meeting that the referendum would be held in the 'autumn' of 2014. The First Minister had earlier dismissed as 'stuff and nonsense' the suggestion it would coincide with the 700th anniversary of the Battle of Bannockburn (on 24 June); instead autumn 2014 was a date (or rather season) that would allow 'the Scottish people to hear all the arguments' as well as giving enough time for all the 'necessary legislation' to be passed. 'This has to be a referendum which is built in Scotland,' Salmond told Sky News, 'which is made in Scotland and goes through the Scottish Parliament.' By announcing the date as Michael Moore outlined his consultation in the House of Commons, Salmond had reclaimed both the media and the political initiative from Westminster. 'Alex announcing the date in that manner', recalled an aide, 'was designed to show that it was up to us, not the UK government.'[28] Ministers and officials in London, meanwhile, were not amused.

Salmond's move also effectively bounced the UK government into accepting its timescale (it had been pushing for a ballot by late 2013) and, although initially annoyed, many came to support the 2014 timing, not least because it gave the Unionist parties, as one MP put it, 'two and a half years to get our act together'. And by naming the season (if not an actual date), Salmond had also ensured any Westminster-initiated referendum was now near impossible. UK advisers, however, insisted it was 'still an option', 'in our back pocket' in the event of the First Minister 'buggering about'.[29] Similarly, SNP advisers held out the prospect of the Scottish government holding a referendum solely on greater powers, 'which we'd sell on the basis of the UK government playing funny buggers about taking us to court'.[30]

A lot of buggering about, meanwhile, concerned the possibility of a second question, which, as the BBC journalist James Naughtie observed, was rather ironic:

> Michael Moore ... says there should – must – be a straight yes/no question on independence on the referendum ballot paper, though he and his party are historically committed to the increase of powers for the Edinburgh parliament within the UK known as 'devo max'. And Alex Salmond, Nationalist and First Minister, whose party regards that option as a false kind of non-independence, says it must be offered as an alternative because many Scots might want to choose it. Work that one out.[31]

The former Labour Chancellor Alistair Darling, meanwhile, began to emerge as the likely leader of any 'no' campaign, although at this point he denied any such ambition ('I'll play my part in it but I hope that others will too'). But there *was* a degree of cross-party consensus. At Prime Minister's Questions on 11 January David Cameron said he was '100 per cent' in agreement with the opposition leader, Ed Miliband, that the UK was 'stronger together and weaker apart' (a phrase that hinted at the eventual campaigning title of 'Better Together'), adding that he believed 'passionately' in the future 'of our United Kingdom'. The First Minister, however, had a dire warning for the Labour Party. If it chose to co-operate with the Conservatives to fight independence, he said, then the Tories would 'suck you in and they'll spit you out as they've done to the Liberal Democrats'.

Alex Salmond discussed his referendum plans with the Deputy Prime Minister (and Lib Dem leader), Nick Clegg, at the British–Irish Council in Dublin the following day. His tone was more constructive, and he made it clear he was 'very happy' to meet either the Prime Minister or his deputy 'to talk through these things in a positive way'. Downing Street, however, said it expected the First Minister to meet the Scottish Secretary in the first instance, not a figure Salmond held in high regard. Also in Dublin were the Northern Irish First Minister, Peter Robinson, and his deputy, Martin McGuinness. 'Peter Robinson and I have a castle in Belfast,' joked the latter. 'I am sure we would be prepared to make it available for peace talks.'

Both sides stressed how terribly 'reasonable' they were being. As a UK government adviser put it, 'Our approach throughout has been to be "reasonable". A Section 30 Order looks very reasonable; we're trying to achieve for them what they promised to deliver, no more, no less.'[32] One Scottish government adviser, meanwhile, said the SNP were 'much more reasonable than everyone gives us credit for', referencing the Good Friday Agreement as 'hugely influential' to SNP thinking. 'Our view is that if you don't have a process everyone accepts as legitimate then it's no use.' He then sketched out a fantasy Salmond–Cameron summit across the Irish Sea:

> The Prime Minister should set aside some time to think about this properly. If he then met Alex privately at a hotel in the west of Ireland, they could reach a deal. If retaining the premiership, world stature and seat at the UN is so important [to the PM], they could thrash something out. We get what we want [devo-max] and Cameron is written up by historians as the man who saved the UK, got his party re-elected, and radically redrew the constitution. We'd compromise so the House of Commons became an English parliament; we'd even send peers to a reconstituted Upper House which would deal with defence and so on … there would be statues of David Cameron on George Street.[33]

The public stance, of course, looked somewhat different, and the only statues in sight were up at Edinburgh Castle, where the Scottish government prepared to launch its own referendum consultation on 25 January – Burns Night. Revealingly, this appeared to concede that a Section 30 Order (it referred to 'an adjustment of legislative competence') would be necessary to pose its preferred question, 'Do you agree Scotland should be an independent country?',[34] although the public position remained that ministers could hold an 'advisory' referendum on anything they desired.

Several experts pronounced the question loaded or biased, particularly the word 'agree', while Alistair Darling highlighted the fact that it made no mention of Scotland actually *leaving* the UK. 'It is asking for trouble', added Darling, 'and if he tries to push through unfair wording someone will go to court.' When the BBC's Andrew Marr challenged Salmond on this point, he argued that as SNP policy was to retain the monarchy, then 'that union, that United Kingdom if you like, would be maintained after Scottish political independence',[35] and therefore could not reasonably form part of the referendum question.

Also marshalling its forces was a short-lived umbrella group called 'Future of Scotland', a loose coalition of 'civic' organisations such as trade unions and the Church of Scotland. Alison Elliot of the Scottish Council for Voluntary Organisations said it was 'not about making the case for independence, devolution, status quo or anything in between. We do not have a fixed view about the outcome of the referendum.' Others, however, suspected it existed to provide the rationale for the SNP's preferred option of a second question. The devo+ campaign also launched formally in February 2012, comprising the MSP troika of Tavish Scott (Liberal Democrat), Alex Fergusson (Conservative) and Duncan McNeil (Labour).

The UK government continued to insist that schemes offering 'more powers' would be considered, but only *after* a single-question referendum was out of the way. 'Independence and devolution are completely different issues,' said one government aide. 'There should be a referendum on independence to get that cleared up before we consider the case for more devolution.' The new Scottish Labour leader, Johann Lamont, appeared to reject the idea of more powers ahead of her spring conference (instead she set up another commission), although Alistair Darling conceded that the full devolution of income tax would be 'relatively easy to implement'.

David Cameron elaborated on this thinking when, on 16 February 2012, he headed north for a carefully choreographed visit to Edinburgh. His well-crafted speech struck the right tone in terms of the arguments ('both of head and heart'), closed down some potential lines of attack (he acknowledged an independent Scotland 'could make its way in the world') and dangled a surprising carrot. 'This does not have to be the end of the road,' announced Cameron.

'When the referendum on independence is over, I am open to looking at how the devolved settlement can be improved further. And yes, that does mean considering what further powers could be devolved.'

The speech received a lot of input from Julian Glover, recently recruited from (unusually for a Conservative) *The Guardian*, and also the Education Secretary, Michael Gove. One minister believed an early draft included 'too much humility', although he reckoned it effectively contextualised the Prime Minister within the Scottish debate, saying 'look, I'm one voice and yes, even though I'm English and posh, I still care'.[36] Lord Forsyth, the rather devo-sceptic former Scottish Secretary, was also shown a draft. He advised removing the section promising more powers, arguing that it would simply end up becoming a hostage to fortune.

Nevertheless it won plaudits; even former SNP advisers admitted Cameron was 'pitch perfect' whenever he ventured up to Scotland. Labour figures were also on side. Cameron met the party's new Scottish leader, a 'very impressed' Johann Lamont (who had specifically requested a private meeting with the Prime Minister), while Douglas Alexander, watching events unfold from Westminster, changed his view of the Tory leadership. 'I used to believe that George Osborne and David Cameron were diehards who'd want to get rid of Scotland,' he said, 'but now I believe they're both sincere about protecting the Union – they don't want to end up like George III.'[37] It was an apt simile. 'This is a priority for the PM,' said one Downing Street adviser. 'To be frank, a lot of the stuff happening at the moment will be forgotten in ten years; but if the UK breaks up that won't be forgotten, it isn't something the PM wants to happen on his watch.'[38]

The First Minister inevitably seized upon the vagueness of the Prime Minister's words when it came to devolving more power, harking back, as was his habit, to a similar pledge from another Old Etonian Tory, Lord Home, who had promised a 'better' scheme of devolution if Scots voted 'no' in the 1979 devolution referendum. Indeed, the events of that year loomed large in parts of the Scottish (not just SNP) psyche, a collective folk memory of having been 'cheated' out of devolution (the legislation had required 40 per cent of the total Scottish electorate to back it rather than a straight majority) by a duplicitous (Unionist) Labour government. Even the creation of a Scottish Parliament by another (Unionist) Labour government in 1999 could not make up for events eighteen years earlier. 'The shadow of Sir Alec Douglas-Home I think is cast very large over this,' said Salmond. 'What's the old saying: "fool me once, shame on you, fool me twice, shame on me"? Scotland, I don't believe, will be fooled twice.'

This was all to be expected. Privately, however, UK and Scottish government officials had already opened a dialogue on the referendum, which continued during the launch of 'Yes Scotland', the formal pro-independence campaign, in May 2012, and 'Better Together', the umbrella 'no' campaign, the following month. While there were occasional signs of movement on both sides, it became increasingly clear that the expected groundswell of support for a second question – from the Future of Scotland group and others – had not materialised, and at a Scotland Office reception in May 2012 Cameron admitted, to the evident surprise of his advisers, that he was 'not fussed' about the timing of the referendum. The Scotland Office also wielded its referendum consultation as proof an 'overwhelming' number of Scots wanted to be asked a single, clear question on independence, while highlighting flaws in the Scottish government's then ongoing exercise, which appeared to accept multiple submissions without even asking for an address. When that closed on 11 May, the Scottish government delegated analysis to an independent body, thereby kicking any formal response into the long autumn grass (it was eventually published *after* the Edinburgh Agreement).

'When I was at Wimbledon watching Andy Murray I actually challenged Alex Salmond to a game of tennis to settle the issue once and for all,' the Prime Minister joked at a Downing Street reception in July 2012. 'He [Salmond] didn't seem very keen on the idea for some reason.' More seriously, UK ministers continued to pile pressure on the First Minister to rule out a second question and agree to a straight in/out ballot. This was, according to a Downing Street adviser, 'the biggest prize'.

Although officially the SNP did not favour a 'more powers' option,[39] it was still 'kept on the table' during negotiations. As someone involved in the talks recalled:

> A[lex] S[almond] pushed a second question all the way. He required the possibility always be kept open in our discussions. In discussions with Bruce [Crawford, the responsible Scottish minister] we couldn't make an assumption about the number of questions. They will claim they never formally asked for a second question, but nor did they allow discussion to proceed on the basis of there only being one.[40]

And while Bruce Crawford and Scotland Office minister David Mundell were able to sort out most of the non-contentious issues surrounding the referendum, it was clear the former 'didn't have the authority to seal the deal'. The key shift, therefore, came in September 2012, when a Scottish government reshuffle saw the former Health Secretary Nicola Sturgeon replace Crawford as minister for the referendum. As someone close to the negotiations remembered:

> It was never obvious throughout winter 2011/spring 2012 that the Scottish [government] wanted any kind of Section 30 Order or Edinburgh Agreement. It was only with the reshuffle

that things suddenly unblocked. Something clearly happened behind the scenes in the SNP which led them to conclude 'let's go for this referendum, let's make it happen'. What that something was I doubt we will ever know, but there was a huge shift in attitude once Sturgeon was in post.[41]

'At that meeting she [Sturgeon] made clear everything was on the table,' remembered another source, 'particularly the single question; at one point Nicola talked as if there would be a single question and had to correct herself, saying "of course our preference is for two".'[42]

As Sturgeon herself later recalled, it was 'very clear they [the UK government] would not agree to a Section 30 order unless it was on a single question ... I still wish that hadn't been their red line.' Similarly, while maintaining he had 'never said there should be a second question', Salmond explained he 'wasn't hostile to it ... but ... wanted the [Scottish] Parliament to decide'. To confuse matters further, after the Edinburgh Agreement had been signed the First Minister admitted it 'would've been strange from my perspective if I'd said I'm not going to have this Agreement ... to get a second question which I might not necessarily be in favour of'.

But then, as one of Salmond's advisers put it, he was an 'expert at riding two or three horses at the same time'. In reality, by this point the First Minister was aware all the 'second question' kites he had flown since the previous May had floated away. 'Initially there was a sense a second question would be useful,' recalled an aide; 'what held him [Salmond] back was a sense the [SNP] party conference would reject it. So we began to think their red line was actually okay.' Indeed, by stringing UK government ministers along on this front, Salmond believed he had kept their eyes off how the question would actually be worded. 'So our red line became that the question asked didn't mention leaving the UK.'[43] This, however, was in the hands of the Electoral Commission rather than ministers in London.

At the Conservative Party conference in Birmingham, meanwhile, the Prime Minister indicated the end was in sight. After waxing lyrical about the 2012 Olympics and English, Scottish, Welsh and Northern Irish athletes draping themselves 'in one flag', Cameron announced he would be seeing Alex Salmond the following week 'to sort that referendum on independence by the end of 2014'. 'There are many things I want this coalition to achieve, but what could matter more than saving our United Kingdom?' he asked delegates rhetorically. 'Let's say it: we're better together and we'll rise together – so let's fight that referendum with everything we've got.'

This provoked an enthusiastic response, perhaps surprisingly from a party that had long ago retreated to its southern English heartlands. Two days later a referendum 'deal' was finally agreed by the Scottish Secretary and Deputy First Minister, the final sticking points – over campaign finance and the question of the franchise – having been amicably resolved. The Prime Minister had cause to feel pleased with himself; no longer was Alex Salmond an unstoppable force of political nature, and the UK government's 'red line' – that the referendum ought to ask just one question – had been secured. Michael Moore, hitherto seen as a rather nondescript Secretary of State for Scotland (the 'worst combination of the Manse and accountant', said one critic), also emerged from the referendum negotiations with an enhanced reputation. In contrast to the First Minister, Moore had ended up looking like an honest broker.

As for Alex Salmond, he had spent most of 2012 on the defensive. His opponents were frequently derided as 'anti-Scottish' or accused of 'talking Scotland down', while the three Unionist parties were lumped together as 'anti-independence' or, as Nicola Sturgeon later put it, 'a coalition to hold Scotland back'. But despite the rhetoric, the SNP also had much to feel pleased about, not least having secured a legally binding referendum which might result in Scotland becoming an independent country – the party's goal for nearly eight decades. For the pro-UK parties, meanwhile, there was the potential 'prize' of winning the referendum and, as an official put it, 'settling the issue for a generation', much as (in a very different context) a referendum on the Good Friday Agreement had done in 1998.

It was important to remember that, whatever the SNP's electoral prowess, the referendum had not come about because of a groundswell in support for independence, but rather as a result of inter-governmental machinations. The Edinburgh Agreement did, at least, provide some sort of clarity to the process by which Scotland *might* become independent, with two significant gaps: the wording of the question and the date on which it was to be asked. In early 2013 the Electoral Commission finally gave its verdict on the Scottish government's preferred wording, 'do you agree Scotland should be an independent country', judging it to be leading. Instead it suggested the 'more neutral' question: 'Should Scotland be an independent country?' Yes Scotland and Better Together – together with Scotland's 'two govern-ments' – accepted it without a murmur of complaint, although in many ways it was not really a good way of resolving a complex issue, neglecting what a swathe of Middle Scotland actually wanted (more powers) and failing to qualify the word 'independent' in any meaningful way.

But two months later, on the eve of the SNP spring confer-ence in Inverness, Alex Salmond presented draft referendum legislation to the Scottish Parliament and finally named the day as 18 September 2014. 'It's worth reflecting, just for a moment,' he told MSPs, 'on the privilege this nation and this generation will have: nothing less than choosing the future course of our country.' It was also worth reflecting that while other nations had gone to war as a result of independence movements, or refused point blank to acknowledge the possibility of secession (as in Spain), the UK government had not only conceded the point but also equipped a devolved parliament with the legal powers to deliver it. It had been a very British compromise, but one – ironically – that might end up recalibrating centuries-old notions of what being 'British' actually meant.

CHAPTER 2

WHITHER THE UNITED KINGDOM?

Each of the constituent parts of the United Kingdom has entered into Union with the others by a different route. Each has its own distinctive history, from which the very distinctive qualities of its own community today derive. Great benefits have come to the people of each of its parts from the Union, while the peoples of the United Kingdom have been able to achieve great things largely because they have been together. This is why the government's commitment to the unity of the Kingdom is so deep.
The Scottish Office, *Scotland in the Union: A Partnership for Good* (1993)

But are such break-ups of multi-national or other large states inevitable? ... Let us leave aside the counter-tendencies which have, in the past fifty years, made e.g. the federations of Brazil, Mexico and the USA probably more unitary or centrally controlled than before. Let us omit the – so far – successful examples of postwar devolution as opposed to break-up in West Germany and Italy ... In fact, the great bulk of the new states since 1945 have not arisen by the division of existing states, but by the formal separation of already separate dependent territories, within pre-established frontiers, from their metropoles.
Eric Hobsbawm, 'Some reflections on "The Break-Up of Britain"' (1977)

It was quite a moment. In May 2011, just weeks after the SNP had formed a majority government in Scotland, Queen Elizabeth II and the Duke of Edinburgh touched down in Dublin for a state visit to the Republic of Ireland. It was the first visit by a British monarch since 1911, when the Queen's grandfather, King George V, visited the island – then part of the United Kingdom of Great Britain and Ireland – as part of his accession tour. His granddaughter had come, as the journalist Andrew Marr later observed, to put 'a little history to sleep'.

Widely seen as the symbolic normalisation of British–Irish relations following the signing of the 1998 Good Friday Agreement (the Republic's previous territorial claim to Northern Ireland had made a royal visit virtually impossible), the Sinn Fein leader Gerry Adams was nevertheless critical, saying he did not 'think this is the right time for the English Queen [sic]' to visit. Sir John Major, a key figure in the talks that led to peace in the province, rejected this, arguing that a royal visit 'puts a seal on the past and builds for the future'.

The most memorable moment of the tour was a dinner in the Queen's honour at Dublin Castle, the seat of British authority prior to Irish independence in 1922. Mary McAleese, the Irish President, made the toast, to which the Queen replied with a speech on relations between Ireland and the United Kingdom. She began by speaking a few words of Irish Gaelic: 'A Uachtaráin, agus a chairde' ('President and friends'). McAleese was so taken aback she turned to others on her table and said 'wow' three times. 'With the benefit of historical hindsight', said the Queen later, 'we can all see things which we would wish had been done differently or not at all.'[1] It was correctly interpreted as a diplomatic way of saying 'sorry'.

When the Queen opened the new session of the Scottish Parliament a few weeks later, Alex Salmond quoted another line from her Dublin speech, in which she had celebrated 'the ties between our people, the shared values, and the economic, business and cultural links that make us so much more than just neighbours, that make us firm friends and equal partners'. Whatever constitutional path Scotland chose to take, he added, 'we will aspire to be, in your words, "firm friends and equal partners"'.

It was a clever line in an eloquent speech; to the First Minister and the movement he led, Ireland offered proof that independence from the UK was not only possible, but also likely to result in a warmer, perhaps more constructive relationship between Scotland and the rest of the country. As Salmond put it:

> So there is much we share, that is a given. But the nations of these islands are also distinctive, with our own unique history and culture, our own economic challenges and our own opportunities. Some of us believe the best way to articulate that uniqueness and tackle those challenges lies within ourselves – and should be fully expressed within the work of this [Scottish] Parliament.[2]

Although he approached it from a different direction, the historian Norman Davies shared Salmond's belief that Scottish independence was inevitable. In an introduction to his book *Vanished Kingdoms: The History of Half-Forgotten Europe*, Davies said the actions of previous politicians had 'left the political architecture' of the UK in the early twenty-first century 'inherently unbalanced', observing that the English in particular were 'blissfully unaware' that the wider state they inhabited had begun to break up with the secession of the Irish Free State in 1922, and would 'probably continue'. 'Hence, if the end does come, it will come as a surprise,' argued Davies. 'Those who seriously believe "There'll always be an England" are whistling in the dark.'[3]

Indeed, even in the early twenty-first century the terms 'England', 'Britain', 'Great Britain' and 'United Kingdom' were carelessly used, and often interchangeably within the same sentence or interview. During his inquiry into media ethics, for example, Lord Justice Leveson alluded to the 'English parliament' (ironically as he cross-examined Alex Salmond), while the *Daily Mail* routinely referred to Prince William as the 'future king of England'. Of course, there was no such thing as an English parliament or an English monarch. Such slips irritate Scots, both Nationalist and Unionist, and rightly so. The perception generated is that many regard the UK as little more than England with bits added, as had Walter Bagehot in writing his 1867 tome, *The English Constitution* [*sic*].

Few realise, for example, that the UK as currently constituted is a little over nine decades old. The secession of the Irish Free State in 1922 – which, as Davies suggests, the rest of the UK appears to have forgotten about – not only established a new Irish nation (thereafter known as Eire or Ireland) but reconstituted the old British state, which was renamed the United Kingdom of Great Britain and *Northern* Ireland. So far from being something new – as many puzzlingly claim – the possible independence of Scotland not only has a direct precedent, but one very close to home.

There is general agreement that the UK comprises four 'Home Nations' – England, Scotland, Wales and Northern Ireland – three of which have specific layers of government and therefore distinct political traditions. (Danny Alexander calls them the 'four constituent nations of the UK', Nick Clegg the 'family of nations that is the UK'.) While in the United States or Germany this is given constitutional clarity by a formal federal structure, the UK is not a federation, informally or otherwise; it is a unitary state with an *ad hoc* or asymmetric system of devolution (as in Spain).

Political scientists have attempted to make sense of the UK's four unions – 1536, 1603, 1707 and 1801 – by talking about a 'multinational state', or a 'state of unions', but it remains much misunderstood, not least because both sides tend to see 'the Union' as a two- rather than four-way relationship. The political scientist Richard Rose noted that it was difficult even to name the nation associated with the government of the UK. 'One thing is for certain,' he wrote. 'No one speaks of the *UKes* as a nation.' The United Kingdom, in other words, is a very odd country.

Will the real Act of Union please stand up?
To understand fully the constitutional status quo, we have to travel back several centuries to a point at which the political map of the British Isles looked very different. The largest component part, and most populous, is of course England. Around 927 AD England became a unified state and, in 1066, London its capital. More than two centuries later Edward I of England completed his conquest of Wales, and although Owain Glyndŵr briefly restored its independence in the early fifteenth century, the whole of modern Wales was effectively annexed by England under the Laws in Wales Acts of 1535–42. Between then and the nineteenth century, to all intents and purposes, Wales was considered part of England. Thus the infamous encyclopedia entry which read: 'For Wales, see England.'

Scotland's efforts to retain a distinctive status were rather more successful, having emerged as an independent sovereign state in the early Middle Ages, something captured in the hugely popular, if historically inaccurate, 1995 film *Braveheart*. Gradually, its ties with England developed and grew, and by 1603 the 'Union of the Crowns' meant that Scotland, England and Ireland all shared the same monarch while remaining separate countries, i.e. a 'personal union' which meant King James VI of Scotland was also James I of England (and Ireland).

For the purposes of the contemporary independence debate, the most important change took place in 1707 when that personal union also became a political one. After lengthy negotiations Scotland and England – and their respective parliaments – ceased to exist as distinct sovereign entities on 1 May 1707, when the new kingdom of 'Great Britain' was created. This included Wales (as part of England) but not Ireland. And although the Acts of Union passed in both countries created a 'united Kingdom', that was not the name of the new state, the Scottish Act of Union being quite clear that a new kingdom and country, 'by the name of Great Britain', had been established. As Professor David Walker put it in volume V of *A Legal History of Scotland*, in 1707 'the kingdoms of Scotland and of England extinguished themselves as distinct political entities and united themselves forever into a new entity, a kingdom by the name of Great Britain, to be represented by one and the same parliament, to be styled the Parliament of Great Britain'. Article 1 of the Treaties of Union, meanwhile, referred to England and Scotland being united 'for ever after'. Many contemporary supporters of independence (and even many opponents) believe the current 'United Kingdom' was created in 1707 and consists just of England and Scotland, but that is incorrect.

Importantly, as the historian Colin Kidd has pointed out, the ideology of British 'Unionism' originated in Scotland. Invented in the 1520s by the philosopher John Mair of Haddington, his Unionism, wrote Kidd, was the original 'Third Way' in British politics, steering a middle course between the competing claims of Scotland and England and putting an end to 'two centuries of intermittent but economically destructive warfare'.[4] The SNP later rejected such notions, generally subscribing to the notion that Scots complicit in Union had been 'bought and sold for English gold' (a myth busted by the historian Christopher Whatley, among others).[5] Nicola Sturgeon depicted 1707 as 'formed out of the self-interest of the elites of both nations', while the SNP MSP Joan McAlpine controversially likened it to a marriage in which a 'well-educated girl' (Scotland) eventually 'recognises the relationship for what it is – an abuse of power'.[6]

But in the context of the early eighteenth century, the Anglo-Scottish Union had actually been a progressive one, for unlike Wales, Scotland was not considered part of England, but part of a new, larger nation called Great Britain. Furthermore, distinct features of the old, independent Scotland were specifically retained under the terms of Union, chiefly a separate system of Scots law, a semi-established church (the Kirk, or Church of Scotland) and a separately administered education system. Scotland, meanwhile, dispatched forty-five MPs and sixteen 'representative' peers to the Westminster parliament.

The status of Ireland was much more complicated. Although England's involvement in Ireland began with the arrival of Norman settlers in the twelfth century, its direct authority over Irish affairs – via an Irish parliament – had varied from century to century. In 1541 King Henry VIII of England created himself 'King of Ireland' and a century later Oliver Cromwell became Lord Protector of England, Scotland and Ireland following the 'War of the Three Kingdoms', uniting all three for the first time in one London parliament (albeit under threat of force). With the restoration of the Stuart monarchy and King Charles II in 1660, Cromwell's 'Commonwealth' was abolished and the Irish parliament reconvened the following year.

Although Ireland, particularly the northern counties of Ulster, was settled by Scots and English Protestants in the late seventeenth century and onwards, it retained legislative independence (often more theoretical than real) throughout the eighteenth century. Only in early 1801 was Ireland formally united with Great Britain – with an Act of Union similar to that of 1707 – forming the 'United Kingdom of Great Britain and Ireland', a fusion only formally repealed by (the Republic of) Ireland in 1962 and 1983, and which of course still exists in the six counties of Ulster.

Like its 1707 predecessor, the 1800 Act of Union abolished the ostensibly sovereign Irish Parliament and meant Ireland sent a certain number of MPs (100) and 'representative' peers (thirty-two) to the new UK Parliament at Westminster. The Kingdom of Ireland, meanwhile, remained distinct from that of Great Britain, although a new emblem, the Union Jack or, more accurately, 'Union flag', flew over both nations. This is arguably the forgotten union, with most historical studies – and most contemporary debate – focusing on the events of 1707 rather than 1800/01. As the historian Alvin Jackson has observed, there is no 'creation myth' associated with the 1707 or 1800/01 unions; indeed, the former's tercentenary in 2007 and the latter's bicentenary in 2001 were not commemorated in any way.[7]

Nevertheless, Ireland looms large in the constitutional history of the UK, not least due to the events of the early twentieth century. It was the Irish Home Rule debate of the late nineteenth century that gave rise to terms still used today like 'Nationalist' or 'Separatist' (describing those who desired Irish devolution or independence) and 'Unionist' (those who wanted to retain the Union between Great Britain and Ireland, although the term had been coined during the American Civil War). 'I hear constantly used the terms Unionists and Separatists,' complained Gladstone in 1886. 'But what I want to know is, who are the Unionists? I want to know who are the Separatists?'[8] The Irish Home Rule movement was mirrored, albeit modestly, by similar movements in Wales and Scotland. A Scottish Home Rule Association – of which the future Labour Prime Minister Ramsay MacDonald served as president – was established in 1886.

That year Gladstone, the 'Grand Old Man' of Liberal politics, initiated a decades-long controversy by committing to 'Home Rule' for Ireland, or rather, a devolved legislature within the United Kingdom. Although by modern standards this appeared a moderate concession, in the late nineteenth century it was considered revolutionary. The Liberal Party promptly split, between Liberals (who backed Gladstone's scheme) and 'Liberal Unionists' (who did not). Over time the latter grouping coalesced – formally and informally – with the Conservative Party, and by 1912 had merged to form the 'Conservative and Unionist Party', which remains the full name of the modern Tory Party to this day.

The 'Irish Question' dominated UK politics between 1886 and 1922.[9] Three different Home Rule Bills failed to clear both Houses of Parliament, and only after the First World War, when pressure for devolution had hardened into a desire for full independence, did matters come to a head. Finally, in 1920 the Government of Ireland Act created two 'Home Rule' parliaments in Northern and Southern Ireland, a scheme that failed to satisfy majority Nationalist opinion. The result was a war of independence, which ended in late 1921 when delegations from Ireland and Great Britain agreed the Anglo-Irish Treaty.

This, contrary to popular conception, did not grant Ireland full independence but 'dominion status' within the British Empire, something akin to the constitutional position of Canada, Australia and New Zealand. Although the 'Irish Free State' had full autonomy over domestic affairs, there were important, and controversial, caveats. Northern Ireland had the opportunity (which it predictably sought) to opt out of the Free State, while the British monarch, King George V, was to remain head of state in both parts of Ireland. This (rather than partition) sparked a civil war between those for and against the treaty. Following much bloodshed, pro-treaty forces emerged victorious.

Pro-independence supporters, for obvious reasons, do not often cite the Irish experience. When, in 2012, Alex Salmond said 'the people of Ireland' would know that 'bullying and hectoring the Scottish people from London ain't going to work', he was rebuked by the former SDLP leader Seamus Mallon, who pointed out that Scots had been 'part of the bullying that took place in Ireland', from the Ulster plantation, as members of the Black and Tans, prior to the civil war, and even as 'recently as fifteen years ago' as the Troubles drew to a close. 'I think Alex is a very able performer,' added Mallon, 'but his knowledge of history is a little weak.'[10]

Salmond also gave the impression that the Irish economy had boomed immediately after achieving 'independence' in 1922, when in fact it had stagnated for the more than half a century, even relying upon the UK's currency to a greater extent than before the Treaty. Indeed, Ireland illustrated a paradox for Nationalists, the theory of independence being frustrated by its reality, chiefly constraints imposed upon the sovereignty of small nations by external forces.

Only in 1927, meanwhile, did the Royal and Parliamentary Titles Act change the British monarch's royal style, titles and the formal name of the UK Parliament to the 'United Kingdom of Great Britain and Northern Ireland'. That is the name that appears on UK passports until present, and is therefore the name of the state that might be altered if Scotland becomes independent. But what form that change might take is not altogether clear, for Scotland only forms an integral part of Great Britain rather than the United Kingdom.

Alex Salmond has also argued that as the SNP wants to retain the monarch, it would be inaccurate to talk of Scotland *leaving* the United Kingdom. Similarly, the 2007 Scottish government document *Choosing Scotland's Future: A National Conversation* made clear [with my italics] that 'the current parliamentary and political union of Great Britain and Northern Ireland would become a monarchical and social union – *United Kingdoms rather than a United Kingdom* – maintaining a relationship first forged in 1603 by the Union of the Crowns'.[11] All of this, to say the least, is open to question.

The 'independence' of Ireland was only completed in 1949 when the UK Parliament passed the Ireland Act, recognising the departure of Eire (as the Free State was renamed in 1937) from the British Commonwealth and thus severing the last remaining ties with Westminster. That same Act reaffirmed the 'territorial integrity' of Northern Ireland (which Eire's constitution did not recognise) while making it clear the Republic of Ireland (as the UK now chose to call Eire) was, for certain purposes, 'not a foreign country' – allowing its citizens full access to UK benefits and the right to vote if they could demonstrate a 'substantial connection' to the UK[12] – something the SNP has made much of in response to Unionist charges that those in the rest of the UK would become 'foreigners' if Scotland became independent.

So even Irish independence, which many assume to have taken place, suddenly and comprehensively, in 1922, actually took almost three decades to reach full fruition. The same might also be true of Scottish nationhood. As Norman Davies put it, 'Just as the construction of the British state and nation took place by stages over many years, its deconstruction can only be expected to proceed in like manner – in an extended process involving successive lurches, lulls and landslips.'[13]

Many Nationalists concurred with this analysis, pushing a Whig-like interpretation of post-war Scottish history as an inevitable progression towards ever greater national freedom. On the tenth anniversary of the Scottish Parliament in May 2009, for example, Alex Salmond claimed Scotland was 'two-thirds' of the way towards independence, while Iain Macwhirter's three-part television series *Road to Referendum* took a similar approach, looking at recent Scottish history through 'the prism of the national question'. As the former Labour MP and minister Brian Wilson pointed out, 'The vast majority of the political history that has affected people's lives in Scotland since the Second World War had absolutely nothing to do with "the national question".'[14]

'A daily referendum'

So what is a nation? The nineteenth-century French historian Ernst Renan posed that question (*Qu'est-ce qu'une nation?*) in an 1882 essay of the same name, and concluded it was

> a soul, a spiritual principle. Two things, which are really one, constitute this soul and spiritual principle. One is in the past, the other, the present. One is the possession in common of a rich trove of memories; the other is actual consent, the desire to live together, the will to continue to value the undivided, shared heritage ... To have had glorious moments in common in the past, a common will in the present, to have done great things together and to wish to do more, those are the essential conditions for a people. We love the nation in proportion to the sacrifices to which we consented, the harms that we suffered.

Nevertheless, an important element in nationhood, argued Renan, was consent, thus his oft-quoted line about the 'existence of a nation' being 'a daily referendum'. Renan's central premise, that a 'spiritual principle' constituted a nation rather than race, religion or geography, was incredibly influential, as was his related concept of 'civic nationalism', an identification with a particular state apparatus, a concept embraced by the SNP under the leadership of Alex Salmond.

Renan also had something to say about the contemporary Scottish Question. 'A nation never has a veritable interest in annexing or keeping another region against the wishes of its people,' he wrote. 'If doubts arise about national borders, consult the population of the area in dispute. They have the right to an opinion on the issue.'[15] So following his advice, the UK government recognised 'that Scotland has the right to leave the UK if a majority of people vote for it in the referendum in 2014'.[16] This, of course, would involve creating a new 'nation'. On that point, both the UK and Scottish governments were clear in general terms, although they differed on specifics.

For example, there was disagreement as to whether Scottish independence would leave 'the rest of the UK' (hereafter 'rUK'), i.e. England, Wales and Northern Ireland, as the successor state, the country recognised in international law as the continuing 'UK'. The UK government was of the view that it would, while the Scottish government made conflicting noises, including the suggestion that both Scotland and rUK might be viewed as successor states. To clarify the situation Westminster asked two constitutional authorities, James Crawford, Professor of International Law at the University of Cambridge, and Alan Boyle, Professor of Public International Law at the University of Edinburgh, for a detailed opinion.

They concluded that assuming a 'yes' vote in 2014, then 'in the eyes of the world and in law' Scotland would become 'an entirely new state'. 'It is not', judged Profs Crawford and Boyle, 'legally possible for two new states to inherit the international personality of the former state', thus the 'remainder of the UK (comprising England, Wales and Northern Ireland) would continue as before, retaining the rights and obligations of the UK as it currently stands'. Crawford and Boyle cited the following in support:

- the majority of international precedent, with examples spanning the creation of an Irish state from within the UK, and the break-up of the Soviet Union;
- the retention by the continuing UK of most of the population (92 per cent) and territory (68 per cent) of the UK;
- the likelihood that other states would recognise the continuing UK as the same legal entity as before Scottish

independence, not least because of the UK's pivotal role
in the post-war world order; and

- the fact that, on the rare occasions when one state is
dissolved and two new states are created peacefully from
it, this tends to happen by mutual agreement.

Furthermore, Crawford and Boyle concluded that rUK's
membership of organisations like the European Union,
North Atlantic Treaty Organization, International Monetary
Fund, G8 and G20 'would be largely unaffected by Scottish
independence'. As a new state, on the other hand, an independent Scotland 'would be required to apply to and/or
negotiate to become a member of whichever international
organisations it wished to join'.

A newly independent Scotland, therefore, would also
'have to work through its position on thousands of international treaties and agreements to which the UK is currently
party and which would default to the continuing UK'. Some,
of course, would be 'uncontentious', although when it came
to important bilateral arrangements concerning national
security, 'the position of an independent Scottish state would
be unclear'. Finally, the 'body of law' passed by the UK
Parliament would continue to apply in England, Wales and
Northern Ireland, but not Scotland (although an independent Scotland would obviously retain UK legislation, as in
the case of Ireland, until it was replaced or repealed). 'So the
UK's key national institutions – for example, the Bank of
England and the security and intelligence agencies – would
operate on behalf of the remainder of the UK as before, but
would have no power or obligation to act in or on behalf of
an independent Scottish state.'

All of this, of course, would be subject to negotiation,
although Crawford and Boyle were at pains to emphasise
just how complicated this process might be. They gave the
example of Czechoslovakia, whose successor states, upon

its dissolution following a 'Velvet Divorce', had to negotiate some thirty-one treaties and 2,000 sub-agreements, leaving many issues unresolved even seven years after the process started. 'In a UK context,' they wrote, 'hundreds of issues would surface, reflecting three centuries of integration.'[17]

This would obviously take time. Although the UK government was reluctant to estimate exactly how long (for that would appear to concede defeat), the Scottish government set out a timescale of sixteen months, enough, they said, for negotiations and the development of a written constitution (of which more below). Following a 'yes' vote in the referendum, the Scottish government intended to invite representatives from other parties in the Scottish Parliament and representatives of Scottish civic society 'to join the government in negotiating the independence settlement and in ensuring the continuity of those public services which are in reserved areas'.

The culmination would be an 'independence day' on 31 March 2016 followed by the first elections to a fully independent Scottish Parliament that May. A Scottish government paper cited examples such as the reunification of Germany in 1990, as well as independence for the Czech Republic and Slovakia in 1993, to demonstrate that 'countries can make significant constitutional changes happen in months rather than years'. Of the states that had used independence referendums since the Second World War, it argued, the average length of time 'between the referendum and independence day' had been roughly fifteen months, although the constitutional academic Adam Tomkins dismissed this as 'risible' in the case of Scotland.

Although this was not necessarily comparing like with like (many former colonies, for example, had not been institutionally fused with their metropoles), the Scottish government was confident its timetable – which would 'form the final independence settlement' – was sufficient to cover negotiations on the division of assets and liabilities (including oil, military bases and 'overseas assets'), transfer of political authority over institutions previously controlled by Westminster, ongoing 'co-operative arrangements' with rUK, 'and the timetable for the speediest safe removal of weapons of mass destruction from Scotland'.

As both the UK and Scottish governments agreed, 'Scotland would continue to be part of the UK – and, therefore, an integral part of the EU – during these negotiations.' In parallel with independence negotiations, meanwhile, the Scottish government claimed 'pre-independence' negotiations would take place with 'international organisations that Scotland is already a member of as part of the UK'. Ministers assumed this was a foregone conclusion, not least in the case of the European Union (see Chapter 4), arguing that current membership (as part of the UK) would 'ensure that Scotland will become an independent member of these organisations as quickly as possible'.[18]

Unsurprisingly, the UK government took a less optimistic view of this process, in both domestic and international terms. On the timescale for inter-governmental talks, it said it was 'not possible to predict now the outcome of the negotiations, nor how long they would take' (although James Crawford told the BBC eighteen months sounded 'reasonable'). A key sticking point was the 2015 general election, the point being that negotiations could not really begin in earnest until *after* that date, given there might be a change of administration. And while Westminster did not really question whether an independent Scotland would be granted membership of the EU, NATO and so on in due course, it consistently questioned on what terms and under what timescale.

Another point of disagreement was the need for pre-referendum talks. The Scottish government wanted these to happen, but the UK government did not, the latter arguing that it would not 'pre-negotiate independence'. The Electoral Commission, however, urged both governments to provide clarity as to what would follow a 'yes' vote, and while initially Westminster was not inclined to play ball, Nicola Sturgeon later revealed talks were under way, although they amounted to little more than discussions over a paragraph of text for an Electoral Commission leaflet. The Scottish government set out how it saw the 'transition to independence' but, as the UK government pointed out, that did 'not address the critical issue of a Scottish state's position in international law'.

Nicola Sturgeon simply described international law on state succession as 'ambiguous', and blogged [with my italics] as follows:

> For the UK government to argue that the UK will be a 'continuing state' and that an independent Scotland would have no rights betrays *a near colonial attitude* to Scotland's position as a nation and gives lie to any suggestion that they see Scotland as an equal partner in the UK. It also raises a very important question for the UK government – if they are prepared to lay claim to the assets of the UK are they also prepared to take on all of its liabilities, such as the UK national debt?

Despite Sturgeon's use of the word 'colonial' (another SNP minister, Alex Neil, had accused UK Culture Secretary Jeremy Hunt of being 'imperialist' during a row over broadband funding) her latter point about national debt was a reasonable one, for there were precedents under international law that only a recognised successor state could inherit debt liabilities (see Chapter 3 for further discussion of this).

The legal opinion of Crawford and Boyle was, added Sturgeon, was 'just that – an opinion. It is not fact.' Instead she quoted former US ambassador Professor David Scheffer – 'the break up would be viewed as two successor states of equal legitimacy' – and Dr Andrew Blick of King's College

London – 'there is a legal case for saying the UK is dissolved and that there are two successor states' – although it is possible this view was based on the erroneous understanding, shared by some European experts, that the 'United Kingdom' simply comprised Scotland and England.

In reality, concluded Sturgeon, the status of Scotland and rUK following a 'yes' vote would be 'determined not by assertions of law, but by negotiation and agreement'.[19] There was certainly a basis for that assertion. Serbia and Montenegro, for example, had jointly agreed to Serbia becoming the continuing state, as had the ex-Soviet republics in the case of Russia, while in the case of the Czech Republic and Slovakia, both countries had agreed to be 'co-equal successor states'. Scale was important in this respect, it being easier to deal with similar-sized countries – such as the Czech and Slovak republics – which was not the case with the UK.

Nevertheless, such examples were in a minority. When the Irish Free State (later Ireland) was established in 1922, for example, no one doubted that the UK continued to exist, while even the separation of Pakistan and India following independence in 1947 was regarded as creating only one new state (Pakistan). The same view was taken after Eritrea separated from Ethiopia in 1993, and when South Sudan split from Sudan in 2011, following a referendum in which the 'yes' campaign secured 98.8 per cent of the vote, a margin of victory the SNP could only dream of.

A true union of equals

The French historian Albert Sorel divided politicians into two groups, those 'who seek to change the world to suit their ideas' and those 'who seek to modify their actions to suit the world'. He was thinking of Montesquieu, but Alex Salmond certainly belonged in the latter category. Sorel's aphorism was particularly apt when it came to explaining the SNP leader's definition of 'independence'.

In many ways, Salmond's movement on this point reflected a decades-old debate within the SNP. Initially committed to dominion status for Scotland (à la Ireland), the party's formation had been a compromise between two different strands of Nationalism, loosely defined as gradualists (those who believed in taking things slowly, supporting devolution and so on) and fundamentalists (who believed in a 'big bang' approach, generally regarding devolution as a Unionist 'trap'). This tension persisted until the late 1990s when the SNP finally backed the creation of a Scottish parliament, which it had opposed, along with the Scottish Conservatives, between 1979 and 1997 – something the party has largely succeeded in airbrushing from contemporary history.

Persuading the SNP to stop worrying and learn to love devolution had been a major feature of Salmond's first decade as leader. As mentioned in Chapter 1 the referendum policy was adopted shortly before he resigned as leader in 2000, while the word 'independence' only appeared in the party's constitution in 2004 (until then it had been 'self-government'), when Salmond returned to the helm three years before winning the 2007 election. But the experience of government, if anything, forced the SNP to think about its founding vision of independence in a more nuanced way.

Important in this respect was Stephen Noon, a former aide to Salmond and later Yes Scotland's chief strategist. The ideal, he argued, was the creation of a 'true union of equals', something he preferred to call 'co-operative independence' – 'the sort of independence', he argued, 'that works exceptionally well elsewhere'.[20] Professor James Mitchell, following interviews with around eighty senior Nationalists, concluded that the party's 'notion of independence' was 'in transition' [with my italics]:

I think we're going to move to an ever looser Union, that's what the SNP will understand; there will always be a United

Kingdom in some shape or form. The SNP isn't yet ready to say that, but that's where they're heading, I suspect [to] *a more confederal type relationship*. Maybe, maybe this election result will give the SNP leadership the courage to say what I believe they already think.[21]

Sovereignty – the ultimate authority to decide – was the key difference between *federalism* (power devolved)[22] and *confederalism* (power shared). In other words, under a confederal UK Scotland would retain its statehood or sovereignty, while in a federal set-up it would not (the United States fell somewhere in between, a formal federation but with three sovereign entities: the federal government, fifty states and American Indian communities). As Salmond put it [again with my italics], 'The resumption of independence is the resumption of political and economic *sovereignty*. How you then *choose to exercise that sovereignty* reflects the inter-relationships with principally the other countries in these islands.'[23]

Thus even if an independent Scotland chose to leave its currency in the hands of the Bank of England, pool sovereignty with the EU, retain the British monarch and join NATO, the point was that Scotland would be making that decision and not the UK. As the SNP pointed out, no one seriously argued Norway was *more* independent than Germany simply because it sat outside the EU. To supporters of independence this was no mere abstraction, but essential to how they perceived an 'independent' Scotland, even one maintaining a strong relationship with the rest of the UK.

The SNP candidate and pro-independence commentator George Kerevan saw it thus:

Salmond is offering a new British confederation in everything but name. There would be a free trade, a common currency, a common head of state, and a common security strategy through Nato. The individual nations of the British Isles would have their own parliaments and domestic tax arrangements, meaning (crucially) that Middle England regains its direct political voice. The common monetary system would anchor the confederation economically. An English parliament would assuage English populism and let traditional English liberal values shine.[24]

This more nuanced thinking helped explain SNP sensitivity over Labour's use of the words 'separatist' and 'separatism' to describe Nationalists. The Chambers dictionary defined this as 'one who withdraws or advocates separation from an established church, federation, organisation etc.', which seemed an accurate enough assessment of the party's aims, but it objected on the basis, as SNP MP Pete Wishart put it, that 'no one is advocating "separation"', in which case it was not clear what he and others *were* advocating.

But just as there was a range of views within the Conservative Party about what form the UK's membership of the EU might take, there was a range of views as to what independence meant within the SNP. Questioned by Professor Mitchell, some senior SNP members even suggested there was 'no such thing as independence' (although they quickly qualified that statement with 'as sometimes/usually understood').[25] As a Scottish government adviser put it, 'If you remove Scotland from the equation, how do you define "independence"? It's, at best, a messy and contradictory concept.'[26] But attempts to clarify the party's thinking were clearly driven by the leadership rather than the grassroots, although they were generally pragmatic about such things. Herbert Morrison once said socialism was whatever the Labour Party did; between 2007 and 2014 'independence' became whatever the SNP – or more accurately what Alex Salmond – said it was.

If we want things to change, things will have to stay as they are
Constitutional triangulation was, of course, nothing new. When Ireland prepared to secede in 1922 there was much dancing on the head of a pin about the difference between dominion status (the UK's preferred option) and 'external association' with the British Empire (Ireland's), while throughout the 1980s and 1990s the Parti Québécois offered voters, successively, 'sovereignty', 'sovereignty-association', 'economic and political partnership' and finally 'confederative union'. As the political scientist Jo Murkens observed of the Canadian experience, 'One may reasonably doubt whether the nuances are appreciated by all political scientists and constitutional lawyers, let alone by ordinary citizens.'[27]

The same could have been said of Scotland, but this thinking helped explain the SNP's movement in a number of areas. On the royal family, for example, Alex Salmond had gone from advocating a 'Scottish Socialist Republic' in his youth to an almost zealous pro-monarchism as First Minister. And although the SNP had always been, to some extent, a pro-monarchy party, this neither pleased its small republican wing nor sat comfortably with general rhetoric about creating a modern, democratic nation. On currency, the SNP switched from wanting to join the euro to proposing a 'currency union' or 'sterling zone' after independence, while more importantly it also backed continued membership of the European Union (1988) and, later, NATO (2012).

The aim in all of this was to stress continuity rather than upheaval, guiding moderate Scottish opinion towards viewing independence as *no big deal*. In doing so, Nationalists were turning Tomasi di Lampedusa's dictum – 'If we want things to stay as they are, things will have to change' – on its head. But then constitutional change in a Scottish context had always been conservative with a small 'c', promising to protect Scots from 'change', chiefly perpetrated by big 'C' Conservatives at Westminster. SNP strategists were conscious this strategy could be a double-edged sword: if the party kept stressing how consistent the new Scotland would be with the old, then voters might shrug and say 'what's the point?' Equally, of course, an adequately reassured electorate might think, 'well, why not?' It was a fine balancing act.

Concepts of the United Kingdom had also shifted since the Second World War. For much of the twentieth century political Unionism had a powerful appeal, not only for Conservatives but also for Labour, for whom, as H. C. G. Matthew observed, 'the Unionist Constitution was something of a left-wing paradise'.[28] And although Nationalists had a tendency to depict the UK as overly centralised (although ironically the Scottish government was often accused of centralising power itself) and inflexible, by the early twenty-first century it was increasingly less so, although still far behind many comparable states such as Germany. The creation of the Scottish Office in 1885 initiated a long period of 'administrative devolution', the dispersal of civil servants and government machinery to Edinburgh (1939) and Cardiff (1965), while in 1920 Northern Ireland was granted significant administrative *and* legislative autonomy within the UK (relinquished under direct rule in 1972). Finally, following the 1997 general election legislative power (of varying degrees) was granted to Scotland and Wales (1999), London (2000) and restored to Northern Ireland (1998). And it was extended thereafter, most notably in the Government of Wales Act (2006) and Scotland Act (2012).[29]

Thus Unionists argued that the status quo gave 'people in Scotland the best of both worlds'. As the UK government put it in its first 'Scotland Analysis' paper:

Scotland has always maintained its own distinctive identity, legal and education systems, and other aspects of civic life. But devolution has, in little more than a decade, brought political decision-making on key issues closer to the people affected by it, within the framework of a single UK. This means that a

Scottish Parliament and Scottish government are empowered to take decisions on a range of domestic policy areas, such as health, education and policing, so that specific Scottish needs are addressed.

But, it continued, devolution also meant Scots continued 'to benefit from decisions that are best made on a UK-wide basis', notably 'providing significant economic opportunity, representing their interests in the world and allowing resources and risks to be shared effectively'.[30]

And although the SNP belatedly supported devolution in 1997, it had always maintained its inadequacy, highlighting the 'democratic deficit', under which Westminster policies (such as Trident and the 'bedroom tax') were 'pushed through' in Scotland despite the views of Scottish MPs. Even though devolution was supposed to address that deficit, Salmond argued in 2013 that it 'still exists today'. He continued:

It is worth remembering that in 1999 comparatively few additional powers were granted to the Parliament in Scotland that had not previously been devolved to the Secretary of State for Scotland. The shift from administrative to legislative devolution was, of course, momentous in itself. But it still left Scotland with fewer powers than the German Länder, most American states, parts of Spain such as the Basque Country or Catalonia, or, within these islands, the Isle of Man.[31]

We're all Nationalists – and Unionists – now

The terms 'Unionist' and 'Nationalist', therefore, no longer adequately captured what those two political tribes actually stood for in the early twenty-first century. As the historian Colin Kidd argued in his 2008 book, *Union and Unionisms: Political Thought in Scotland 1500–2000*, the two traditions had more in common than either cared to acknowledge. Just as the SNP had a strand of 'Unionist' thinking, so too had the Conservative Party a strain of small 'n' Nationalism, from a 1949 policy document entitled *Scottish Control of Scottish Affairs* to Edward Heath's 'Declaration of Perth' in 1968 (which committed the Conservatives to a devolved Scottish Assembly). As the blogger Alex Massie argued, the 'better kind of Unionism – the confident type – can accept nationalist tools (Home Rule, greater fiscal responsibility) while putting them to Unionist ends (rendering independence unnecessary)'.[32]

By the late twentieth century Nationalists also had a simplistic habit of lumping together everyone deemed opposed to Scottish independence as 'Unionists', which included not just Conservatives but also Labour and the Liberal Democrats. This made little sense considering a Labour government had delivered devolution – hardly behaviour befitting hardline Unionists – while the Liberal Democrats were federalists, envisaging a much looser union that would accommodate many Nationalist demands, including fiscal autonomy. As Scottish Secretary Michael Moore – who denied being a 'Unionist' at all – pointed out, every UK party had long ago accepted that the 'old-fashioned centuries-old version of the UK is horribly outdated'.[33] Indeed, the three Unionist parties adapted to Scotland's changing constitutional landscape by moving towards small 'n' nationalism and, as the journalist Paul Hutcheon put it, embracing 'everything Scottish'. As Peter Mandelson might have said, 'We're all Nationalists – and Unionists – now.'

Nothing had illustrated this phenomenon more eloquently than Donald Dewar's speech at the opening of the Scottish Parliament in May 1999. In a brief oration laced with references to Robert Burns and Sir Walter Scott, he said devolution was 'about more than our politics and our laws. This is about who we are, how we carry ourselves.' He continued:

In the quiet moments today, we might hear some echoes from the past: the shouts of the welder in the din of the great

Clyde shipyard; the speak of the Mearns, rooted in the land; the discourse of the Enlightenment, when Edinburgh and Glasgow were a light held to the intellectual life of Europe; the wild cry of the Great Pipe; and back to the distant noise of the battles of the days of Bruce and Wallace.

The past, concluded Dewar, 'is part of us, part of every one of us and we respect that, but today there is a new voice in the land, the voice of a democratic Parliament. A voice to shape Scotland, a voice above all for the future.'[34] It was a speech Alex Salmond – sitting a few feet away from Dewar that day – could have made, and indeed any self-respecting Nationalist.

Fourteen years later, Salmond delivered a series of speeches that stressed his Unionism as much as Dewar had his Nationalism. The political union, he said in Nigg during summer 2013, 'is only one of six unions that govern our lives today in Scotland, and the case for independence is fundamentally a democratic one. But that will still leave five other unions intact.' Salmond also presented himself as a reforming Unionist, hoping to 'change' those five unions and 'improve them' but at the same time 'basically maintain' them.[35] As the commentator Alf Young pointed out, the SNP leader had revealed himself to be 'five-sixths a unionist'.[36]

Despite this overlap, *nationalist* Unionists and *unionist* Nationalists viewed devolution through very different eyes. While the Labour politician George (later Lord) Robertson believed devolving power to Scotland would 'kill nationalism stone dead', a remark he never quite lived down, the SNP had in mind Michael Collins, who said the 1921 Anglo-Irish Treaty – however imperfect – embodied the 'freedom to achieve freedom'. As Norman Davies observed of the Austro-Hungarian Empire, 'Life in autonomous provinces provides a school for separatists, who see their autonomy as a step towards national independence.'[37]

Many Nationalist paradoxes were captured in the 'Independence Declaration', unveiled in May 2012. 'Being independent means Scotland's future will be in Scotland's hands,' it declared.

> There is no doubt that Scotland has great potential. We are blessed with talent, resources and creativity. We have the opportunity to make our nation a better place to live, for this and future generations. We can build a greener, fairer and more prosperous society that is stronger and more successful than it is today. I want a Scotland that speaks with her own voice and makes her own unique contribution to the world: a Scotland that stands alongside the other nations on these isles, as an independent nation.

But the key line was the first: 'I believe it is fundamentally better for us all, if decisions about Scotland's future are taken by the people who care most about Scotland, that is, by the people of Scotland.'[38] As the BBC's Douglas Fraser pointed out, 'The logic behind that is that Scotland would be better out of the European Union as well as the British one.'[39] The true meaning of 'sovereignty', as Ireland knew only too well post-2008, was a fiendishly complicated business.

'We the people…'
The 'Independence Declaration' was consciously modelled on the constitution of the United States (which, ironically, had been inspired by the 1707 Act of Union),[40] and indeed a few months after it was launched the Scottish government announced plans for a written constitution should Scotland vote 'yes' in 2014. This was hardly a radical aim, for only the United Kingdom, New Zealand and Israel lacked codified constitutions. The SNP had first produced such a document in the 1970s, drafted by Neil MacCormick,[41] while in 2002 it published 'A Constitution for a Free Scotland'.[42]

Shaping the SNP's thinking on this – then and now – was a strong belief in what it called a 'distinct Scottish constitutional tradition', the argument that in Scotland (pre-1707) sovereignty rested with the Scottish people rather than the monarch, whereas in England the reverse was true. This had historical validity, as demonstrated in 1953 when the Lord President of Scotland's Court of Session observed that 'the principle of unlimited sovereignty of Parliament is a distinctively English principle and has no counterpart in Scottish constitutional law',[43] although in practice sovereignty of the people was rather harder to pin down.

Thus it followed that a 'sovereign' Scottish people had the right to 'self-determination', a term Nationalists often used interchangeably with 'independence'. In truth, however, it was difficult to argue – as the SNP sometimes did – that Scots had somehow been deprived of the right to self-determination given that the UK had enjoyed full and free democratic elections since the introduction of the universal franchise in 1918. Arguably every general election since 1935 (when the SNP managed just 1.1 per cent of the vote) had enabled self-determination in respect of independence, it was just that a majority of Scots chose to self-determine in favour of the Union. Nor was the concept contingent upon a referendum which, after all, the SNP had only adopted in 2000. Even Margaret Thatcher wrote in her memoirs that Scots possessed an 'undoubted right to national self-determination'. 'Should they determine on independence', she added, 'no English party or politician would stand in their way, however much we might regret their departure.'[44] John Major, meanwhile, admitted 'no nation can be kept in a union against its will'[45] while David Cameron said 'we believe in self-determination' after Falklanders voted overwhelmingly to remain a British Overseas Territory following a March 2013 referendum.[46]

Nevertheless, a written constitution was viewed as a means by which the 'sovereignty of the Scottish people' could be enshrined in a codified document. Unlike the independence negotiations, however, the drafting of a written constitution was envisaged by the Scottish government to begin only once Scotland had elected its first independent parliament, for a written constitution 'should be prepared in a spirit of national unity', i.e. after the referendum and negotiations were out of the way. This, the SNP argued, would facilitate the drafting of a constitution reflecting 'the values of the people of Scotland'. And although the Scottish government would 'propose provisions that encapsulate the collective expression of values that we hold dear in Scotland', it would not be the only, or indeed dominant, voice in the process.

As well as the usual suspects, civic organisations, business interests, trade unions and others would, the Scottish government said, 'have a direct role in shaping the constitution'. There were several precedents for this process, similar citizen-led assemblies and constitutional conventions having been convened in British Columbia (2004), the Netherlands (2006), Ontario (2007), Iceland (2010) and, most recently, Ireland, which summoned a convention to review the Irish constitution in late 2012. Alex Salmond also argued such a document would follow the 'constitutional tradition' of the 1320 Declaration of Arbroath and the 1988 Claim of Right (which, ironically, the SNP had refused to sign). The Claim (which had demanded a devolved Scottish Parliament), however, had been a political gesture rather than a binding constitutional document.

But while the Scottish government repeatedly stressed how open and participative this process would be, it was at the same time prescriptive, proposing that certain 'individual rights' ought to be enshrined in a written constitution, including housing and education, and the right not to be involved in 'weapons of mass destruction' or 'illegal wars';[47]

LGBT rights, according to one of Yes Scotland's campaigning sub-groups, were also likely to feature, taking its lead from the groundbreaking South African constitution.

This, critics pointed out, conflated constitutions and public policy (a bad SNP habit in any case), with several experts pointing out the obvious dangers of including a 'right to housing' or a 'right to education' in a constitution, for if a future Scottish government failed in either respect (which seemed likely), then those affected would be able to sue. Scottish Secretary Michael Moore was rather dismissive, saying such talk (so long before referendum day) was 'like framing and hanging a picture that is yet to be painted. No matter how gilded and fancy the frame, the missing image is the essential part.'[48]

Building a nation

One element of nation-building the SNP generally played down (in public) were the start-up costs associated with building a newly independent state. Although it made the reasonable point that Scotland already had many of the institutions required, i.e. a parliament (no need to construct a new building), a government, a judiciary and legal system, decoupling elements of the executive and civil service (currently Great Britain-wide, Northern Ireland having its own) would of course be both complex and expensive.

In June 2013 the UK government published a list of 200 public bodies it believed would need to be replicated in an independent Scotland, having already confirmed that neither the Post Office nor the Royal Mail would continue to operate in an independent Scotland (although since the latter was about to be privatised, this was a moot point). The Scottish government pointed out that some on the list, such as Public Health England, the British Library and Visit Britain, already had Scottish equivalents, while it seemed likely a lot of charities and even trade unions would continue to cover the British Isles with or without independence (the National Union of Journalists, for example, covered the UK and Ireland). The SNP MSP Kenny MacAskill called this the 'DVLA Question', by which he asked if it would really be necessary for an independent Scotland to establish its own DVLA, National Statistics Office, and so on, when it could simply share existing services,[49] although that analysis, of course, assumed the co-operation of rUK.

A Yes Scotland video released the same month claimed the 'initial start-up costs' of independence would total just £300 million, an amount it said would be covered by scrapping Trident (£250 million) and no longer sending MPs to London (£50 million). Given that constructing a Scottish parliament building had cost £400 million, this seemed rather optimistic. Privately, however, Finance Secretary John Swinney acknowledged that 'undoubtedly there will be a cost associated with setting up and running the necessary institutions and in some cases these are likely to be significant'[50] (including around twice Yes Scotland's figure on 'tax administration' alone), although publicly the Scottish government blithely claimed any transition costs 'would be completely outweighed by the benefits that would accrue to Scotland as a result of independence'.

The £50 million saving from ditching Westminster referred to Scotland's current representatives in London, chiefly fifty-nine MPs, around eighty-five peers and two Justices of the Supreme Court. The judges would obviously go, transferring to a new Scottish Supreme Court (which would assume the criminal appeal function of the UK Supreme Court), although the status of parliamentarians was less clear-cut. With a UK general election due to take place in May 2015, roughly halfway through the period likely to be given over to independence negotiations, then it seemed likely those elections would be contested in Scotland, only for those elected to depart less than a year later. In Ireland the situation had been easier. The last election contested by every Irish constituency had been in 1918 (when forty-seven Sinn Feiners were elected, mostly from prison), and by the time of the next poll in 1922 the Irish Free State had been formed and thus only candidates standing in the six counties of Ulster remained.

The Irish precedent was also instructive when it came to the House of Lords. Curiously, neither the Anglo-Irish Treaty of 6 December 1921 nor the Irish Free State (Agreement) Act (1921) contained any provision for the Irish peers, twenty-eight of whom had been 'elected' by the whole Irish peerage since the 1801 Act of Union with Great Britain. After 1922, therefore, the Irish representative peers continued to sit in the House of Lords, although they were allowed to die out. Thus the last survivor, the Earl of Kilmorey, passed away nearly forty years later in 1961.

The Peerage Act of 1963 finally excluded the Irish peers from the House of Lords entirely, while giving all Scottish peers – who, like the Irish, had hitherto been 'elected' representatives – a seat in the House of Lords as of right (as new 'UK peers').[51] This would create problems in the event of independence for there are no longer specifically Scottish peers, as there were Irish in 1922. Most of the hereditary peers were expelled in 1999, although ninety-two – including a few Scots – remain in the unreformed Upper House. Life peers, meanwhile, are all United Kingdom creations, and thus identifying, and presumably expelling, those classified as 'Scottish' would be an inexact science. Many Scots, for example, were given a peerage in recognition of careers spent predominantly in England or overseas. It seemed likely, therefore, that the Irish example would be followed: existing 'Scottish' peers would remain, but no more would be created.

The SNP cares little about any of this, for its policy is abolition of the House of Lords while, in the event of independence, the Scottish Parliament would continue as a unicameral institution, in common with around half the world's legislative bodies. Although Lord Steel, a former Presiding Officer, at one point mooted a small second chamber (comprising worthies rather than peers), it had minimal political support and even more minimal public interest. That said, the process of decoupling Scotland from the UK, as with Ireland in 1922, would require legislative authorisation by the Westminster parliament. Just as the Act of Union making Scotland part of Great Britain in 1707 required ratification by both the English and Scottish parliaments, so too would an Act extracting Scotland from the UK in 2016. The Scottish government recognised this and pointed to the Malta Independence Act of 1964 and the Statute of Westminster as precedents.

The statute had established legislative equality for the British Empire's self-governing dominions, Canada, the Irish Free State, the Union of South Africa, Australia, New Zealand and Newfoundland, in 1931. In all those dominions the British monarch continued to be head of state (although only until 1949 in Ireland and 1961 in South Africa), with domestic representation by a governor general. While an independent Scotland would not strictly be a 'dominion', it followed that a similar arrangement would apply, for there is not a single British Crown territory, dependency or country in the world where the Queen reigns without an intermediary.

The constitutional expert Vernon Bogdanor cited the Irish Free State and Northern Ireland as precedents, governors having represented the Queen in both following the 1920 Government of Ireland Act. In southern Ireland the governor was generally hidden from view, although in Northern Ireland the last (Lord Grey of Naunton) only left office in 1973. Similarly, the UK's self-governing 'Crown Dependencies' – the Isle of Man, Guernsey and Jersey – all have lieutenant governors (none are part of the UK or EU), as do 'Crown Territories' like Bermuda, the Falklands and Gibraltar. And assuming an independent Scotland remained a member of the Commonwealth (in August 2013 Secretary General Kamalesh Sharma said it was 'not something that would automatically apply'), a high commissioner rather than an ambassador would most likely represent rUK in an independent Scotland, and vice versa.

Unsurprisingly, the SNP is not keen on this sort of talk, the term 'governor' or 'governor general' sounding, as Nicola Sturgeon might say, 'near colonial'. 'Bogdanor is mistaken,' a spokesman said in response to news reports. 'The Queen is regularly in Scotland, she is obviously extremely close to Scotland to be able to carry out ceremonial duties, and has always opened each session of the Scottish Parliament. When the Queen is not present in Scotland, the elected Presiding Officer of Parliament would represent her.' This meant Tricia Marwick, or her successor as Presiding Officer, would be the *de facto* head of state in the Queen's (often lengthy) absences from Scotland. This was in line with a 1995 SNP policy paper called 'Citizens Not Subjects', which proposed that the 'speaker' of the Scottish Parliament would assume the monarch's duties when he or she was out of the country.[52]

Her Majesty's private views on Scottish independence were, of course, subject to a lot of idle speculation. Naturally, these were not exactly telegraphed from Buckingham Palace, 'The Firm' having learned its lesson from a previous intervention during the 1977 Silver Jubilee, when devolution and independence chatter had been at its height. Addressing both Houses of Parliament in Westminster Hall, the Queen said [with my italics]:

> The problems of progress, the complexities of modern administration, the feeling that Metropolitan government is too remote from the lives of ordinary men and women, these among other things have helped to revive an awareness

of historic national identities in these islands. They provide the background for the continuing and keen discussion of proposals for devolution to Scotland and Wales within the United Kingdom. I number Kings and Queens of England and of Scotland, and Princes of Wales among my ancestors and so I can readily understand these aspirations. *But I cannot forget that I was crowned Queen of the United Kingdom of Great Britain and Northern Ireland.* Perhaps this Jubilee is a time to *remind ourselves of the benefits which union has conferred, at home and in our international dealings, on the inhabitants of all parts of this United Kingdom.*[53]

Criticised at the time as unconstitutional (probably correctly) by the SNP, a similar speech in the same location for the Diamond Jubilee in 2012 played it safe, the only slight controversy arising from the 2013 Queen's Speech, which included the line 'my government will continue to make the case for Scotland to remain part of the United Kingdom', although that was the coalition's sentiment rather than the head of state's. Even so, the SNP MP Pete Wishart complained it was 'politicising the monarchy unnecessarily'.[54]

Otherwise, reports following the SNP's landslide election victory in 2011 suggested Her Majesty had sought 'detailed briefing' from Downing Street as to the implications of a split, while Alex Salmond went to extraordinary lengths to expunge a 1997 SNP conference resolution (confirmed in its 2002 constitution) to hold 'a referendum in the term of office of the first independent Parliament of Scotland on whether to retain the monarch'. The First Minister claimed the policy had changed, but no one could quite pinpoint when. While content with jettisoning what Bagehot called the 'efficient' parts of the English constitution [*sic*], Salmond was determined to retain this particular feature of its 'dignified' form.

What, then, of nomenclature? An independent Scotland would, of course, be called 'Scotland', while the Scottish parliament would presumably become simply 'Parliament', unless the new administration wanted to save money on stationery. The rest of the UK was trickier. In 1922 the matter was fudged, with a partial name change formalised in 1927 but little else. The 'United Kingdom' or 'Great Britain' was still the accepted shorthand, while the Union flag (which included the St Patrick's Cross of Ireland) continued to fly over public buildings. There might be a strong case for a similar approach in the event of Scottish independence, for the UK and its flag would still be an internationally recognised brand. Just as the Scottish government emphasised continuity even after independence, so too might the rUK government. The subheading, however, might require revision, for as the academic Robert Lane concluded: 'Without Scotland there is no "Great Britain" and without Great Britain there is no "United Kingdom".'[55] Might rUK go for 'United Kingdom of England, Wales and Northern Ireland', finally recognising Wales in its own right? On the other hand, a policy of business as usual – for both Scotland and rUK – might be the most likely outcome.

What would an independent Scotland actually be like?

The most pressing question of the independence debate, of course, transcended 'process' issues and concerned what an independent Scotland would actually be like. 'The only sensible answer', as the economist John Kay wrote in 2012, 'is that no one really knows.' He continued:

> because the outcome would be the result of protracted negotiations between the putatively independent country and its international partners, particularly the EU and the continuing government of the UK ... To ask either proponents or opponents of independence to explain how these issues would be resolved is a waste of time. A waste of time because both groups are presenting exaggerated pictures to

rally support. A waste of time because initial positions are negotiating stances, not expectations of outcome.[56]

This was an important point, for neither side could actually give definitive answers to perfectly legitimate questions when they could not possibly know what independence looked like until the negotiations had concluded in 2016, while, as the SNP often pointed out, there were also 'uncertainties' (relating to the economy, welfare and so on) associated with remaining part of the UK. As Nicola Sturgeon said in a November 2012 speech:

> There isn't always an absolute objective truth to be found on issues where negotiation and the policy choices of governments yet to be elected will help shape Scotland. There are facts that will be set out, of course, but the referendum will not simply be a contest of competing 'facts'. Instead, when the Yes and No campaigns set out their stalls, people will be asked to make a qualitative judgment about which is more credible and compelling and about who they trust most with Scotland's future.[57]

But it was possible to examine those initial 'stalls' in quite a lot of detail, something both the Scottish and UK governments felt compelled to do before 2014. In the autumn of 2012 Whitehall announced its intention to assemble a 'manifesto for the UK' by publishing a series of thirteen policy papers (under the uninspiring banner 'Scotland Analysis') throughout 2013 and 2014. Co-ordinated by Sir Nicholas MacPherson, the Treasury's Anglo-Scottish permanent secretary (who was personally fascinated by the 1922 Anglo-Irish independence process), the first covered the constitutional status of an independent Scotland, the second looked at currency, a third financial services and banking, a fourth examined business, a fifth macroeconomics, and a sixth defence, while the rest would cover tax and spending, debt and borrowing, EU membership and international matters, energy and North Sea oil, security, welfare, culture, heritage and identity, borders and immigration.

A week later the Scottish government made it known its officials were working on sixteen similar policy 'work-streams' that would amount to a blueprint for a 'successful, independent' country. A series of working groups (which had actually been set up in November 2011) were to look at external affairs, EU membership, macroeconomic policy (this was published as the Fiscal Commission Working Group in February 2013), business and enterprise, the structure and capacity of government, as well as health, welfare, and defence and security. All of these, it was planned, would feed into an 'independence prospectus' – a 500-page Scottish government white paper setting out its negotiating position – to be published in November 2013. This, as one former Scottish government adviser put it, would 'be quite some document', covering so many topics it might even 'include the meaning of life, the universe and everything'.[58] Deputy First Minister Nicola Sturgeon preferred to see it as 'a fantastic prospectus for the case for independence'.

But there was an imbalance: while practically the entire, well-oiled, Whitehall machine was channelling its energies into making the case for the UK, the Scottish government had only its own officials, whose expertise did not extend to non-devolved areas. Not only that, but while the UK government simply had to describe the status quo and hypothesise about the consequences of independence, the Scottish government had to explain why the status quo was inadequate *and* set out a coherent and (if not always) costed alternative. Although many Nationalists resented this uncomfortable reality, the burden of proof lay with them. This book will now examine these areas in greater detail.

CHAPTER 3

THE ECONOMICS OF INDEPENDENCE

Scots have many virtues, but constructive self-criticism is not their strong point. This reflects a basic lack of confidence, which in the discussion of economic matters is revealed by two extreme viewpoints. The first, and historically the predominant, argument is that the Scottish economy is so weak and dependent on England that self-government would result in serious economic disadvantage. The obverse argument, which has recently been gaining ground, is that Scotland's economic difficulties are someone else's fault; specifically, the result of the political union with England.

D. I. MacKay, *Scotland 1980: The Economics of Self-Government* (1977)

If the economy is doing well ... that's an argument for independence.
If the economy is doing badly ... that's an argument for independence.
If our banks are doing well ... that's an argument for independence.
If our banks are in crisis ... that's an argument for independence.
If unemployment is low ... that's an argument for independence.
If unemployment is high ... that's an argument for independence.

Douglas Alexander, Judith Hart Memorial Lecture (2013)

Claims and counterclaims about the economic effects of independence have been a fixture of the Scottish constitutional debate since the emergence of the SNP as a significant political force in the late 1960s. Turbocharged by the discovery of North Sea oil late in that decade, it was this debate that first enthused the young Alex Salmond, who later made his name in the party by formulating what he called 'The Economic Case for Independence'. He calculated that without succeeding in this respect – convincing Scots that an independent Scotland could stand on its own two feet – independence remained a pipe dream.

Although Salmond was often guilty of talking up his economic expertise (he had briefly been an agricultural economist at the old Scottish Office and an energy economist at the Royal Bank of Scotland, both several decades ago), he spoke the language of business fluently and convincingly, earning success in one important respect: while until the 1980s – even after oil revenue began flowing into the Treasury – many Unionists had argued an independent Scotland would not be economically viable, by the time Salmond became First Minister in 2007 most of his opponents, including senior UK politicians, had conceded that it would.

Thus the debate became one not of viability, but relative economic benefit. It was, as the historian Colin Kidd put it, 'a cost analysis – does the Union enrich or impoverish us?', while Professor Robert Young, in a paper on 'peaceful secessions', cast it more widely, observing that 'in the absence of oppression, citizens of a sub-unit who contemplate secession carefully weigh the benefits and costs of different outcomes'.[1] And so it was with Scotland.

Celtic neo-liberalism

In the spring of 2013 the First Minister attempted to explain his economic and political philosophy during a speech at Princeton University. The nub of his argument was that Adam Smith's seminal work, *The Wealth of Nations*, should not be considered in isolation but alongside the Scottish Enlightenment writer's earlier – and in Salmond's opinion – 'equally significant' work, *The Theory of Moral Sentiments*. 'Taken together,' he said, 'the moral philosophy of the first and the science of economics of the second provide the balanced outlook that the world needs to confront the major challenges of today.'[2] 'What Smith consistently appeals to', added Salmond, 'is what should be called an enlightened self-interest.'

The First Minister then applied this point to Scotland, arguing that Westminster's toleration of inequality demon-strated the 'empathy gap' between the UK and Scottish governments. 'And my own view is that in Scotland,' he posited, 'that sense of empathy will motivate us to take and use the powers we need to change the direction of the coun-try.'[3] But in drawing a distinction between Smith's 'invisible hand' and advocacy of altruism and benevolence, the leader of the SNP was hardly doing anything new. US Democrats had called it the 'Third Way', as had Anthony Giddens, Tony Blair et al. in the UK.

Alex Salmond chose to think of it as 'social democracy', which he defined as 'believing in a competitive economy' but also 'a just distribution of resources'.[4] This was, however, a lop-sided social democracy, more concerned with spend than tax, an imbalance exacerbated by running a devolved government which – by virtue of its Westminster 'block grant' – involved more spending than taxing. Critics dubbed the SNP's preferred economic model the 'Scandimerican' plan, Scandinavian-style social services paid for by US-level tax rates, while the journalist Iain Macwhirter called it 'Celtic neo-liberalism'. In 2006 two Nationalists, former MSP Mike Russell and businessman Dennis MacLeod, had even set out a programme of tax cuts matched by reductions in public spending in a book called *Grasping the Thistle*, although Russell (who was re-elected in 2007) later repudiated much of its neo-liberal agenda.[5]

In truth, the SNP (or Labour for that matter) was not offering anything akin to Scandinavian social democracy. Rather, it believed that by making markets more competitive the cream could be skimmed off the top and distributed to the less fortunate in society. As a leaked Scottish Cabinet paper [with my italics] made clear, 'our approach *at this point* should be to develop taxes that support economic growth, rather than explicitly raise additional revenue'.[6]

This position neatly captured what might be called Salmonomics, an uncomfortable blend of Keynesianism (spending your way out of a recession) and neo-liberalism (cutting taxes to stimulate growth). At Westminster, for example, the SNP luxuriated in supporting deficit reduction but not spending cuts, arguing that growth – stimulated by capital spending – would, over time, reduce the UK's debt pile – Salmond's so-called 'Plan McB'. Strongly influenced by the apparent success of the Irish model throughout the 1980s and 1990s, Salmond remained wedded to Laffer Curve economics and what Tony Judt called 'the delusion of endless growth' long after the great crash of 2007–08. Indeed, had the Blair–Brown boom years continued, the economic arguments for independence might have looked very different in 2012–14.

This economic mindset naturally trickled down to the party more widely. As the political scientist Michael Keating observed, the SNP had 'yet to make up its mind about whether it believes in the neo-liberal or the social democratic model', instead mixing up 'very different economic and social models ... low-tax and low-welfare Ireland [and] high-tax and high-welfare Sweden'. And, of course, it extended beyond the SNP. As the former Cabinet Secretary Gus O'Donnell reflected ruefully, 'Everyone wants to spend more and tax less, and at the national level that does not add up to a sustainable fiscal policy.'[7]

The 'Scottish economy'
Politicians on both sides of the independence debate frequently referred to the 'Scottish economy', although

in a technical sense there was no such thing. The prefix 'Scottish' implied something distinct from the rest of the UK, which, although true in certain respects, did not quite capture the reality. The National Institute of Economic and Social Research (NIESR), for example, concluded that while Scotland was 'a small and very open economy', it was at the same time 'more integrated with the rest of the UK than with Europe or the rest of the world'.[8]

North Sea oil, whisky and financial services all loomed large, employing between them more than half a million people. Two thirds of Scottish exports went to rUK (around £45 billion) and the remainder overseas (around £22 billion), figures roughly mirrored by its imports. Despite regional variation (Aberdeenshire, for one, vastly outperformed the rest of the country), the 'Scottish economy' as a whole closely mirrored that of the UK, and has done so since the late 1980s.

Thus there is a central tension in the SNP's pitch on the contemporary economic case for independence, between conceding that Scotland is economically the best-performing part of the UK outside London and the south-east, and arguing that Scotland's economy is being *held back* by 'the Union'. Alex Salmond has also argued that independence, or rather greater fiscal autonomy, would *in itself* stimulate the economy, an assertion on which the economic jury is still out. Rather, it depends on policy decisions taken *after* independence, which might be either good or bad. As the Scottish government's former chief economic adviser Dr Andrew Goudie put it:

Economic power does not necessarily imply the determina-tion of good economic strategy and good economic policy or, conversely, of poor strategy and policy ... Unless it is argued that the UK as presently constituted will always – or typi-cally – have administrations that are deemed to pursue poor policy, and, with an independent Scotland, future Scottish administrations are assumed to always – or typically – pursue policy that will be deemed good, the argument for constitutional change, on this count, is weak.

And, of course, vice versa. 'It is, therefore, important not to confuse the poor use of economic power within an existing constitutional arrangement as necessarily implying the weakness of that constitution,' added Goudie, 'just as the poor use of new powers within an alternative constitutional arrangement does not necessarily imply an inherent failing of that new arrangement.'[9]

Indeed, a lot of Scottish government arguments betray a strong belief in the hypothetical sagacity of independent Scottish policy makers. As the economic consultant Dan Gay blogged, the SNP 'think that Scotland is going to escape all the failings of Westminster, and that stupidity and greed won't exist in the new nation'.[10] But of course plenty of other 'small nations' (to use the SNP's preferred terminology) had overspent and deregulated too much, most notably Iceland and Ireland – two nations in Alex Salmond's much-mocked 'arc of prosperity'.

It could, of course, be argued that independence might unleash 'animal spirits' that would stimulate economic growth. The SNP, for example, cited research it claimed showed Scotland could expect a surge in foreign direct investment simply by virtue of leaving the UK. It drew parallels with the nations that gained autonomy from the USSR in the early 1990s, although their economies had of course been far less developed than Scotland's. At the same time there would be downsides, with even a leaked Scottish Cabinet paper acknowledging that the 'fiscal dynamics of an independent Scotland' would be 'subject to more volatility in future as the block grant approach comes to an end'. Gaining control of expenditure, the paper continued, would offer 'more opportunities for innovation and prioritisation but also more responsibility, for example for benefits and for defence'.[11]

It is also worth noting the Scottish government already controls many of the policy levers pro-independence campaigners claim to desire, certainly more so than the Welsh Assembly or English regions. A devolved Scotland can already undertake, as one economist put it, 'a co-ordinated growth strategy with appropriately targeted public expenditures and administrative structures'.[12] After 2015/16, meanwhile, the Scottish government will have even more flexibility, including the power to create more taxes, borrow and even levy a Scottish rate of income tax (although several economists warned of unintended consequences in this respect; see Chapter 7).

Similarly, frequent calls for tax-raising powers have rather ignored the fact the Scottish Parliament had originally, via the 'Scottish variable rate' (SVR) been able to alter the basic rate of income tax up or down by 3p in the pound, a fiscal lever it chose not to pull. Although there were legitimate criticisms of what the Conservative politician Michael Forsyth famously called the 'tartan tax', its neglect was consistent with a Scottish government that generally downplayed the fiscal levers it already possessed. That said, Scottish ministers could credibly claim, as another document put it, that Scotland's economic performance had 'improved' because of its ability 'to use even limited levers in the interests of Scotland'.[13] By the middle of 2013, for example, Scottish unemployment was 0.7 per cent lower than the UK average, while the rate of private-sector job creation was ahead of every part of the country except London, something economists attributed to £323 million of accelerated capital spending in 2008–10, followed by £2.5 billion of private funding for road, rail, school, hospital and house building work. This helped explain a 10 per cent increase in Scotland's construction workforce during 2010–13 (compared with a 3 per cent reduction elsewhere), and although 'job quality' was declining, the Fraser of Allander Institute expected Scotland to create more jobs than Wales, Northern Ireland or the north of England between 2013 and 2018.

The debate has also focused more on which fiscal powers might be transferred to Scotland, rather than exploring how they might be used. Although there are notable exceptions (such as corporation tax), this reflected a generally poor level of economic literacy in Scottish political discourse. 'Where these questions have been addressed,' observed Dr Goudie, 'the responses have typically suffered from a paucity of evidence to support specific propositions and, instead, have often lapsed into cavalier assertions with little or no foundation.'[14] Economics, in the context of the independence debate, played second fiddle to politics.

Fiscal Commission Working Group

The most substantial statement of economic intent from the Scottish government was an initial report on an independent Scotland's 'macroeconomic framework' from its Fiscal Commission Working Group (FCWG).[15] Although intended to 'work from the first day of independence', its authors conceded the 'exact' framework would be 'subject to negotiation', much of which would probably not take place until after the referendum in September 2014.

By international standards, the FCWG concluded, Scotland was 'a wealthy and productive country'. Noting that under the status quo the Scottish government had no 'distinct input' into UK's fiscal policy, monetary policy, financial regulation and key elements of industrial policy, the report said under independence Scotland could 'organise and manage' its own macroeconomy. The early years of independence would be crucial, with a new Scottish state having to demonstrate 'stability, competence and fiscal sustainability' while also getting to grips with a significant increase in the 'economic and social policy levers at the disposal of policymakers in Scotland'.

The report, however, did not quite depict an independent Scotland enjoying the best of all possible worlds, warning of further austerity and of North Sea oil revenue doing little more than servicing its share of UK national debt. An independent Scotland ought, therefore, to make cautious budget assumptions to allow for volatility. This implied a significant cut in current spending levels, although the report suggested the change could be implemented in the medium rather than the short term.

The FCWG also agreed with the Scottish government's policy of leaving monetary policy in the hands of the Bank of England (BoE), although it said a currency union would require a 'fiscal sustainability agreement' that would inevitably place limits on both Scotland's and the rUK's tax and spending levels. The FCWG noted that EU rules would require an independent Scotland to regulate its own financial sector (Finance Secretary John Swinney had proposed leaving this 'solid framework' in the hands of the BoE),[16] perhaps called the Scottish Monetary Institute, while a 'Fiscal Commission' could advise future Scottish governments on public finances, something akin to the UK's Office of Budget Responsibility.[17]

These recommendations, said FCWG chairman Crawford Beveridge, offered 'a workable blend of autonomy, cohesion and continuity', and although that 'continuity' involved a lot of ongoing oversight from rUK institutions, the authors were confident Scottish ministers would still be left with considerable fiscal flexibility. Alex Salmond seemed quite content with what he called a 'substantial piece of information'. 'Our central argument is that if we match our great natural resources with the fantastic human resources of Scotland,' he told Sky News, 'we can build both a prosperous economy and, equally importantly, a just society.'

'Nothing to fear and everything to gain'

While the FCWG report had been a very public statement of economic intent, a Scottish Cabinet paper leaked the following month (March 2013) revealed the SNP's private thoughts. Somehow obtained by the Better Together campaign, the by then year-old briefing betrayed a rather more phlegmatic take on the likely state of Scotland's economy post-independence. Written by Finance Secretary John Swinney, this acknowledged heavy dependence on (volatile and declining) oil revenues, and thus uncertainty when it came to future spending power. Not only that, but the paper accepted that tax and spending would have to be in line with any 'fiscal pact' agreed with the Bank of England, while paying off Scotland's share of the UK's national debt would be a significant feature of the Scottish budget post-independence.

The former Labour Chancellor Alistair Darling seized on the document as proof that the SNP 'will tell tales to the people of Scotland even although, in private, they know the opposite to be true'. Few of the issues discussed in the paper were revelatory, but as Darling suggested, several had been vehemently refuted by Salmond et al. The Scottish government said the paper had been 'overtaken by events', while Swinney said it demonstrated 'just how seriously the Scottish government is approaching the task of managing Scotland's finances' as it approached the referendum.

He quoted a more upbeat portion, that Scotland had 'nothing to fear and everything to gain' in grasping the opportunities of independence, while an 'international comparison' indicated Scotland would be the eighth wealthiest country in the Organisation for Economic Co-operation and Development (OECD), compared with the UK in seventeenth place. 'The question every voter in Scotland must ask themselves between now and the autumn of next year,' concluded Swinney, 'is whether, given all these facts, Scotland can afford not to be independent.'[18]

Other reactions to the leaked paper – which was clearly embarrassing for the SNP – came from the Scottish Trades Union Congress (STUC). As Stephen Boyd wrote, the 'SNP's stubborn devotion to low taxes and apparent reticence in embracing anything that hints at radical change seems to constrain imaginative thinking'.

> From a trade union perspective, it would be appreciated if some solid ideas were forthcoming on ways in which independence, or indeed additional powers for Holyrood, might be used creatively to develop Scotland's economy – providing more and better jobs, reducing inequality, poverty and economic insecurity, building a financial system that supports productive investment and nurturing a new innovation system. There's been precious little of this stuff so far.[19]

Salmond affected to be relaxed about such criticism, saying he welcomed 'voices to the left of the SNP's social democratic position speaking up in favour of independence', just as he welcomed support 'from the entrepreneurial and more free-market perspective'. It highlighted, he added, that 'post-independence the people of Scotland will have the opportunity to choose from a range of political perspectives and parties'. Only occasionally did reality intrude; for example when Nicola Sturgeon admitted in late 2012 that independence would not 'magic away financial difficulties'.

'We're all Thatcherite now'

When it came to the question of taxation the SNP was conservative in some respects and more radical in others. In April 2012 Alex Salmond said an independent Scotland was 'likely to align our income tax rates [to those] across these islands', while almost a year later John Swinney said he did not 'envisage increases in personal taxation in an independent Scotland'. Nor did the Finance Secretary envisage

increasing tax on corporations or the North Sea oil industry; rather, he planned to foster a 'competitive business tax
regime' that would 'grow the economy and thereby grow the
tax base'.

Business taxation was a different matter. Cutting corporation tax, most likely by around 3p, had been a long-standing
SNP pledge, another fiscal idea borrowed from the Irish
model. This, according to a 2011 Scottish government
discussion paper (described by the STUC as 'an excruciat-
ingly awful piece of work') would create 27,000 jobs and a
1.4 per cent increase in output over a two-decade period.[20]
And when the UK government announced plans to cut the
rate to 20 per cent (also Salmond's target) by 2015, the SNP
leader simply committed to undercutting the UK rate by
3 per cent.

This policy presented a number of problems for the SNP.
The Scottish Labour Party quoted Salmond's economic
adviser Joseph Stiglitz, who warned cutting certain taxes in
order to increase revenue was 'just a gift to the corporations
increasing inequality in our society' (a rather curious point
given the previous Labour government had also reduced the
rate), while several experts believed the European Union
would simply block the move. Salmond also ducked questions about the resulting gap in government revenue (at
least in the short term), while left-wingers complained about
mixed messages. As the former Labour MSP John McAllion
put it, the pitch appeared to be that in an independent
Scotland 'we choose to embrace neo-liberalism ourselves
rather than having it imposed upon us from the outside'.[21]

Ireland illustrated the difference between headline and
effective rates of corporation tax, with most companies
headquartered in Dublin paying far less than 12.5 per cent
while employing few (and generally low-paid) workers, a
phenomenon known as 'brass plaque' syndrome – a symbolic
presence but often little more. And while David Cameron

embarked upon a (largely rhetorical) crusade to clamp down
on tax avoidance by international firms, Salmond rather half-
heartedly argued an independent Scotland would be 'better'
than the UK at collecting tax from the likes of Amazon,
Google and Starbucks, without actually explaining how.

At various points in 2013 the Scottish government also
floated the idea of tax breaks for film makers, targeted VAT
reductions for Scotland's restaurateurs and 'a reduction, or
indeed even an elimination' of air passenger duty, which
Salmond told the *Wall Street Journal* would 'more than pay
for itself in terms of gross domestic product growth, increase
in tourism and the increase in the take in other taxes such as
VAT', another example of Laffer Curve economics. This was
of course arguable, and more to the point hardly compatible
with the Scottish government's ambitious carbon-reduction
targets.

On this, as in other areas, Salmond was inconsistent. His
government had, after all, introduced a supermarket levy and
opposed Westminster's reduction in the 50p rate of income
tax, while at the first elections to the Scottish Parliament
in 1999 the SNP had enlivened an otherwise dull campaign
by promising to introduce a 'Penny for Scotland', a 1 per
cent increase in the SVR to fund additional public services.
Thereafter, however, suggested tax increases from Salmond
were rare, while the word 'redistribution' did not seem to
feature in the First Ministerial lexicon. Labour began accusing the SNP of wanting to turn an independent Scotland into
a 'tax haven', and it had a point.

As for how tax might be collected and administered in
an independent Scotland, a leaked Scottish Cabinet document suggested ministers would draw on 'international best
practice' to come up with 'a modern and efficient tax system
for an independent Scotland' (perhaps revealingly, it cited
Ireland as an example of 'best practice'). The paper estimated
it would cost £575–625 million, not an inconsiderable sum,

to establish and operate a system capable of handling around £50 billion in annual revenue.

Finance Secretary John Swinney, meanwhile, had already begun establishing a new body called 'Revenue Scotland' to handle the fiscal responsibilities due to be devolved under the 2012 Scotland Act, including stamp duty and landfill tax. Again, the emphasis was on administrative efficiency rather than redistribution. 'It is clear', judged Swinney privately, 'that clarity and simplicity in taxes help reduce the cost of administration.'[22] As Peter Mandelson once remarked, 'We're all Thatcherite now,' something echoed by a celebrated Salmond slip in 2008. Scotland, he argued, 'didn't mind the economic side' of Thatcherism 'so much', but did not 'like the social side at all' as if – somehow – the two were not related.[23]

In May 2013 the Scottish government published *Scotland's Economy: The Case for Independence*, an attempt to flesh out its economic case for independence, something that often relied on debating points rather than detailed policy. It divided the argument into four parts:

- Scotland can afford independence, not just because of oil but because Scottish finances are in better relative strength than the rUK's.
- Scotland has lots of potential, based on natural and human resources, and key productive sectors such as life sciences, tourism, renewable energy, food and drink and financial services.
- The Union is holding Scotland back, creating inequality and concentrating economic activity too closely in London.
- Independence would help Scotland fulfil its potential, for small countries are more nimble and better able to respond to changing global conditions.

Scottish government economists went further by identifying

ten fiscal levers (mainly taxation) and eight non-tax policies (mainly regulatory) that could be used in the event of independence. One economist praised such a 'strategic, developmental approach', although that ignored obvious contradictions between lowering many of the fiscal levers (taxes) while lifting others (welfare, capital borrowing etc.). Economic policy-making, the paper argued, would move away from the one-size-fits-all approach of the UK Treasury and towards a more decentralised, context-sensitive system. Renewables, which Salmond once claimed would 'reindustrialise' Scotland, was cited as a key industry of the future.

But the central tension in SNP economic policy manifested itself about halfway through *Scotland's Economy*. Having spent Sections 1 and 2 setting out 'the advantages and strengths of the Scottish economy', it suddenly changed tack in Section 3 and declared that UK government economic policy was 'letting Scotland down', as evidenced by the 'growing gap between rich and poor' and a disproportionately buoyant London and south-east. This attempt to argue that Scotland suffered from being in the Union while also pointing to a healthy economy was the inverse of the Unionist position, which asserted that a devolved Scotland was thriving within the Union but could end up being worse off under independence, a delicate balancing act neither side pulled off entirely successfully.

And while the Scottish government's point about inequality was all well and good, it rarely set out exactly what a future (and independent) SNP government would do – as the STUC's Stephen Boyd put it – 'to make a serious and enduring dent in inequality'. Challenged on this point, Alex Salmond and Nicola Sturgeon could only offer abolition of the 'bedroom tax'. 'This is about change for the long term,' she said elsewhere. 'It is about ending, once and for all, the cycle of deprivation so that our people can enter a thriving economy and contribute more meaningfully to their own well-being and that of the world.'[24] They were fine words, but the SNP's centre-right economic agenda did not strike left-wing observers as a sensible way of tackling growing inequality, independent or not.

The 'Union dividend'

Governing the Scottish government's budget was the Barnett Formula, conceived in 1978 to calculate the old Scottish Office block grant and based on UK public expenditure and Scotland's population share rather than tax raised or actual 'needs' north of the border. This system had survived under devolved government and meant that public spending in Scotland (excluding social security and debt interest) was, according to the Institute of Fiscal Studies, nearly 17 per cent higher per head,[25] something often referred to, with a touch of hyperbole, as the 'Union dividend'.

All this was raked over during an annual bun fight concerning Government Expenditure and Revenue Scotland (otherwise known as GERS, not to be confused with the Glasgow football club). Conceived in 1991 by the then Secretary of State for Scotland, Ian Lang, as a way of demonstrating what a good deal Scotland got from being part of the UK, by 2007 the Scottish government (which had gained control of statistical analysis in 1999) was equally determined to wield GERS as proof of how well off an independent Scotland might be.

It was rather difficult to argue Scotland was hard done by. Only by dwelling on certain categories of payments and ignoring or touching lightly on others could GERS be depicted as a raw deal: total (Scottish and UK) government spending north of the border had more than doubled to £64.5 billion between 1999 and 2011/12 (partly, of course, due to inflation), and while a total of £40 billion was due to be stripped from Scottish budgets up until 2025, that was a lower reduction, in relative terms, than most UK government departments.

Some of this overspend was easily justified, for the cost of delivering public services in a predominantly rural part of the UK such as Scotland was disproportionate, while social security spending in deprived parts of, for example, Glasgow, was well above the national average. Even taking into account all these factors, however, Scotland still got more than it ought to on a strict 'needs' basis. Wales, for example, regularly received 2 or 3 per cent less than it would have been entitled to if judged on need.

This obviously created resentment, not least among English taxpayers, whose frustrations were regularly aired – in simplistic terms – in newspapers like the *Daily Mail*. That those south of the border 'paid for' higher public spending in Scotland was both true *and* false; true in that the Scottish block grant was paid out of general taxation, and of course most of the UK's taxpayers were based in England, but false in that Scotland was not the only part of the UK to benefit from Barnett. Northern Ireland, for example, regularly received more per head, while even London benefited from a Barnett dividend similar to that of Scotland.

The SNP said the 2011/12 GERS figures demonstrated that Scotland was financially stronger than the UK as a whole to the tune of £4.4 billion, equivalent to £824 per person.[26] This was significant, for opinion polling had suggested being £500 a year better off would be enough to significantly increase support for independence (although equally the prospect of being £500 a year worse off reduced the likely 'yes' vote to just 18 per cent). Although Alex Salmond and John Swinney were careful to note this was a 'relative surplus', i.e. a lower deficit than in the rest of the UK, other independence supporters behaved as if it meant the average Scot would have more money to spend as they pleased. A deficit, of course, was still a deficit.

Yes Scotland (and SNP MSPs) also repeated the favoured – but ultimately misleading – statistic that in 2011/12 Scotland had generated 9.9 per cent of UK tax revenues but received only 9.3 per cent of total UK spending. As Better Together pointed out, 9.3 per cent of UK expenditure (£64.5 billion) was still a larger sum than the total tax take in Scotland (£56.9 billion, including a share of oil revenues). It was, in non-economic parlance, like comparing apples with pears.

But there were, of course, lies, damned lies and statistics, and inevitably both sides claimed victory. Labour's Ken Macintosh said the GERS figures showed 'the benefit to all Scots of remaining part of the UK', while Blair Jenkins, chief executive of Yes Scotland, said they demonstrated that Scotland had 'one of the best sets of national accounts of any country in the developed world'. But GERS simply described the fiscal position of a *devolved* Scotland and therefore, as Dr Andrew Goudie pointed out, revealed 'little, if anything, about the state of the public accounts were a radically different constitutional arrangement to be put in place'.[27] The Centre for Public Policy for Regions, meanwhile, urged the Scottish government to develop a Scottish measurement of gross national income (GNI) rather than GDP, which it said 'would provide the clearest picture of the level of Scotland's prosperity and how it is changing over time'.[28]

It's Scotland's oil

The argument over North Sea oil revenue is almost as old as the modern independence debate, and central to many of these calculations. The SNP capitalised early on, crying, 'It's Scotland's Oil', a memorable slogan which helped the party win seven and eleven MPs respectively at the two general elections of 1974. The discovery of 'black gold' gave the Nationalists the confidence to make an economic case for Scottish independence for the first time. As the authors of *Scotland's Choices* observed, 'But for North Sea oil, Scotland would probably not now be facing the choices it is.'[29]

Private civil service advice appeared to confirm some

Nationalist arguments. A 1974 memo written by the Scottish Office's chief economist, Dr Gavin McCrone, said it was

> quite clear ... the balance of payments gain from North Sea oil would easily swamp the existing deficit whatever its size and transform Scotland into a country with a substantial and chronic surplus ... [it] would tend to be in chronic surplus to a quite embarrassing degree and its currency would become the hardest in Europe, with the exception perhaps of the Norwegian kroner.[30]

Although McCrone's analysis was heavily caveated with warnings about the risks oil wealth could present to an independent Scotland (in terms of monetary policy, inflation and wages), Harold Wilson's government – determined to take 'the wind out of the SNP sails' – made sure the document remained classified.[31] In 2005 the SNP secured it under Freedom of Information legislation, and has made much of what Alex Salmond called its 'duplicity' ever since. In 2013, the former Labour Chancellor Denis Healey appeared to confirm Nationalist suspicions, saying 'we did underplay the value of the oil to the country because of the threat of nationalism'.

There was, in fact, very little evidence that this was so. Some government forecasts of likely oil revenue in the 1970s were certainly incorrect, while others were reasonably accurate, a disparity which simply demonstrated how difficult it was to predict. McCrone believed it was poor analysis by the then Department for Trade and Industry, while Professor Alex Kemp, the official historian of North Sea oil, believed the UK government had been upfront about its economic potential. There were, however, consistent claims the oil would quickly run out,[32] although this was a widely held view based on independent analysis. It just turned out to be wrong.

So of the benefits there was little doubt, then or now, but Scotland's legal position was less clear-cut. Given that Scotland was not a sovereign state, it clearly had no direct claim to the North Sea's oilfields. The existence of two separate legal systems in mainland Britain, however, provided a theoretical boundary between the Scottish and rUK sectors, with the Continental Shelf Act 1964 and the Continental Shelf (Jurisdiction) Order 1968 defining the area under jurisdiction of Scots law. Also pertinent was the Scottish Adjacent Waters Boundary Order 1999, which had (controversially) moved Scotland's marine and fishing boundary north.

It was, however, generally accepted that around 90 per cent of the UK's oil resources lay in 'Scottish waters', and assuming the principles of the United Nations Convention on the Law of the Sea – used in defining the maritime assets of newly formed states, as well as disputes between existing ones – were applied, then an independent Scotland would get roughly that share. Two experts at Dundee University, however, argued that the International Court of Justice would 'likely' favour a more northerly line, pushing certain reserves into English waters, a negotiation which they predicted could take several years.[33] A per capita division, on the other hand, would give an independent Scotland just 8 per cent of oil revenues. Unsurprisingly, the SNP seemed content with a population share of every other UK asset except oil, an inconsistency the former SNP strategist Stephen Noon explained thus: 'The coal under Yorkshire or Wales was not put there by the Union. Scotland has no claim to it. And the Union didn't put oil and gas under Scottish waters, so, quite simply, the rest of the UK has no claim to that.'[34] This was both a curious distinction, and, of course, a convenient one.

Another aspect of the SNP's argument was that Scotland has not benefited from the oil revenue that has flowed into Treasury coffers since the late 1970s. This did not quite stack up, for the Scottish block grant was of course funded by the Treasury, and as the GERS figures made clear, per capita spending in Scotland had generally been above the UK average for a similar period, if not longer. As several economists pointed out, taken together over the past three decades this Barnett 'consequential' was roughly equivalent to Scotland's geographical share of the proceeds from North Sea oil. The economist Gavin McCrone reckoned an 'assumed geographical share of the oil and gas revenues in the last few years would approximately compensate for this [higher spending], though not to the extent of eliminating all of the present deficit'.[35]

And so the argument went on, and while the SNP no longer cried 'it's Scotland's oil', it continued to claim an independent Scotland would be extremely wealthy as a result. Using a GDP measurement, this was certainly true (with Scotland galloping up the OECD charts), but assessed by GNI per head, an independent Scotland and rUK actually ranked joint thirteenth. The difference was due to the sheer extent of foreign ownership, a point Alex Salmond and his colleagues usually skirted over, constantly reminding voters the North Sea might yet yield £1 trillion worth of oil, ignoring the fact that most of that would go to private companies, *not* an independent Scottish Treasury, something that did not stop the First Minister claiming that 'marvellous bonus' would amount to '£300,000 for every man, women and child in Scotland'. The SNP, however, was conscious that generating the impression an independent Scotland's economy would depend upon oil was a weakness in their pitch, thus Salmond's change of tone in the summer of 2013, when he said that if oil revenue was 'taken out of the equation, then Scotland's economic output per head is almost identical to that of the UK. The benefit we get from oil and gas will be a huge bonus.'

The idea of investing some of this oil revenue for future use also survived from the 1970s, although unhelpfully the SNP often gave the impression tax receipts could both be invested *and* used in general expenditure. Initially, Salmond spoke of channelling £1 billion a year into an oil fund,[36] although he later added the caveat 'when fiscal circumstances allow' to a couple of speeches in early 2012.[37] A leaked Scottish Cabinet paper also conceded the obvious point that investing in an oil fund would 'require some downward revision in current spending'. Nevertheless, it was generally acknowledged that shrewdly managed sovereign wealth funds could yield significant rewards. A report from the Fiscal Commission Working Group recommended the creation of both a short-term stabilisation fund and a long-term savings fund, while the Scottish government pointed repeatedly to Norway, whose oil fund stood at a massive £330 billion, dwarfing its debt and annual economic output.

It had, however, taken six years for Norway to make its first investment, while its oil industry – unlike the UK's – was government owned; building up a genuinely beneficial endowment, in other words, could be both slow and expensive, while Norway had also enjoyed a lower deficit and higher oil revenue than Scotland. Even so, had a Scottish wealth fund been established in 1980 (with 10 per cent of tax receipts invested each year), then its value in 2008 would have stood at £47 billion, almost equal to Scotland's total tax receipts in a single year. Eventually, former Chancellor Alistair Darling acknowledged the missed opportunity, reflecting that 'if we had our time over again, perhaps we should have [set up a fund]'.

That said, there was obviously no guarantee a hypothetically independent Scotland would have followed the Norway model, and what had *not* happened in the 1980s could hardly be undone. Salmond claimed it would '*perhaps* handle the oil and gas better than the government at Westminster' [my italics], while an oil fund would act as a fiscal buffer should the Scottish economy experience peaks and troughs. The

Westminster government's fifth 'Scotland Analysis' paper argued that the UK already shielded Scotland from fiscal fluctuation, while the historian Graham Stewart took an unfashionable view, arguing that given the lower price of oil post-1985, 'far from squandering future revenue, the Treasury had maximised petroleum revenue tax at exactly the right moment' without any need for a sovereign wealth fund.[38]

The major benefit from North Sea oil had come between 1980 and 1986, when the UK's fiscal deficit would have rocketed without the resulting revenue, but after 1987 there had been no real difference because oil had been on a declining trend. Forecasts of future revenue varied, but it generally pointed downward, the Office of Budget Responsibility (OBR) taking a particularly pessimistic view in predicting a sharp drop to just £4 billion a year by 2017. Most projections showed steady depletion until the middle of the twenty-first century, although Nationalists said they had heard it all before. The Scottish energy minister Fergus Ewing, for example, told a Houston conference that in his 'personal view' oil and gas production would continue until the year 2100.

There was also a lack of clarity about decommissioning costs, estimated to be as high as £30–35 billion. Ewing implied the UK government would have a 'moral' duty to foot the bill (even after independence), an argument that rather ignored its significant investment in North Sea oil extraction throughout the 1970s. Professor Kemp, however, believed the 'great majority of the decommissioning expenditures' would 'be incurred in what would become the Scottish sector',[39] while a Scottish government paper said it would ask rUK to stump up a share of North Sea decommissioning tax relief 'subject to negotiation'.[40] The UK government, however, warned that while Scots would have to pay £300 a head (for the £20 billion it had committed towards decommissioning costs) as part of the UK, with independence that would rise to £3,800 per head.[41]

And while the Scottish government acknowledged (privately) that the OBR's projections had 'not been seriously challenged by the industry or by independent commentators', ministers decided to publish their own forecasts which, not surprisingly, showed a much higher revenue level, perhaps as much as £57.1 billion by 2017/18. Although this appeared pretty shameless, Professor Kemp believed the SNP had a point in taking on the OBR, although perhaps not its talk of a 'second oil boom'.

There was no implication, meanwhile, that independence would radically alter the UK Continental Shelf's tax regime, which amounted to a total effective tax rate of between 62 and 81 per cent (depending on the age of the field), considerably lower than Norway's. 'The whole system', remarked Professor Kemp with typical understatement, 'is very complex.' Nevertheless Unionists claimed the referendum caused uncertainty (a survey suggested a third of North Sea oil and gas companies considered the outcome relevant to their future plans), while David Cameron asked Scottish businessman Sir Ian Wood to examine ways of unlocking the potential of remaining reserves. The industry, added the Prime Minister, was the 'jewel in the crown of the United Kingdom economy', an example of the generally more positive tone taken by UK ministers when not speaking in the context of the independence referendum.

The renewables capital of Europe

There was also a wider environmental point. Basing an independent Scotland's economy on the burning of fossil fuels hardly sat easily with ambitious carbon-reduction plans (though these proved more theoretical than real, with the Scottish government repeatedly missing its own targets). Yet at the same time the First Minister was apparently dedicated to encouraging 'clean' renewable energy, which he claimed gave Scotland the potential to become the 'Dubai of the north'.

With a pledge to generate most of its electricity needs from renewable sources by 2020, firms such as Areva, Gamesa and Samsung noticed the Scottish government's enthusiasm (and therefore subsidies) for the sector, while the First Minister proved a charismatic salesman. But however bold and positive his vision of a renewables-fuelled Scotland, Salmond was also guilty of overstating the potential benefits. He had to apologise after telling MSPs the renewables sector had created 18,000 jobs in Scotland when in fact the figure was 11,000, while Professor John Kay – together with several industry experts – flagged up an inconvenient truth: that even though Scotland was 'wet and windy', renewable energy 'was inherently unprofitable, and viable only through cross-subsidy from electricity consumers, mainly English ones'. This was a key point. Indeed, Brian Wilson, a former UK energy minister, praised Salmond's renewables vision but argued his whole energy strategy was 'profoundly Unionist in character'.[42]

Eventually the SNP conceded that a single UK energy market ought to exist even after independence. As *The Economist* put it, 'all sides benefit from a system that allows the easy transmission of electricity from England's power stations to Scotland when the winds are calm up north, and from Scotland's wind farms to the south on days when they have excess capacity'. The Scottish government also chose not to quibble with the UK government's Energy Bill, which would govern the subsidies for green energy well beyond September 2014. A leaked Scottish government paper (which described North Sea oil as a 'damaging, price-volatile fossil fuel') argued that as renewable technologies were a 'shared objective of Scotland and the rest of the UK' then it was 'equitable that these costs continue to be shared among consumers in Scotland and the rest of the UK'.[43]

Whether – and indeed why – the rUK government would agree to an 'energy union' was a moot point; the Energy

Secretary, Ed Davey, warned that an independent Scotland would 'have to compete with other foreign countries' in providing renewable energy, although the UK and Scottish governments, as the Scottish government paper observed, had similar aims to reduce greenhouse gas emissions, ensure security of supply and minimise costs while increasing reliance on renewable energy. One point of difference was nuclear energy, which the SNP refused to entertain as part of a future energy mix, promising only to sustain existing power stations but not build any replacements.

Keep the pound!

But the SNP's 'energy unionism' was nothing compared to its plans for sterling. Adopted with little fanfare in 2005,[44] the proposed 'currency union' was very much in keeping with Alex Salmond's 'gradualist' approach to independence. This argued that retaining the pound in the event of a 'yes' vote would be the 'best option' for both parties. In taking another leaf out of the Parti Québécois playbook (which had pledged to retain the Canadian dollar even after 'separation'), the SNP had ended up subconsciously echoing William Hague's 2001 cry of 'Keep the Pound!'

This was curious, for the SNP leader had spent much of his career attacking the Bank of England for ignoring the needs of Scotland as it set interest rates and monetary policy. As the pro-independence economists Jim and Margaret Cuthbert concluded, 'ceding control over monetary policy' would result in it being 'delivered primarily in the interests of the south-east of England'.[45] Taken together with dire warnings about sterling 'sinking like a stone', Salmond's gradual conversion to retaining the pound was naturally derided by his opponents. The Scottish government might consider it a 'strong and coherent economic narrative', but the crucial point was this: from the point of view of those seeking self-determination, monetary policy in an independent Scotland would not be self-determined; two of the things Salmond wanted for Scotland, independence and a shared currency with the rest of the UK, were simply irreconcilable.

Thus Salmond sought to play down its importance. 'I don't think monetary policy – that is the control of the exchange rate – is a *sine qua non* of independence,' Salmond told *Time* magazine in late 2011, while the following year he said people 'often exaggerate the importance of monetary policy; fiscal policy has primacy in the modern world'. The 'essence' of economic independence, he added in April 2013, was the ability to control tax rates, which, under 'independence in Europe' meant Scotland would control 100 per cent of its taxation base, rather than 8 per cent under the status quo.

The economist John Kay, however, believed the choice of currency 'would be the most important economic decision for an independent Scotland', all other aspects of economic policy being 'contingent on that choice'.[46] Scotland had only enjoyed a full currency union with England since 1805, when the 'pound Scots' was finally fixed against sterling and transaction costs abolished. Ireland, meanwhile, had not used the pound until 1846, and carried on doing so for six years following its secession in 1922. It only established a central bank in 1943, and did not break the link with sterling until 1979.

Despite this precedent, the UK government initially claimed an independent Scotland would *not* be able to use sterling. The SNP rightly said it was a fully convertible currency, citing other countries that used another nation's currency, even under less than ideal circumstances: Montenegro might use the euro without being a member of the eurozone, and El Salvador the dollar without being a US state, but that did not mean their respective interests were taken into account by the European Central Bank and US Federal Reserve.

But once the UK government conceded sterling *could* be used by an independent Scotland, it redirected its fire to what that might mean in practice. 'Scotland within the monetary union, but fiscally independent,' commented Danny Alexander in late 2011, 'creates similar risks to those we see in the Eurozone.' The Fiscal Commission Working Group later rejected this, pointing out that while the differences between Germany and Greece were stark, the same could not be said of Scotland and rUK. Even so, Alexander's analogy was valid, and there were also concerns from other parts of the UK, Wales's First Minister, Carwyn Jones, warning there 'would be a real risk for the continuing UK if it were to enter a euro-style currency zone with an independent Scotland'.

All of this had been played out at some length before the Chancellor of the Exchequer travelled to Glasgow in April 2013 to launch the second of the UK government's 'Scotland Analysis' papers, this time on currency. An independent Scottish state, he argued, would have four main currency options:

- continue to use sterling with a formal agreement with the continuing UK (a sterling currency union);
- use sterling unilaterally, with no formal agreement with the continuing UK ('sterlingisation');
- join the euro; or
- introduce a new Scottish currency.

Each of these options, the paper argued, would 'affect transaction costs, fiscal and monetary policy and financial stability in an independent Scottish state'. It also made clear that the UK government believed the best option was not actually on the list, i.e. the status quo.

Of the SNP's preferred currency route, it had this to say: 'In practice this [currency union] would be likely to require rigorous oversight of Scotland's economic and fiscal plans by both the new Scottish and the continuing UK authorities.'[47] Indeed, as the rUK's GDP would be about seventeen times that of Scotland, it seemed likely an independent Scotland's negotiating position would not exactly be strong. Ministers also made the point that goodwill might not be enough. After all, the Czech–Slovak monetary union had broken down just thirty-three days after the 'Velvet Divorce' in 1993.

Under questioning, the Chancellor went even further, saying it might 'not be worth it' for the UK to join a currency union. Such a drastic approach in the event of a 'yes' vote seemed unlikely, although the key – and most pertinent – question concerned the conditions rUK would impose as a *quid pro quo*. Alex Salmond accused Osborne of 'political sabre-rattling', later implying in a speech on the Isle of Man that his Plan B might be an informal currency union with the rest of the UK, even though his Fiscal Commission had specifically ruled this out. 'Advanced economies of a significant scale tend not to operate such a monetary framework,' it stated. 'Though an option in the short-term, it is not likely to be a long-term solution.'[48]

Salmond also raised the stakes in another respect. 'If the Westminster government's position is that we should not be entitled to our own currency and other shared assets,' he argued, 'then the only logical extension of that argument is that an independent Scotland will not inherit any share of the UK's debts.' The First Minister had a point on this, for if the UK insisted on being the sole successor state then international precedents suggested *only it* would be liable in terms of debt. 'We would be liberated', said John Swinney, 'from a population share of the UK's debt of £125 billion.' The UK government did not really respond to this point, instead suggesting an independent Scotland would be considered a 'basket case' by international markets.

Although the SNP used to claim an independent Scotland had already paid off its share of the UK's debt via North Sea oil revenue, ministers generally accepted an 'equitable' share would need to be negotiated should voters back independence.

The Fiscal Commission Working Group suggested it might be 'gradually transferred', while the leaked Scottish Cabinet paper conceded that 'interest payments on inherited debt [would] be a significant feature of Scotland's budget after independence'. But the former permanent secretary to the Scottish Government, Sir John Elvidge, also reckoned the 'benign gaze' of the international community would ensure Scotland was not short-changed by London over the division of national debt. 'Various international partners have no interest in inequitable economic outcomes,' he told a House of Lords all-party group. 'One might think that Europe and the rest of the world had enough limping economic passengers without wishing to see any more created.'[49]

But then, if an independent Scotland was forced to shoulder a share of UK debt, it was only logical it should share its assets too. These had been set out in 2007, including total fixed assets (under devolved control) worth nearly £23 billion in Scotland.[50] These would likely be carved up in two ways: immovable assets within each territory accruing accordingly, while shared assets (for example overseas possessions and the Bank of England) would be split according to a formula.

And while Salmond accepted the need for a 'sustainability arrangement' with rUK's central bank, he denied this would give it 'oversight' of an independent Scotland's budget. As Alistair Darling (who had at one point conceded a currency union would be 'logical') put it, 'They don't seem to understand if you have a currency union, there are terms and conditions about your taxation, about your borrowing, about your spending. Whatever else that is, it is not independence.'[51] The Scottish Labour leader Johann Lamont also mocked the First Minister, saying he wanted 'a divorce but to keep the joint bank account'. On the other hand, Gus O'Donnell argued it was in rUK's 'interest to have a flourishing Scotland'. 'If, by choosing slightly different tax rates,' he continued, 'and allocating spending differently, Scottish growth is higher, then this should also raise UK growth.'[52]

The First Minister pointed to two precedents without obvious fiscal constraints: the Isle of Man ('a living example of a territory that is not part of the UK but which is effectively in a currency union with the UK') and the Belgium–Luxembourg currency union that existed between 1922 and 1999. Not only had the latter accommodated significant tax differentials, but Luxembourg – with no central bank of its own – had shared monetary management with its larger neighbour. There was an obvious problem with both these examples: size. As the book *Scotland's Choices* put it, 'Small offshore tax havens have a real but limited effect on UK tax revenue. A tax haven of five million people with a land border and excellent communications with the rUK would be a greater challenge.'[53]

The currency union stance also prevented the SNP attacking the UK's economic record quite as strongly as it might have. Rather, the Scottish government appeared to be arguing both *for* and *against* maintaining a close relationship with the economic status quo, as the Bank of England would naturally continue to set interest levels – and therefore Scottish mortgage rates – even after a 'yes' vote. A rather defensive Scottish government repeatedly cited the FCWG's first report, claiming an independent Scotland would take a 'shareholding' of nearly 10 per cent in the Old Lady of Threadneedle Street, which, after all, had been publicly owned since 1946.

Although talk of a 'shareholding' was misleading (a percentage share of the asset would have been more accurate), the SNP said it would amount to 10 per cent more than Scotland had as part of the UK. But on this point Scottish ministers resorted to assertion. When Nicola Sturgeon claimed an independent Scotland could appoint a representative to the Bank's nine-strong Monetary Policy Committee

(MPC), all she could find to back it up was a half-hearted quote from former MPC member David Blanchflower, who said the Scottish government's position was 'probably not unreasonable'.

Even if that were true, however, a Scottish representative faced being outvoted by 8–1 on any future point of disagreement, while an independent Scotland would have little or no influence over legislative changes decided by the Westminster parliament. John Swinney, meanwhile, claimed he had enjoyed a 'very helpful dialogue' with the Bank of England over future arrangements, something formally denied by the Bank itself. And although Sir Mervyn King paid Alex Salmond a courtesy call during his 'farewell tour' as governor, Danny Alexander said the UK government had still to receive any correspondence from the Scottish government on the subject. Professor Brian Quinn, a former deputy governor of the Bank of England, said a currency union would introduce 'administrative complexity, confused governance and flawed decision-taking' into Scotland's financial system. 'Trying to stand astride two horses heading in diverging directions', he added, 'could lead, sooner or later, to an expensive accident.'[54] In all the referendum debates about economics, this was undoubtedly the point on which the SNP was weakest.

Euro, groat, scottie, or S£?

Prior to 2005, the SNP had made positive noises about joining the European single currency, but even before the eurozone crisis Salmond had begun to distance himself, instead keeping it in reserve as a long-term prospect. This too would have meant constraints, although a reasonable case could be made that the European Central Bank in Frankfurt might apply a lighter touch than the Bank of England in London, for the European Union already tolerated considerable fiscal variation between member states.

There was also much talk about whether membership of the EU would compel an independent Scotland to join the euro. The balance of expert opinion seemed to think it would, but it was, at least in the short term, rather academic. Economic and political turmoil in Cyprus – which supplied an uncomfortable backdrop to the currency debate in the spring of 2013 – probably hardened SNP minds against joining that particular European club. Besides, party policy required 'the sanction of the people in a referendum', a device Sweden had also used to get round membership of the single currency. The FCWG had, however, left open the option of an independent Scotland pursuing the fourth of the Treasury's options: adopting a new Scottish currency. Indeed, giving evidence to a Scottish Parliament committee, Joseph Stiglitz said the FCWG had weighed up 'transition' currency arrangements 'versus the long run'. He added:

> It will be important to have a structure that has flexibility, so that over time the institutions will be able to adapt to the change in circumstances. As we thought about that issue, the two notions that were influential were the smoothness of the transition and the flexibility to move eventually to the institutional structure that is appropriate for Scotland.[55]

The implication was clear and, perhaps revealingly, when asked Alex Salmond refused to rule out adopting a Scottish currency at some point in the future. The need for stability was key. Even a vague commitment to going down such a road, immediately or in the near future, might produce what John Kay called 'speculative activity'. As the economist Michael Dooley put it in 1998, 'Monetary arrangements are given birth at conference tables, and laid to rest in foreign exchange markets.'

On the other hand DeAnne Julius, a founder member of the MPC, said a new currency (which she called the 'scottie') would 'not depend on uncertain negotiations' and was 'the only option that would allow Scotland to set its own monetary policy and make its own trade-offs with fiscal policy'.[56] And while its exchange rate might fluctuate wildly if the new country's government lacked credibility in international markets, Norway, Sweden, Denmark and Switzerland all demonstrated that it *was* possible, in practice as well as in theory.

The currency debate also produced the first tangible split in the pro-independence camp when Yes Scotland chairman Dennis Canavan said a Scottish currency would give an independent Scotland 'more flexibility, more freedom' than keeping the pound. The Jimmy Reid Foundation, a left-leaning think tank, agreed, as did the Scottish Greens and Socialists. Some commentators even (half-jokingly) suggested Scotland might adopt the bitcoin, a then fast-growing virtual currency.

Sustainable and responsible financial services

'The near collapse of the Royal Bank of Scotland was psychologically very damaging,' recalled a former employee, 'not just for those of us who worked there, but for independence and the SNP. It was supposed to be Scotland's success story.'[57] Indeed, Salmond's long association with RBS had not always been helpful. A letter he had written to Fred (previously Sir Fred) Goodwin offering support for the bank's acquisition of ABN Amro frequently came back to haunt him. And while the First Minister made vague noises about 'consistent taxes on bonuses' and 'greedy' bankers, he never sounded particularly sincere.

When it came to the bailout, the SNP argued an independent Scotland would only have been liable for around 5 per cent of the £65 billion cost, reasoning that (assuming a currency union) the Bank of England would have been compelled to step in and help. It also implied that the constitutional status quo, rather than Scottish bankers, had been to blame. 'The events of the past few years aren't the result of independence,' blogged Stephen Noon, 'they are the consequence of the Union.'[58] Salmond, of course, had not demurred in any meaningful way from UK banking policy, while at points he had even advocated lighter financial regulation, telling *The Times* in April 2007 that an independent Scotland would pledge 'a light-touch regulation suitable to a Scottish financial sector with its outstanding reputation for probity'. Only several years later did the First Minister admit that 'with the benefit of hindsight we'd [have done] things differently'.

Alistair Darling, meanwhile, presented his rescue of RBS and HBOS as part of the 'Union dividend':

> In the United Kingdom, we share opportunities and we also share risks. Four years ago Scotland's banks were on the brink of collapse. The size and strength of the UK meant that we could stop that and also that Scottish taxpayers carried only a small part of the cost. Ireland and Iceland were not so fortunate.[59]

Similarly, the economist Gavin McCrone reckoned had Scotland already been independent in 2008, 'it would not have been able to cope with the losses incurred by its banks, whatever arrangements had been put in place ... the Scottish government's finances would have been overwhelmed and, like Ireland, it would have had to seek a bailout from international organisations.'[60]

The UK government's third 'Scotland Analysis' paper on banking and financial services pointed out that a Scottish banking sector would be 'exceptionally large compared to the size of an independent Scotland's economy',[61] thus making it more vulnerable to financial shocks. At the document's launch in Edinburgh, Scottish Secretary Michael Moore and Economic Secretary to the Treasury Sajid Javid even raised the spectre of Greece.

More widely, the paper pointed out that an independent Scotland would need to establish its own regulatory and consumer protection schemes, something John Swinney rebutted with plans for a 'Scottish Consumer Authority', which he envisaged assuming the functions of more than ninety bodies, including the Furniture Ombudsman, National Caravan Council and the Carpet Foundation, a model derived from the Netherlands' *Geschillencommissie* system.[62]

Javid, meanwhile, warned that many firms might relocate given that 90 per cent of their customers were based outside Scotland. Sir John Gieve, a former deputy governor of the Bank of England, suggested Scotland's banking giants would face 'considerable market pressures' to leave their Edinburgh headquarters. The Scottish government talked vaguely of a 'thriving financial service sector' making 'the right services available to all of Scotland's people',[63] but its pitch was essentially a conservative one: everything would stay the same, not least a sympathetic tax regime. In his introduction to another document called *Sustainable, Responsible Banking*, Salmond referred obliquely to addressing the 'issues of the past' and building a 'new relationship' with customers 'firmly based on traditional Scottish banking values'.[64] The STUC's Stephen Boyd was unconvinced. 'A too large banking sector absorbs resources (e.g. engineers, mathematicians etc.) that could be more productively deployed elsewhere,' he blogged. 'It contributes to higher inequality, destabilises the wider economy and exerts a degree of political influence that cannot be reconciled with a healthy democracy.'[65]

Boyd had a point, for there was little in the Scottish government's banking paper that appeared to challenge the status quo under the Union. Only proposals for a Scottish Business Development Bank stood out as new or original. But the wider point was this: what scope would an independent Scotland, particularly one in a currency union with rUK, actually have to recalibrate its banking sector? The paper claimed independence would 'allow Scotland access to the necessary levers to encourage a responsible, sustainable banking sector that better meets the needs of the Scottish people', but there was precious little detail as to how.

Good for business?

Scottish businesses, always a cautious group when it came to constitutional change, certainly favoured as much fiscal and monetary continuity as possible. With this in mind, the UK government stressed that Britain's 'true single market' was another compelling reason for Scotland to reject independence. A UK government paper argued that even EU membership would not compensate for the loss of such a liberal regime governing the flow of goods, services, capital and people, whereas trade between newly independent nations would likely incur additional 'red tape'. A fifth 'Scotland Analysis' paper highlighted what it called the 'border effect', warning that the long-term effect of independence would reduce Scotland's GDP by 4 per cent over the next three decades,[66] although of course the British Isles already tolerated several borders – not least in Ireland – with no demonstrable impact on its economy. 'There is a useful piece of work to be done on the trading implications, positive and negative, of prospective independence,' remarked John McLaren of the Centre for Public Policy for Regions (CPPR). 'This isn't it.'

Following the SNP's landslide in May 2011, the Scottish and UK governments had engaged in a prolonged ding-dong about whether or not the referendum was good (or indeed bad) for business. George Osborne claimed it was damaging the Scottish economy (without giving specific examples), while the First Minister cited an Ernst & Young report listing Scotland as the top-performing location in the UK for inward investment in 2010/11.

And although most businesses kept their own counsel (Rupert Soames of Aggreko said business leaders feared attracting 'rains of bile and ire' from angry Nationalists), others stuck their heads above the parapet. Citigroup warned clients not to invest their money in Scottish renewables, while the energy giant Scottish and Southern Energy (SSE) said uncertainty risked damaging economic growth in Scotland and the rest of the UK. CBI Scotland – a particularly unpopular body with the SNP – concurred, as did the Weir Group and industry body Scottish Engineering. Yes Scotland was unimpressed, with its chief strategist Stephen Noon even tweeting (under the hash tag 'lessonlearnt') that 'big business said No to devolution in 97 – if we'd listened we'd have NHS privatisation, student fees, no free personal care'.

Standard & Poor's, Moody's and Fitch, meanwhile, suggested an independent Scotland would not automatically inherit the UK's high credit rating, although when this was downgraded in February 2013 it proved embarrassing for Better Together, which had produced campaign material listing this as a benefit of the Union. Jim McColl of Clyde Blowers urged a 'management buy-out' to break London's dominance of the UK economy and threatened to withdraw his business from Scotland if it did not vote 'yes'; the Ultimo bra supremo Michelle Mone deployed an identical threat if it did.

The backing of businessmen like McColl was important in giving the SNP's economic arguments wider credibility. In March 2013 Alex Salmond, Nicola Sturgeon and John Swinney all attended a dinner at the five-star Gleneagles Hotel, where the violinist Nicola Benedetti entertained executives from leading firms. Other select gatherings were planned, with the First Minister arguing the referendum had increased Scotland's profile and was, therefore, good for business. 'Once we get onto people's radar,' he told France 24, 'then we've got the international agencies ... which can offer people not just incentive packages but more importantly the skills they're looking for to do the job.'

There was also the wider question of business confidence during both the 2014 referendum campaign and its aftermath. Devolution in 1999 had caused some uncertainty among businesses but nothing too serious, although during the final two weeks of the 1995 Quebec sovereignty referendum there had been a fall on the Toronto Stock Exchange and in the value of the Canadian dollar, and rises in interest rates, all related to polls showing the 'yes' campaign to be ahead in voting intentions. After the narrow 'no' vote had been declared, all three returned to pre-referendum levels.

Scotland was not Quebec, which accounted for a greater proportion of Canada's population, but nevertheless 'capital flight' under such scenarios was a recognised phenomenon, having occurred in Ireland in 1922 and Slovakia in 1993. Even assuming both sides stressed continuity and stability, not least via a currency union, it would be naïve to assume nothing similar would happen should Scotland secede from the UK. Even a year before the referendum, for example, Glasgow City Council complained that two English local authorities had refused it loans beyond September 2014, a decision taken as a sign of 'market uncertainty'.

The economic consequences of independence could, of course, be argued either way, and had been for more than four decades, although as the journalist Peter Geoghegan observed it was a rather narrow debate, an endless fixation on corporation tax speaking 'volumes for the poverty of the economic discussion on independence'.[67] And while Professor John Kay accepted an independent Scotland 'would clearly be economically viable', he argued that on 'both politics and economics, the advocates for full independence have tended to overstate their case'. 'The reality is that Scotland would gain little by full independence,' he added. 'In the modern world, economic sovereignty for small nations is inescapably limited, and political sovereignty is largely symbolic.'[68]

Even so, in a June 2013 lecture Kay posited that independence was not 'primarily an economic issue'. 'Anyone who goes to the ballot box in 2014 believing either that they should vote no because independence for Scotland would be likely to be an economic disaster or vote yes because they believe it is likely to lead to an economic bonanza,' he argued, 'has failed to review the issues sensibly.'[69] The referendum expert Dr Matt Qvortrup also challenged the orthodoxy that voters would reach a view primarily on the basis of economics. 'That may well be the case for general elections,' he reasoned. 'But referendums about independence are birds of another feather and require a different tactic.'[70] The economics of independence was undoubtedly important, but it could only take the debate so far.

CHAPTER 4

DEFENCE AND FOREIGN AFFAIRS

Metropolitans have often accused those who (like myself) both supported entry to the European Community *and* self-government for smaller nations. There is no contradiction in this. None, that is, unless one thinks the Community and the old British state are equivalent healthy and acceptable 'larger units' – so that it must be illogical to accept the one and reject the other. In fact there is no common measure between them ... whatever the shortcomings and contradictions of the new Europe, it is still a modern, voluntary, genuinely multi-national organisation, capable of great farther progress and of playing a positive role in a new world order. By contrast, the United Kingdom long ago ceased to be a multi-national entity in any ennobling or forward-looking sense: the nerve of its larger unity passed away with empire, and should not be mourned or resuscitated for that reason.
Tom Nairn, *The Break-Up of Britain* (1977)

All men are by nature free; you have therefore an undoubted liberty to depart whenever you please, but will have many and great difficulties to encounter in passing the frontiers.
Voltaire, *Candide* (1759)

Alex Salmond was hardly alone in wishing to conquer the United States, a well-trodden transatlantic path for Prime Ministers, First Ministers and leaders of the opposition; winning over Washington – though rarely achieved – was perceived as the *sine qua non* of credibility in terms of foreign policy. As SNP leader and more recently as First Minister, Salmond had visited the US many times. Like much of the UK political class he was fascinated by American politics. His visit in the Easter of 2013 followed the usual itinerary: talks in New York City, a lecture at Princeton and visits to think tanks in the capital. The aim was to raise money for the SNP and, more to the point, change the Hill's view of Scottish independence.

Recent events had made this harder than it might have been. The Scottish government's release of Abdelbaset al-Megrahi, the only man convicted of the 1988 Lockerbie bombing, had not exactly won the cause any American friends, while a series of hostile newspaper editorials since 2011 demonstrated that independence was viewed with, at best, apprehension. The *Christian Science Monitor* warned it 'sent a dangerous "go it alone" message', the *Washington Post* said an 'independent Scotland would significantly weaken the foremost military and diplomatic ally of the United States' (a leader column apparently derived from a US State Department briefing), while a longer piece in the journal *Foreign Affairs*, by Charles King of Washington's Georgetown University, struck a similarly downbeat note: 'Scotland once embodied the belief that local distinctiveness, united governance, and democratic practice were mutually reinforcing. It would be a shame if the Scottish model became something else: a handbook for transforming muscular regionalism into territorial separatism.'[1]

On the eve of the First Minister's visit, meanwhile, the *New York Times* looked at the 'financial woes of small, independent European states like Cyprus and Iceland' and concluded that 'Scottish voters may want to think twice about going it alone'.[2]

Similarly, Madeleine Albright, Bill Clinton's Secretary of State, had warned against what she called 'fragmentation', which suggested the US preferred its main European ally – its conduit to the European Union – to remain united. The US government made it clear, however, that unlike 1995 when the President had cautioned against Quebec independence, it would 'watch' events in the UK but not 'take sides'. 'We are neutral and we will just have to see what will happen,' said Louis Susman, the former US ambassador to the Court of St James. 'But obviously there are ramifications either way.'[3] Indeed, the potential break-up of the United Kingdom cast doubts on what the journalist David Leask called 'old certainties, old alliances and old friendships', not least Trident.[4] Even so, a personal intervention from President Obama, apparently feared by some senior Nationalists, was unlikely to transpire publicly, whatever the movement behind the scenes. There were also warmer words from his predecessor but one. 'You just have to run up the pluses and minuses,' said President Clinton on a visit to Scotland in mid-2013, 'and do it in a way that doesn't tear the place apart while you're trying to reach an agreement.'

On touching down at JFK a few months earlier, the First Minister had been at his most ebullient and looking forward to 'setting out Scotland's ambition to enter the global community of nations'. Having already put right aspects of the *Washington Post*'s editorial (the 'claim that an independent Scotland would be unable to contribute meaningfully to global security … is untrue'), Salmond was determined to correct impressions that his vision of autonomy was somehow isolationist or anti-NATO (the *Post* had erroneously assumed the latter).[5]

The centrepiece of the visit, however, had been less geopolitical and more cultural: 'Tartan Week' celebrations in New York and Washington, an annual shindig that, despite the best efforts of those on both sides of the Atlantic, had never quite matched St Patrick's Day celebrations in terms of impact. Salmond also participated in the official US launch of Homecoming 2014, which the First Minister hoped would attract the 'tens of millions of people across the US' who claimed Scottish ancestry. A visiting UK minister, meanwhile, took away a different message from that Tartan Week. 'There's no real support in the US for independence,' he said. 'They just don't get it.'[6]

Salmond also addressed the Carnegie Council, named after Scotland's most famous American export, the philanthropist Andrew Carnegie. There, the First Minister later wrote, he had detected 'an appreciation of the peaceful and orderly way in which our century-long debate on self-determination has been conducted',[7] without, as Culture Secretary Fiona Hyslop added in a 4 July speech, 'so much as a nose bleed'. As an SNP spokesman had put it the previous November, 'We look forward to an independent Scotland being a friend and ally of the United States – as we will be with the rest of the UK – and to the day when Scotland can play a full part in meeting the many challenges facing our interconnected world.'

'The best of neighbours, the best of friends'

The Scottish government's commitment to a referendum on independence, meanwhile, had been a world news story. The consultation launch in early 2012 had attracted international media attention and, addressing a phalanx of foreign journalists at Edinburgh Castle, the First Minister had waxed lyrical about the number of independent states – fifty – when the United Nations (UN) had been inaugurated in 1945. 'Today, that figure has risen to almost 200,' he added. 'Of the ten countries that joined the European Union in 2004, a majority had become independent since 1990, and Scotland is bigger than six of them.'

His point, of course, was to depict Scottish independence as an entirely natural, if not inevitable, event. In fact, there was no precedent for secession in a modern, successful (loosely defined) welfare state. As Professor Robert Young pointed out, it had only occurred in the case of political or religious oppression (Ukraine, Bangladesh), where economic integration was basic (Norway/Sweden) or in flux (Czechoslovakia), or in countries only recently unified (Singapore/Malaysia).[8] Or, it might be added, in former colonies – it was rather fitting that as Scotland contemplated its future an independence referendum was also pending in the tiny French Pacific colony of New Caledonia.[9]

But if successful, Scotland would become the 194th member of the UN (South Sudan having joined in 2011), taking its seat between Saudi Arabia and Senegal. Perhaps surprisingly, the UK's former ambassador Sir Jeremy Greenstock said, 'Scotland would be very welcome at the UN, which is highly in favour of self-determination and a new people expressing itself.' Article 1 of the 1945 United Nations Charter also referred to the 'equal rights and self-determination of peoples', although that was generally taken to mean those under colonial rule.

As to how an independent Scotland would express itself on the world stage, however, Salmond was usually rather vague, telling Sir David Frost on Al Jazeera that an independent Scotland was 'determined to be [a] good world citizen',[10] while Angus Robertson invoked Robin Cook in saying it should have an 'ethical foreign policy'.[11] The Army officer and former SNP candidate Stuart Crawford interpreted this rather more bluntly: 'The SNP hasn't got a foreign policy apart from being nice to everybody.' And to paraphrase Abraham Lincoln, in terms of foreign policy you can never hope to be nice to all of the people all of the time.

The party had long espoused internationalism. During the 1967 Hamilton by-election Winnie Ewing had cried 'stop the world, Scotland wants to get on', while in 1977 Tom Nairn noted approvingly that 'the Scots are endeavouring to reattach themselves to an outside world'. Inevitably, this had been challenged by Unionists, who argued that Scotland already punched above its weight on the world stage as part of the UK. During his 2012 visit to Edinburgh the Prime Minister claimed the 'shared Union' counted 'for more together in the world' than it would apart. He added:

> We have a permanent place on the UN Security Council, real clout in NATO and Europe, and unique influence with key allies all over the world. Scottish pilots helped us to free Libya from tyranny and prevented a failed pariah state festering on Europe's southern border potentially threatening our security and creating a more dangerous and uncertain world for Britain and for all our allies.

David Cameron also touched on international aid, a subject 'very close' to his heart:

> And this is an issue where Scottish people have a huge influence. Together as a UK we have the second biggest aid budget in the world. Through the UK, Scotland has global reach. And with that we are saving thousands of lives and helping people in some of the poorest parts of the world to forge a new future. From the famine in the Horn of Africa to the support for people in North Africa and the Middle East as they seek new freedoms that we and others take for granted.[12]

On the former point, Salmond was dismissive, claiming international status symbols – which he called 'baubles of prestige' – meant little to Scots lacking jobs or benefits, while on the latter the First Minister pointed to the Scottish government's own, admittedly more modest, aid efforts in countries like Malawi, which Salmond's predecessor as First Minister, Jack McConnell, had pioneered as part of his distinctive Scottish 'foreign policy'. Later, Alistair Darling also echoed Cameron's point about 'clout', although confusingly he chose to do so a few days after the House of Commons chose not to exercise the UK's via military action in Syria. This was a sort of influence the SNP leader seemed content to do without. 'We don't have pretentions to be a superpower,' he told AFP, adding dryly, 'We're not going to launch invasions of Iraq.' On Syria, Salmond was careful not to repeat his 1999 'unpardonable folly' comments about Kosovo, although equally confusingly he appeared unhappy that the House of Commons had chosen to reject an 'illegal' war (i.e. one without a UN mandate) and said an independent Scotland would not have ruled out military action. Curiously, few questioned the First Minister's ability to peer into alternate realities, but Syria showed the difficulty of trying to crowbar foreign policy into an independence mould.

The SNP was also critical of the UK government's record on international aid, despite its budget having been shielded from coalition cuts. In January 2013, Humza Yousaf, the Scottish Minister for External Affairs, outlined post-independence plans to increase aid commitments to meet (or even exceed) UN targets for developed countries. At 0.7 per cent of total spending, this was obviously quite a significant commitment, although even under the status quo Scots contributed about £1 billion to UK overseas aid spending of £10.7 billion via general taxation, the second largest aid budget in the world. Independence, as Unionists pointed out, also placed a question mark over more than 500 Department for International Development (DFID) jobs located in East Kilbride.

Angus Robertson, the SNP's foreign affairs spokesman, thought a little more creatively about Scotland's place in the world. He talked of reorientating an independent nation away from southern Europe and towards Scandinavia, paying particularly close attention to the 'High North and Arctic' where the seas were warming at 'an alarming rate' (although Robertson noted this would also bring 'significant economic opportunities', including new international shipping routes, oil, gas and mineral extraction, and new fishing grounds). 'Our neighbours to the north and east have already made a good start and work constructively together,' Robertson said. 'We need to join them and play our part.'[13] Even so, the House of Commons Foreign Affairs Committee was probably correct when it identified significant gaps in the SNP's foreign policy. Not only did it have no clear plan for establishing its own foreign office but, it observed, Salmond's policies appeared 'to be underpinned by a belief that where problems emerge, goodwill for Scotland will trump difficulties'.[14]

During his 2013 US trip the First Minister had spoken of Scotland's 'friendships' with the USA, Canada, Australia and New Zealand being 'based on a deep shared history, but also on modern ties of trade, people and values'. 'Closer to home,' he added, 'the remaining nations of the United Kingdom, and Ireland, will remain our closest friends as well as our closest neighbours.'[15] But that would obviously be qualified by self-interest. Following a Ditchley Foundation conference on the 'international implications' of Scottish independence, the *Irish Times* columnist Paul Gillespie reckoned a 'self-interested official Ireland still recovering from financial crisis' would want the UK to stay part of the EU, London to continue subsidising Northern Ireland, and view 'an independent Scotland as a potential competitor for investment more than a Celtic soul-sister'.[16]

The First Minister was better at behaving as if he already led an independent nation. He enjoyed addressing the Foreign Correspondents' Club in London, and presented a kidnapping incident at an Algerian gas plant as if he had direct responsibility for Scots among the hostages. What he could do without any objections from the Foreign Office was promote international trade. This Salmond did with aplomb, putting overseas visits at the heart of his second term as First Minister. He encouraged Californian businessmen to invest in Scotland and travelled to the Gulf to promote Scottish business and educational links, while he had some success in cultivating a particularly close relationship with the Chinese government, making several visits to lobby for deals such as an agreement to protect the patent rights of Scotch whisky. The Scottish government even published a five-year plan for Sino-Scottish 'engagement' which spoke of 'shared values, partnership and trust'.[17] For China's part, as an editorial in the *Global Times* (a Chinese government paper) observed, 'cultivating more contacts with separatists in Northern Ireland and Scotland would make London quite uncomfortable'.[18]

But the burgeoning Sino-Scottish partnership also gave Salmond a taste of the diplomatic trade-offs he might be faced with as leader of an independent nation. In the summer of 2012, for example, he declined to meet the Dalai Lama during a private visit to Scotland. The First Minister refused to say if the matter had been raised when he had met China's UK ambassador, Liu Xiaoming (it had), and when asked if his meeting Tibet's spiritual leader might have threatened Chinese investment in Scotland, Salmond replied, 'We do what is appropriate for the benefit of the Scottish people.' For a centre-left party that championed the self-determination of small nations, it was clearly an uncomfortable situation for the SNP leader to have found himself in.

Documents released under the Freedom of Information Act suggested Salmond had relied heavily upon the UK diplomatic network during his visits to China and, indeed, the Scotland Office minister David Mundell claimed British embassies around the world opened 'doors for Scotland', although when the Foreign Secretary suggested they would no longer promote whisky if Scotland became independent, Salmond claimed the Scottish government already paid for the privilege. The SNP, meanwhile, floated the idea of sharing embassies and diplomatic networks with the rUK in the event of a 'yes' vote, something it already did via Scottish 'ambassadors' based within the US, EU (UK Representation) and Chinese embassies. Scottish Development International, the Scottish government's overseas trade agency, was also mooted as the core of a Scottish 'foreign service'.[19]

The UK government was not inclined to play ball, instead implying Scotland would require 'some sort of border check' if it became independent, not least because the Scottish government had made clear its intention to pursue 'a proactive immigration policy – with a Scottish green card for skilled, committed new Scots'.[20] David Mundell even visited the border between Ireland and Northern Ireland (covered by a long-standing Common Travel Area) to emphasise the point, although the pro-independence website 'Wings over Scotland' had a bit of fun with a photoessay on Europe's border crossings: formal checks were rare, dusty (but open) roads and fields *de rigueur*.[21] But then twenty-six European countries were in the borderless Schengen Area and thus effectively shared an immigration policy, something Home Secretary Theresa May implied an independent Scotland within the EU might be compelled to sign up to.

The Republic of Ireland, of course, allowed UK citizens resident in the north to apply for an Irish passport, an arrangement Salmond told a New Zealand television station he might be willing to extend to expat descendants of Scots. 'We have a reach internationally across the world,' he said. 'We want the maximum entitlement to citizenship and the Irish model is one we have admired.' An independent Scotland,' Salmond also told Mumsnet, would issue its own passports offering 'shared or dual citizenship'. The SNP MP Pete Wishart even wondered why 'anyone would want anything other than a Scottish passport' after independence, given how 'dynamic' the new nation would be.

Nicola Sturgeon, meanwhile, told the House of Commons Foreign Affairs Select Committee an independent Scotland planned to establish its own versions of GCHQ, MI5 and

MI6. Start-up costs were skirted over, but Stuart Crawford estimated GCHQ alone costing more than £200 million. Sir David Omand, a (Scottish) former head of GCHQ and the Home Office, concurred, saying it 'would take years to build up the capability'. The historian Rhodri Jeffreys-Jones suggested an independent Scotland could instead 'join in the clamour' for a European intelligence service to pool resources.

On a visit to Edinburgh in June 2013 the Foreign Secretary, William Hague, sought to tie all these different strands together. 'Travelling from Afghanistan to Brazil, and from Canada to Australia,' he said, 'I encounter bafflement that anyone would try to break up a union that has been so resilient, so successful and so admired as ours.'

> On the one hand is continued membership of the world's sixth largest economy, represented at the G7, G8 and G20, with a permanent seat of the UN Security Council, and an established, influential and growing diplomatic network that is increasingly focused on trade and building up links with the Commonwealth and the fastest-growing parts of the world economy. On the other is an uncertain future where Scots would have to face the inconvenience and tremendous burden of having to start again in world affairs, with a different passport for future generations, without that global network and enviable diplomatic position in the world.[22]

Yes Scotland was scathing in response, arguing that one word – 'Iraq' – made a nonsense of the Foreign Secretary's arguments. 'The reason we have to become independent is to increase the wealth of the people of Scotland,' blogged chief strategist Stephen Noon. 'After a Yes in 2014, Mr Hague will continue to tour the world, projecting power, and he will be joined by a Scottish government that reaches out to the world to project peace and prosperity.'[23]

Nationalist international

The SNP's electoral success and referendum plans naturally interested other independence movements around the world, although these required delicate handling. The Parti Québécois – which had staged two secession referendums in Canada – was particularly keen to get in on the act, and dispatched its leader, Pauline Marois, elected Premier of the French-speaking province in September 2012, to meet Salmond in Edinburgh. Although the Canadian press had hopes of high political theatre, instead the two nationalist leaders met privately, more a 'courtesy event' (as one Scottish official put it) than a nationalist summit. 'It is encouraging because when you see people [such] as the Scottish population,' commented Marois, 'decide to ask the question on their future in a referendum, I think it is hope for us.'

The *Montreal Gazette*, however, called the encounter 'tepid', while a cartoon in the French-language newspaper *Le Devoir* depicted Marois meeting a kilted man with a bag over his head. As the *Guardian* journalist Severin Carrell observed, the SNP was 'far more attuned to, and energised by, Scotland's close bonds through more than a century of emigration with English-speaking Canada, not the Francophone Québécois',[24] while the PQ's emphasis on language and ethnicity did not sit comfortably with the SNP's 'civic' Nationalist agenda. Following a narrow defeat in 1995, for example, the then Quebec Premier, Jacques Parizeau, had controversially blamed the result on 'money and ethnic votes'.

Spain, with its Catalan and Basque separatists (neither Catalans nor Quebeckers shared the SNP's aversion to that term), produced similar tensions. Catalans in particular were inspired by the UK government's constructive approach to pro-independence sentiment in Scotland, and hoped the more intransigent Spanish government would follow its lead. 'We are going to see new nations all over Europe,' said one. 'I hope that Madrid allows us the same democratic choice as Britain has allowed Scotland.' Following Catalan elections in November 2012, in which various nationalist parties secured a majority, a referendum was subsequently mooted for 2014, shortly before Scotland's, although the Spanish government was not exactly keen to play along. 'Just contrast our approach', commented a Downing Street adviser, 'with that of the Spanish governments; Spanish generals quoted in *El Pais* saying they'll invade Catalonia and so on.'[25]

There were also strong links between the Catalan delegation in London and the SNP, and therefore obvious resentment when Salmond used a radio interview to publicly distance himself, his party and Scotland from the Catalan push for independence, stressing it was a 'different' case, lest he annoy the Spanish government. 'Scotland and Catalonia are old nations of Europe,' Salmond had written at a less complicated moment. 'We have written part of the history of Europe as free and independent countries.'[26] Unionists like William Hague, meanwhile, repeatedly implied Spain – fearful of creating a secessionist precedent – would veto Scotland as a new member of the European Union (EU), a view echoed by the European Parliament vice-president and Catalan MEP Alejo Vidal-Quadras. Spain was officially neutral on the matter, although noises from Madrid indicated Hague et al. might have a point. In October 2012 the Spanish Foreign Minister, José Manuel García-Margallo, told the Spanish senate that an independent Scotland would have to 'join the queue' in order to get into the EU. The signal to regions of his own country was unmistakable, although the former Slovak Foreign Minister Eduard Kukan said he was sure the 'overwhelming majority [of EU members] would welcome this new country and new state'. This was a little ironic, for both Slovakia and Spain (and three other EU member states) had refused to recognise Kosovo's 2008 declaration

of sovereignty, making its membership of the union virtually impossible. One objection – as Croatia discovered with
Slovenia – was all it took.

'Independence in Europe'

'For the second time in her history', declared a *Scotsman*
editorial on 2 January 1973, 'Scotland has joined a larger
union.' It had been a reference, of course, to the United
Kingdom's membership of the European Economic
Community (EEC) the day before. For the next forty years,
the resulting loss of sovereignty dominated the internal politics of at first Labour, then the Conservatives, and even the
Scottish National Party. It split public, as well as political,
opinion, often aggressively so.

The SNP's relationship with Europe was typically complex.
Initially, it was hostile, its MPs voting against continued
membership on the basis that Scotland should only be in
the EEC on its own terms. 'Feeling was also heightened by
European centralisation', recalled the SNP politician Gordon
Wilson in his memoir of the period, 'that was anathema
to SNP members who had been fighting London control
and saw little benefit in exchanging that jack boot for a
European model.'[27]

A UK-wide referendum on 5 June 1975 (a constitutional
first at that time) was supposed to settle the membership
issue once and for all. At St Andrews University a young
Alex Salmond railed against the 'excesses of Brussels bureau-
cracy'. 'Scotland's bright economic future', he told one
meeting, 'will be jeopardised by the remote and centralised
policies of the Common Market.'[28] But the referendum
outcome was decisive. More than 67 per cent of voters said
'yes' to continued membership on a 65 per cent turnout,
although in Scotland the 'no' vote was significantly higher
than the UK as a whole, with the Western Isles and Shetland
each voting against by a majority.

Over the next decade or so, the SNP gradually toned down its hostility to the EEC and, by 1988, Salmond was an enthusiastic proponent of a new stance dubbed 'independence in Europe', in reality more of a slogan designed to counter Labour charges of 'separatism' than a detailed policy. Although this resulted in a minor split,[29] within a few years it had become an article of faith for Scottish Nationalists that an independent Scotland would be warmly welcomed into the European Union. The Conservative Party, of course, had its own – much more traumatic – ructions during this period, dominating its last two terms in government, and in opposition thereafter.

A few weeks after the UK marked forty years of EU membership, David Cameron attempted to draw a line under those ructions, not to mention the rise of the United Kingdom Independence Party (UKIP), by committing to an in/out referendum once the UK's relationship with the EU had been renegotiated (shades of Harold Wilson in 1975) by 2017. Under questioning, the Prime Minister explicitly linked his EU referendum with that on Scottish independence. 'I want to be the British Prime Minister who confronts and gets the right answer for Britain on these sorts of issues,' he told his audience at Bloomberg in central London.

> Take the future of our United Kingdom. Many people said to me, obviously you just have to ignore what's happening in Scotland and the fact there's an SNP government and I said 'no'… and I think it's the same in some ways on this issue: you can put your head in the sand, you can pretend that somehow this issue will go away and that somehow events will turn out alright; I think that is simply incredible.[30]

The common issue to both the First and Prime Ministers was political sovereignty. As Jo Murkens and Peter Jones wrote on a London School of Economics blog, they 'both want more of it'.

Salmond wants to claim it from the UK, Cameron wants to claim it from the EU. In that narrow sense, they are both nationalists: Salmond a Scottish one, Cameron a British one. Both also want, they claim, to be good European citizens but have to contend with the problem that the European club they want to be members of has rules which conflict with their visions of the idealised version they imagine it should be.

Murkens and Jones added that it

> puts Salmond in the odd position of being, simultaneously, a Scottish nationalist, a European federalist, and a British unionist. He wants Scotland to have untrammelled use of its own credit card to dine at the same time in the British and European restaurants, but refuses the *table d'hôte* menu and insists on picking from two *à la carte* menus, which neither chefs seem willing to offer.[31]

Murkens had noted more than a decade earlier the 'paradox involved in that the SNP seeks sovereignty first and, having achieved it would then hand it over to the EU';[32] indeed, in 1988 Salmond himself had conceded that EU membership would involve 'a degree of sacrifice of sovereignty'.

Unwilling to cede anything was the UKIP leader, Nigel Farage, whose party's threat to the Conservatives had been the major impetus behind the Prime Minister's speech. Interestingly, this shared motivation ended up producing rhetorical – if not policy – similarities between the Conservatives, UKIP and the SNP. Many of the lines in Cameron's Bloomberg speech could easily have been uttered by Salmond in a different context, while Farage's regular pleas to let Britain run its own affairs having nego-tiated a new 'relationship' with the EU were, substituting 'Scotland' for 'Britain', familiar Nationalist refrains. A UKIP campaign poster highlighted what it believed to be the logical contradiction at the heart of the SNP. 'Swapping London for Brussels is NOT "independence",' it warned. 'You'll be out of the frying pan and into the fire.'

Nevertheless, Salmond attacked what he called 'a fundamentally confused speech' and made it clear the Scottish government did not support Cameron's planned referendum, despite around a third of Scots supporting withdrawal (similar to the proportion who backed pulling out of the UK). But although UKIP was electorally weak in Scotland, the SNP's frequent assertion that Scots were more pro-European than the rest of the UK deserved more scrutiny than it generally received. In general terms, most polling showed this was true, although it also indicated the gap was not very large. Surveys by Ipsos MORI demonstrated that Scottish and Welsh attitudes generally mirrored those of England, where 50 per cent supported withdrawal and a third staying in (whereas in Scotland and Wales 34 per cent wanted to leave and 53 per cent stay put).

Professor John Curtice, however, judged the gap to be more like five points, based on ten YouGov polls conducted since January 2013, with – on average – 37 per cent wanting out and 42 per cent intent on staying in. 'So Scotland is more Europhile than Britain as a whole,' concluded Curtice, 'but nothing like as markedly so as you might assume … there is still in reality a substantial vein of Euroscepticism north of the Border.'[33] A majority of Scots, meanwhile, appeared to support the Prime Minister's plan for an in/out referendum by the end of 2017. Importantly, those for and against EU membership cut across yes/no and traditional Scottish party lines.

Cameron's pledge was both good and bad for supporters of independence. Good because the Prime Minister's line about the Scottish referendum causing 'uncertainty' now looked hypocritical, but also bad because the First Minister's reaction revealed a certain defensiveness. If Salmond was confident Scots would vote 'yes' to independence in 2014 (and thus become so by around 2016), then why was he concerned with plans for a referendum on the UK's membership of the EU in 2017? On the other hand, it allowed Salmond et al. to contrast the 'certainty' of the SNP's position on EU membership (staying in) with the 'uncertainty' of the UK government's new stance (possible withdrawal).

Indeed, a long-standing assumption underpinning the SNP's European policy was the belief that a newly independent Scotland would 'automatically' become a member of the European club (Sir Neil MacCormick, for example, called this prospect 'internal enlargement'). In 2007 Nicola Sturgeon told MSPs that 'Scotland would automatically be a member of the European Union upon independence. There is legal opinion to back that up. I don't think the legal position is in any doubt.' Only it was. This came to a head in March 2012 when the BBC's Andrew Neil asked if Salmond had 'sought advice' from his Scottish law officers. The First Minister said, 'Yes, in terms of the [debate],' adding that he could not 'reveal the legal advice of law officers'.

Curiously, however, when in July 2012 the Scottish (Freedom of) Information Commissioner ruled that ministers had to publicly state if they had asked for advice on this point, the Scottish government decided to challenge it in court. And although Salmond cited 'authoritative' sources to support his claim that Scotland would 'automatically' remain in the EU as a successor state, as the Labour MEP David Martin pointed out, most of them were dead and their 'advice' was more than two decades out of date.[34] In other words, no serious work had been done on the SNP's European policy for quite some time. As one Salmond aide admitted, advisers had been conscious of the need to 'sort out the Europe issue' but the First Minister had refused. 'There's an obsession with internal consistency,' said the source. 'We should have just fessed up.'[35]

The automaticity claim fell down on the point that 'while the people and territory of Scotland' was already in the EU (as Murkens and Jones wrote), the Scottish government was not, and in order for it to be so it required 'its votes in the European Council and other entitlements to be written into EU treaties', which could only be done with the unanimous consent of all other member states, not to mention assent by the European Parliament and ratification by all twenty-eight legislatures (Croatia became the EU's twenty-eighth member in July 2013). In reality the SNP was fully aware of this, reports later suggesting the Scottish law officers (the Lord Advocate and Solicitor General for Scotland) had consistently warned ministers that an independent Scotland's membership of the EU would not be automatic but a 'policy objective' requiring 'detailed negotiations'.[36]

Nevertheless, the Scottish government stuck to its guns until that October, when Sturgeon dropped a bombshell by informing the Scottish Parliament that contrary to Salmond's March interview, no such advice from the Scottish law officers existed. Although Salmond insisted his comments had been taken out of context, the result was the First Minister's worst barrage of headlines since taking office in 2007: 'EU LIAR' screamed the front page of the hitherto friendly *Scottish Sun*. Sturgeon, characteristically, attempted to limit the damage, telling the BBC that creating the impression 'we had legal advice, that we were not prepared to reveal because somehow it didn't suit our purposes' had been 'unfortunate', while the SNP MEP Alyn Smith later called the lack of legal advice 'an unforgiveable own goal'.

With those notes of contrition, the EU story died down; an opinion was requested from the Lord Advocate and received, although the Scottish government later confirmed it would not be made public (the UK government, to be fair, was similarly secretive). Helping the SNP, for the time being, had been the European Commission's reluctance to get involved in the internal constitutional politics of the UK – that is, until a parliamentary question from David Martin asking for the Commission's view required a response, as did a letter from the House of Lords' Economic Affairs Committee.

It was *The Scotsman* that broke the silence with a notable scoop revealing the essence of the Commission's position in a reply to the Lords committee. The crucial passage stated:

> The EU is founded on the Treaties which apply only to the member states who have agreed and ratified them. If part of the territory of a member state would cease to be part of that state because it were to become a new independent state, the Treaties would no longer apply to that territory. In other words, a new independent state would, by the fact of its independence, become a third country with respect to the EU and the Treaties would no longer apply on its territory.[37]

Although this was not new – the Commission had used the same wording in response to a parliamentary question as far back as 2004 – it represented a significant challenge to the SNP's assertion that an independent Scotland would 'automatically' become a new member state.

Under considerable pressure, the SNP did not handle the situation well. The Scottish government accused *The Scotsman* (in a formal press release) of running a 'fabrication' (meaning the Commission's reply to the Lords committee), while Alyn Smith took to the airwaves to accuse the newspaper of indulging in the 'black arts'. Various straw men were assembled, chiefly that opponents of independence claimed Scotland would be 'kicked out' of the EU (few, in reality, had seriously suggested this),[38] but just as the SNP's charges appeared to be gaining some traction, the Commission's response to David Martin's question was published online – its wording identical to that in the *Scotsman* story.

Once again it fell to Nicola Sturgeon to clean up the mess.

The word 'automatic' disappeared from view, and instead she told MSPs an independent Scottish government 'would seek to ensure that our intention to remain within the EU was achieved'. In a cogently argued article for the *Sunday Herald* ('Scotland is an ancient European nation'), she claimed the SNP's 'consistent position – as attested to by documents published since 2007' was that 'the specific terms of Scotland's continued EU membership' would 'need to be negotiated'.

On the face of it, Commission President José Manuel Barroso's statement was accurate. It was, after all, the UK – not Scotland – that was a signatory to the EU treaties and therefore a member state. Consequently, if Scotland decided to leave the UK then it would also leave the EU (there was in fact a precedent – though not perfect – in this respect: when Algeria achieved independence from France in 1960 it also left the then Common Market). But it also seemed likely that more than EU law would actually decide what happened in the event of a 'yes' vote. As *The Economist* put it, 'In the end, the political will of EU member states is likely to count for more than what the law does, or does not, say.' Not only was the legal position rather opaque, but the EU had been faced with similar dilemmas in the past, not least semi-autonomous Greenland's exit from the EEC in 1985.

There had also been Germany's reunification in 1990, an example of *Realpolitik* that Sturgeon wielded as proof that the EU was, whatever the legal position, a 'flexible institution'. 'When the Berlin Wall fell in late 1989,' she wrote, 'few at that point would have expected a united Germany to be part of the then European Community within less than twelve months – but that is exactly what happened when German reunification took place on October 3, 1990.' Scotland's case, she added, was 'more straightforward' given its forty years of 'existing membership'.

That much was true. Scots were also European 'citizens', a legal identity that could not easily be withdrawn, while its domestic laws and legislation – courtesy of the 1998 Scotland Act – were already obliged to comply with both EU law and the European Convention on Human Rights. As a joint paper from the Royal Society of Edinburgh and British Academy stated, 'There is no reason why an independent Scotland would fail to meet the Copenhagen criteria (the basic standards required to be eligible for EU membership, including democratic governance, the upholding of human rights and a functioning market economy).'[39]

Scotland, argued Sturgeon, also possessed around 90 per cent of the EU's oil reserves, a 'huge share' of the Continent's renewable energy, and some of the richest fishing grounds in Europe. 'Would Brussels really want to lose such assets at a time when energy security is one of the dominating political and economic issues of the early twenty-first century?' she asked. 'Would Spanish, French and Portuguese fishermen want to be blocked from fishing the lucrative waters in Scotland's sectors of the North Sea and West Atlantic?'[40] This was a weaker argument, for unless an independent Scotland was actually threatening to withdraw (as Greenland had over fishing rights), the bargaining chips listed by Sturgeon were pretty worthless. 'Both in terms of a feasible negotiating position and political realities,' concluded the pro-independence economists Jim and Margaret Cuthbert, 'the current SNP position appears incomprehensible.'[41] Furthermore, as the UK government pointed out, Spain and Portugal were not actually able to fish in the North Sea.

The question of treaties and opt-outs was also hard for the SNP to deal with convincingly. Sturgeon instead resorted to assertion, arguing it was 'perfectly reasonable' to claim Scotland would 'jointly inherit' the existing UK opt-out of the single currency; the country could not 'be forced into euro membership', while Scotland's EU partners 'would understand' its desire to stay out of Schengen and instead co-operate with Ireland, the rUK and Crown Dependencies

via the Common Travel Area (Sturgeon later claimed, erroneously, that Croatia's membership of the EU would not
compel it to join either the euro or Schengen). None of this,
of course, was by any means certain, merely an aspiration.
Most experts, meanwhile, considered it almost impossible
that an independent Scotland would hold on to a proportion
of the UK's EU budget rebate, Professor John Kay writing
that it was 'about as likely as making the kilt the national
dress of Europe'.

The SNP also brandished the opinion of Graham Avery,
an honorary director general of the European Commission,
who had stated that for 'practical and political' reasons an
independent Scotland could not be asked to leave and apply
for readmission. 'Negotiations on the terms of membership
would take place in the period between the referendum and
the planned date of independence,' suggested Avery. 'The EU
would adopt a simplified procedure for the negotiations, not
the traditional procedure followed for the accession of non-
member countries.'[42]

This was all well and good, but Avery was not exactly a
senior – or even serving – Commission official, and indeed
his former employers later explicitly rejected his view. But
the SNP had something to hold on to, and the line gradually shifted from claiming membership would be 'automatic'
to one of negotiating accession from 'within' the EU (i.e. as
part of the UK), in the sixteen months between a 'yes' vote in
2014 and 'independence day' in 2016. The former European
Court of Justice judge Professor Sir David Edward proved
a more reliable witness. He argued that an independent
Scotland's EU membership would only require the amend-
ment of existing treaties, not the usual 'accession treaty'
required for new members.[43]

And while John Swinney rejected Barroso's statements as
having 'no foundation', Sturgeon took a more constructive
approach, saying his opinion was 'important' and ought 'to

be respected'. But it was, she added, 'by no means the only or the decisive opinion in the matter of Scotland's future in Europe', as if somehow the Commission President's view was on a par with that of Avery, a handful of constitutional lawyers and a retired judge. Instead Sturgeon embarked upon a European charm offensive, asking Barroso for a meeting and writing to the heads of the EU's other twenty-six member states. This did not exactly go to plan, with the Irish minister for Europe saying an independent Scotland would require 'painstaking and complex' negotiations to get into the EU (she later 'clarified' her remarks without actually contradict-ing them) and Brussels refusing to play ball. Not only did Barroso steer clear of meeting the Deputy First Minister, but in a BBC interview he stood by the Commission's position and specifically refuted the notion of negotiating member-ship 'from within' the EU. When asked if an independent Scotland's membership would be 'nodded through' as some experts had suggested, he replied, 'If one part of a country – I am not referring now to any specific one – wants to become an independent state, of course as an independent state it has to apply to the European membership according to the rules – that is obvious.'[44]

Jim Sillars, a former deputy leader of the SNP, proposed membership of the European Free Trade Association (which comprised non-EU members like Norway and Iceland) as an alternative to EU membership, which would give an independent Scotland access to the 'four freedoms' of goods, services, capital and persons without obliging it to join the Common Fisheries and Agricultural Policies (CFP and CAP). The SNP was committed to arguing for a 'replacement' of the former, a task it claimed would be made easier by its new status at the 'top table'.

An independent Scotland would of course gain its own Commissioner (as had Croatia in 2013), an influential position within the European maze, votes in the Council of

Ministers akin to those of Denmark, Finland and Ireland, perhaps double its current number of MEPs and 'generally an ability to make the case for funding and influence' (as the former SNP adviser Stephen Gethins put it). An independent Scotland would also take its turn at holding the presidency of the European Council, nominate a member of the European Court of Justice, take its share of European Commission posts and increase its membership of bodies like the Committee of the Regions. Its (inevitably smaller) share of European social funds, meanwhile, would come directly to Scotland rather than via Whitehall.

Nevertheless, as Jo Murkens noted in 2002, small states within the EU tended to 'suffer from structural disadvantages – less political power and fewer administrative resources – compared to larger member states',

> and many have argued that the trend has been for smaller states to have less influence in areas like foreign and security policy, and economic and monetary policy. Nevertheless, countries like Finland and Ireland have shown that small states can effectively advance their national interests, albeit selectively, by exploiting the intergovernmental bargaining process through co-ordination or alliances with other small countries and partnerships with larger member states.

In other words, an independent Scotland would get its own voice in Europe, but that voice ran the risk of carrying less weight. 'Scotland would not have a stronger voice in the EU if it found no allies and was constantly outvoted,' judged Murkens. 'If it ended up voting with its natural ally – the United Kingdom – the gains of independence in Europe would be apparent rather than real.' And if, he added, an independent Scotland started 'cherry-picking, adopting the legislation it likes and rejecting the legislation it does not', it would likely meet 'with resistance from and tough negotiations with other members'.[45] The economist John Kay also pointed out that Scotland's financial contribution to the EU could rise more than five-fold under independence, landing taxpayers with an extra £550 million bill, although Alex Salmond also claimed independence meant Scotland would gain additional farm payments from the EU worth £850 million between 2013 and 2019.

Nationalists often appeared to regard the EU as little more than a loose collection of sovereign states, co-operating on trade but little more (not dissimilar to Mrs Thatcher's vision as outlined in her Bruges speech). But in reality a lot had changed since 1988, not least increasing moves towards political union, and there was a sense SNP policy-making had not quite caught up. The 1992 Maastricht Treaty had committed to 'ever closer union', which seemed an odd aspiration for a Nationalist party to sign up to, particularly when the trajectory in the UK (certainly post-1997) was, if anything, ever looser union. As Professor Andrew Goudie put it:

Certainly the indications arising from the financial and euro crises is that there will be moves towards greater union across most areas of economic policy and management, including fiscal policy. This would suggest an environment in which member-states would individually have less power at national level to diverge significantly from the centrally determined limits.[46]

In that context, 'independence in Europe' made as much sense as William Hague's old mantra of 'in Europe, but not run by Europe'.

Nor had the SNP given any serious thought to the very real problems faced by the EU in the early twenty-first century, not least in terms of democratic legitimacy, grow-ing inequality and so on. The party, so critical of the UK in similar terms, was generally silent when it came to Brussels, Salmond weakly promising to 'seek reform' from within. But did he really believe the EU – with no elected executive body – was *more* democratic than the UK? He certainly did not think its currency was more desirable than sterling, while the implications of retaining the pound if rUK withdrew from Europe at some point in the future had not occurred to even the party's brightest thinkers. Dr Fabian Zuleeg of the European Policy Centre said there would arise the 'fundamental question' of whether a currency pact between Scotland and a non-EU member would be 'compatible' with EU membership.[47] 'The Scottish government doesn't understand European politics,' admitted one former adviser, 'they think it's like politics at home, but it's not. Barroso doesn't think about Scotland, and if he *does* think about secession it's Catalonia that comes to mind rather than Scotland.'[48]

But did Scotland really lack influence within the status quo? The UK government, naturally, argued not. When the European Parliament backed a reform of the Common Agricultural Policy in June 2013 Michael Moore boasted that the UK had 'one of the most inclusive arrangements in the EU for devolved administrations to contribute to decision-making'. 'This formal recognition by the EU hard-wires our ability to enable a strong, local Scottish voice for agriculture,' he said, 'with a clear, unified UK voice exerting shared clout at the top table in Europe as the third largest member state.'

The events of late 2012 had amounted to a bruising few months for the SNP, in which not only Salmond's trustwor-thiness, but his party's preparedness for the international consequences of independence, had been put under intense scrutiny. Senior Nationalists made the best of a bad situation. 'The sense of – and reporting of – Scotland negotiating our interests in a European context', suggested one, 'takes us on to the ground of Scotland beginning to think, sound and feel like an independent country. It's what independent countries do.' Another insider was rather more frank. 'It was a stupid way of phrasing things by him [Salmond] and by us [the SNP],' he said of the 'automatic' EU membership claim. 'It should have handled it better; fortunately, it was miles before the referendum.'[49] As in other areas, pro-independence supporters hoped time would heal a multitude of sins.

A Scottish Defence Force

Defence, together with foreign policy, was often presented as one of the defining characteristics of a sovereign state, while analysis by Glasgow University showed it to be the second most reported aspect of the independence debate after economics. A dominant theme was international conflict. In March 2013 Alex Salmond said 'independence would mean we would not be dragged into another illegal war', while a party document put it more accurately, saying that with independence Scotland could 'decide whether or not our young men and women are sent to fight in wars abroad … legal or illegal'.[50]

Beyond that, the SNP was best known for what it opposed in terms of defence, rather than what it supported. And while it gave the general impression of being pacifist and anti-war (which was certainly true of many SNP activists), the actual position was rather more nuanced. The party, for example, had supported Mrs Thatcher's Falklands crusade in 1981–82, while more recently it had backed allied action in both Afghanistan and Libya. Perhaps better known, however, was Alex Salmond's high-profile opposition to military action in Kosovo (which he called an act of 'dubious legality') and later Iraq, over which he and others attempted to 'impeach' Tony Blair.

Iraq in particular was continually wielded as proof that while the 'British state' remained intent upon imperial-ist aggression regardless of UN sanctions, by contrast, an independent Scotland would not allow itself to be 'dragged' into any more 'foreign wars' (a similar argument had been used by Irish nationalists in the early 1920s). As in several other areas, 'sovereignty' was key. And more than a decade after the event, Iraq still had the capacity to make Salmond's blood boil. During a Holyrood debate which condemned 'reckless, illegal military conflicts with incalculable human and material costs', the First Minister turned on Labour MSPs (who had voted for military action in 2003, as had the House of Commons), telling them 'people died' because of their votes.

But the upshot remained a confused defence policy in which the SNP simultaneously argued for some kind of Scottish Defence Force and co-operation with the UK Ministry of Defence (except over Trident) while making it clear it would not commit Scottish troops to any 'illegal' conflicts. The former SNP MSP Christopher Harvie called it 'military Unionism', and indeed it smacked of loving 'both the cake and the eating', as *The Guardian*'s Ian Jack put it: 'No to Trident and ludicrous post-imperial pretension, yes please to aircraft carriers and RAF fighter bases on the east coast.'[51] Again, Salmond was in Panglossian mode, consciously seeking the best of all possible worlds.

On the first plank – conventional forces in Scotland – the SNP had two contradictory positions. On the one hand it argued the MoD's Scottish footprint ought to be higher, pointing to a consistent 'underspend' north of the border, while on the other it advocated a smaller, nimbler defence force which would offer the same defensive capacity post-independence without costing as much. These two defence policies, at time of writing, had still to be reconciled; only the total budget had been fixed. The SNP argued that within the Union Scotland contributed £3.3 billion to the UK defence budget but only received around £2 billion in spending, thus, conveniently, its commitment to a budget of

£2.5 billion amounted to both a cut *and* an increase, a right-wing accountant's wet dream.

For instance, in July 2011 the SNP made much of UK Defence Secretary Liam Fox's plans to base a multi-role brigade of the British Army (around 6,000 troops) just outside Edinburgh. Dr Fox argued it would 'strengthen the union', while Stephen Noon believed he had made a 'strategic error'. 'The old argument that Scotland would have to create an army from scratch has disappeared,' he blogged: 'we will have one, it will be there for all to see, created and located right here in Scotland.'[52]

But when, in March 2013, Philip Hammond (Fox's successor as Defence Secretary) announced the figure would be nearer 600, Salmond dispatched an angry letter to the Prime Minister. Though embarrassing for the UK government at a sensitive stage in the referendum debate, Cameron flagged up the obvious contradiction between the First Minister's protest and his desire to 'end centuries of our shared British military effort'. As part of the UK, he argued, Scotland benefited from 'every pound' (direct or indirect) of expenditure in the world's fourth largest defence budget.

MoD plans to close two Scottish air bases also illustrated confusion in the SNP ranks. Initially, Salmond bitterly criticised the plans, before U-turning and declaring that the UK Strategic Defence Review's template of one naval base, one air base and one mobile brigade was 'exactly the configuration' required for an independent Scottish Defence Force. 'The idea that you can sort of break off a little bit,' responded Hammond, 'like a square on a chocolate bar and that would be the bit that went north of the border, is frankly laughable.'

So what exactly did the SNP envisage? This was set out, in some detail, in a resolution to its annual conference in 2012. 'An independent Scotland will be an outward-looking nation which is open, fair and tolerant,' it began, 'contributing to peace, justice and equality.' And, it continued, the Scottish armed forces will comprise 15,000 regular and 5,000 reserve personnel, operating under Joint Forces Headquarters based at Faslane, which will be Scotland's main conventional naval facility. All current bases will be retained to accommodate units, which will be organised into one regular and one reserve Multi Role Brigade (MRB). The air force will operate from Lossiemouth and Leuchars.[53]

It also alluded to the 'restored' Scottish regiments, a long-standing SNP pledge to reverse the amalgamation of Scotland's historic regiments into the Royal Regiment of Scotland. This, according to defence expert Phillips O'Brien, was 'in the realms of fantasy'. 'The old regiments no longer exist in a meaningful way, they are nameplates on doors, not real military units,' he wrote in the *Sunday Herald*. 'Trying to maintain a military structure based on regiments that were established during the British Empire in an independent Scotland is about as sensible as trying to re-establish the Raj.' Cost was inevitably an issue, and indeed a leaked Scottish government paper revealed that John Swinney had told those in charge of defence policy to assume 'a much lower budget'.

Critics later pointed out that many Scottish servicemen and women might want to stay in the British Army rather than join a Scottish Defence Force. The Irish precedent, as ever, was illustrative. Not only had many Irish regiments survived the secession of 1922 (mainly those based in the six counties of Ulster), but more than ninety years later Irish citizens could still enlist in the British Army. 'Those who wish to do it do it [join the British Army after independence],' defence analyst Francis Tusa told the Scottish Affairs Select Committee, 'is probably one of the easiest things. If you dust off the legislation from 1921, delete the word "Irish" and insert "Scottish", it should be doable.'[54] The Henry Jackson Society (dismissed by the SNP as 'neo-conservative'), however, reckoned the majority of Scottish soldiers would opt to remain in the British forces,[55] although Angus Robertson promised 'enhanced terms and conditions for military personnel', including trade union representation and 'a more settled basing solution in Scotland' as well as 'the prospect of operations and training in different countries'.[56]

As for what role a Scottish Defence Force might play, the resolution said it would be focused on territorial defence, while the MRB would 'provide deployable capabilities for United Nations sanctioned missions and support of humanitarian, peacekeeping and peace-making "Petersburg Tasks"'. In an article for the Chatham House magazine *World Today*, Alyson Bailes and Paul Ingram said Scotland might even prove more adept than the UK in such a role, referring to the scope for 'clean-handed' mediation in national or regional conflicts 'where the UK might seem less qualified or trusted given its size, alignments and imperial history', although they also warned that emulating 'Norwegian peace activism' would also impose 'heavy costs'.

Of course this was perfectly possible, and indeed Angus Robertson had visited Denmark and Norway to investigate their respective set-ups. An internal party review was ongoing, which meant Unionist critics made much of the running. More than a year out from the referendum, sneered Philip Hammond, 'the commitments from those proposing independence remain almost insultingly vague, implausibly long on ambition and incredibly short on detail and the means to deliver them'.[57] Hammond made these remarks, it ought to be noted, while presiding over unprecedented cuts to the UK's military establishment.

The UK government also targeted another perceived weakness, suggesting up to 4,000 jobs could be lost building warships at Scottish shipyards. More specifically, Hammond warned that the contract for thirteen Type-26 warships, expected to go to Clyde shipyards, would not be awarded until *after* Scots voted 'no' in the referendum. An inquiry by the Scottish Affairs Select Committee shored all of this up, while a report from the Defence Select Committee criticised both the Scottish and UK governments for failing to provide enough information about what would happen to Scotland's – and indeed rUK's – defences in the event of independence.[58]

This assumed, of course, rUK assent. Dr Phillips O'Brien said an independent Scotland would need to strike a deal with the rest of the UK to buy up English military hardware if it was to persuade the Navy to carry on ordering Clyde-built ships, while Nicola Sturgeon seemed confident the yards would thrive no matter what the outcome in 2014. 'I know that the skill and efficiency of its workforce will equip that shipyard to compete,' she said, 'and compete success-fully, regardless of the constitutional arrangements.' O'Brien, on the other hand, believed 'warship building on the Clyde would be damaged by independence'. 'For political reasons,' he explained, 'rUK would not build its warships in Scotland.' UK spending on shipbuilding, however, was about to plum-met, and it was not really clear why politicians on either side believed the future looked rosy either in or out of the Union.

Robertson's defence resolution also stressed 'joint procurement' with the rest of the UK, as well as 'shared conventional basing, training and logistics arrangements'. 'This includes sharing conventional military capabilities,' it added, 'setting priorities and better co-ordinating efforts providing economic synergies, job stability and taxpayer value for money.' 'Our most important partner', promised Robertson at a Royal United Services Institute seminar on independence (the first of its kind), 'will be the rest of the United Kingdom.'

If anything, however, Professor Hew Strachan thought SNP policy a little cautious. 'A new state is the opportunity for new thinking,' he wrote. 'In relation to defence the SNP looks more conservative and traditional than its rhetoric suggests.'[59] Thus in a comprehensive essay for the *Sunday Herald*, Dr Phillips O'Brien urged the SNP to eschew a 'Mini-Me' defence structure and instead do something a bit different. And rather than spending £2.5 billion, he reckoned £1.75 billion would allow an independent Scotland both to defend itself and integrate with NATO (a report by the retired Irish Defence Force colonel Dorcha Lee suggested the even lower figure of £1.4 billion).[60] O'Brien suggested a Scottish navy could model itself on Denmark's, based around three frigates and a number of smaller craft divided into two squadrons, one directed towards domestic patrols and protection, and the other to serve with NATO. An independent Scotland might also base the latter at Faslane (to ease the jobs impact of Trident's departure) and its domestic force at Rosyth on the east coast, 'from where it could quickly reach the North Sea oil fields'.

More difficult in hardware terms would be the size and composition of its air force. O'Brien said an independent Scotland would be best advised to negotiate a share of the present RAF, using one of the Typhoon squadrons at RAF Leuchars as the nucleus of a Scottish air force. 'The political reality, though, is that it would call for considerably fewer or smaller military facilities than currently exist,' warned O'Brien. 'And this is where the Yes campaign could be far more creative than it has been so far.'

Instead of trying to maintain the fiction that an independent Scotland would keep anything like the present force and base structure, it could be stated that the best way forward would be to manage the change. For instance, one could take the £750 million per year saved on defence spending from the proposed £2.5 billion budget to create a defence transition fund for the first ten years of independence. This would give an independent Scotland £7.5 billion to address the economic effects of declining defence spending, for example by regenerating or reconstructing areas affected by the loss of military facilities.[61]

But then the SNP's defence policy was a work in progress. Paul Cornish, Professor of Strategic Studies at the University of Exeter, reckoned it was more of a sketch than a full strategic review (which Angus Robertson promised would follow after independence). This he boiled down to three options: 'Work with the UK; make a token effort; or don't bother.' Think tanks, meanwhile, lined up to criticise SNP plans. Major General Andrew Mackay, whose 'Scotland Institute' paper was based upon dozens of interviews with senior officers and military experts, said he could not 'see how slicing up a competent and well established military will aid either the United Kingdom or an independent Scotland'.[62]

'A good citizen of the world'

One issue the SNP had given a little more thought to was the North Atlantic Treaty Organization (NATO), a mutual defence organisation formed in 1949. In essence: to join or not to join? The question had been hanging over the party for quite some time, with Alex Salmond reluctant to pick a fight with the left of his party, who regarded opposition to NATO as part and parcel of its anti-nuclear stance, particularly the submarine base at Faslane and its Trident-missile bunker at Coulport. Within days of the Edinburgh Agreement, however, he did just that at the SNP conference in Perth. Having toyed with pushing a change in policy through the party's National Council, senior Nationalists instead opted for a public debate, an uncharacteristically risky move for the normally cautious Mr Salmond.

At first he moved slowly, telling the US magazine *Time* that an independent Scotland would consider an 'alliance' with NATO, while two weeks before the conference, the First Minister also tried to reassure critics by proposing to include an 'explicit ban' on nuclear weapons ('or indeed any weapons of mass destruction') in a written constitution. He continued:

> An independent Scotland will be a good citizen of the world – and a good friend to our neighbours and allies. That is why as Scotland prepares to take our place in the world, I believe it is right that Scotland continues our NATO membership as a full member state as one of twenty-nine – subject to an agreement that we will not host nuclear weapons, in line with the vast majority of current NATO members.

Salmond also outlined a 'triple lock' governing future military action:

> First, NATO must continue to respect the right of the government of each member state to decide whether to commit forces or not. Second, the deployment of any armed servicemen and women into combat situations would require to be approved by Scotland's independent Parliament. And third, above all, Scotland would only become involved in actions which carried the authority of the United Nations.[63]

Similarly, Angus Robertson's defence resolution made it clear that a future SNP government would only maintain NATO membership 'subject to an agreement that Scotland will not host nuclear weapons ... In the absence of such an agreement, Scotland will work with NATO as a member of the [non-nuclear] Partnership for Peace programme.' Privately, however, senior Nationalists did not regard that 'Partnership' as 'a serious exercise'. Salmond and Robertson had visited Norway and Denmark often enough to realise that only full NATO membership would satisfy international expectations; shifting gear on this front was therefore about 'sending signals both internally and externally'. 'This is a demonstration that we're serious, not frivolous,' explained someone close to the policy switch. 'For international observers this will be the most significant signal that the SNP is preparing for the referendum and independence. It's about international credibility.'[64]

Some of this was implied in the course of a memorable debate, almost a throwback to party gatherings of the 1970s and 1980s when policy genuinely was decided on the conference floor, but those opposed to NATO membership were not convinced; Angus Robertson was even booed by some delegates as he made a final plea to overturn thirty years of opposition to the Alliance. Tellingly, few speakers actually made a compelling argument *for* membership, simply positing arguments *against* the status quo in the context of the independence referendum. In other words, you might not like this, but it is a necessary evil in order to win the main prize in 2014.

The main motion was passed narrowly, although the SNP had more or less split right down the middle. John Finnie and Jean Urquhart, two Highlands and Islands MSPs who had spoken against NATO membership, later resigned in opposition. For a party that had prided itself on unity and discipline since 2007, this was quite a blow. Indeed, Urquhart got the full works prior to her resignation: phone calls from party chairman Derek Mackay, followed by John Swinney, then Salmond and finally his wife Moira, who tearfully told Urquhart she could not resign because it would 'damage the party'. Urquhart held firm, later joining a new grouping of Independent and Green MSPs in the Scottish Parliament.

But the NATO issue did not end there. While it was certainly the case that not all its members were nuclear powers, NATO was nevertheless, knowingly and unashamedly, a *nuclear* alliance. Why, then, would NATO members accept a new member so openly and actively opposed to nuclear weapons? This was a point made by the former

Defence Secretaries Lord Robertson, Lord Healey and Sir Malcolm Rifkind, as well as a former adviser to President George W. Bush, who described it as 'illogical'. So keen was Salmond to appease US opinion on this point that he told Reuters an independent Scotland might be willing to 'host' NATO bases, provided they did not include nuclear weapons.[65]

This, in certain respects, replayed the EU membership issue, for Angus Robertson's assertion that an independent Scotland would 'inherit its treaty obligations with NATO' unravelled when the Alliance clearly stated the contrary:

> It appears widely agreed that, as a matter of law, a Scotland which has declared its independence and thereby established its separate statehood would be viewed as a new state. In the NATO context, the definitive determination on this question would be made by the member states, acting in the North Atlantic Council. A new state would not be a party to the North Atlantic Treaty, and thus not a member of NATO. If it were to choose to apply for NATO membership, its application would be subject to the normal procedure, as outlined in Article 10 of the Treaty.[66]

This was, as in the case of the EU, not necessarily an insurmountable barrier. Kurt Volker, the former US ambassador to NATO, said there was likely to be 'great goodwill' from existing members towards an independent Scotland's application, although Washington sources later suggested to *The Times* that it would veto Scotland if it insisted on banishing nuclear weapons from its waters. When Scottish government officials visited NATO high command in Brussels, meanwhile, they were given coded warnings that ongoing disputes concerning Trident might constitute a bar to fast-tracked membership.[67] But if Volker was right, and it seemed likely he was, an independent Scotland could conceivably end up as NATO's twenty-ninth member, Albania and Croatia having joined in 2009.

Salmond, meanwhile, did not bat an eyelid, admitting to the BBC there was 'a parallel with the European Union – you notify your intent to remain a member'. 'We are a member [of NATO] by virtue of our membership of the United Kingdom,' he added, 'and we notify in that period between the referendum, and a successful vote, and the adoption of Scottish independence about eighteen months later.' As the First Minister also observed, it was the 'exception rather than the rule to be a nuclear country – only Britain, France and America possess nuclear weapons'. This, however, was not quite the full story. As the former Labour Defence Secretary Lord Browne pointed out, a total of eight NATO member states hosted nuclear weapons on their soil, while another five were not opposed to doing so in principle.

The SNP, meanwhile, indicated it had no intention of making an independent Scotland a nuclear-free zone, for long a touchstone of New Zealand's foreign policy. But even assuming Scotland did not end up sheltering under NATO's protective umbrella, the 'no' campaign had never really been able to articulate why an independent Scotland would be *less* secure outside the UK. Alan Clements's 2010 political thriller *Rogue Nation* had envisaged Russians bankrolling a newly independent Scotland by basing its nuclear missiles on Scottish soil, but in reality who might threaten a newly sovereign state in northern Europe? Even were rogue states to emerge over the next decade, why would Scotland become a target for terrorist activity? In some respects, it could even be argued independence might make it safer.

Ban the bomb
There was also no precedent for a state aspiring to join NATO while simultaneously ridding itself of a key component of its nuclear deterrent. As the defence specialist Professor William

Walker pointed out, even assuming a 'yes' vote in the refer-endum, getting rid of Trident would be expensive and less than swift, and would 'risk incurring the displeasure of the American, French and other governments without whose support Scotland would struggle to gain recognition and respect'.[68] And even with the 'best will in the world', as Sir Malcolm Rifkind put it, it might take ten to fifteen years before the construction of an alternative site could be completed.

Unionists drove home this point relentlessly. Defence Secretary Philip Hammond said the timescale for removing Trident would be in 'the order of a decade', costing at least £3.5 billion and losing around 8,200 jobs in the process (even so, the MoD admitted, it had prepared no 'specific contingency plans'). The SNP, on the other hand, pointed to MoD figures listing only 520 civilian jobs at Faslane, although this ignored considerable indirect employment. It also toned down previous rhetoric about removing Trident within weeks of achieving independence. 'Be under no illusions,' Angus Robertson warned a 2009 conference on nuclear disarmament, 'it is likely to be a long road. Nuclear weapons will not disappear overnight.'[69]

The Unionist argument for maintaining the UK's 'inde-pendent' nuclear deterrent, meanwhile, appeared vague and nostalgic, largely concerned with maintaining a place on the UN Security Council (which in any case might not be lost as a result). As Tony Blair reflected in his memoirs, he could see the 'force of the common sense and practical argument against Trident but giving it up would be too big a down-grading of our status as a nation'.[70] The Scottish Labour Party (predominantly opposed to Trident), meanwhile, often struggled to articulate why it agreed at all, and the former Labour Defence Secretary Lord Browne did not even try, telling the House of Lords it was 'decreasingly effective and increasingly risky'. Even the former Conservative Defence Secretary Lord King told ministers to think 'very carefully'

about whether a Trident replacement was strategically necessary or affordable. It was of course phenomenally expensive,
something resented by parts of the Armed Forces being
forced to endure deep spending cuts. The Liberal Democrats,
meanwhile, argued the UK could maintain a credible nuclear
deterrent while reducing the size of the fleet and ending
round-the-clock patrols, a claim roundly condemned –
for different reasons – by the Conservatives, Labour and
the SNP.

The SNP's position on Trident at least had the virtue of
being clear, if not straightforward. 'A long-standing national
consensus has existed that Scotland should not host nuclear
weapons', declared Angus Robertson's defence resolution, 'and a sovereign SNP government will negotiate the
speediest safe transition of the nuclear fleet from Faslane
which will be replaced by conventional naval forces.' But
while this 'long-standing national consensus' was oft stated,
it was not really backed up by a tremendous amount
of survey data. A couple of polls (including one commis-
sioned by the Scottish Campaign for Nuclear Disarmament)
appeared to show overwhelming opposition to renewal of
Trident, although it depended how the question was framed.
When the Conservative pollster Lord Ashcroft carried out
a much more comprehensive survey in May 2013, it actually found that a majority of Scots supported a new nuclear
weapons system to replace the current Trident missiles,
20 per cent wanting a like-for-like replacement, and 31 per
cent favouring a cheaper nuclear alternative. More Scots
(43 per cent), meanwhile, wanted the weapons system to stay
at Faslane than said it should be moved south of the border
(39 per cent).[71]

The Scottish CND responded rather weakly that this
did not tally with its experience at public meetings, while
the Scottish government (equally weakly) said a majority
of MSPs had voted against Trident at Holyrood. It seemed

likely the SNP was assuming public opinion reflected its long-standing hostility to nuclear weapons, and indeed Salmond's confidence in this respect was clear from his public pronouncements. 'What is unconditional is that Scotland doesn't want to be a nuclear country,' he told Sky News, while asserting elsewhere that it was 'inconceivable that an independent nation of 5,250,000 people would tolerate the continued presence of weapons of mass destruction on its soil'. The UK government, he said, could either decommission Trident, relocate it to another part of the UK (at one point the Welsh First Minister seemed keen on Milford Haven playing host, while Falmouth and Devonport were also discussed) or rely on US or French nuclear facilities. The First Minister flatly rejected the idea of the Cyprus model, under which rUK would retain sovereign territory in Scotland (an option floated by the MoD and sunk by Downing Street in mid-2013),[72] or indeed the temporary 'treaty ports' agreed with Ireland in 1922.

Some experts mooted a compromise by which an independent Scotland would accept the current generation of Trident but not any successor, although that, of course, implied a timescale of several decades. The SNP said the 'lifetime costs' of Trident could approach £100 billion, although its opposition went beyond financial concerns. Many of those who had joined the SNP in the 1960s had done so out of opposition to nuclear weapons, and although newer members – and indeed party leaders – did not share this pedigree, the smarter ones realised the importance of maintaining a rhetorical commitment to banishing Trident for the sake of party unity. After decades of triangulation, meanwhile, it was one of the few authentically left-wing elements of the SNP's agenda, and as such Trident was always spoken of in suitably apocalyptic terms.

As the party also argued in mid-2013, 'only a "yes" vote next September can get rid of Trident for Scotland, so that we can spend Scotland's share of this money helping to build a fairer society and stronger economy'. The SNP's stance on Trident was, above all, a moral one; principled opposition to what it referred as 'weapons of mass destruction'. In 1957, when the UK had embraced nuclear deterrence, it did so precisely because it represented a cheaper form of defence for a small state with a weak economy. As the war historian Professor Sir Hew Strachan reflected, in another context that logic 'might have recommended nuclear weapons to an independent Scotland too'. Instead the independence debate found the SNP wrestling with decades-old arguments over how a sovereign state ought to defend itself while carving out a role for itself on an increasingly crowded, and frequently volatile, international stage.

CHAPTER 5

WELFARE AND PENSIONS

What could reasonably be expected from independence is a sharpening of the sense of Scottish responsibility for Scotland's social health. At the least it would rob Scots of their alibis for failure, increasing the pressure on them to confront the areas in which as a society they fall short of the performance of the best in Europe. And it should make them more receptive to one of the key lessons of the Nordic experience, that a small country has to make its living from its own assets, of which the most critical is its own people.
Stephen Maxwell, *Arguing for Independence* (2012)

'Scotland can be independent,' Nicola Sturgeon told the SNP's spring conference in 2013. 'Any politician who suggests otherwise is being mendacious. *But our argument rests on more than that* [my italics]. Our case for independence is about the kind of country we want Scotland to be. It can be summed up in three words: fairness, prosperity, democracy.' These, added Sturgeon, were the 'three pillars of any decent society'.[1]

Thus continued a relatively new Nationalist strategy of placing welfare at the heart of the independence case. With 'out-of-touch Westminster governments' (not just Conservative ones) intent on undermining and cutting the welfare state down to size, ran the argument, only by voting 'yes' in 2014 could Scots halt – and by implication reverse – the cuts. Ironically, the SNP was attempting to claim elements of the post-war British consensus as its own, presenting itself as the only true defender of welfare, pensions and the National Health Service. As Sturgeon put it in another speech, 'The very institutions which once made us distinct, the welfare state and – in England – the NHS, are under attack from the Westminster system of government.'[2]

This was seldom challenged, for mainstream civic, media and political voices had long subscribed to the belief that in Scotland there existed a more caring, more egalitarian and less market-driven ethos. Although this was not necessarily backed up by public opinion, it nevertheless shaped much of Scottish political discourse. Many Nationalists also took a year-zero approach to welfare in the UK, pinpointing May 1979 as the point at which inequality began.

In that context, a Conservative-led government at Westminster provided the perfect backdrop for certain SNP arguments during 2011–14. In her conference speech, for example, Nicola Sturgeon claimed that, despite coalition estimates that its welfare cuts would total £2.5 billion (in Scotland) by 2015, Scottish government officials reckoned the 'cumulative cut' would actually come in at £2 billion more. '£4.5 billion taken from the purses and wallets of ordinary, hard-working people right across Scotland who can least afford it,' she stormed. 'So there you have it – the awful price of letting Westminster control our resources and take our decisions for us … these welfare cuts are a dagger to the heart of the fairness and social justice that we hold so dear.'[3] The actual figure was closer to £2 billion, lower than the government's own estimate,[4] while a survey of benefit reforms between 2010 and 2015 by the Institute of Fiscal Studies actually calculated they would reduce household incomes in Scotland by less than in the UK as a whole, £480 compared with £560.[5]

Nevertheless, the Scottish government was less than radical in response. The document *Your Scotland, Your Voice* blandly assured readers that in an independent Scotland 'pension and benefits [would continue] to be paid at a similar level as now',[6] which technically committed a future SNP government to reversing billions of pounds of cuts ('now' being 2009, pre-coalition). Otherwise, there were sweeping assertions along the lines that the simple act of becoming independent, in the words of SNP minister Alex Neil, would 'effectively eliminate poverty from our society'.

Another document, *Your Scotland, Your Future*, meanwhile, was similarly vague:

> With independence, we will be able to tailor the system to Scottish needs, creating a fair, flexible and transparent structure that seeks to address both the symptoms and the causes of inequality ... Clearly, our objectives will have to be affordable, with a balance struck between reasonable levels of taxation and commitments which are as broad as possible ... We'll inherit the same benefits arrangements as the rest of the UK and then be able to make them better. The aim will be to establish a sensible system that seeks to eliminate poverty traps and to make working, preparing for work or performing socially useful tasks worthwhile.[7]

Only in early 2013 did the Deputy First Minister establish an Expert Working Group on Welfare, although, again, its remit was imprecise. Rather than designing a Scottish welfare state from scratch, it was charged with looking at benefits in Scotland, considering possible changes in the event of independence and making initial recommendations as to how a new welfare system might best 'reflect Scottish values'.[8]

This reported in June 2013 and devoted a lot of space to describing the status quo. While noting that most welfare policy remained reserved to the UK government, it said the 2012 Welfare Reform Act had 'indirectly provided Scotland with additional responsibilities', including the transfer of funds associated with the old social fund, community care grants and crisis loans (scrapped throughout the UK as of 1 April 2013) to the Scottish government. Ministers at Holyrood had decided to channel these into a new 'Scottish Welfare Fund', while legislating to ensure certain 'passported' benefits (for example free school meals) continued even after the UK government had introduced the universal credit (UC) and personal independence payment (PIP). This gave the Scottish government responsibility for council tax reduction (which replaced the old council tax benefit scheme), a significant devolution of power to Holyrood that more or less passed unnoticed. Ministers preserved this at its previous level, unlike the UK government. Free prescriptions and personal care were also sizeable welfare responsibilities devolved to Edinburgh, and expensive ones, the cost of the latter increasing by 160 per cent between 2003/04 and 2011/12.

In addition to this nascent (and indeed expanding) Scottish welfare state, the Expert Group found that not only were 'almost all' the UK benefits paid to Scots already administered from 'locations within Scotland', but that Scotland also provided 'a wide range of services to England'. Northgate in Glasgow, for example, was the biggest benefits centre in the UK, employing more than 1,000 people, while 900 people in Falkirk administered child maintenance payments not only in Scotland but also to the north of England. The Department for Work and Pensions disbursed a total of £15 billion in Scotland, representing 9 per cent of the UK total. This, then, was the rationale for recommending a 'transitional period of shared administration' until around 2017/18. Beyond that, the report concluded, all 'options for the delivery of welfare at the point of independence – including a stand-alone Scottish system of administration – are possible'.

But there were caveats. Not only was the 'picture painted' a 'complex' one, but the Expert Group warned that a 'downside of continuing to share services might be that an independent Scottish government found itself unable to implement some of its early priorities for change to the benefit system'. This included abolition of the 'bedroom tax' (which the SNP tried hard to make as totemic as the poll tax) and reversing certain aspects of the UC, Work and Pensions Secretary Iain Duncan Smith's flagship consolidation of various separate benefits. As the academic Gregor Gall pointed out, this would simply turn the 'clock back on reforms to the welfare state since the coalition government came into power in 2010' and therefore ignore all the changes – all criticised by the SNP – that had occurred since the early 1980s.[9] Furthermore, the Scottish government was planning a series of policy announcements in the run-up to referendum day in order to illustrate, as Nicola Sturgeon put it, 'clearly and vividly the benefits and possibilities of independence'. Even so, added the report, 'as a way of ensuring that benefit claimants who currently receive services from the UK nations continue to receive those services in the event of Scottish independence (irrespective of where they live), we concluded that this [a transitional arrangement] was the preferable and most pragmatic option'.

Finally, the report also appeared to pour cold water over other aspects of the Scottish government's welfare agenda, noting that the Scottish Campaign on Welfare Reform and the Child Poverty Action Group generally supported the UC reforms, with the latter warning against changing it 'for the sake of doing so'. As for public attitudes, generally presented by the SNP as more 'progressive' than those in the rest of the UK, while the Expert Group cited the 2012 Scottish Social Attitudes Survey figure of 64 per cent support for devolution of welfare to the Scottish Parliament, it also noted that support for redistribution of wealth had fallen in both Scotland and England over the last decade. Scots, meanwhile, were only 'a little more concerned' than the English about income inequality.[10]

In response, Nicola Sturgeon expressed cautious support (a transitional period of shared administration, she said, 'would make sense'), although she qualified this by saying it would 'only be in Scotland's interests if it allows us from day one of independence to address the inequities of the current system', while stressing that a transition arrangement 'is as much, if not more, in the interests of the UK'. She and the First Minister cited the fact that welfare was already administered separately in Northern Ireland as proof that 'such an arrangement is perfectly possible', although the only policy deviation in the province came in the frequency of benefit payments. Talk of a transitional arrangement, meanwhile, jarred with the urgency of Sturgeon's previous claim that 'leaving welfare to Westminster [was] more worrying than ever'.

At Holyrood, Alex Salmond insisted that a shared UK administration delivering 'two radically different systems' (he cited student loans as an example) north and south of the border was perfectly viable. The Scottish Secretary, Michael Moore, was scathing: 'The Scottish government seems to have their heart set on the impossible. They want to leave the UK and keep the UK welfare system. But they only want to keep the UK welfare system if they can insist upon immediate policy changes. I think most people in Scotland will regard this as a self-defeating contortion.'[11]

As for what an independent Scottish government would do once a transitional period had come to an end, the SNP was rather vague. A leaked Cabinet paper had talked of 'exploring the possibility of a combined tax and benefits service in the more medium term', while in the long term Sturgeon depicted it as a journey, 'on the road to a separate Scottish welfare system that meets Scotland's needs'. Pushed for more detail, she described something that was 'fair and sustainable, protects the vulnerable and supports people into work', although that did not sound very different from the

UK government's aim of making 'it fairer, more affordable and better able to tackle poverty, worklessness and welfare dependency'. Sturgeon also announced another expert group that would look at 'the medium- to longer-term options for reform of the welfare system and the delivery models that will best support that'. This included Jon Kvist of the University of Southern Denmark, a nod to the Deputy First Minister's respect for the Danish way of doing such things, although he and the rest of the group were told to bear in mind 'the economic and fiscal circumstances' and consider potential savings as well as the costs of any new policies. Even this report (due in early 2014), Sturgeon later conceded, would not actually firm up details of a new welfare system for inclusion in the autumn 2013 white paper. Voters, she told *The Guardian*, would need to wait until 2016 for that.

More generally, the Deputy First Minister stressed that independence would allow Scotland to have a 'distinctive approach to welfare which at the moment we just don't have'. Salmond argued that under devolution all the Scottish government could do amounted to 'mitigation – nothing more'. He added:

> With devolution, we can create a social wage. But we cannot avoid the anti-social consequences of the UK's austerity measures. With devolution, we can take steps to mitigate the impact of the UK government's welfare reforms. But only with independence can we create a welfare system which makes work pay without reducing people to penury and despair. With devolution, in many key areas we can only lobby Westminster. With independence, we can deliver for Scotland.[12]

Again, Salmond did not go into any specifics, although he was confident that once Scots had 'decided to become an independent nation' then they would also 'choose to become a fairer nation, as well as a more prosperous one'. He made it all sound very straightforward.

The First Minister also did not waste any opportunity to contrast his administration's approach with both that of the UK government (by, for example, abolishing Thatcherite Right to Buy legislation) and, closer to home, proposals from the Scottish Labour Party. In a controversial speech, Johann Lamont invoked (perhaps unwittingly) Conservative rhetoric by calling for an end to what she called a 'something for nothing' culture, by which she meant the SNP's policy of free university tuition. Such schemes, she argued, created a culture in which the 'poorest pay for tax breaks for the rich'.[13] A group (quickly dubbed the 'cuts commission' by the SNP) was set up to examine whether free tuition fees, free prescription charges and a council tax freeze were affordable. This echoed a similar shift at Westminster, where party leader Ed Miliband and his shadow Chancellor, Ed Balls, were attempting to triangulate their way back into Downing Street by accepting elements of the coalition's welfare agenda.

In reality, however, all Scotland's governments since 1999 had extended provision in some form or another, the first Labour–Liberal Democrat Scottish Executive having scrapped tuition fees (which it replaced with a graduate 'endowment'), introduced free personal care for the elderly and phased out charges for eye and dental checks. But although clumsily expressed, Lamont's concern was about spending priorities given the likely reduction in the Scottish government's block grant as Westminster focused on deficit reduction. So the debate was not so much about whether universal benefits ought to exist, but about their extent. Either tax would have to go up, Lamont argued, or services would have to be cut; a devolved government could not have its cake and eat it.

The SNP leader, however, chose to depict this as a full-frontal assault on everything from Scotland's NHS to free pensioner bus passes (another perk introduced by his government). As he put it to the Scottish Trades Union Congress:

> Since it was re-established in 1999, the Scottish Parliament has proved itself to be a champion of progressive policies, with successive administrations promoting and defending universal benefits. But those universal services are under threat as never before. Not only are the punitive policies of the current Westminster government damaging the social fabric of Scotland, our political opponents here in Scotland have said that they regard Scotland as a something-for-nothing country.

'Nothing', he added, 'could be further from the truth.' Scotland was 'a something-for-something country, where people contribute to the common good and are entitled to expect something in return'.

'Progressive', however, was a much-misused word in the Scottish and British political lexicon. Salmond had made it the centrepiece of his Hugo Young Memorial Lecture in early 2012, when he suggested an independent Scotland could 'be a beacon for progressive opinion south of the border and further afield', not least in terms of welfare.[14] (Gordon Brown, on the other hand, suggested 'Britain' could 'become a beacon' in an increasingly 'multinational world'.) There was, of course, a lively debate as to whether some of the SNP's own policies, not least a long-standing council tax freeze, were truly 'progressive', particularly when analysis demonstrated it actually hit the poorest hardest in terms of the impact on council services (there was scant acknowledgement that a freeze naturally deprived local authorities of much-needed revenue).

So policy was frequently conflated with the constitution, and deliberately so, something Labour attempted to disentangle in an interim paper on further devolution: 'Labour has always been the party of the UK welfare state,' it declared.

We take pride in this fact, and will do everything we can to sustain it against the attacks it faces from the Conservatives and SNP. We oppose the Conservative-led government's welfare agenda, but this does not lead us to the conclusion that the solution is to tear up the welfare state that has served us well. We believe it is an argument for Labour governments at both Westminster and the Scottish Parliament.[15]

But on this, as on the SNP's wider macroeconomic strategy, the urge to associate independence with a more generous and 'fairer' welfare state in voters' minds inevitably ran up against Salmond's determination to either cut personal and business taxes or keep them at about the same level once Scotland had achieved independence. A more 'competitive' tax regime, ran a familiar refrain, would grow the tax base and ensure an independent Scotland had enough revenue to provide generous social provision, precisely the same rationale behind 'New Labour' in the late 1990s and early twenty-first century.

Apparently influential in this respect was the US economist Joseph Stiglitz, one of the joint authors of the Scottish government's Fiscal Commission Working Group report on an independent Scotland's macroeconomic framework. The nub of his argument, as outlined in his 2012 book *The Price of Inequality*, was that social and economic inequality directly contributed to stunted economic growth (Richard Wilkinson and Kate Pickett had set out a similar thesis in their influential 2010 tome *The Spirit Level: Why Equality is Better for Everyone*). Reports suggested he had pressed for the inclusion of this observation in the FCWG report, which pointed out that the income gap had grown faster in the UK than in any other developed country since 1975. 'Such patterns of inequality will continue', the report warned, 'to have a negative impact on growth and prosperity over the long-term.' But it concluded that 'without access to the relevant policy levers – particularly taxation and welfare policy – there is little the Scottish government can do to address these trends'.[16]

'That's what the independence referendum is becoming about,' remarked one Yes Scotland strategist. 'And Stiglitz has ended up heavily influencing Alex on this.'[17] But the Nobel Prize-winning economist appeared to be, at best, a partial influence, for Stiglitz was also a staunch critic of trickle-down theory and the very sort of neo-liberal, low-tax economics Salmond had advocated for the past two decades. To the journalist Paul Hutcheon, this was because so-called 'civic Nationalism' was 'a value-free zone'. 'There is no logical Scottish position on wealth inequality, feminism or reforming public services,' he wrote in 2009. 'Most SNP policies are tactical compromises designed solely with the intention of promoting independence.'[18]

The commentator Kenny Farquharson was only marginally more charitable. 'Once again I find myself wondering why we don't know more about how Alex Salmond's mind works,' he wrote during the summer of 2011, 'and what he thinks about some of the key political questions of the age.'

> This is a bizarre position to be in. Salmond has been one of the biggest beasts in Scottish politics for more than two decades. He is part of our landscape. We should know him inside out. Yet we don't. Not even nearly. We know what he thinks about the Laffer Curve, but we have no idea what he thinks about welfare dependency. We know his views on the base load possibilities of Scotland's wind turbines, but we're in the dark about his views on tackling Scotland's appallingly high level of teenage pregnancy.

Farquharson posited that Salmond avoided straying into such territory 'because social and moral issues by their very nature divide opinion'.[19] Same-sex marriage – a high-profile issue during 2012 and 2013 – was a case in point. For all Salmond's talk of 'progressive' values, his administration seemed remarkably reluctant to legislate on something that enjoyed both broad political support (particularly at Holyrood) and public backing. As ever, the First Minister was keen to keep everybody happy, and that included the SNP donor Sir Brian Souter (who had campaigned against the abolition of Section 28 in 2000) and the Catholic Church in Scotland (which was vehemently opposed to gay marriage). This proved an impossible task, and only after the latter had been silenced by a scandal involving Cardinal Keith O'Brien did the Scottish government introduce a Bill in June 2013, expected to pass *before* the independence referendum. Nevertheless it was notable that the supposedly reactionary Westminster had legislated first, the Prime Minister having closely associated himself with the reform, unlike the 'progressive' Alex Salmond.

But then, post-2011 Salmond had obviously come round to the view that pursuing a more progressive agenda would not only be popular electorally, but would help secure victory in 2014. The same logic applied to welfare, on which subject the First Minister never managed to sound particularly convincing (unlike, for example, Nicola Sturgeon). Although critical of the UK government's benefit changes, he made a point of telling the journalist Jon Snow that did not 'mean every single thing about those changes [is] wrong', perhaps conscious that a key section of SNP support – aspirational voters – were generally hostile to generous welfare. Later he went further in saying he supported a benefit cap 'deployed in the right way'.

The Yes Scotland campaign, meanwhile, could afford to be a little bolder. Launching *Yes to a Just Scotland* in February 2012, its chief executive, Blair Jenkins, argued that an independent Scotland could use its tax system to target the wealthiest, investing in universal benefits and welfare to promote a 'social justice agenda'. Clearly influenced (again) by Stiglitz, it envisaged 'a virtuous cycle of enterprise and compassion whereby jobs and investment create growth, creating a more equal and caring society'. It continued:

> The challenge in this debate is to move beyond a point of discussion that focuses solely on what movements up or down might be made to current tax rates – so that a view on independence stands or falls on potential penny changes to income tax or corporation tax, for example. Independence gives us an opportunity not just to play around on the margins with the current Westminster tax system, but over time to design a system that reflects Scottish needs and priorities: a system that can work to reduce inequality and support social justice.

A new approach, it added, 'might include greater integration of the tax and welfare system, debates about the relative value of taxes on employment or land or pollution or consumption, and reassessment of the weighting given to progressive taxes within the overall balance of the system'. Furthermore, it should move away from the assumption that the UK status quo, 'which has enabled a culture of tax avoidance to be fostered', was 'in any way a suitable model for Scotland'.

Although far in advance of anything published by the SNP, not least its cautious suggestion of tax rises, Yes Scotland's welfare pitch rested on what it called a 'balance of consensus around issues of social justice and social democracy' in Scotland, 'a consensus held by citizens, civic groups and organisations, as well as political parties, and indeed by some of our most successful entrepreneurs'.[20]

Regular social attitudes surveys and opinion polling told a rather different story. Far from the caricature of the mean-spirited English hammering the poor while more community-minded Scots looked on in horror, polling showed when it came to support for means-testing, equality and redistribution, attitudes differed only marginally north and south of the border. One YouGov poll (admittedly with a small sample) showed that 82 per cent of Scots supported the UK government's proposed benefits cap, while 81 per cent agreed benefits ought to be removed from those who declined an opportunity to work, similar levels as existed in the rest of the UK. Similarly, ScotCen, a leading independent social research body, found that even among those who believed independence *would* reduce income inequality, only 38 per cent of them were prepared to vote 'yes'. Furthermore, in what some academics termed the 'devolution paradox', while the majority of Scots wanted welfare devolved to the Scottish Parliament, they were less enthusiastic about policies varying across the UK.

The elephant in the room when it came to discussions of welfare reform was, of course, cost. Spending on 'social protection' in Scotland accounted for around 40 per cent of all identifiable expenditure north of the border, while social security spending per head was about 9 per cent above the UK average. Although the Scottish government claimed overall costs were slightly lower than in rUK, it varied from benefit to benefit. A report from the Institute of Fiscal Studies revealed, for example, that expenditure on disability benefits per person was 22 per cent higher in Scotland (£593) than in Great Britain as a whole (£486), while spending on housing benefit and child benefits/tax credits were, respectively, around 12 and 9 per cent lower in Scotland.[21] Research by Stirling University also showed that spending on incapacity benefit (IB), employment support allowance (ESA) and severe disablement allowance (SDA) north of the border was a third higher than in Great Britain, the equivalent of £307 per person of working age compared with £232 in England and Wales.[22]

Any vision of welfare in an independent Scotland not only had to consider the expectations of Scots already in receipt of benefits from the UK, but also the views of those who were not, but saw themselves as financing those who were. As the authors of *Scotland's Future* put it:

> This could pose a substantial political obstacle to change, even if Scotland were to have the powers to amend the system to better meet its preferences. It would not, of course, prevent change – as would be entirely legitimate and, indeed, anticipated with such a constitutional change – but it would suggest that transformation of the welfare system would be both a delicate process and one that might be expected to span many decades.[23]

It also had to be borne in mind that the public sector's recent experience of radical change in terms of delivering public services – particularly when a cumbersome IT system was involved – was not exactly a happy one, or indeed cheap.

'Welfare Unionism'

Even in the context of a welfare-cutting Conservative–Liberal Democrat coalition, Unionists generally regarded the welfare state as one of their strongest hands. On a visit to Glasgow the Work and Pensions Secretary, Iain Duncan Smith, said services would have to be cut and taxes increased in order to sustain a separate Scottish welfare system ('offensive and nonsensical', responded Salmond). To the Prime Minister, meanwhile, the welfare state was 'properly funded' and even 'generous'. Whatever his government's policies, which – like Margaret Thatcher's – amounted to tweaking rather than a wholesale assault, state provision 'from the cradle to the grave' remained in place for all UK citizens, regardless of postcode or devolved government, and if it was cut in one place it was also cut in every other. As the economist

Gavin McCrone pointed out, one of the main consequences of independence would be an end to welfare redistribution and the Barnett Formula. 'If Scotland were wealthier than other parts of the UK,' he wrote, 'it would not be expected to contribute support to them and, if Scotland was poorer, it could not expect any help from them.'[24]

Thus Unionists stressed Scotland's 'solidarity' with the rest of the UK. Scotland had been an integral part of the UK's welfare state since it had been founded, in nascent form by Lloyd George's Liberal governments, extended by paternalistic Tories before the Second World War, and brought to full fruition by a combination of Liberals (Beveridge and Keynes), visionary Labour politicians (such as Nye Bevan) and Conservatives (for example Harold Macmillan) committed, at least until the 1970s, to the post-war Butskellite consensus of full employment and generous social provision.

Unpicking all that would naturally prove challenging (when Ireland seceded from the UK in 1922 there had been less of a welfare state to disentangle). The National Health Service was a case in point. Established in 1948, it had always been administered separately north of the border – on the basis of the National Health Service (Scotland) Act 1947 – while remaining fully integrated with the rest of the UK. After entering government in 2007 the SNP went to great lengths to present itself as the true defender of Bevan's vision (given that he hailed from Tredegar, Wales's Labour First Minister Carwyn Jones did likewise), a task made easier post-2010 as the coalition embarked on a controversial NHS reform agenda (none of which applied in Scotland). As Health Secretary, Nicola Sturgeon also gave the impression the NHS was already fully independent, which rather skirted over the fact that patients from the rest of the UK, and indeed Scots in rUK, were all entitled to free service at the point of delivery. If Scotland became independent, then that would cease to be the case unless a reciprocal agreement was reached with the NHS in the other parts of the UK. Better Together highlighted the case of its volunteer Sally Russell, who had benefited from a rare double-lung transplant at Freeman Hospital in Newcastle, a procedure unavailable in Scotland,[25] although the Scottish government claimed such arrangements with hospitals in rUK 'would not change' under independence.

Since the war, Scots had also paid into a UK-wide national insurance fund (the 1911 legislation actually established a separate Scottish fund, although this was later centralised by Clement Attlee's government) and general taxation, and thus drawn on pensions and benefits as they became entitled to them. An independent Scotland, Unionists pointed out, would no longer be part of the UK welfare state and would thus not receive any benefits from it. 'Benefits for people living in Scotland would be the responsibility of the new Scottish state,' judged the authors of *Scotland's Choices*. 'Whether they were more or less generous would depend on the decisions of an independent Scotland, and on what it could afford. A more complex question is whether there is scope for devolving further aspects of welfare within a continuing UK.'[26] Indeed it seemed curious that health – given its reach, expense and importance – had been devolved to Scotland in 1999, but not welfare.

The authors also cited the Calman Commission, the cross-party group (including Labour, Lib Dem and Conservative members) which had recommended extending devolution following the SNP's 2007 election victory. This emphasised the need to protect a number of shared UK-wide entitlements as part of what it called the 'social union' (a term used frequently by Alex Salmond in a slightly different context). And although it advocated further powers for the Scottish Parliament, these did not include the redistributive aspects of the welfare state. To do so would, in the words of Calman, 'break the bonds of common social citizenship'.[27] This might be termed 'welfare Unionism', as opposed to the 'welfare Nationalism' advocated by the Scottish government.

Pensions

Although any changes to welfare – as part of the UK or not – would impact upon thousands of Scots, the question of what would happen to pensions in the event of independence was much more potent, for it had the potential to affect almost everyone. As with benefits, all the Scottish government had said on this was that 'in an independent Scotland', pensions would 'be paid at a similar level as now', although Nicola Sturgeon had also hinted they would be more generous.

Beyond that, there was scant detail. Pro-independence campaigners argued that as Scotland (as part of the UK) spent a smaller share of GDP (14.4 per cent) on 'social protection' than the UK (15.9 per cent) then, if anything, pension (and welfare) payments would be 'more affordable' in an independent Scotland. This, as ever, depended upon how one measured it, and using proportions of GDP, as the Centre for Public Policy for Regions pointed out, was not necessarily the best guide as it included the total value of North Sea oil rather than the resulting tax revenue. Professor David Bell of Stirling University, for example, calculated that actual spending (per head) on social protection in 2010/11 was actually higher in Scotland at £3,972, compared with £3,658 for the UK.[28]

Yes Scotland, as well as the SNP, did its best to be reassuring. 'Your private pension will not be affected by Scotland becoming an independent country,' read the relevant section on the campaign website. Even more reassuringly, given the Scottish government's proposal to retain sterling, 'your pension would be paid in the same pounds and pence as it is today'. Public pensions were addressed separately. These too would 'not change', with the Scottish Public Pensions Agency continuing to administer NHS and teachers' pension schemes, as well as regulating police, fire and local government funds administered on a regional basis. An independent Scottish government, meanwhile, would take on the pension liabilities of civil servants (including the Royal Mail) currently in UK-wide schemes. Again, these would 'not be affected' by Scotland becoming independent.

The Yes Scotland position on the state pension – estimated to cost £6.5 billion a year – followed a similar script. Entitlement to this or pension credits 'on Day One of an independent Scotland' would be 'the exact same' as entitlement before, only they would be paid through the Scottish government rather than the UK Department of Work and Pensions (DWP), perhaps using two large DWP centres in Dundee and Motherwell, respectively the fourth and fifth biggest in the UK. As Johann Lamont pointed out to a visibly irritated Alex Salmond during an exchange at the Scottish Parliament, he would soon be able to draw on five separate pension schemes himself, from his careers in the civil service, at RBS, in two parliaments and as First Minister.

Continuity and reassurance was the name of the game, although a leaked Cabinet paper by John Swinney told a rather different story. Far from emphasising how little things would change with independence, this stated that spending 'on state pensions and public sector pensions is … driven by demographics, and is set to rise' (the Scottish government's Christie Commission had estimated that additional demand for health, social care and justice over the next fifteen years would amount to £27 billion).[29] The paper also acknowledged that while, under the status quo, the Treasury and DWP absorbed 'the risk of growth in demand' and therefore 'all associated costs', in future an independent Scottish government would 'assume responsibility for managing such pressure'. 'This will imply more volatility in spending than at present,' noted the paper, especially as there was little an independent Scotland could do 'from a public policy perspective' in the short to medium term to 'manage Scotland's demographic position'. Swinney even tasked the Fiscal Commission Working Group with considering 'the affordability of state pensions',[30] which hardly seemed consistent with repeated claims that nothing would change following independence.

This was a less rosy view of the prospects for pensions than that presented by the SNP or Yes Scotland, but probably a more realistic one. The UK government was also keen to emphasise uncertainty. Pensions Minister Steve Webb (a rare creature in that he actually understood pensions) echoed Swinney's point about the rising cost of state pensions being 'absorbed' by the UK via fiscal transfers. A 'fragmented' system operating across a 'porous' border, he argued, would make the system immeasurably harder to operate. Webb also linked independence with his own pension reforms:

> We're setting up a system so that when you change job your private pension goes with you. So instead of having a pension here and a pension there, there's a pot that follows you and grows. That's fine if you're one country, but if you work in Scotland and build up a pension, then work in England and build up a different one, then go back to Scotland – you've got a pension here, a pension there, national insurance records here, something else in Scotland.

For Webb, the UK-wide pensions system was 'welfare Unionism' in action. 'The Scottish population is ageing faster than in England, but we have automatic stabilisers,' he said. 'The pensions will flow to wherever the pensioners are, it doesn't matter which bit of the UK they're in, although the taxation may come from elsewhere. That works.'[31]

Withdrawing Scotland from a UK pensions system in which Scots had accrued rights since before the First World War was, unsurprisingly, complex. There were also other

cross-border issues. In a report that appeared to catch the
Scottish government completely off guard, the Institute of
Chartered Accountants of Scotland (ICAS) pointed out that
while, under European Union rules, defined-benefit (DB)
company pension schemes operating in a single nation
could be underfunded, those serving pensioners in two or
more EU member states could not. Given that independence
would create a border between Scotland and rUK, the consequences were obvious: UK employers with beneficiaries on
both sides of the border would have to stump up to cover
all their liabilities, estimated at around £250 billion.[32] The
pensions specialist David Davison warned that many Scottish
charities would 'potentially have to close' if compelled to
eliminate their pension deficits following independence.

On this issue, the Scottish government's line that nothing
would change post-independence was simply unsustainable.
Responding in the Scottish Parliament, Alex Salmond implied
the EU would be relaxed about an independent Scotland
breaking the existing rules by spreading the cost over a transition period of several years, while later Finance Secretary
John Swinney sought to defuse anxiety by announcing a
'triple lock' guarantee, under which an independent Scottish
government would uprate the new single-tier flat rate state
pension by whichever was highest, earnings growth, inflation or 2.5 per cent.[33] Swinney was less impressive under
a barrage of hostile questioning from his opponents. 'The
pensions issues that the country faces today', he said at one
point, 'have not been created by independence, they have
been created by the Union.'

The Scottish government's pensions paper, finally
published in September 2013, nevertheless committed to
using the current UK state pension system as the 'foundation' for an independent Scotland, and guaranteed that all
state, private and public sector pensions would be paid in
full and on time after 2016. Ministers also dangled another

pre-referendum carrot by appointing another expert group
to review Westminster's plans to raise the state pension age to
67 between 2026 and 2028, the implication being that Scots
might be able to retire a year earlier than those in the rest
of the UK, a move the UK government claimed would cost
around £6 billion. On fully funded cross-border pensions,
meanwhile, the paper said an independent Scotland would
'negotiate for appropriate transitional arrangements' with
the EU,[34] although that ignored – as Better Together pointed
out – that the Czech Republic had recently been fined for
ignoring those same regulations.

The Scottish government's paper also appeared not to
have given much thought to what might happen to the UK's
complex regulatory infrastructure, for example the Financial
Services Compensation Scheme (FSCS), the Pension
Protection Fund (PPF) and the Pensions Regulator (TPR),
all of which protected against the loss of pension savings,
including those of thousands of Scots. ICAS recommended
creating a Scottish Pension Protection Fund, but of course,
doing so would cost money. Swinney conceded that any
regulatory structure would have to have 'a compatibility
with the rest of the regulatory infrastructure in the UK',
particularly given that an independent Scotland planned to
retain sterling.

The task facing those arguing for independence was
a formidable one. In terms of both the welfare state and
pensions, they had to come up with the Scottish equivalent
of the Beveridge Report in the space of two years (it took Sir
William almost as long, though admittedly he was starting
from scratch), while demonstrating to voters that benefits
would, at least initially, continue as normal in an independent Scotland. Not used to doing the legwork on reserved
matters, however, the Scottish government proved itself
rather better at identifying what Beveridge called 'Giant Evils'
associated – in their eyes – with Westminster governance,

rather than coming up with creative alternatives. Indeed, it seemed odd that a party pushing independence since the 1960s had done little or no detailed work on developing alternative welfare models.

Yes Scotland and the SNP also lazily conflated inequality with 'the Union', when by most measurements inequality in Scotland was very much in the middle of the UK range. Independence *in itself* would of course do little to tackle welfare dependency and rising pensions bills – indeed, in the short term there was a good argument that spending on both those areas would come under added pressure (as a leaked Cabinet paper acknowledged). Rather, it depended on policy decisions taken *after* independence. The SNP could, of course, point to its track record in government as evidence that those decisions would depart from the status quo, although not radically so; in government, its spending choices (for example on free prescriptions) had been taken in a fiscal vacuum, a luxury the Westminster government did not enjoy. And given its emphasis on co-operation in other policy areas, the Scottish government struggled to explain why an essentially redistributive welfare state should stop at the Anglo-Scottish border.

Nevertheless the welfare aspect of the independence debate did not necessarily leave the cross-party 'no' campaign in a stronger position. It was relatively strong on the benefits of existing structures and raising related concerns about the consequences of taking Scotland out of the pan-UK status quo, but weaker when it came to explaining how unprecedented benefit cuts pursued since 2010 meant Scotland and the rest of the UK were truly 'Better Together'.

The referendum, if anything, encouraged a more open debate about those wide-ranging reforms (which included many long overdue changes), but in acknowledging the challenges facing an ageing population amid sustained economic turmoil, neither side offered much in the way of game-changing solutions. The direction of UK travel was clear, while even the veteran Nationalist Stephen Maxwell concluded there was 'nothing in Scotland's recent political record to suggest a pent-up demand for radical social and economic change waiting to be released by independence'.[35]

CHAPTER 6

CULTURE AND NATIONAL IDENTITY

Having a national identity is a bit like having an old insurance policy. You know you've got one somewhere but often you're not entirely sure where it is. And if you're honest, you would have to admit you're pretty vague about what the small print means.

William McIlvanney, *The Herald* (1999)

It is no use looking to the intentions of the SNP or any other separatist movement for answers to questions like these. However new nationalism may differ from old, it has inherited much of its ideology; and it is a standard law of such ideology that '*our* nationalism will be different' – i.e. not aggressive, not narrow or 'inward-looking' but progressive and 'outward-looking', not turning back the historical wheels but urging them forward (and so on).

Tom Nairn, *The Break-Up of Britain* (1977)

'I am here to stand up and speak out for what I believe in,' declared the Prime Minister on a visit to Edinburgh in February 2012. 'I believe in the United Kingdom. I am a Unionist, head, heart and soul. I believe that England, Scotland, Wales, Northern Ireland, we are stronger together than we ever would be apart.' Although Unionists such as Cameron were adept at making practical – chiefly economic – arguments for the preservation of the UK, they had long neglected the cultural or spiritual dimension. That, expressed in terms of history or national identity, had generally been the preserve of Nationalists.

In an eloquent and ostentatiously ecumenical speech, however, the Prime Minister sought to reclaim some of that ground. He spoke of the Scottish air hanging 'heavy with history', the 'injustices' visited upon victims of the Highland Clearances and the 'mercantile greatness of the Empire's second city' (Glasgow) while giving Adam Smith and Keir Hardie joint billing in the Scottish hall of fame. And far from simply being a 'great historical construct', argued Cameron, the case he intended to make was 'partly emotional'.

> Because this is a question of the heart as well as the head. The United Kingdom is not just some sort of deal, to be reduced to the lowest common denominator. It is a precious thing; it is about our history, our values, our shared identity and our joint place in the world. I am not just proud of the Union because it is useful. I am proud because it shapes and strengthens us all.

Individual nations could, of course, 'adhere around ancient myths, blood-soaked memories, and opposition to others', but the Prime Minister believed the UK cohered around better 'values', those 'embodied in standing up for freedom and democracy around the globe'. He continued:

> A United Kingdom which is not monoglot, monochrome, and minimalist but multi-national, multi-cultural, and modern in every way. Our United Kingdom, founded on the strengths, yes, of our constitutional monarchy, our parliamentary democracy, and the rule of law. But it is also the birthplace of the NHS, the BBC and Christian Aid. We have shared achievements that more than match those of any country anywhere in the world.

The Prime Minister then turned to the matter of national identity. 'The ties of blood', he argued, were 'actually growing thicker'.

> Far from growing apart, we are growing together. There are now more Scots living in England, and English people living in Scotland, than ever before. And almost half of Scots now have English relatives. I am something of a classic case. My father's father was a Cameron. My mother's mother was a Llewellyn. I was born and have always lived in England: I am proud to be English. But like so many others too, I am proud to be British as well.[1]

There are, however, endless debates as to whether there is any such thing as 'Britishness'. Nationalists often depict it as a hollow, artificial construct with little public traction, but in a 1992 book, *Britons: Forging the Nation 1707–1837*, the historian Linda Colley argued that a common British identity had been forged by a shared Protestant faith (in contrast with a predominantly Catholic Europe), status as an Imperial 'mother country' and rivalry with France. Although this ignored the role of (Catholic) Ireland and the fact, as Colin Kidd pointed out, that Protestantism had in fact been a divisive issue for the Scots, Colley's thesis contradicted a Scottish school of history which emphasised centuries-old differences rather than common pan-UK bonds.

It was the Labour MP and academic John P. Mackintosh, meanwhile, who best captured the curious dynamic of Scottish national identity by advancing the concept of 'dual nationality', the idea that Scots could be both Scottish *and* British, something illustrated (albeit in a slightly muddled way) in the 2012 James Bond film *Skyfall*. Initially, in a word association test, 007 responds to the question 'country' with 'England', although later in the film he is seen heading to northern Scotland to revisit his childhood home; the movie ends with Bond amid fluttering Union flags on a Whitehall rooftop. David Cameron also explored this 'dual identity' at the 2012 Scottish Tory conference. 'Not only can you drape yourself in the Saltire and the Union Jack,' he told delegates, 'but you can be even prouder of your Scottish heritage than your British heritage – as many in Scotland are – and still believe that Scotland is better off in Britain.'[2]

Unionists also borrowed a related strategy from the Canada/Quebec experience. 'We've been looking at Canada,' said one Downing Street adviser, 'and a big part of the 1995 result was the rest of Canada saying to Quebec, "Don't go." It's a simple narrative: we're trying to empower Scots to say I just "am", i.e. Scottish and British, or British and Scottish.'[3] They had in mind a massive 'United Canada' rally in Montreal on the eve of the 1995 referendum, when thousands of people from across Canada urged Quebeckers to stay, an emotional event many believed tipped the balance on polling day. In that vein, when the Prime Minister visited Diageo's aptly named Cameronbridge distillery in Fife, he claimed that 'deep in the English psyche there is a love of the UK and a deep respect for what Scotland brings to the UK', later ordering his ministers to 'spread the word about the Union in English constituencies' during the 2013 summer recess.

Pinning down what being 'English' or 'Scottish' actually meant, however, was tricky, although the historian Tony Judt had a stab at the latter by positing that the Scots' 'sense of self' rested upon a 'curious admix of superiority and *ressentiment*'.[4] Since the 1970s the number of Scots identifying primarily as 'Scottish' had increased significantly although, paradoxically, support for independence had not risen with it; in other words, if a 'yes' vote depended upon national identity then Scotland would have become independent long ago. Britishness, of course, still existed, but was subordinate to Scottishness, while as feelings of Scottishness and Welshness had grown, many white Britons had turned to Englishness as an alternative identity, some 60 per cent giving their national identity as 'English' only (compared with 19 per cent who said 'British' only) in the 2011 census.[5] 'Scottishness', however, was generally assumed to be virtually irrelevant in the context of the independence debate. 'Any attempt to make this purely about national identity', predicted a Better Together insider, 'is set up to fail – on both sides.'[6] But while research by Professor John Curtice concluded feelings of 'Scottishness' made 'remarkably little difference' to voting intentions, he also found that how 'British' voters felt was important, helping to explain the disproportionately large numbers of older people who opposed independence.

Although in 2003 the SNP's then leader, John Swinney, had told 'the Brits' to 'get off', in the intervening decade the party had gradually embraced elements of 'Britishness', not least by stressing the 'social union' that would persist even after independence. 'We want to be part of the monarchical union, have the Queen as head of state,' Salmond told *Channel 5 News*, continuing [with my italics], 'We want Scots with English families to still travel from Scotland to England. All these aspects, the valuable bits, *the things we really love*. The social union will be retained.' Beyond that, however, the First Minister rarely moved beyond banal statements of the obvious, positing that 'ties of family and friendship with our neighbours on these islands' would 'never be obsolete', which was, of course, self-evidently true. Alistair Darling meanwhile said the historical, social and cultural ties that bound UK citizens together were not 'just something that is a nice bonus, a warm feeling around royal occasions and sporting triumphs – they underpin our economic union'. 'Our social union', countered Yes Scotland rather simplistically, 'has nothing to do with Westminster.'

In terms of Britishness, meanwhile, the SNP MP Pete Wishart moved from claiming that 'all vestiges of Britishness' would go (2008), to arguing it would 'exist in Scotland long after we become independent'. In fact, he added, 'it could well be enhanced with independence' (2011). Similarly, Alex Salmond admitted having 'a British aspect' to his identity. 'I've got a multilayered identity,' he told the *New Statesman*. 'Scottishness is my primary identity but I've got Britishness and a European identity.' And Alex Neil, who had once likened the Labour politician George Robertson to the English Nazi propagandist Lord Haw-Haw, said Scots could 'still call themselves British' after independence. One SNP strategist even went so far as to claim that Scotland would remain a 'British nation' by virtue of its geographical location. Danny Alexander's identity was even more layered: 'I'm a Highlander, I'm a Scot, I'm a Brit, I'm a European too and all those identities can sit comfortably within one United Kingdom.'

Pro-independence supporters worked hard to shift the referendum discourse away from issues like national identity and towards political 'values', stressing the *why* (policy objectives) of independence rather than the *how* (process). But this shift 'disconcerted' guardians of the Union in Downing Street. 'The Nationalists I'm used to are blood-and-soil types; "we were wronged historically and need to correct it",' explained one adviser. 'But the SNP aren't like that, they talk about values, social justice and the economy.'[7] Indeed the preamble to 'An Act Respecting the Future of Québec', passed by the Quebec National Assembly ahead of its 1995 sovereignty referendum, illustrated a rather different kind of nationalism:

> The time has come to reap the fields of history. The time has come at last to harvest what has been sown for us by four hundred years of men and women and courage, rooted in the soil and now returned to it. The time has come for us, tomorrow's ancestors, to make ready for our descendants harvests

that are worthy of the labours of the past. May our toil be worthy of them, may they gather us together at last.[8]

The SNP would not have been caught dead framing independence in such terms, something the late Sir Neil MacCormick described as the difference between 'existential' and 'utilitarian' Nationalists; the former desiring independence *for its own sake*, the latter in order to deliver a better society. (The former Labour minister Brian Wilson was rather cynical about this distinction, believing there were simply existentialist Nationalists who posed as utilitarians 'in order to tempt the unwary with wonderful promises and disappearing problems, when what they are actually after is a vote for independence by hook or crook'.[9])

Deputy First Minister Nicola Sturgeon explored this in a thoughtful speech at Strathclyde University towards the end of 2012. Referencing MacCormick's comments, she suggested that 'today most SNP members are an amalgam of these two strands'. She continued:

> For my part, and I believe for my generation, I have never doubted that Scotland is a nation … but for me the fact of nationhood or Scottish identity is not the motive force for independence. Nor do I believe that independence, however desirable, is essential for the preservation of our distinctive Scottish identity. And I don't agree at all that feeling British – with all of the shared social, family and cultural heritage that makes up such an identity – is in any way inconsistent with a pragmatic, utilitarian support for political independence.

Rather, Sturgeon's belief in independence stemmed from principles, 'not of identity or nationality, but of democracy and social justice'.

Down the years, many people have asked me why I ended up

in the SNP and not the Labour Party. Why did a young girl, growing up in a working-class family in the west of Scotland – a part of the country where in those days, they would joke that the Labour vote was weighed rather than counted; someone who was, just like Labour was in those days, anti-Trident and pro-social justice and went on to work as a social justice lawyer in Drumchapel – why does that person end up in the SNP instead of Labour. The reason is simple. I joined the SNP because it was obvious to me then – as it still is today – that you cannot guarantee social justice unless you are in control of the delivery.

Given that Sturgeon had joined the SNP aged sixteen, it seemed she had reached this 'utilitarian' view of independence at a remarkably young age (indeed, she later told *The Guardian*'s Ian Jack her early Nationalism 'might have been more of a heart rather than a head thing' given her love of Nigel Tranter's historical novels). Nevertheless her 'central argument' remained that independence was 'more than an end in itself' and that only by being independent could Scots 'build the better nation we all want'. 'And I ask you ... to base your decision,' she added, 'not on how Scottish or British you feel, but on what kind of country you want Scotland to be and how best you think that can be achieved.'[10]

It was an interesting contrast: a Unionist Prime Minister making an emotional, almost nationalist pitch on behalf of the UK, and a Nationalist Deputy First Minister eschewing sentiment and making a hard-headed, practical case for Scottish independence. Not all Nationalists, of course, agreed with her analysis. Asked by Sir David Frost to articulate the essence of his political philosophy, the First Minister replied, 'I think the case for independence is a fundamental one. It is about Scotland as a nation and nations have a right to self-determination. [They] usually are better to govern themselves as opposed to let somebody else do it for them.'

And when asked on the Gransnet online forum if he believed independence was 'in itself of supreme value', and would be worth having 'even if it meant that Scottish people gain no economic advantage from independence', he replied [with my italics]:

> Couldn't have said it better myself. I fully agree. *A sense of identity*, a new confidence in a proud nation with a strong sense of social justice, a good global citizen: these are all attributes which Scotland aspires to through independence. And of course the fact that we will flourish economically is also a welcome bonus!

And when it came to giving the 'best expression' to that 'sense of identity', Salmond did not agree with former US President Bill Clinton, who said the biggest challenge of the twenty-first century was for people to reconcile different identities while recognising that common endeavours 'matter more'. 'It doesn't necessarily need to have an independent country,' argued the First Minister, 'but I think it is best expressed through an independent country because people's identity and feelings are often expressed through the field of politics.'

So while Salmond leaned more towards existential Nationalism his deputy claimed to be more of a utilitarian. A 2012 survey of the SNP's membership, however, appeared to put most members in the former camp. When asked if 'all else should be secondary' to the 'primary goal' of independence, 71 per cent said they agreed or strongly agreed.[11] But then of course Sturgeon's pitch, and the party's generally, looked beyond the converted.

The Nationalist impulse, and to an extent also that of the Unionist, was perhaps better understood as an article of faith, and faith – like the religious variety – owed more to instinct than utilitarian analysis. Unionists were a bit like lapsed Catholics, strongly committed to their faith despite many obvious failings, while Nationalists resembled Wee Frees, determined to plough their own furrow regardless of public indifference and theological inconsistencies. The Scottish Tory leader Ruth Davidson even said Conservatives shared 'the nationalists' faith in Scotland's future; but our faith is not blind to the facts'.[12] The religious analogy was not new. As Michael Kelly argued in *The Scotsman*, independence to Nationalists was 'an act of faith'. 'They have no need to explain it or defend it among themselves,' he wrote. 'But they are outraged when those not of their religious persuasion challenge the very basis of their belief.'[13]

Similarly, the former Canadian Prime Minister Jean Chrétien (who informally advised the UK government on its referendum strategy) recalled that it became 'almost a religion for them [Quebeckers] to have their country, so on the "no" side you're breaking the dream of someone ... breaking the dream of a kid is difficult; breaking it of an adult is more difficult'. Dr Matt Qvortrup used the Canadian province to illustrate his belief that referendums were 'won by emotions, not by economics'. In the 1980 referendum the Parti Québécois had pushed economic arguments and lost by 20 per cent, while in 1995 the charismatic Lucien Bouchard had stressed the cultural differences between Quebec and the rest of Canada and come within a whisker of victory. One Downing Street adviser appeared to concede this point. 'What the Canadians tell us is they handled badly the emotional angle,' he reflected, 'and that's what caused the dramatic narrowing late on in the day.'[14] British Unionists, it seemed, were determined not to repeat the same mistake.

One nation or two?

One article of Nationalist faith had it that England and Scotland, or rather Scotland and the rest of the UK, were 'distinctly different' (according to the SNP MSP Fiona Hyslop), electorally, politically and culturally, something implied by Alex Salmond's complaint in the summer of 2011 that the BBC kept referring to 'UK riots' when in fact they were specifically 'English' (there existed, he argued, 'a different society in Scotland'). In electoral terms, of course, Scotland and England had indisputably grown apart during the last half-century. Political scientists had first noticed a divergence in the 1960s when the 'Scottish Unionist' (or Conservative) vote began to decline and the SNP vote started to rise.[15] The turning point came in the October 1974 general election when the SNP got 30 per cent of the vote and eleven MPs. Although the Nationalist vote subsequently declined, Scotland – for much of the next few decades – had a four-party system of politics.

The 1970 general election had also given rise to the 'no mandate' argument, although it did not really take hold until the 1980s. Until then, UK governments generally enjoyed a majority of seats in both Scotland and England, but Edward Heath's Conservatives had just twenty-three Scottish MPs, prompting grumblings that his administration's writ did not extend north of the border. This was curious, for when the reverse had been true – for example, in 1964 – the English had not complained about an arguably greater electoral injustice. As the political scientist Richard Rose put it, 'The Tories did not issue demands for the creation of a devolved English assembly to meet in Winchester, on the grounds that Labour was unrepresentative of England. Losers as well as winners accepted that the power of government belonged to the party winning the most seats in Britain overall.'[16]

That consensus, however, broke down from 1979 onwards and reached its peak in 1987 when Margaret Thatcher secured a third term with just ten MPs in Scotland (and 25 per cent of the vote). Ironically it was pushed by Labour opponents of the Iron Lady as well as Nationalists, but it was always a problematic point, for Scotland was not then an independent country, and the elections in question were

UK-wide ballots. But it undoubtedly gained resonance, not least because Thatcher was perceived, whatever her constitutional legitimacy, to lack 'consent' to govern. And although she never achieved a majority of either seats or votes (as Anthony Eden had in Scotland in 1955), nor was support for the Conservatives as weak as mythology now dictates: for most of the 1980s the party had around 30 per cent of the vote and about twenty MPs (indeed, she won almost as many votes in 1979 as the SNP did in 2007).

Devolution was supposed to settle this 'democratic deficit', for if Scots were able to control education, health and so on then they could opt out of the Thatcherite agenda (proponents rather skirted over the obvious point that in other important respects, most notably the economy, this would not be the case). And although Scottish public opinion had been rather lukewarm about devolution when polled in 1979, by 1997 it was, in the words of John Smith, the 'settled will' of the Scottish people. Ironically, the Labour landslide that year resolved in one fell swoop the 'mandate' question, for Scotland was – for the first time in eighteen years – once again in agreement with the rest of the UK.

The new Scottish Parliament, almost by design, ensured no single party would have an overall majority in terms of seats. Labour was only able to govern in coalition with the Liberal Democrats for two terms, while in 2007 the SNP formed a minority administration without a majority of seats or the popular vote (interestingly, no one accused it of lacking a 'mandate' to govern). Although Nationalists could hardly question Tony Blair's mandate to rule Scotland, he did find his moral authority under almost constant attack, particularly in the wake of the Iraq War. Again, this never quite stacked up, for Blair won the 2005 general election in Scotland *and* the UK, which of course was a comprehensive test of his mandate to govern at every level, whatever the SNP thought of his foreign policy legacy.

Only after 2010, with the emergence of a UK coalition government, did the 'no mandate' argument resurface. Even factoring in the Liberal Democrats, the new administration had just twelve MPs in Scotland (including only one Conservative) and around 35 per cent of the popular vote. As Nicola Sturgeon put it in 2012:

> I simply do not believe that Scotland should have to put up with long periods of UK government led by a party we did not vote for. It is – surely – democratically indefensible that although the Tories have never won a majority of votes or seats in Scotland in my entire lifetime – or even come anywhere close – they have nevertheless governed Scotland for more than half of my lifetime.[17]

Thus it was a central argument of the pro-independence case that having opted out of the Westminster system then Scotland would *always* get the government it voted for. Sturgeon et al. frequently pointed to surveys showing the Scottish government to be 'trusted' by a larger proportion of Scots than that at Westminster (71 per cent compared with 18 per cent according to the 2011 Scottish Social Attitudes Survey). This was undoubtedly the case, although Scottish turnout in UK elections since devolution had actually been consistently higher than those for the Scottish Parliament (63.8 per cent in 2010 compared with 50 per cent in 2011), which implied Scots still considered Westminster elections of greater importance.

The rise of UKIP in England (and to a lesser extent Wales) also provided the SNP with a convenient narrative. Again, this had validity in electoral terms for UKIP had virtually no presence north of the border so when, in May 2013, UKIP secured a quarter of the vote in English council elections (and came second in the South Shields by-election), the SNP's Kevin Pringle tweeted that Scottish politics 'looks very different from Westminster politics this morning'. And when, in the wake of this election, the Conservatives indulged in a predictable bout of infighting over the prospect of an in/out referendum on membership of the European Union, the SNP spoke of the 'different directions' being taken by Scotland and Westminster. 'UKIP's success south of the border is dragging the whole Westminster agenda further and further to the right,' said Angus Robertson, the party's Westminster leader, 'far away from what the people of Scotland want.'

The journalist Lesley Riddoch wrote of 'two sets of values … grinding away at each other' in 'almost every aspect of life',[18] something Labour's Douglas Alexander argued was part of a general attempt to convince Scots 'that the rest of the UK has become so foreign a place with such different values, a foreign place so lacking in points of deep connectedness, and with so little sense of being neighbours, that we should split apart'. He continued:

> The Nationalists' claim relies on the implicit but spurious assertion not only that we as Scots are committed to social justice, but that our friends, family and colleagues across the rest of the UK are not … I reject a cultural conceit that relies upon a single stereotype of voters in the rest of the UK – the stereotype of voters south of Gretna as Conservative in character, somehow irredeemably different from Scottish voters.[19]

Despite Alexander's critique, his mentor Gordon Brown had also laid claim to distinctive Scottish attributes in his 2012 Donald Dewar Memorial Lecture. He framed his 'Scottish values' in terms of the 'democratic intellect', an egalitarian belief in making educational opportunity available to all, and also the 'idea of civil society, of a community where we have mutual obligations to each other and where there is a moral core to the public realm'. Furthermore, Brown argued that those 'distinctive Scottish values' had shaped not only Scottish society but the 'British Union'. Thus Scottish values were also 'shared values' in a 'multinational' state.[20] Similarly, Alistair Darling said he welcomed the independence referendum as a 'chance to reaffirm Scottish values and our expression of them in our partnership with our neighbours'.

In policy terms there had, of course, been some notable divergence since devolution in 1999. Nicola Sturgeon described it thus:

> In the thirteen years of devolution, great changes have occurred. We lose sight of them in the pell-mell of politics – but unlike the privatisation process south of the border, our health service remains true to Nye Bevan's founding principles; our education system has a new curriculum fit for modern teaching and learning; our universities offer education based on the ability to learn not the ability to pay; and our older people have more security in their later years.[21]

A deficit-cutting Tory-led government since 2010 had naturally provided the SNP with an even more potent contrast. Stephen Noon referred to 'a tale of two countries, of two very different visions of society', while Salmond said he was focused on creating a 'fair society' rather than David Cameron's 'Big Society':

> Elsewhere on these isles, the tolerance of the poor is being tested, budgets slashed, priorities changed, hope crushed in the braying tones of people who claim to know best. We should aspire to be different. In Scotland the poor won't be made to pick up the bill for the rich. When we control our natural assets as a sovereign power, the profit from the land shall go to all. Too many of them have been ill served by the union as it currently stands. There is a better way.

Cynics, of course, might have interpreted this emphasis on a 'better way' governed by 'Scottish values' as being a nicer way of saying 'we don't like the English', and although Anglophobia (once cited by Hugh MacDiarmid as a 'hobby' in his *Who's Who* entry) had been a prominent feature of pre-1960s Scottish Nationalism, Alex Salmond – who often described himself as an 'Anglophile' – had worked hard to reconstruct his party along more inclusive lines. By 2011 the SNP had several English (or English-born) MSPs and special advisers, and while anti-Englishness certainly existed in Scotland, it was, according to Murray Watson's book *Being English in Scotland*, episodic and isolated. There were occasional lapses, not least when the First Minister emphasised the nationality of senior judges in a prolonged attack on the UK Supreme Court (Justice Secretary Kenny MacAskill, who had once jokingly referred to England as the 'Great Satan', said their knowledge of Scots law was 'limited to a visit to the Edinburgh Festival'), while the former SNP leader Gordon Wilson urged his party to pitch one part of England against the other, campaigning 'with the moral support of the north' to 'strike' at what he called 'the southern cancer'.

Some pro-Union figures even implied racism, the Labour-aligned lawyer Ian Smart suggesting on Twitter that Nationalists would 'turn on the Poles and the Pakis' if independence failed to deliver economic benefits (Smart later explained he was 'making a rhetorical point about the language used by others'). This was taking things too far, for as the playwright David Greig explained:

I have equated nationalism with racism, xenophobia, inward-looking-ness and militarism. I have spent my adult life voting and campaigning for a British Labour party. All the while, I've kept my eye on Scottish nationalism, watching and waiting, distrusting it, expecting it to reveal its true dark heart. But it never has. They have openly campaigned for *more* immigration. The SNP proudly asserts the multicultural nature of modern Scotland with its MSPs taking the parliamentary oath in Urdu, Gaelic, Italian and English.[22]

As an SNP press release put it, 'We have a wide range of identities in modern Scotland – Scottish, British, Pakistani, Chinese, Polish, French, Irish and many, many more. Independence is the broad, inclusive and positive option for Scotland, in which all these identities can be reflected and celebrated.'[23] Although, as the journalist Andrew Marr observed, the SNP's was 'an exclusive rather than an inclusive notion of identity', requiring 'much more of the incomer than, for instance, Britishness does'.[24]

'Settlers and Colonists'

'There is only one argument for Scottish independence,' declared Professor Alan Raich in early 2013: 'the cultural argument.'

> It was there long before North Sea oil was discovered, and it will be here long after the oil has run out. It is the only distinction that matters. No one denies the importance of economics – putting bread on the table, jobs and health – but they are all matters of material fact unless occupied and enlivened by imagination. The arts – music, painting, architecture and, pre-eminently, literature – are the fuel and fire that makes imagination possible. Neglect them at your peril.[25]

This was probably an accurate reflection of Scotland's cultural community, many of whom were long-term supporters of independence. Indeed, support among this group tended to be much higher than among Scots as a whole. In 2012, for example, the pro-independence 'National Collective' (NC) produced a list of fifty 'Artists and Creatives for Independence';[26] it would have been much harder to produce a similar list of, say, fund managers who shared the same view, although Eddie McGuire, chairman of the Musicians' Union in Scotland, vowed to organise pro-Union events during 2014.

The writer and artist Alasdair Gray was one of the best-known names on the list, although he did not express his support for independence in terms mainstream Nationalist politicians were comfortable with. Indeed, he provoked controversy with his contribution to a book called *Unstated: Writers on Scottish Independence*, a chapter entitled 'Settlers and Colonists'. Gray divided English people living in Scotland into two groups, those who took up temporary jobs (mainly in the arts) in order to advance their careers in London were called 'colonists', while those staying long term were categorised as 'settlers'.

This rather ignored that the phenomenon also existed in reverse, many Scots occupying prominent arts posts in London, including Sir Neil MacGregor at the British Museum and fellow Scot Penelope Curtis at Tate Britain. Gray's essay was undoubtedly embarrassing for the SNP, for not only did Alex Salmond and Nicola Sturgeon often quote Gray's line about living in the 'early days of a better nation',[27] but it appeared to be a throwback to the sort of ethnic, blood-and-soil nationalism the party had made strenuous efforts to jettison over the past thirty years. But then artists and writers were almost impossible to keep on message. The Scots-born writer Shena Mackay, for example, told *The Observer* she wanted Scotland to be 'Scottish through and through', adding that she hated 'to hear English accents in the shops there'.[28]

Gray, meanwhile, compounded the controversy by naming names, including the then outgoing artistic director of the National Theatre of Scotland (NTS), Vicky Featherstone, who he noted was 'leaving in 2013 for work nearer London'. At around the same time Gray's essay was published,

Featherstone admitted criticism of her appointment based on her Englishness had forced her to question her position. After much prompting the SNP formally distanced itself from Gray's comments (who repeated the 'colonist' charge when an Englishwoman, Janet Archer, was appointed chief executive of Creative Scotland), although he was supported by many mainstream Nationalists and 'yes' supporters, including the former publisher Kevin Williamson (later a Yes Scotland board member), who used Twitter to call for a 'social audit' of government officials and administrators to discover 'who they speak for'. Williamson later admitted his comments sounded a 'bit fascistic' but did not withdraw them. Gray, meanwhile, announced he was preparing a new book on Scottish independence, having published the short polemic *Why Scots Should Rule Scotland* in 1992.

Featherstone's successor at the NTS was also English, although Laurie Sansom said he had avoided reading Gray's essay and had been made to feel 'nothing but welcome' in his new post. In June 2013 he announced a year-long programme inspired by the independence debate, including a new variety production called *The Great Don't Know Show*. All NTS shows in 2014, meanwhile, would tackle that 'unusual and remarkable event', although Sansom was conscious the debate could cause 'some quite serious fissures'. Two leading Scottish playwrights, David Greig (who was pro-independence) and David MacLennan (who was anti), were also working on a referendum-themed play to be launched in the summer of 2014 and staged around Scotland until the eve of the independence poll.

Just weeks before Sansom's appointment at NTS, meanwhile, an open letter – signed by 100 leading figures from the Scottish arts world – had condemned Creative Scotland (formerly the Scottish Arts Council) for 'ill-conceived decision-making; unclear language, and a lack of empathy and regard for Scottish culture'. Andrew Dixon, the arts body's first chief executive (also English), resigned shortly after. Although the controversy stemmed in part from mismanagement by the Scottish government (which had established Creative Scotland), the SNP moved quickly to repair the damage.

In what Sansom called a 'magnificent and bold' speech, the Scottish Culture Secretary, Fiona Hyslop, said she did not want Scotland's artists to make 'a new economic or social case to justify public support for their work'. 'Despite these challenging times, we do not measure the worth of culture and heritage solely in pounds and pence,' she said, 'we value [them] precisely because they are so much more, because they are our heart, our soul, our essence.'[29] It was a deliberate response to UK Culture Secretary Maria Miller, who had earlier warned that in the context of austerity, the UK government's focus had to be on 'culture's economic impact'. Thus another point of contrast had been opened up between north and south, Scotland and England. It must have been music to the ears of Scotland's (already independence-leaning) arts establishment.

Alex Salmond believed that while Scotland and England shared the same language ('albeit with different accents'), 'you couldn't get two more different cultures'. Nobody, he added, 'would mistake a Scottish novelist for an English novelist', while claiming the Scottish bard Robert Burns (a '100 per cent Scottish patriot') and Sir Walter Scott ('I'd like to think he might have moved towards a "yes" vote') as posthumous supporters of independence. This was, of course, a debate for literary experts, although rarely acknowledged were two inconvenient truths. First, the greatest Scottish contribution to global culture – the Scottish Enlightenment – had occurred under the Union, while a post-1979 renaissance in writing, poetry and song had taken place in the 1980s and 1990s, without even a devolved parliament for support.

Some of the beneficiaries inevitably reflected on the

independence debate in the early twenty-first century. The crime writer Ian Rankin, for example, was careful to feature both pro- and anti-independence characters in his books (Inspector Rebus intended to vote 'no'), while James Robertson's *And the Land Lay Still* (which Salmond named his book of 2011) was an epic narrative of post-war Scotland with many familiar Nationalist refrains. 'I do not subscribe to nationalism as an ideology', Robertson wrote on the Scottish Review website, 'but I do believe in the right of peoples and nations, if this is how they perceive themselves, to determine their own political futures.' 'Despite the abandonment of principle and dodgy behaviour of the SNP government,' he went on, the British state's apparent obsession with illegal 'foreign wars and invasions, an economic war on the most vulnerable in our society through benefit cuts, endless toadying to the USA, a determination to build another generation of weapons of mass destruction, and the sycophantic adoration of royalty' all inclined him towards a 'yes' vote.[30]

Similarly, Iain (M.) Banks said he had spoken to a number of Scottish writers, all of whom felt 'we would vote for independence purely never to be part of any more unnecessary illegal, immoral wars'. Elsewhere he explained that the Thatcher era had

> made a lot of Scots begin to realise that we were, after all, meaningfully different en masse from the English; more communitarian, less convinced of the primacy of competition over co-operation ... These days, I support the idea of an independent Scotland. It's with a heavy heart in some ways; I think I'd still sacrifice an independent Scotland for a socialist UK, but ... I can't really see that happening.[31]

Unfortunately for Banks, he did not live long enough to vote 'yes' in the referendum (which, by the time of his last interview, he believed would be lost), for he died of cancer in June 2013. Irvine Welsh, meanwhile, got a bit carried away in saying, 'I'm totally for independence, totally. I think everyone is – even the unionists. It's the process which is being argued about, not the principle.' With a nod to Shelley's remark about poets being the 'unacknowledged legislators of the state', the SNP even floated the idea of getting the 'tartan noir' novelist William McIlvanney to draft an inspiration précis of its white paper on independence (he claimed to be 'totally in the dark' about it).

Other Scottish writers, meanwhile, intended to vote 'no'. 'I don't want to be divided from a Yorkshireman or Cornishman,' the poet John Burnside told the BBC, 'I want to work together', while the Edinburgh-based writer J. K. Rowling ('I'm pro-union') and the historical novelist Allan Massie (whose son Alex was a prominent referendum commentator) were rare Unionist voices in Scotland's literary community. The thriller writer C. J. Sansom took a rather different approach in his alternative Nazi history *Dominion*. In this, the UK has become a satellite state of the Third Reich and the SNP (whose wartime leaders had, in reality, flirted with the far right) were collaborators. In a lengthy 'historical note' at the end of his novel, Sansom made sure no one had missed his point: 'A party which is often referred to by its members, as the SNP is, as the National Movement should send a chill down the spine of anyone who remembers what those words have often meant in Europe.'[32] Little more than a 'casual glance' at the party's history, he told a journalist, shows 'the SNP have never had any interest in the practical consequences of independence. They care about the ideal of the nation, not the people who live in it.' In response, James Robertson said Sansom seemed to 'be singling out the SNP as particularly dangerous, whereas their history shows them to be one of the mildest-mannered of "national movements" that ever existed'. Scottish publisher Hugh Andrew, meanwhile, said nationalism represented 'the worst of all worlds for our writers and culture', erecting an 'artificial wall' between Scotland and the London-dominated book industry, which would lead to Scottish writers being viewed as 'foreign' by the rest of the UK.[33]

The independence debate also filtered through to the BBC's popular radio soap *The Archers*, with its token Scottish character, Jazzer, diligently avoiding taking sides (not that he would have a vote in any case, being resident in Ambridge), while questions arose as to how the arts would be administered and funded if Scotland ceased to be part of the UK. In reality (assuming stable revenue), there would likely be little change, for culture had been devolved to Scotland in 1999. The future of cross-border organisations, however, was less clear-cut, as was nomenclature in respect of London-based institutions like the 'British' Museum and 'British' Library. The SNP tended to address these as they arose, for instance when a Conservative MSP raised the future of the National Lottery, John Swinney responded blandly that an independent Scotland would 'continue to have a lottery and lottery infrastructure'.

As in many areas, the cultural – certainly pop culture – tastes of most Scots could not be said to differ markedly from the rest of the UK, as evidenced by their viewing and cinema-going habits, not to mention the bestseller and pop music charts. Pat Kane of the 1980s duo Hue and Cry accepted a place on Yes Scotland's advisory board; Fairground Attraction singer Eddi Reader tweeted in support of Scottish independence; Sheena Wellington – who delivered a memorable performance of Burns at the opening of the Scottish Parliament in 1999 – said she would be voting 'yes' on a non-partisan basis; while Annie Lennox said an independent Scotland 'could take a stand in a wonderful way, ecologically and morally and ethically'. Scots-Italian Texas singer Sharleen Spiteri, however, was a declared 'no' ('as far as I'm concerned, I'm British'), as was *Trainspotting* actor

Ewan MacGregor ('I love Scotland with all my heart. But I also like the idea of Great Britain') and the comedian Billy Connolly ('I love Scotland but I hate the way nationalists think they own the place'), although the Big Yin decided to keep a low profile during the long referendum debate, saying Scots were 'very capable of making up their mind' without his 'tuppence worth'. The comedian Hardeep Singh Kohli, meanwhile, revealed he had moved back to Scotland after two decades in London to 'bang the drum for independence'.

In sport, too, Scotland was as much a footballing nation as England, although with more of a national disposition towards rugby rather than cricket. The outgoing and much-lauded Manchester United manager Sir Alex Ferguson looked likely to be a fixture of the 'no' campaign, branding independence a 'distraction from what really matters – the economy, jobs, schools and hospitals', while the SNP's approach to the London Olympics, the world's largest international sporting event, proved instructive. For several years MP (and former Runrig drummer) Pete Wishart had set the tone with remarks like Scotland getting 'absolutely zilch from the London Olympics', 'a Games for London and the south-east', 'all we are going to get is the opportunity to bask in the reflected glory from London', 'Scotland has absolutely no interest in Team GB', and so on.

There was an abrupt change of tone the weekend before the Olympics kicked off in the summer of 2012, SNP politicians having been surprised at the reception for the Olympic torch relay as it made its way around Scottish towns and cities. One UK minister recalled watching Nicola Sturgeon praise, 'through gritted teeth', sizeable crowds in Glasgow. 'Scotland just doesn't have the theatre there is in London,' he explained, 'and people like being part of that. In some mystical way, the torch gave people a connection with not just the Olympics but the UK.'[34]

The Scottish government belatedly set up 'Scotland House'

in Pall Mall to showcase the best Scotland had to offer to overseas visitors, international business people and journalists. Five Scottish Cabinet ministers even produced a video message for Scotland's fifty-four Olympians and twenty-three Paralympians, whom Alex Salmond rather clumsily dubbed 'Scolympians', while Shona Robison, the Scottish sports minister, gushed, 'London 2012 is a huge opportunity to showcase Scotland to the world.'

Danny Boyle's colourful opening ceremony also gave a psychological boost to pro-UK politicians, equipping them with an inclusive, cultural and rather left-wing vision that resonated beyond dry lists of facts and figures. As an editorial in *Scotland on Sunday* put it:

> What Danny Boyle's opening ceremony did on Friday night was provide an alternative narrative of what it means to be British. What it takes from history are the virtues of innovation, industriousness and shared endeavour – but its defining feature is the enormously rich legacy of half a century of British popular culture, and particularly pop music. Dynamic, democratic, stylish and creative, it is Britain's gift to the modern world. And crucially, Boyle expressed this through the prism of a contemporary Britain that is racially and culturally diverse, and all the better for it.[35]

The response to the Olympics, argued Douglas Alexander, 'inadvertently but powerfully crushed' one of the SNP's chief narratives while, following Edinburgh cyclist Sir Chris Hoy's gold medal win, London Mayor Boris Johnson got a little carried away in claiming the Olympics had 'retarded' the 'yes' campaign. He tweeted: 'The Scots are never going to vote for independence ... these games have done for Salmond ... vote Hoy.' Sir Chris, however, denied rumours he would be helping the Better Together campaign. 'I'm British. I'm Scottish and British,' he told *Channel 4 News*.

I think you can be both – they are not mutually exclusive. All I can say is I'm very proud I've been part of this team, to be part of the British team, to be alongside my English and Welsh and Northern Irish, guys on the Isle of Man – everybody. It's been a great team and I'm proud to be part of it.

Similarly, tennis pro Andy Murray – who promised to declare his voting intention before the referendum – said he was 'proud to be Scottish but ... also proud to be British', and that he did not 'think you should judge the [referendum] on emotion, but on what is best economically for Scotland'. At Wimbledon in July 2013, meanwhile, he described himself as 'a British winner' despite the First Minister's best efforts. Indeed, despite telling several SNP conferences that he fought 'not for flags or anthems', Salmond had 'photobombed' the Prime Minister by unfurling a large saltire behind him, in contravention of All England Club rules.

Television images the previous summer of Hoy and Murray literally wrapping themselves in the Union Jack (a flag once described by an SNP researcher as 'the butcher's apron') had certainly been inconvenient for Scottish Nationalists, no matter how much they had affected to be relaxed about Britishness. Polling, however, suggested the success of the Olympics had done little to bolster support for the Union (some even said it made them more likely to vote 'yes' in 2014), although only 29 per cent said they wanted Scotland to remain part of Team GB if voters backed independence. The First Minister confirmed his intention to field a separate Scottish team at the Rio Games in 2016, pointing out that Scotland already competed separately in the Commonwealth Games, due to be staged in Glasgow in the summer of 2014, a sporting event Salmond hoped would boost Scotland's profile and self-confidence ahead of the referendum.

In terms of football, Scotland was already independent in the eyes of EUFA and FIFA, ensuring minimal disruption in the event of a 'yes' vote; the historian Chris Harvie reckoned the formation of the Scottish Football Association in 1887 – a declaration of sporting independence from the English league – had been more significant than any formal Home Rule movements during the same period. Indeed, various sports reflected the UK's multi-layered unions and national identities: the Olympics (called 'Team GB' but drawing from across the UK), rugby's Lions team (Great Britain and Ireland) and football (Scotland). Scottish Nationalism in all those contexts could, of course, outstrip the political sort, a phenomenon the SNP's Jim Sillars once characterised as involving 'ninety-minute patriots'.

The rocks will melt in the sun...

In three other domains Scotland was also effectively independent. The 1707 Act of Union had recognised – and protected – its pre-Union systems of law, religion and education, which the political scientist James Kellas said 'became the transmitters of Scottish national identity from one generation to the next'.[36] Indeed, Scots law had continued to enjoy significant regulatory and operational autonomy even before legislative power was devolved to Scotland in 1999. Even the UK Supreme Court, established in 2009, was predominantly 'supreme' when it came to civil law in Scotland, the High Court of Justiciary in Edinburgh remaining the final court of appeal for most Scottish criminal cases. The 'not proven' verdict, meanwhile, was often cited as a linchpin of a more enlightened legal system, as was the Scottish government's release of Lockerbie bomber Abdelbaset al-Megrahi in 2009 on 'compassionate' grounds.

In the spiritual domain, meanwhile, Alex Salmond and the SNP had not, as might have been expected, championed Scotland's 'National Church', otherwise known as the Church of Scotland (the 'Kirk' was not quite established, but then nor was Scotland secular).[37] During the devolution debates of the 1980s and 1990s the Church of Scotland had enjoyed a prominent role in Scottish politics, its annual General Assembly acting (in the eyes of some) as a surrogate Scottish parliament (the journalist Iain Macwhirter called it 'a form of clerical self-government'), while Kirk figures had also been involved in the Scottish Constitutional Convention, which prepared a blueprint for the Scottish Parliament eventually established in 1999. Although the First Minister had been raised in an active Church of Scotland family and had spoken at the General Assembly, he generally ignored Kirk affairs.

Instead, he devoted huge attention the Roman Catholic Church in Scotland. The motivation in this respect was chiefly political, for until the mid-1990s allegations of anti-Catholic sectarianism dogged the SNP, most famously in the Monklands by-election which followed the death of Labour leader John Smith in 1994 (Billy Wolfe, a former party leader, had also infuriated colleagues by publicly opposing Pope John Paul II's visit to Scotland in the early 1980s). By detoxifying the party, Salmond hoped to build support among Scotland's Catholic communities. In this, the SNP enjoyed some success: by 2013 sectarianism was the preserve of football terraces rather than politics, and while Catholic support for the SNP was difficult to quantify, voting behaviour had certainly shifted as a result.

The apex of this approach had been Pope Benedict's visit to the UK in September 2010, which began in Scotland. And even when allegations surrounding Cardinal Keith O'Brien, the UK's most senior Catholic, damaged the Scottish Catholic Church's reputation during the conclave to elect Benedict's successor in early 2013, the First Minister was ostentatiously loyal. He was the only senior politician to back O'Brien in public, paying tribute to him as 'a good man for his church and country' and lamenting the possibility that 'a lifetime of positive work' might be overshadowed by the 'circumstances of his resignation'. More widely he praised Catholics as 'an important and highly valued part of the fabric of Scotland', later telling the weekly Catholic newspaper *The Tablet* that the Church had been 'at the heart of the independence movement in Scotland' in the past, and even that 'without the Catholic Church there would be no Scotland'.[38]

Finally, Scotland's distinct education system was dominated by the myth it was the 'best in the world', arguably something truer several decades ago than it was in the early twenty-first century. Under devolved control since 1999, most policy-making was therefore unlikely to be affected by independence, and while Scotland's fifteen universities – four of which were termed 'ancient' – were also under Scottish government control they also remained integrated with the UK system, not least when it came to applications and research grants.

In funding terms, the 'abolition' of tuition fees by the first devolved government had been perhaps the first significant policy divergence from the rest of the UK. Following the SNP's election victory in 2007, any charge for higher education was scrapped altogether (although a related pledge to write off all student debt was conveniently ditched), becoming another key element in the oft-invoked contrast between the political culture in Scotland and England; the rocks, said Salmond (quoting Burns) on more than one occasion, would 'melt in the sun' before he introduced charges for higher education. Nationalists saw this policy as a defining feature of how Scotland did things differently, even though various studies in 2013 showed the abolition of fees had done little to attract more students from disadvantaged backgrounds (the number had actually fallen over the last decade). In schools, too, research by the London School of Economics found that educational inequality was 'a huge problem that devolution has been unable to solve' although it posited that 'with independence Scotland would be better able to tackle' the problem.[39]

The Scottish government also struggled to explain what would happen post-independence, when EU rules (assuming membership) would mean students in rUK would for the first time be entitled to free tuition in Scotland, alongside those from other member states who already enjoyed that perk. Paradoxically, Brussels was relaxed about discrimination *within* a member state but not *between* them. A Scottish government spokeswoman said there were 'a range of options', although at the time of writing none had been set out in any detail.

The only aspect of Scottish higher education controlled from London, meanwhile, was research funding, which remained the preserve of David Willetts, the UK minister for universities, who had warned of a possible 'brain drain' should Scotland vote 'yes' in 2014. Several prominent figures also pointed out the obvious consequences of independence in this respect, not least the fact that Scottish institutions usually secured 15 per cent of public and charitable research funding (totalling £229 million in 2011/12), well above Scotland's 8.5 per cent share of the UK's population. Microbiologist Professor Hugh Pennington said cutting-edge science research in Scotland could 'take a knock' in the event of independence, a concern shared by the Royal Society of Edinburgh (RSE) and Royal Society of Chemistry, while the principal of St Andrews University, Alex Salmond's *alma mater*, warned that if it was 'cut off from national research councils it would be catastrophic for this institution'. Scottish Science Minister Dr Alasdair Allan had previously suggested an independent Scotland could co-operate with the rest of the UK and continue to pay into a joint research council, while a Scottish government spokesman said it fully understood 'the importance of long-term stability' and would set out its plans for higher education 'in due course'.

The independence referendum, meanwhile, prompted a plethora of academic activity, including a public information programme at Dundee University (Five Million Questions),[40] Cardiff University's 'UK's Changing Union' project, a collaboration between the British Academy and RSE, and an Economic and Social Research Council-sponsored research programme encompassing several different universities, around £1.5 million in funding and nine fellowships exploring different aspects of the constitutional debate.[41]

'Rise now and be a nation again'

'Scotland will never be free', predicted Tom Nairn in the late 1960s, 'until the last [Church of Scotland] Minister is strangled by the last copy of the *Sunday Post*.'[42] Although this reflected the views of many Nationalists (even half a century later), the media was another distinct aspect of Scotland's cultural life, although one without – at least at the end of 2013 – any political underpinning. Its variety was most striking in the printed media, with several national newspapers, the *Daily Record* (Scotland's largest tabloid), the Glasgow-based *Herald* and Edinburgh-orientated *Scotsman*, dominating Scottish newsstands. Although the circulation of the latter two was relatively small (circa 30,000 in each instance), both were important in shaping the political agenda, *The Scotsman* (pledged in 1817 to 'impartiality, firmness and independence') being the closest Scotland had to a *Times*-style newspaper of record. The Scottish political press corps, or Lobby, also operated more informally than its Westminster counterpart. Tony Blair even did them the honour of calling them 'unreconstructed wankers'.

The Times produced a Scottish edition with a significant amount of distinct content, as did the *Daily Telegraph*, *Sun* and *Daily Mail*, and to a much lesser degree *The Guardian* and *Independent*. Sunday was also a crowded market, with the *Sunday Mail* (a tabloid), *Sunday Post*, *Sunday Herald* and *Scotland on Sunday* all competing with the Scottish editions of London-based titles. Regional dailies like the *Courier and Advertiser* in Dundee and the *Press and Journal* in Aberdeen, meanwhile, lacked political clout but easily outsold their Edinburgh and Glasgow equivalents, which only enjoyed a combined circulation equivalent to about 1.5 per cent of the total Scottish population. Many Nationalists believed independence would boost the Scottish print media, giving it more to report on and therefore increased sales (that, of course, did not necessarily follow), although many in the sector regarded the referendum as a temporary reprieve, after which the industry would seek to consolidate. 'The people who would be most radically affected by independence are the political and media elite, which is perhaps why they are so obsessed by constitutional change,' was Andrew Marr's more optimistic view. 'For journalists and ambitious politicians working in Edinburgh, independence would be Christmas and a lottery payout gift-wrapped together.'[43]

Politically, a distinction had to be drawn between titles that supported the SNP in devolved elections (a majority in 2007 and 2011) and independence (none, although the *Sunday Herald* was considered a possible backer in 2014). Many Nationalists firmly believed *The Scotsman*'s refusal to back independence explained its declining circulation, something that did not stand up to much scrutiny. Not only did the pro-independence *Scottish Standard* fold after just seven editions in 2005, the aforementioned *Scottish Daily Mail* managed to sell more than most quality Scottish newspapers despite its vehement opposition to independence. The websites newsnetscotland.com and wingsoverscotland. com, meanwhile, both attracted thousands of hits with often trenchant rebuttal of perceived 'MSM' (mainstream media) bias, with the latter even crowdsourcing funding for its own opinion poll.

Feelings often ran high. In mid-2013 the word 'TRAITORS' was spray-painted on *The Scotsman*'s Edinburgh HQ, while

Alex Salmond said *The Economist* would 'rue the day' it depicted Scotland as 'Skintland' on its cover. 'This is Unionism boiled down to its essence', he thundered, 'and stuck on a front page for every community in Scotland to see their sneering condescension.' Elsewhere support for independence came from surprising quarters, the hitherto Labour-aligned Kevin McKenna, an *Observer* columnist, writing that with 'each passing week' the Union became 'more difficult to support', an article shared almost 15,000 times on Facebook.

But while quite a few newspaper columnists (including several at *The Scotsman*) backed independence (even the Labour-supporting *Daily Record* gave a regular column to the SNP MSP Joan McAlpine), attempts by the SNP to cultivate editorial support were mixed. The Scottish edition of *The Sun* had famously backed independence in the run-up to the 1992 general election ('RISE NOW AND BE A NATION AGAIN' proclaimed a splash), but lapsed soon after, depicting the SNP logo as a hangman's noose during the 2007 Holyrood election.[44] Salmond had high hopes of rediscovering past glories in the run-up to the referendum, but this too came to nothing when, despite having backed the SNP ahead of the 2011 election, the *Scottish Sun* decided the SNP and Yes Scotland had 'so far failed to make a convincing case for Scotland to go it alone', although it also criticised Better Together for becoming 'bogged down in scaremongering stories'.

Unsurprisingly, Salmond later played down the importance of newspapers' allegiances in the referendum campaign as 'not a great issue', commenting in a speech that the 'the bulk of the press is clearly in the Better Together "operation fear" camp'. Many Nationalists, meanwhile, were uncomfortable at the extent to which the News International (NI) chief, Rupert Murdoch (whose mother had been born in Rosehearty), appeared to enjoy the First Minister's company. While Labour politicians and the Prime Minister deliberately distanced themselves from the Murdoch empire ('I think we all got a bit too close,' admitted Cameron), Salmond if anything moved closer (Murdoch was, he said, 'the most substantial figure in British journalism'). And even after the Milly Dowler hacking scandal prompted Murdoch to close down the *News of the World*, Salmond invited him to Bute House for tea, and played down the resulting Leveson Inquiry in the first edition of the *Scottish Sun on Sunday*. The 'questions the probe is looking at relate to the industry,' he wrote in a notably friendly op-ed piece, 'not one newspaper or company'.

And when the *Scottish Sun on Sunday* claimed to know the date of the referendum (Saturday 18 October 2014, exactly a month out), it prompted accusations of an inappropriate relationship between the First Minister and NI. This was later subject to prolonged scrutiny when the Leveson Inquiry published emails that appeared to show Salmond's willingness ('striking' was Leveson's adjective) to lobby the UK government in support of Murdoch's bid for a takeover of BSkyB. The implication was that this had been a *quid pro quo* for having secured the *Scottish Sun*'s support prior to the 2011 Holyrood election. The First Minister vehemently denied any such deal, maintaining his sole aim had been protecting 'jobs and investment' in Scotland, a line he reiterated during his own low-key appearance at Leveson on 13 June 2012. On neither occasion, however, did he produce firm evidence that either was under any immediate threat.

Thereafter, Salmond suddenly discovered an interest in press regulation, which had been devolved (probably unintentionally) to the Scottish Parliament in 1999. This was curious, for the First Minister had told Scottish newspapers a couple of years earlier that it barely figured on his list of priorities. It was tempting to conclude that the volte-face owed more to Scottish exceptionalism than a reasoned assessment of the situation. At first, Salmond proposed setting up a new Scottish voluntary regulator, underpinned by statute and modelled on Ireland's press ombudsman, with a separate Scottish press council. He told the BBC:

> The Irish press council system, or at least something like it, would seem to be at least an area where we can talk about and bring about a distinctively Scottish solution that protects absolutely the freedom of the press but still allows people, particularly people without the means to carry forward a defamation action, proper redress.

But, faced with widespread scepticism (it emerged that the Irish model was far from ideal), the First Minister asked a review panel chaired by another judge, Lord McCluskey, to find a Scottish model for the voluntary body recommended by Leveson. But McCluskey and his colleagues (who included the journalist Ruth Wishart, a recent convert to independence) rejected that, instead urging mandatory regulation including, controversially, online news media and possibly even social media sites such as Twitter. Rejected by everyone including Salmond, who put it to sleep as 'an important contribution' to the debate, he then tried (and failed) to forge cross-party agreement on a voluntary system before finally acknowledging that Scotland's participation in the Royal Charter model agreed at Westminster was the only realistic option.

Broadcasting, meanwhile, *was* reserved to Westminster, along with a regulatory regime governed by statute and the industry watchdog, Ofcom. Commercially, Scotland was covered by ITV Border in the south and STV (formerly Scottish and Grampian Television) in the north, the latter producing a three-part historical series called *Road to Referendum*, which aired on STV and the whole ITV network during 2013. The *British* Broadcasting Corporation, however, dominated the media in Scotland, with BBC Scotland one of the most prominent of the network's 'nations and regions', although Alex Salmond told the 2012 Edinburgh Television Festival he planned to replace it with a new public sector broadcaster, potentially part funded by advertising, should Scots back independence in 2014.

A new broadcaster, argued the First Minister, would build on the existing assets and staff of BBC Scotland. 'Television was invented by John Logie Baird and the very concept of public service broadcasting was shaped by Lord Reith,' he said, stressing the medium's Scottish heritage. 'But Scottish viewers and TV production talent are today being short-changed. Viewers are clearly voting with their remote controls for more Scottish content. Yet we do not have an English-language public service broadcasting channel of our own.'

Pressed as to how the network would be funded, Salmond said it would rely on the existing £325 million licence fee fund while adding that commercial avenues were 'not necessarily a problem in principle' (he cited Ireland's RTE network, which had mixed public and private financing). Finally, the First Minister reassured his audience that popular BBC shows like *EastEnders* and *Top Gear* would still be available to Scottish viewers, as was the case in Ireland.[45] Unionists, however, pointed out that viewers in the Republic had to pay a £7 fee to watch content on the BBC's iPlayer, implying the same might be the case if Scotland became independent. The former Labour MP (and journalist) Brian Wilson, meanwhile, was appalled by Salmond's idea of aping Irish broadcasting. 'We will abandon public service broadcasting', he wrote, 'founded by a Scot, disproportionately enhanced by Scots, staffed throughout its many outposts by Scots – in order to be like RTE. This is where madness leads us.'[46] Alistair Darling said if the SNP had its way then Scots 'would reduce ourselves to becoming eavesdroppers to one of the world's most successful broadcasting corporations'.

BBC Scotland was the focus of complaints from both

Nationalists (over bias) and Unionists (over bias) which, if anything, indicated its editorial guidelines worked rather well. Craig Murray, a former rector of Dundee University, complained about repeated use of what he called 'negative language', while Alex Salmond also raised concerns with BBC chairman Lord Patten over the use of words 'separation' and 'separatist'. 'My deeper concern is that these incidents stem from an editorial approach', he added in a 2012 letter, 'which falls short in explaining the current constitutional context objectively and in the round.' Labour's Ian Davidson, meanwhile, dubbed the nightly current affairs programme *Newsnight Scotland* (live on air) 'NewsNat Scotland'.

Broadcast four nights a week, *Newsnight Scotland* and STV's *Scotland Tonight* provided the most comprehensive day-to-day coverage of referendum activity, examining the minutiae and personalities of the long campaign. The BBC's flagship *Question Time* also turned into a bit of a minefield whenever it was broadcast from Scotland. Not only did Nationalists demand the panel be evenly divided between 'yes' and 'no' supporters (something broadcasters were not obliged to do, particularly outside the formal campaigning period), there were also contortions over how extensively independence could be debated given the programme's UK-wide remit (a concern that did not seem to prevent discussion of specifically English issues). On one memorable edition from Edinburgh in June 2013 the SNP MP Angus Robertson accused host presenter David Dimbleby of having 'mucked about' independence supporters by stacking the guests five-to-one against (although fellow guest Lesley Riddoch outed herself as a 'yes' supporter in the course of the programme). Dimbleby protested that the audience was evenly split, but the presence of George Galloway and Nigel Farage, who represented parties (Respect and UKIP) without any Scottish representation, prompted formal complaints from the SNP and Scottish Greens (which had two MSPs) to

BBC director general Tony Hall, who said his aim was 'not just that we do it [cover the referendum] really well but also we do it for all of the UK'.

Speaking at a Westminster lunch, Lord Patten said it was 'plainly a big problem for the BBC' to ensure it covered the referendum in as 'impartial and balanced a way as possible'. He ducked questions about what might happen to BBC Scotland post-independence, simply adding that the debate was 'the most important issue that has come up domestically in my political lifetime'.

Alex Salmond had not exactly fostered good relations when he accused BBC staff of being 'Gauleiters' – a term used to describe Nazi officials in occupied France – after being barred from appearing in its coverage of a Scotland–England rugby match on grounds of impartiality. Quality was also a persistent concern. The BBC's 2013 annual report found that only 48 per cent of Scots believed the corporation achieved an appropriate balance between Scottish and non-Scottish news in its current affairs output in Scotland. BBC Scotland responded by appointing the former *Independent on Sunday* editor John Mullin to head up a £5 million schedule of 'multiplatform' referendum coverage, while the *Today* programme's James Naughtie ('Mr Referendum') was seconded to *Good Morning Scotland* (a morning radio programme known as 'Good Morning Separatist' by some UK government advisers) for two days a week as of September 2013, a role the veteran broadcaster combined with leading BBC Radio 4's referendum coverage. Although presumably not part of any internal strategy, it also happened that the lead role in the Beeb's popular science fiction show *Doctor Who* would be played by a Scot (Peter Capaldi, fresh from *The Thick of It*) throughout 2014.

Both BBC Scotland and STV broadcast a series of debates on different aspects of the referendum in the run-up to September 2014, in which Nicola Sturgeon did most of the heavy lifting for the 'yes' side. A year out from the referendum, for example, the BBC network broadcast an ambitiously staged debate in front of the Union Bridge across the river Tweed on the Anglo-Scottish border. Alex Salmond, meanwhile, pushed for a televised confrontation with the Prime Minister as soon as they had signed the Edinburgh Agreement in October 2012. The First Minister argued – and it was a reasonable point – that his and Cameron's signatures were the principal names blessing that document and therefore they ought to have it out in person, perhaps on 30 November 2013 – St Andrew's Day. Downing Street initially appeared open to this idea, but quickly retreated. 'This is not a debate between the SNP and the UK Conservative Party,' said the Prime Minister, 'it's a debate between people in Scotland.' He claimed a television debate was a 'diversion tactic' and made the equally reasonable point that despite Salmond spending most of his time 'telling me to butt out of Scotland's business, now he seems to want me to butt back in again'.

Many 'yes' supporters imagined that television series like *Borgen*, which featured a charismatic Scandinavian Prime Minister called Birgitte Nyborg, would be the result of an independent Scottish broadcaster with a more generous budget. Culture Secretary Fiona Hyslop spoke of offering tax incentives to film and TV production companies after cable network Starz and Sony Pictures Television announced plans to make a fantasy series called *Outlander* in Scotland (lured, ironically, by UK tax breaks), while Nicola Sturgeon's fascination with *Borgen* extended to personally interviewing the series' lead actress during a special screening at Edinburgh's Filmhouse. She and other independence supporters often projected their hopes for Scotland's future on to the surprise television success from Denmark. 'For the first time,' wrote the journalist Iain Macwhirter, 'Scottish viewers were able to see what political life might be like in a small country.'[47]

CHAPTER 7

'DEVO-MAX' AND OTHER OPTIONS

The result, and the norm, is incremental constitutional change. Anticipated economic loss is a powerful motive for constitutional flexibility, and a strong inhibition to radical constitutional change.
Robert A. Young, 'The Political Economy of Secession: The Case of Quebec' (1994)

Although clearly a compromise, a quasi-federal agreement might be seen as a useful interim solution to Britain's constitutional challenges. It would be much more stable and balanced than the current system of devolution because it would have largely addressed the English anomaly, sometimes called the 'West Lothian' question. In time it might evolve into a full federation, but from the start it would divide sovereignty between the Home Nations and the British state.
David Melding, *Will Britain Survive Beyond 2020?* (2009)

'**O**f course devolution – to Scotland, Wales and Northern Ireland – was … an attempt to renew the UK state,' reflected Nicola Sturgeon in a 2012 speech at Strathclyde University. '*But the UK's ability to re-invent itself is spent. The Westminster parties are at best sceptical, and at worst hostile, to further substantial reform in Scotland's interests*' [my italics]. This phrase represented the point at which the SNP formally abandoned so-called 'devo-max', otherwise known as 'full fiscal autonomy', a sort of constitutional halfway house the party had backed to varying degrees since

2000. 'As a Nationalist, I accept that fiscal autonomy is not independence,' the then leader John Swinney had said. 'But I also accept it would be progress for Scotland.' After 2012, however, 'progress' in Nationalist eyes was independence or nothing.

A few months before Sturgeon's speech she and her colleagues had been pushing for 'devo-max' to be included in the independence referendum as a second question, putting the SNP in the curious position of articulating the main *non-independence* alternative to the status quo. This, however, proved unsustainable. 'We were never going to be the ones in the position of campaigning for devo-max,' reflected a former SNP adviser, 'there was always going to be another body doing the legwork on that. It reflects where we are as a party; if people don't want independence but do want devo-max we'll accept that. That's what drives us, moving Scotland forward.'[1] Even so, that outcome had often appeared to be the First Minister's preferred option. As one occasional adviser said, perhaps off guard, 'devo-max *was* Alex's ideal scenario'.[2]

Instead the Scottish government pressed on with its related strategy of *presenting* independence as devo-max, and vice versa. As a Scottish government adviser admitted in early 2012, the mere sight of the UK government and Unionist parties at Holyrood 'talking about more powers' allowed the SNP to 'reposition' itself in that respect. 'And', he added, 'it gives us two years to get the public into the same place.'[3] That, however, was easier said than done, for articulating exactly where devolution ended and independence began required the squaring of innumerable political circles.

Good international precedents for devo-max were, in any case, difficult to find, although the Basque Country, described as having 'full fiscal autonomy', came close: it collected most taxes and controlled personal and corporate taxation, although not VAT, social security or excise duty. The 2009

Scottish government white paper *Your Scotland, Your Voice*, meanwhile, defined what it called 'full devolution' thus:

> Under full devolution the existing devolution framework would be retained, and Scotland would remain within the United Kingdom. The United Kingdom government and institutions would continue to have responsibility for many matters, for example the currency and monetary policy, and decisions on peace and war. Full devolution would give Scotland more responsibility for domestic matters, and would extend the range of measures the Scottish government and the Scottish Parliament could take to encourage greater sustainable economic growth. Nonetheless, there would be continued interaction with matters reserved to the United Kingdom, for example foreign affairs, defence, macroeconomic policy, some taxation and, possibly, social protection and pensions. Existing areas of disagreement would continue.[4]

Importantly, 'devo-max' was *not* independence and would, as the white paper implied, have left defence and foreign affairs (two existing 'areas of disagreement') in the hands of a Westminster government, which, considering the emphasis given by the SNP to banishing Trident and avoiding 'illegal wars', seemed an obvious point of tension. Unionists were generally quite negative about devo-max (although Sir John Major surprised many Nationalists by backing it in a July 2011 speech); the authors of *Scotland's Choices* deemed it 'not deliverable as a form of devolution',[5] while Westminster advisers dismissed it as without precedent in a unified state, rather ignoring the fact Northern Ireland had been granted something akin to devo-max in the early 1920s (although this had proved more theoretical than real).

Nevertheless it *was* possible. The UK's three Crown Dependencies, the Isle of Man, Guernsey and Jersey, also enjoyed considerable autonomy within the British Isles. In 1973 the Royal Commission on the Constitution had called their status 'unique'. 'In some respects they are like miniature states with wide powers of self-government,' it observed, 'neither part of the United Kingdom nor colonies.'[6] Alex Salmond, who regularly rubbed shoulders with the islands' chief ministers at meetings of the British–Irish Council (the Standing Secretariat of which was based in Edinburgh) was clearly struck by the balance they achieved between fiscal autonomy and close links with the UK via its monarchy and currency.

Polls also suggested Scottish public opinion was ahead of the political classes on this front, survey after survey demonstrating a desire for neither the status quo nor independence but instead greater autonomy. Although there was often confusion as to what form that might take (some of those surveyed said health and education, which of course had been devolved since 1999), a clear majority of Scots wanted the Scottish Parliament to assume control of taxation and welfare. Salience, of course, was harder to assess – in other words how strongly voters felt about gaining more powers. And even in the absence of detail, 'devo-max' had credible proponents. The economist John Kay (a vocal critic of SNP policy in other respects) reckoned that faced with three options, most voters would choose the middle course. 'It is also a desirable one,' he added. 'Scotland can get many of the advantages claimed for independence if it negotiates for more autonomy, while still staying part of the Union.'[7] Jim McColl, meanwhile, pitched this to fellow businessmen as 'an independent Scottish Parliament within the United Kingdom', which was not a million miles removed from Donald Dewar's late 1980s concept of devolution as 'independence in the UK'.

This, to Unionist die-hards such as former Labour MP Tam Dalyell, meant a constitutional settlement 'indistinguishable' from independence, and indeed Downing Street had rejected devo-max on precisely that basis. As a result, the SNP tried to depict the Unionist parties as intransigent, positing that voting 'no' in September 2014 would therefore mean 'no' constitutional change (again, a perceived folk memory of the 1979 devolution referendum was deployed). But presenting Scotland's other parties as 'at best sceptical and at worst hostile' to further devolution was a bit of a stretch. Labour had, after all, delivered a Scottish Parliament in 1999, while all three had sponsored an extension of that devolution settlement – however modest – in the years since. As Martin Kettle (an advocate of devo-max) pointed out in *The Guardian*, the prospect of a referendum had not so much strengthened the mood for independence, but produced a 'sudden buoyancy' in the other parties and parts of civic Scotland. The independence referendum, he observed, 'far from acting as a springboard for a much more confident and assertive nationalism, seems to have become the catalyst for some significant and welcome rethinking about the nature of unionism'.[8]

The biggest transfer in 300 years

That 'rethinking' had begun in late 2007 when, in response to the SNP's narrow election victory earlier that year, the three Unionist parties had co-operated via the Calman Commission to agree a package of further devolution.[9] Following the 2010 general election this took legislative form as the Scotland Bill and, in 2012, the Scotland Act.[10] Coalition ministers frequently hailed it as the 'the biggest transfer of fiscal power and responsibility to Scotland' since the creation of the Scottish Parliament in 1999, if not since the 1707 Act of Union. But despite the rhetoric, it never really captured the public imagination, although ministers hoped – at least initially – that it would satisfy apparent demands for more devolution. In early 2012 the Prime Minister complained that it had not 'got the attention yet that it deserves'.

Its rationale was sound enough: that any truly account-able parliament ought to be responsible for raising money as well as spending it. There was also a cruder political motive: devolving more fiscal powers to Holyrood was perceived – wrongly as it turned out – as a means of shooting the Nationalist fox. The main features were as follows:

- Holyrood would take charge of half the income tax raised in Scotland, creating a new Scottish 'rate' by the Treasury deducting 10 pence from the standard and upper rates of UK income tax and a related cut in the Scottish govern-ment's block grant.
- The Scottish Parliament would also gain control over stamp duty, land tax and landfill tax. Future devolution of aggregates levy and air passenger duty (as desired by the SNP) was not ruled out.
- Scottish ministers would for the first time gain powers to borrow, from either HM Treasury or commercial institutions, to fund capital expenditure (powers already possessed by local authorities). The Scottish government would also have the power to issue bonds.
- The power to set national speed limits, control drink-driving laws and legislate on the control of airguns (the latter had been a long-standing SNP demand) would also be transferred to Holyrood.
- The Scottish Parliament would also be able to create completely new taxes subject to UK agreement.
- Finally, the Scottish Parliament would be given powers over appointments to bodies governing the Crown Estate and broadcasting in Scotland, as well as new procedures for Scottish criminal cases referred to the UK Supreme Court.

The SNP's view of the Scotland Bill fluctuated between its introduction on St Andrew's Day 2010 and May 2012, when it received royal assent. It initially described the proposals as 'dangerous', arguing the tax powers and block grant cut would have a 'deflationary effect'. Post-2011, however, Alex Salmond and his colleagues took a friendlier view, talking up the legislation as 'significant' but arguing it ought to be given 'economic teeth'. Even when it was not, the SNP still backed its third reading in June 2011 (conscious that it could not be seen to oppose additional powers, however weak), while in 2012 the Scottish government changed tune again, saying the Act had been 'bypassed by events', which of course was true. The general aim was not to dignify the Scotland Act with any significance in the eyes of voters, lest they actually notice and be satisfied that the greater autonomy they apparently desired had actually been delivered.

Although certainly significant, it was also woolly and academic, the former because it did not follow the logic of its own analysis (in which event income tax would have been devolved in its entirety) and the latter because the tax-varying powers already possessed by the Scottish Parliament (the so-called Scottish Variable Rate) had been neglected by every devolved government since 1999. Although the Scotland Act had derived inspiration from international precedents, for example Canada's experience of dividing taxation between Ottawa and the provinces, it was not exactly a voter-friendly – or easily understood – scheme.

Nevertheless, an SNP-controlled Scottish government had been handed additional powers and it had to prepare to use them. In June 2012 Finance Secretary John Swinney announced the creation of Revenue Scotland, a new agency to collect taxes devolved to Holyrood. Not only did he claim the organisation would be at least 25 per cent cheaper to run than the UK's HMRC, but he promised the SNP would 'make full use of these powers' and introduce replacements that 'reflected Scottish values and Scottish circumstances'. 'In setting up Revenue Scotland we are developing an innovative approach to taxation,' he told MSPs, 'to deliver Scottish taxes, set by this Scottish Parliament, and to save the Scottish taxpayer money. This is an example of the advances that could be made if Scotland had the powers to determine its own future.'

A year later MSPs backed plans to replace stamp duty with a new land and buildings transaction tax which would apply to all property sales as of April 2015. Swinney, however, said the rates and tax bands would not be announced until September 2014 at the earliest (perhaps hinting at a pre-referendum bribe), although ministers had indicated these would be more closely linked to property value. (Power to set the new Scottish rate of income tax, meanwhile, would be available as of April 2016.) The Scotland Act was thus subject to the law of unintended consequences. Contrived to shoot the Nationalist fox, it had instead given it a new lease of life, a convenient mechanism for demonstrating how an independent Scotland might look and act.

A line in the sand
It was the Scottish Conservatives, rather grudging partici-pants in the post-2007 Calman/Scotland Act process, who had made the longest journey in respect of devolution for Scotland. Although Edward Heath had been the first main-stream party leader to back devolution in 1968, the election of his successor, Margaret Thatcher, had ushered in a gradual erosion of that commitment, to the extent that by the mid-1990s the Conservative Party was rightly perceived as a hardline Unionist party, opposed to legislative devolution in any form. The successful 1997 referendum acted as a reality check in this respect, and from that point onwards the party became reluctant converts to a Scottish Parliament. But they were still perceived as lacking enthusiasm – even after the first elections in 1999 – for the new institution and its work.

Only after the May 2011 Holyrood election was there substantial movement. In his bid to become leader following the resignation of Annabel Goldie in May 2011, Murdo Fraser argued that greater autonomy for Scotland ought to go hand in hand with a completely new centre-right party in Scotland, and while Ruth Davidson, the victorious candidate, described the Scotland Bill (not yet an Act) as a 'line in the sand' on the constitutional front, within months of her election David Cameron had washed it away with his Edinburgh speech, which promised more powers in the event of a 'no' vote.

Curiously, Davidson gradually came round to Fraser's way of thinking, at least in relation to the constitution. One speech extolled the virtues of US-style federalism, while by March 2013 she had committed – with the Prime Minister's agreement – to greater fiscal autonomy for the Scottish Parliament. She reasoned:

> A parliament with little responsibility for raising the money it spends will never be properly accountable to the people of Scotland. It can never have the proper incentive to cut the size and cost of government, or to reduce tax bills. So that means in future a far greater share of the money spent by the Scottish Parliament should be raised by it. We will examine the mix of taxes best suited to achieving that goal, but the principle is clear. If you spend the public's money, then you must be accountable to the public both for how it is spent and how it is raised.

The detail was to be worked out by a commission due to report well before the 2014 referendum. 'With the benefit of hindsight,' said Davidson, 'I believe we found ourselves on the wrong side of history in 1997. We fought against the idea of a Scottish Parliament long after it became clear it was the settled will of the Scottish people.'[11] The recommendations of the commission – which was to be chaired by former House of Lords leader Lord Strathclyde (who was, ironically, no great fan of devolution) – were also to be included in the party's 2015 general election and 2016 Holyrood manifestos.

It seemed an eminently reasonable prospectus, although to an extent it was too little too late. At the 2011 Holyrood election the Scottish Tories had managed to secure just 14 per cent of the constituency vote and 12.4 per cent of the list vote, enough to elect fifteen MSPs. At the last UK general election the party had done only slightly better, polling 16.7 per cent of the vote but electing just one MP, the Scotland Office minister David Mundell. The party's support had fluctuated at each election since 1997, although the general trend was downward. This was important, for Scotland's oldest Unionist party being so electorally weak hardly made a defence of the Union any easier. Compounding Davidson's problems was a largely unreconstructed Scottish Tory grassroots, many of whom had never learned to love the Scottish Parliament, let alone further powers.

Home Rule all round

The Scottish Liberal Democrats, meanwhile, harked back to their Gladstonian heritage of 'Home Rule', initially proposed for Ireland but later extended – though never to any serious extent – to the rest of the UK, so-called 'Home Rule all round'. The Grand Old Man, however, had never advocated true federalism, which would have required a new constitution; 'Home Rule' in his eyes was a compromise between federalism and full autonomy for Ireland, Scotland and Wales. Nevertheless, in the course of the twentieth century the Liberals, and later the Liberal Democrats, were generally regarded as a federalist party in the Gladstonian mould.

After the 2011 Scottish Parliament election the SNP even tried to make further inroads to Liberal territory (having benefited greatly from its collapse at the election). 'The old Scottish Liberal Party was the independent party of Home

Rule,' said Salmond, going on to argue that 'that honourable tradition' was now reflected in the SNP's constitutional ambitions. Recognising the need to reclaim the 'Home Rule' mantle, the Scottish Liberal Democrat leader, the former Westminster MP Willie Rennie, established a 'Home Rule and Community Rule Commission' (chaired by former UK leader Sir Menzies Campbell) to look 'at a settled distribution of powers between London, Edinburgh and local councils'.

Building upon a 2006 report by the former Liberal leader David Steel called *Moving to Federalism: A New Settlement for Scotland*, which he described as a 'new, modern settlement for Scotland in the UK based on more federal principles', *Federalism: The Best Future for Scotland* was published shortly after David Cameron and Alex Salmond signed the Edinburgh Agreement in October 2012, and was thus intended as a deliberate riposte to the SNP argument that the Unionist parties were offering Scots no constitutional progress in the event of a 'no' vote. It called on Scottish Liberal Democrats to 'reassert' their federalist beliefs 'in favour of home rule for Scotland within a reformed, federal UK' but recognised that other parts of the UK 'may wish to move at different speeds'. The status of each devolved body, meanwhile, would be made permanent under a new federal treaty.

Powers over all of income tax, as well as control of rates and bands, would also be devolved within a federal UK, as would inheritance and capital gains tax. Corporation tax would not be devolved (for it would potentially fall foul of EU rules), but the proceeds (i.e. the tax raised in Scotland) would be 'assigned' to the Scottish Parliament. Welfare and pensions, however, would be retained by Westminster, ensuring 'a common set of living standards and entitlements' across the UK. *Federalism* also looked beyond central government, proposing 'extensive autonomy' for local government, including the transfer of power over council and business rates back to councils.[12]

A few months after Sir Menzies published his report, Tavish Scott, a former Scottish Liberal Democrat leader and the MSP for Shetland, went even further and proposed 'home rule' (or rather Crown Dependency status) for Orkney and Shetland, two northern Scottish archipelagos which were not only consistently sceptical of London, Brussels and even Edinburgh rule, but which could lay claim to a considerable proportion of North Sea oil revenues should they secede. 'Two thirds of the North Sea and west of Shetland reserves are in Shetland's coastal waters,' said Scott. 'The Northern Isles don't need nationalists negotiating Scotland's oil share. We have plenty of our own leverage.'

This, of course, was largely mischief-making, for the prospect of more autonomy for the islands had figured nowhere in the party's *Federalism* report. Scott – together with Orkney and Shetland MP Alistair Carmichael (who would become Scottish Secretary in October 2013) – were trying to out-Nationalist the Nationalists with their own logic. As Eric Hobsbawm had observed in 1977, 'The irony of nationalism is that the argument for the separation of Scotland from England is exactly analogous to the argument for the separation of the Shetlands from Scotland; and so are the arguments against both separations.'[13]

Initially, the SNP appeared uncertain of how to react, but later claimed to have always been open 'to greater autonomy for the Northern Isles in an independent Scotland'. 'We are confident that Orkney and Shetland will vote Yes to Scottish independence', added a spokesman, 'along with the rest of the country in autumn 2014.' That was unlikely. Not only had both islands voted 'no' to devolution in 1997, they had also rejected continued membership of the EEC in 1975 and the devolution proposals in 1979; a *Press & Journal* poll found 82 per cent of the islanders believed they should remain part of Scotland, with only 8 per cent desiring outright 'independence'. In June 2013 Comhairle nan Eilean Siar, Orkney

Islands and Shetland Islands councils launched 'Our Islands, Our Future', a formal campaign for more autonomy within the UK and EU, to which the First Minister responded with a rather grandiose 'Lerwick Declaration', promising a ministerial working group to explore greater decentralisation but little that was concrete.[14]

As with the Scottish Conservatives, the Liberal Democrats envisaged their constitutional proposals securing 'consent' at the 2015 general election. But the party (again, like the Scottish Tories) was increasingly weak in electoral terms. Tavish Scott had presided over a meltdown in his party's vote at the 2011 Holyrood election, securing just 8 per cent of the constituency vote and 5.2 per cent of Holyrood's regional list vote, a result that deprived the party of twelve of the seventeen seats it had won in 2007. With eleven Scottish MPs, including several coalition ministers, the 2015 general election was not exactly hotly anticipated. Reasserting federalism was all part of the party's pre-election fight-back, with Nick Clegg promising his party would stand 'on a platform of further powers to the Scottish Parliament'.

'Low-hanging fruit'

The biggest challenge, however, was faced by the Scottish Labour Party. It, by 2011, found itself in the curious position of being perceived as hostile to (further) devolution, despite having legislated for a Scottish Parliament in 1997 and supported – together with the Conservatives and Liberal Democrats – further powers via the 2012 Scotland Act. Its official position was more or less in line with the former Welsh Secretary Ron Davies's aphorism that devolution was a 'process' rather than an 'event' (a line often misattributed to Donald Dewar), but beneath that progressive stance were internal splits, not only between Edinburgh-based Labour MSPs and the party's Glasgow-based HQ, but more damagingly between London-based MPs – many of whom despaired of their Edinburgh colleagues' desire to 'appease' the SNP – and the Labour group in the Scottish Parliament, who by and large viewed further devolution as a tactical necessity ahead of the 2014 referendum. In a thoughtful 2007 speech, the former Scottish Labour leader Wendy Alexander said the movement had always been split between 'home-rulers of the heart' and 'home-rulers of the head', suggesting it had taken 'a home-ruler of both the heart *and* the head', the late Donald Dewar, to actually deliver a Scottish Parliament.[15]

Many hoped the election of Johann Lamont as leader in late 2011 – the first formal *leader* of the Scottish Labour Party – following an internal reorganisation would draw a line under some of these tensions. It was only partially successful – a murky row involving the Unite union and Falkirk Labour Party in summer 2013 exposed, said Alex Salmond, 'the total pretence that she leads Labour in Scotland' – and Lamont had to tread carefully as she plotted her party's next constitutional move. In this she was largely left to her own devices by UK Labour leader Ed Miliband, whose 'One Nation' philosophising often appeared heavily Anglocentric. The party, in other words, had a narrative problem as well as an electoral challenge. As the political scientist David Runciman put it, lacking 'a convincing account of the reason different national communities need to be joined together in a larger whole', the UK Labour Party might well be 'finished as an electoral force'.[16]

And as the largest pro-Union force in Scotland, with more than forty MPs, and the SNP's main opposition at Holyrood, the onus was on Scottish Labour to take the lead. This it did tentatively. Lamont established another internal commission, although it was tardy in convening and cautious in scope. Devo-max had already been ruled out, Gordon Brown having warned it would lead to higher taxes (heaven forbid) and cuts to frontline services. Devolution of welfare and pensions, he had added, would simply produce a 'race to the bottom'.

Similarly, the Scottish Labour devolution commission's interim report, *Powers for a Purpose: Strengthening Devolution*, dismissed 'full fiscal autonomy' as 'no more than a thinly disguised version of independence'. But, at the same time, it singled out income tax as 'clearly the best candidate for further devolution' and said it was 'minded' to devolve it 'in full'. The report continued:

> We do, however, wish to consult widely on this issue. The advantage of devolving income tax – a revenue stream that provides a substantial, stable tax yield – is that it would provide a broader range of fiscal choices, enhancing accountability and responsibility for decisions made by the Scottish Parliament on taxation and public expenditure. It would also enable the Scottish government to make the tax system more progressive.

As for other taxes, devolving national insurance ('given its linkage to old age pensions and other contributory benefits') remained, in the commission's view, 'open to question', while ceding corporation tax to Holyrood would simply extend the 'pernicious practice' (a clear dig at the SNP) of helping businesses reduce 'their overall tax burden by moving profits between different tax jurisdictions'.

Air passenger duty, meanwhile, had a 'strong case', as did excise duty, although the commissioners were 'less convinced' when it came to devolving alcohol and tobacco duty. Inheritance and capital gains tax were also possibilities, although the sums raised would be 'small' and might present 'administrative challenges', and while it would be technically possible to devolve oil taxation, the report feared that might build a 'fiscal cliff' of 'uncertain size and timing' into Scottish public spending plans. Finally, the report committed to 'maintaining common pensions and benefits across Britain'.

Powers for a Purpose had begun on a defensive note:

> Scottish Labour is the party of devolution. Labour's support for devolution pre-dates the existence of the SNP – we have been making the case for devolution for over 100 years. Devolution is a cause we advocate out of deep-rooted conviction, not pragmatic necessity. Any debate on our constitutional future cannot be a political fix: it must be about what is best for Scotland. Devolution is not a journey that leads to independence – it is a journey towards true home rule. Nothing we say in this report will placate the SNP – they will only ever be satisfied by separation.[17]

But when the report appeared ahead of the Scottish Labour Party's April 2013 conference, it seemed many Scottish Labour MPs were not satisfied either. 'It's not going to happen as it does not stack up,' said one, while another malcontent warned against 'making ourselves more nationalist than the Nationalists'. Johann Lamont said the report provided a 'starting point', although given that Labour MPs would be required to pass the necessary legislation at Westminster, the SNP naturally felt vindicated, repeating its charge that Labour – and Unionist parties in general – were not serious about devolving more power. All of which made it harder for Lamont to carve out a non-constitutional narrative. 'I didn't get into politics to defend the Union,' she remarked in the summer of 2013. 'I got into politics to change people's lives for the better.'

Speaking at a Lobby lunch at Westminster, meanwhile, the former Chancellor Alistair Darling appeared to pour cold water over the interim report, stressing that whatever recommendations emerged they were unlikely to be radical. 'Most of the low-hanging fruit of devolution has been picked,' he said, although adding that – unlike some of his colleagues – he had no 'philosophical objection' to the complete devolution of income tax. Finally, in line with his Tory and Lib Dem Unionist colleagues, Darling was quite clear any plans for further devolution required a 'mandate' at the 2015 general election.[18]

A UK constitutional convention?

One might have thought this Unionist unanimity on presenting proposals to the electorate ahead of 2015 would have amounted to a common position on further powers ahead of the referendum. The Scotland Office minister David Mundell had hinted as much, indicating that such an agreement could even be concluded before the SNP published its 'independence prospectus' in the autumn of 2013. But others under the Better Together umbrella distanced themselves from this suggestion, keen to preserve party autonomy and therefore 'ownership' of the constitutional agenda. 'We're not going to have an agreed package before the referendum,' confirmed a UK government source in mid-2013, 'but there's a political consensus between the three parties to legislate for more powers.'[19]

There were, however, modest but increasing calls for a UK-wide constitutional convention to take a more holistic look at the machinery of government should Scots reject independence in 2014. This had support within the three Unionist parties, and had been explored by Ruth Davidson as she announced her party's devolution commission:

> Fundamentally, we must find a means whereby we do not lurch from one commission to another, year after year; where the constitutional and commercial certainty we all crave is never reached. Where devolution is not viewed as a bilateral arrangement between Holyrood and Westminster, Cardiff Bay and Westminster or Stormont and Westminster. But a mechanism which reviews devolution across – and within – our whole United Kingdom.[20]

This implied support from Downing Street, although the UK government diligently avoided a formal commitment. 'A few of us have been pushing for a royal commission or a convention,' said one minister. 'We should set out a vision of a 21st-century UK, one in which there is a coherent place for Scotland, with proper processes, but the elephant in the room is the way in which England is governed' (of which more below).[21]

Labour's Lord Foulkes also concurred. 'All the constitutional changes undertaken by several governments have been piecemeal and we have ended up with a range of anomalies,' said the former Scotland Office minister. 'We now need to look at the constitution in a comprehensive way.' Supporters envisaged the convention being established shortly after the 2015 general election to examine more powers for Holyrood, greater devolution for England, the Barnett Formula and long-overdue reform of the House of Lords, something more or less backed by the House of Commons' Political and Constitutional Reform Committee. The SNP, of course, would be invited to take part, although it did not have good form in that respect, having boycotted similar cross-party talks in 1979, 1988 and 2007.

It remained cynical in 2013. 'A "no" vote in the referendum', predicted Nicola Sturgeon, 'would result in the London government filing Scotland away in some pigeon-hole and not wanting to come back to the issue.' Various Unionist outliers gave their opponents plenty of ammunition. Tam Dalyell, a consistent opponent of both independence and devolution, said it was 'fraudulent' of his colleagues to talk of greater powers, while his preferred option was to 'take the bull by its horns' and 'abolish the Holyrood parliament'. The *Scotsman* columnist Michael Kelly agreed. 'Losers', he wrote, 'should lose', his 'dream consequence' of a majority 'no' vote being 'a steady erosion of Holyrood's powers until it can be abolished and the previous efficient unitary form of government restored'.[22]

But Dalyell and Kelly were fringe Unionists, relics of the

pre-devolutionary era with as much relevance as funda-
mentalist Nationalists like Gordon Wilson. The Scottish
Secretary, Michael Moore, said as a Liberal Democrat he
supported 'neither extreme', although predicting post-2014
scenarios was what he called a 'mug's game'. 'Will we take a
small step or a large step next time,' he said, 'who knows?'
The economist Gavin McCrone, meanwhile, had a warning
should independence be rejected. 'Proposals for increased
devolution might then be shelved,' he predicted. 'That is
quite a likely outcome but it would be a huge mistake. It
would probably mean that the next time there was a big
surge in support for independence for Scotland, maybe in
ten or twenty years' time, it would carry the day in a second
referendum.'[23] The Yes Scotland strategist Stephen Noon was
less gloomy than the SNP but reached a similar conclusion:

> We could possibly get bits of welfare and bits of taxation,
> but only of a very limited scope. So, even with the best will
> in the world, a No vote next year might mean more powers,
> at some stage, but insufficient powers when they come. The
> desires of the majority will, once again, be unmet.[24]

A pocket-money parliament

The Devo+ (Devo-Plus) group, an offshoot of the centre-right
think tank Reform Scotland, attempted to rise above the
constitutional fray. Its scheme – advocated by single MSPs
from Labour, the Conservatives and Liberal Democrats if not
their respective parties – envisaged Holyrood raising more than
60 per cent of its own revenue with the UK providing 'equalisation support'. Income, corporation, insurance premium and
capital gains tax would all be devolved, while VAT and national
insurance would remain reserved to Westminster.

It only proposed devolving a geographical share of North
Sea oil and gas revenue, meanwhile, once there was 'widespread agreement across all nations in the UK', although

importantly it was the only group to countenance this at all. Devo+'s welfare proposals were, however, more modest, proposing that Westminster retain control of most social provision with only the Work Programme, winter fuel payments, attendance and carers' allowances being devolved to Holyrood. Taken together, it argued, this provided the basis for 'a New Union' in which the Scottish Parliament's status was (like the Liberal Democrat proposals) made permanent. 'Why should Scotland, with its thousand-year history,' ran the essence of the Devo+ pitch, 'be treated like a teenager with a pocket money parliament? It should take responsibility for what it spends.'[25]

Devo-more

As if to demonstrate the agility of the word 'devo', the IPPR think tank unveiled its 'Devo More' project in early 2013 with the rationale that Scottish voters 'like devolution and want more of it'. Many of its conclusions and language were similar to that produced by Devo+. The challenge, argued the author of Devo More (the constitutional expert Alan Trench), was to take a holistic approach, explaining the benefits devolved parts of the UK derived from remaining part of the Union. A 'new union', it concluded, 'needs to be sustained by shared interests and structures as well as devolved ones'. Trench's proposals, therefore, were designed to be applicable to Wales and Northern Ireland as well as Scotland.

The project's first report, *Funding Devo More: Fiscal Options for Strengthening the Union*, proposed:

- The outright devolution of personal income tax.
- An assigned share of ten 'points' of VAT (as it could not be devolved for EU legal reasons).
- Devolution of taxation on alcohol and tobacco, given their relationship with already devolved health (although

Trench noted 'formidable legal and administrative problems with doing so').

- Air passenger duty and aggregates levy (as recommended by the Calman Commission) ought to be devolved.

- HM Treasury should 'adopt a permissive approach to the establishment of any further tax relating to land, and look at the practicalities of devolving capital gains tax in relation to land'.

- Employer's national insurance contributions could also be devolved 'if needed', as they accounted for between 9 and 13 per cent of current devolved spending.

This package, argued Trench, would put around 55–60 per cent of devolved public spending 'directly in the hands of devolved governments', 43–50 per cent of which would be taxes 'fully' under their control (as opposed to around 30 per cent under the 2012 Scotland Act). The remainder of Scottish spending would, as at present, be funded by a grant from the UK government, although Trench suggested this should be 'calculated on the basis of spending need rather than fiscal equalisation', thus spelling the end for the Barnett Formula.[26]

The economist Gavin McCrone, meanwhile, resisted the temptation to come up with yet another variation on 'devo' for his plan, detailed in his 2013 book *Scottish Independence: Weighing Up the Economics*. Building on the Scottish Liberal Democrat and Trench schemes, McCrone envisaged devolving three quarters of income tax, all of VAT (minus a contribution to the European Union), insurance premium tax, the aggregate levy, landfill tax, stamp duty land tax and air passenger duty, which, together with council tax and business rates, meant the Scottish government would control 57.4 per cent of its own expenditure.[27] Only the trenchantly Unionist commentator Alan Cochrane, meanwhile, was prepared to make the case for what he called 'devo-minus'.

'Common Weal'

Others, meanwhile, wanted to smash the British state rather than rejuvenate it. Colin Fox, leader of the Scottish Socialist Party (a tiny force since the 2007 Holyrood election, when it lost all its seats) and a member of Yes Scotland's advisory board, said a 'yes' vote would represent a 'significant defeat for the British state and its stranglehold over our economy, society, culture and politics'. 'The referendum can be won if it offers independence as change,' he added, 'not dressing up the political status quo as radical.'

> The prospect of an SNP government employing the same economic and political levers as any other Western European state to exploit the working-class majority will clearly do nothing to ensure success in 2014. But if socialist ideals are raised clearly and unequivocally in the independence debate, there is every chance real change can take hold.[28]

Many on Scotland's small but vocal left agreed with Fox's analysis, although more in hope than expectation. In mid-2013, meanwhile, a group of economists and academics outlined a model they called the 'Common Weal' (a term often used by Alex Salmond), something more akin to social democracy than socialism. They believed Scotland could become a Nordic-style country by cherry-picking the best features of Denmark, Norway, Sweden, Finland and even Germany, breaking with neo-liberal orthodoxy in order to build a more equal and harmonious society. And, importantly, unlike the usual SNP allusion to 'social democracy', the report was upfront about the need for higher taxation.

The Common Weal model included six key elements:

- A gradual shift in the balance of taxation, with the wealthier paying more, and a move away from low-skilled and low-pay work. More nationalised industries, for example those governing oil production (as in the 1970s).

- A larger and more comprehensive welfare state akin to the Nordic 'Folkhemmet', with universal cradle-to-grave benefits, greater emphasis on childcare, social housing and local amenities.

- Less reliance on finance sector and a national investment bank offering long-term loans to grow Scottish firms and rebalance the economy towards manufacturing. Mortgage lending would also be reconfigured to avoid housing booms.

- Moves to encourage more small and medium-sized businesses (on the family-owned German 'Mittelstand' model) and fewer large multinationals. State support for more mutual and co-operative enterprises to help buffer the economy against cyclical downturns.

- Stabilising the economy by weakening overreliance on the financial sector and opting out of EU rules in order for the state to buy more goods and services from Scottish firms.

- Democracy and governance.[29]

Officially, the Yes Scotland campaign said it was 'an interesting contribution to the debate', while the SNP agreed to debate the proposal at its 2013 annual conference. Nicola Sturgeon was said to be 'broadly supportive' though 'wary of its tax implications' while the First Minister, unsurprisingly, was 'cooler', clearly anxious about anything that could link the independence project with high taxes or, indeed, expose a left/right split within his party. One idea floated by the group, levying a wealth tax on super-rich companies and individuals to pay for universal childcare, did not exactly sit comfortably with Salmonomics. Yes Scotland chairman Dennis Canavan, who did not need to worry about such things, was more enthusiastic, saying it was 'the kind of creative thinking which can ensure that an independent Scotland is based on sound economics, as well as sound principles of social justice'.

In that sense, it was notable that a coherent left-of-centre vision of independence came not from the SNP but from a group of academics operating under the umbrella of the Jimmy Reid Foundation, set up to promote the ideas and thinking of the late, and iconic, Scottish trade unionist. He had once spoken of the 'rat race' in a famous rectorial address, now a body established in his name was trying to come up with ways to ensure an independent Scotland did not join it.

The dog that finally barked

Most of the constitutional thinking post-2011 naturally emanated from Scotland and, equally naturally, concerned only Scotland. But other parts of the UK, chiefly Wales and Northern Ireland, also responded in their own ways to the prospect of a truncated – or reconfigured – Union.

In Wales there was little sign that independence was catching, one poll putting support for Welsh autonomy at just 7 per cent (rising to 12 per cent if Scotland jumped first). Leanne Wood, the new (and republican) leader of Plaid Cymru, took a leaf out of the SNP's book by expressing contentment with the notion of 'Britishness' while calling for 'Anglo-Celtic Accords' to refashion the UK state after the referendum. The former MP Adam Price, viewed as Plaid's Salmond-like king over the water, floated a 'confederal' arrangement under which the Welsh Assembly would delegate control over defence and foreign affairs to Westminster.

This reflected Plaid's more modest short-term goals. Plaid MP Jonathan Edwards, for example, admitted frankly that a Welsh independence referendum could not be won due to the poor state of the Welsh economy, instead advocating 'parity with Scotland' as a 'strategic objective'. As the political scientist Richard Wyn Jones put it, the much-quoted encyclopedia entry 'for Wales, see England' should more accurately read 'for Wales, see Scotland'.

The former Welsh First Minister Rhodri Morgan had once spoken of putting 'clear red water' between his devolved administration in Cardiff and the UK government in London, a policy maintained by his successor, Carwyn Jones (a believer in 'asymmetric quasi-federalism'), who said Scottish independence, if successful, ought to provoke 'a fundamental rethink of the nature of the relationship between the three nations left within the UK to ensure ... fair representation'. He suggested an upper house reconstituted as a US-style senate with an equal number of English, Welsh and Northern Irish representatives in order to balance out a lower house dominated by England. A former Assembly Presiding Officer, the veteran Plaid politician Dafydd Elis-Thomas, concurred with Jones's senate proposal, surprising many in his party with a speech that included the line: 'I'm an out and out UK federalist ... There was never a project for Welsh independence, anyway.'

UK federalism continued to be promoted most effectively by another member of the Welsh Assembly, its Deputy Presiding Officer, David Melding. The SNP was not necessarily hostile to such thinking, with Alex Salmond constantly referencing the British–Irish Council as a possible forum for a kind of inter-state 'confederalism'. As one Scottish government adviser reflected in early 2012, 'it's a no-brainer'. 'They [the UK government] could say, look, working all this out [a federal system] would take us years,' he said, 'and that would completely remove the wind from our sails.'[30] Even the UKIP leader Nigel Farage spoke of 'a vibrant Scotland within a federal independent Britain' as his party gradually dumped its anti-devolution of old. He also backed a geographically reconstituted upper house.

But the UK government – even its ostensibly federalist portion – simply was not interested, despite its antecedents having produced several federal schemes for other countries after the War (the West German constitution had been a notable success). 'This isn't about imposing some Identi-Kit blueprint on each and every part of the UK,' protested Danny Alexander, 'we have to address ourselves to ... the issues that seem to make [most] sense in these areas; where does the political consensus lie?' Melding, in his book *The Reformed Union: The UK as a Federation*, argued that not only would federalism achieve that political consensus but it would be 'an organic development of Britain's parliamentary tradition'. He recommended convening a Speaker's conference after the 2014 referendum in which the Commons Speaker and the three Presiding Officers of the UK's devolved institutions might agree a new Act of Union. Ideally, this would declare that each 'home nation' separately and the UK collectively were 'sovereign' over their respective jurisdictions (Gordon Brown also argued for legislation that made clear the Scottish Parliament was 'permanent ... irreversible ... indissolvable'), while the House of Lords would be geographically reconstituted (something else supported by Nigel Farage) to give 'voice to each home nation in influencing and scrutinising state matters such as defence, foreign affairs, and the operation of the British constitution'. Remarkably for a Conservative politician, Melding hoped the UK would 'in a very British way' stumble 'towards common ground that could accommodate the most constructive elements of unionist and nationalist thought'.[31]

Support came from parts of the Scottish left not already signed up to a 'yes' vote. *Class, Nation and Socialism: The Red Paper on Scotland 2014* (a conscious attempt to echo Gordon Brown's seminal book from 1975) concluded that the Scottish Parliament and the Welsh and Northern Irish assemblies provided 'the basis for a federal arrangement with power devolved within the UK', while Jim Gallagher, the principal architect of the Calman scheme, said it was 'time for a better articulation of the UK as a union state'. He added:

All the components are there, but their implications need to be better understood. First of all, the Union has to retain the combination of economic integration and social solidarity that creates both the domestic market and a well-functioning social market. Subject to that, it should be home rule all round and, as in federal countries worldwide, national parliaments should be funded by a mixture of a share of UK taxes, which give effect to social solidarity, and their own tax resources.[32]

But while Yes Scotland's chief strategist, Stephen Noon, conceded that federalism 'would give people in Scotland a great deal of what we want', 'in reality' he considered a federal UK to be 'out of reach', requiring change 'elsewhere on these isles that is nowhere in sight'.[33] And to those who said 'wouldn't federalism be a nice idea', observed Alex Salmond, 'their timing is slightly late'.[34]

In Wales, despite a 2011 referendum on law-making powers,[35] constitutional change moved slowly. At the time of writing, the Silk Commission, an accidental by-product of the 2010 coalition negotiations, had quickly come to resemble a Welsh Calman Commission, reaching similar conclusions in terms of partial fiscal autonomy although without enjoying the same degree of political support. The UK government, despite the views of Conservatives and Liberal Democrats in Cardiff Bay, was distinctly lukewarm, recent developments in Scotland having made London-based Unionists more cautious.

The same dynamic applied to Northern Ireland, where moves to devolve control of corporation tax had more or less been put on hold due to the fear of a knock-on demand in Scotland. Meanwhile what Tony Blair called the 'hand of history' loomed large. The province's First Minister, the Democratic Unionist Party leader Peter Robinson, used a gathering of the British–Irish Council at Dublin Castle to appeal to his 'Ulster Scots brethren and sisters' to reject independence, although when he spoke of 'the Union' (which he called 'a patchwork quilt of identity') the DUP leader was obviously referring to 1801 rather than 1707. Although the evidence suggested Northern Ireland's place in the UK was secure (even a majority of Catholic voters were content with the constitutional status quo), Sinn Fein hoped to stage its own referendum on reunification in 2016.

But there was a gap in the debate about constitutional change in the United Kingdom and that gap was England-shaped. Alex Salmond tried to fill it by making positive noises about English regionalism, as did a report, *Rebalancing Britain: Policy or Slogan?*, by the Tory peer Lord Heseltine and former Tesco chief executive Sir Terry Leahy,[36] although Michael Keating warned regional government was 'not the answer to the United Kingdom question; it is the answer to a question about the internal organisation of England'.[37] The London Mayor, Boris Johnson, had long argued for consti-tutional parity with Scotland and Wales, a 'city state' agenda with which Labour's Ken Livingstone more or less agreed. London had always been a little semi-detached.

The LSE's Tony Travers, who chaired Johnson's London Finance Commission, found 'no evidence that devolution had damaged the economic progress of Scotland or Wales'. The 'practicalities of establishing [a new] Scottish tax regime', added Travers in the *Financial Times*, 'suggest there are no insuperable obstacles to the devolution of tax powers to any other part of the UK'.[38] Scotland had now become a model not only for Wales, but for the imperial capital too, not something many Nationalists would necessarily have welcomed. They generally resented London's 'gravitational pull', although John Swinney suggested independence would act as a counterweight. Even that, suggested the Nationalist thinker Stephen Maxwell, 'would not insulate Scotland against the dominance of London'.[39]

But as Disraeli once quipped, England was 'governed

not by logic but by parliament', and despite enthusiastic backing from Westminster, most of England's great urban centres rejected London-style elected mayors in a series of referendums held in May 2012. The localism agenda – as with the 2004 ballot on devolution for the north-east – foundered as a result of ill-thought-through schemes and electoral apathy. Nevertheless some English regions felt particularly remote from 'Planet London'. The north-east, according to Professor Keith Shaw, was 'caught in a pincer movement between a reinvigorated Scottish government and a very powerful London economic development machine',[40] thus his 'Borderlands' report urged twelve local authorities to see greater Scottish autonomy as an opportunity rather than a threat.[41] IPPR North suggested the region needed its own Alex Salmond-style figure to prise more powers away from Westminster. It certainly worked in reverse, the region understandably resenting the loss of an Amazon customer service centre to Edinburgh after Scottish Enterprise lured it away with a £1.8 million training grant.

The IPPR suggested, in another report, that England was the 'dog that finally barked', a new 'political community' emerging in response to the perceived privileges of Scotland and a (related) growing sense of English identity. Not only had the number of English voters who believed devolution had worsened 'British' governance doubled since 2007 (to 35 per cent), but 45 per cent of voters in England believed Scotland got 'more than its fair share of public spending' (another doubling, this time since 2000), while more than 50 per cent believed the Scottish economy benefited more than England's from being in the UK.[42]

Support for Scottish independence among English voters, however, remained low, only 22 per cent backing full autonomy, although they did appear to be enthusiastic proponents of devo-max, a staggering 80 per cent supporting it, 44 per cent of them 'strongly'. John Curtice reckoned this meant the English, for the most part, wanted the UK to survive, 'but probably would not die in a ditch to keep it preserved'. Seventy-nine per cent of those surveyed also said Scottish MPs ought to be barred from voting on English laws, something the UK government's 'Commission on the Consequences of Devolution for the House of Commons' (chaired by the former House of Commons clerk Sir William McKay, yet another Scot) partially addressed with a report in March 2013.

The former Lord Chancellor Derry Irvine once remarked that the best thing to do about the West Lothian Question was not to ask it. Backbench MPs in every party, however, were not inclined to follow his advice, and although McKay noted that it was, in fact, very rare for a UK government to rely on Scotland and Wales for its majority (only in the short-lived Parliaments of 1950–51, 1964–66 and February–October 1974 had this been the case), nevertheless he identified 'a clear and enduring sense that England is materially disadvantaged relative to the other parts of the UK, especially Scotland'. Sir William also noted that England-only legislation was rare, with most laws and policies applying to the UK's largest component part having 'consequential cross-border legal and policy effects'.

McKay went on to rule out several potential solutions including, not surprisingly, reversing devolution ('not on the political agenda'), maintaining the status quo ('a long-term risk), federalism ('has compelling objections') and electoral reform ('fails to tackle the underlying issue'). His recommendations, therefore, were inevitably unsatisfactory. A legislative consent motion in Grand Committee or on the floor of the House prior to a Bill's second reading was, argued McKay, the 'minimum ... effective means of allowing the voice from England (or England and Wales) to be heard'. Space in the Queen's Speech debate should also be devoted to the government's 'proposals for England', and likewise in party manifestos, while a 'Devolution Committee' of the House of Commons might consider the consequences of decisions on each part of the UK.[43]

Press briefing in the summer of 2013 suggested the UK government planned to go further than McKay's modest proposals by introducing a new 'fourth reading' of Bills at which only English MPs would be able to vote. A senior minister (probably Oliver Letwin, who was in charge of the process) told *The Independent*:

> The idea is to give English MPs the right to ratify legisla-
> tion that concerns England ... Scotland has had devolution
> and is now voting on independence. Wales is going to get
> more powers. It would be wrong not to address the issue of
> England too. This is a neat solution to a problem that has not
> been satisfactorily addressed since devolution.

Her Majesty's Opposition, however, described it as a 'hair-brained [*sic*] scheme',[44] no doubt conscious of the likely impact on future Labour governments, while the SNP's Pete Wishart pointed out there was 'one clear answer to the West Lothian question – independence for Scotland'.

But while such constitutional untidiness bothered a few Conservative backbenchers (although Jacob Rees-Mogg argued it was a 'price worth paying' for having Scotland in the Union), the English generally showed little inclination towards devolution, regional or otherwise, and certainly not independence, despite Simon Heffer's impassioned plea in his 2000 book, *Nor Shall My Sword: The Reinvention of England*. Ed Miliband had dismissed the 'simplistic consti-tutional symmetry' of an English parliament or assembly in a June 2012 speech, proposing instead 'taking power out of Whitehall and devolving it down to local authorities'; only the maverick Labour MP Frank Field – and the Campaign for an English Parliament[45] – demurred. In July 2013, meanwhile, the Local Government Association suggested merging six Whitehall offices in order to create a minister (and department) for England to take its side in negotiations with the devolved nations for funds.

The IPPR report's authors concluded that 'the main problem is not that the English question is now finally being asked by the country's electorate, but rather that the British political class has failed to take it, and them, seriously'. A second survey, *England and its Two Unions: The Anatomy of a Nation and its Discontents*, confirmed all the findings of the first while detecting a strong correlation between Euroscepticism and what it called 'devo-anxiety'. In terms of salience, meanwhile, it found the governance of England ranked second only to the EU in the eyes of English voters.[46]

Clearly this presented a challenge for all the UK's political parties, although the constitutional historian Vernon Bogdanor reckoned Labour – 'the only major party with substantial representation in Scotland, Wales and England' – faced the biggest. 'It will campaign hard against Scots independence,' he wrote in *The Guardian*. 'But it needs to campaign equally hard to ensure that the Unionist slogan "Better Together" works as well for England as it does for Scotland and Wales.'[47] Some Welsh and Scottish Nationalists even envisaged Scottish independence prompting a realignment of English politics. Plaid Cymru leader Leanne Wood urged England to discover its left-wing voice by forming a new political party, while the SNP's Stephen Maxwell imagined 'a centre-left majority of progressive Labour, Liberal Democrats and Greens committed to challenging the sources of inertia in English public life',

the first-past-the-post voting system, the dominance of the City and of English public schools and Oxbridge, the centralisation of power in London, the obsession with Britain's great power status and its expensive accoutrements such as the nuclear deterrent. By demonstrating that there are different ways of organising society and of being a useful member of the international community, an independent Scotland could make its own modest contribution to that realignment.[48]

The political scientist Michael Keating took a different view. 'The end of the United Kingdom is unlikely to come about from the secession of Scotland as long as the Scots have other options,' he predicted. 'It is more likely, strange to say, to come from the secession of an England that is no longer prepared to pay the political or economic price of union.'[49]

CHAPTER 8

BETTER TOGETHER VERSUS YES SCOTLAND

It must be remembered that there is nothing more difficult to plan, more doubtful of success, nor more dangerous to manage than a new system. For the initiator has the enmity of all who would profit by the preservation of the old institution and merely lukewarm defenders in those who gain by the new ones, and so it is that whenever those who are enemies of a new order have a chance to attack, they do so ferociously, while others defend it half-heartedly.

Niccolò Machiavelli

Little do ye know your own blessedness; for to travel hopefully is a better thing than to arrive, and the true success is to labour.

Robert Louis Stevenson, *Virginibus Puerisque* (1881)

Mario Cuomo's most repeated aphorism holds that politicians ought to 'campaign in poetry' but 'govern in prose'. The former New York Governor was making an obvious point: that while the business of government necessarily involves the explanation of public policy in ordinary, layman's language, actually securing victory in the first place was often made easier through the use of poetry, oratory designed to inspire and therefore secure the necessary majority of votes.

But despite Scotland's independence referendum regularly being trumpeted as the most important decision in 300 years, the biggest grassroots campaign in history, and other assorted hyperbole, there was precious little poetry as the 'yes' and 'no' campaigns set out their stalls from May/June 2012 onwards. Rather, both were subject to what the economist John Kay termed 'Franklin's gambit'. 'So convenient a thing is it to be a reasonable creature,' Benjamin Franklin had observed, 'since it enables one to find or make a reason for everything one had a mind to do.'[1] In other words, campaigning amounted to hindsight rationalisation, building evidence to match pre-existing narratives. Both Nationalists and Unionists generally began with a conviction and then worked backwards, contriving whatever arguments and 'facts' were available to justify a constitutional belief already firmly held, while readily disregarding any inconvenient truths.

And they had a long time to do so. Even though a referendum became a reality after the SNP secured an overall majority in the Scottish Parliament at the May 2011 elections, there was a phoney war until about January the following year, when the Prime Minister intervened to get things moving (or so he thought). It was another five months before 'Yes Scotland' launched on 25 May 2012 and six before 'Better Together' was unveiled on 25 June. With a referendum expected in the autumn of 2014, that meant each campaign had more than two years to make its case, together with a sixteen-week formal campaigning period in the run-up to polling day.

For the first year, at least, it proved a rather understated, workmanlike affair. There was a sense the campaigns were locked in the equivalent of political trench warfare, with little progress (on either side) and a lot of casualties in the field of public engagement. Both 'yes' and 'no' were in different bubbles, preaching to the converted, something reflected in stubbornly unshifting opinion polls. Part of the problem was time – there was too much of it. The battle for Scotland in 2012–14 amounted to one of the longest, if not *the longest*, campaigns in modern political history.

The best of all possible worlds

The launch of Yes Scotland at an Edinburgh cinema was a curious affair. Uneven and even a little rushed, it set out the main 'yes' pitch but at the same time hinted at divisions that would emerge over the next year or so. Alex Salmond unveiled the 'Independence Declaration', while backing came from the actors Brian Cox ('Scotland has earned the right ... to determine its own destiny') and Alan Cumming ('independence can only add to our potential and release a new wave of creativity and ambition'), even though both were resident in the United States. While Cumming indicated he was 'planning' to return to Scotland in order to vote, Cox (who later said he really came 'from a federalist point of view') admitted his relocation was unlikely. The most famous pro-independence expat, Sir Sean Connery, sent only a short written message.

The event was also heavy on a lot of things the SNP claimed independence was *not* about, chiefly sentiment, national identity and nostalgia. Dougie MacLean sang 'Caledonia', Liz Lochhead read from her play *Mary Queen of Scots Got Her Head Chopped Off* (which included the line about Scotland: 'National pastime: nostalgia'), and so on. There was also a distinctly leftish tenor, which indicated Yes Scotland would try to differentiate itself from the SNP in ideological terms, symbolised by the presence of former Ravenscraig trade union leader Tommy Brennan.

At the same time the Yes Scotland launch demonstrated just what a broad church the independence movement had become. Former Royal Bank of Scotland chairman Sir George Mathewson contributed supportive comments to a special film, as did Colin Fox, leader of the pro-independence Scottish Socialist Party (SSP). This was packed with hackneyed tartan imagery, something that jarred given the SNP's long-standing efforts to jettison such shortbread-tin clichés. Furthermore, there was scant acknowledgement of the economic and social challenges facing every nation in the world except, it seemed, Scotland.

Fantasy politics loomed large, each speaker reeling off their wish list of the wonders independence would or could achieve. Only the *Rab C. Nesbitt* actress Elaine C. Smith injected some realism by conceding that independence 'would be no magic pill'. Scottish Green Party leader Patrick Harvie, meanwhile, spoke of the need for a 'new political culture' in order to win a 'yes' vote, the implication being that the SNP was still rather wedded to the old. Both the Greens, who said they backed 'full independence based on a written constitution', and the SSP, which was 'striving to create an independent, nuclear-free, multi-cultural, Scottish socialist republic', stressed support for independence rather than Nationalism.[2] 'I am looking forward to voting Yes,' blogged Harvie shortly after the launch. 'Just for very different reasons than Mr Salmond.' While Dennis Canavan, the former Labour MP later drafted in as chairman of Yes Scotland, frequently proclaimed, 'I am not a Nationalist, I am an internationalist.'

In a rather pedestrian speech, meanwhile, Alex Salmond said the next two years were needed to give 'form and substance' to the desire for independence, via a 'brick-by-brick' campaign. He continued:

We're at the start of something very, very special: the beginning of a campaign to restore nationhood to the nation of Scotland. Our opponents are rich and they're powerful and therefore to win and to win well, we're going to have to galvanise the whole community of the realm of Scotland … by the time we enter the referendum campaign in autumn 2014, our intention is to have one million Scots who have signed the independence for Scotland declaration. Friends, if we achieve that, then we shall win an independent Scotland.

Not only was that aim rather quixotic (by May 2013 the declaration had attracted only 372,103 signatures), for even if a million Scots signed *and* voted 'yes' in September 2014 it would not be enough, as Salmond contended, to win. It also emerged at the launch that Yes Scotland had no significant organisational structure, no paid staff, campaign director or board of management; some involved went out of their way to emphasise that the launch had been put together quickly by a small, overworked team. Widely acknowledged to be the most important political event in modern Scottish history and, following the May 2011 election, hardly unexpected, such sloppy preparation seemed odd, not to mention out of character for the normally slick and well-organised National Movement. If launch events were important in terms of establishing tone and momentum, Yes Scotland had failed.

Generating some minor news headlines was the appointment of Blair Jenkins, a former head of news at BBC Scotland and Scottish Television, as head of Yes Scotland. More or less aloof from party politics (although he had headed up the Scottish government's 2008 Scottish Broadcasting Commission), Jenkins had no campaign experience and was not exactly a household name beyond Glasgow's media fraternity. But although it took a while for him to find his feet, the Yes Scotland chief was courteous and committed, and his lack of political baggage was undoubtedly an advantage in the tribal world of Scottish politics.

Even then, Yes Scotland suffered from early impressions it was little more than an SNP front (the Greens' Patrick Harvie threatened to withdraw on that basis), something it tried to combat in August 2012 with the appointment of a politically ecumenical board, including former Scottish Labour member Susan Stewart as director of communications (she left a year later to take up an 'ambassadorial role' amid rumours she had been sidelined) and Stan Blackley, formerly of the Scottish Green Party, as her deputy. Jacqueline Caldwell, a former RBS manager, was later appointed director of operations but quit after just six months. At points, Yes Scotland did not give the impression it was a happy ship.

Also involved were figures associated with the SNP such as the Essex-born marketing consultant Ian Dommett and former SNP MSP Shirley-Anne Somerville. Left-wingers including Kevin Williamson (formerly of the publisher Rebel Inc.), Colin Fox and the former Hue and Cry singer Pat Kane, meanwhile, added ideological balance. Sporadically involved, and more heavily in 2013/14, was the executive coach Claire Howell, an important figure in the SNP's 2007 and 2011 election campaigns. Not only did she get along well with Alex Salmond, but she knew how to hone winning messages, a talent Plaid Cymru also hoped to exploit ahead of the 2016 Welsh Assembly elections.

There were related – and significant – personnel changes within the SNP and Scottish government. Kevin Pringle, good cop to Salmond's bad for more than two decades, quit as the First Minister's official spokesman to become the SNP's head of strategic communications before finally transferring to Yes Scotland in the summer of 2013. Deputy First Minister Nicola Sturgeon, meanwhile, was charged with directing the Scottish government's – as opposed to Yes Scotland's – referendum strategy. Although this chiefly involved concluding negotiations with the UK government, it was recognition that Sturgeon was one of the SNP ministerial team's most gifted communicators.

It also marked a subtle sidelining of Alex Salmond as the public face of the independence campaign. Although his approval ratings remained remarkably high, advisers privately conceded the party had 'maxed out' on the First Minister. In other words, there were few more pro-independence votes to be gained by pushing the panda-faced SNP leader down voters' throats. Sturgeon had blossomed since becoming Salmond's deputy in 2004 and particularly since serving as Health Secretary between 2007 and 2011. Less chippy than she had been in opposition, the Govan MSP had become pragmatic, persuasive and less prone than her boss to semantic slip-ups. By May 2013 Ipsos MORI polling even showed her edging ahead of Salmond in terms of voter approval.

Although the First Minister had been present at the launch of Yes Scotland he had hardly dominated the cinema that afternoon in May 2012. 'Does it make democratic sense for the future of a country to depend on the human flaws of one person?' pondered *The Herald*'s Ian Bell, a pro-independence columnist. 'Beyond question, he's a remarkable man. But we are, and must be, better than that.' The independence campaigner and actress Elaine C. Smith also urged the 'yes' campaign to 'reclaim' the debate from the First Minister, declaring, 'This is not about Alex Salmond.'

In 2009 the journalist Paul Hutcheon referred to him as the Tony Benn or Enoch Powell of Scottish politics: 'a maverick politician who, by force of personality, makes unreasonable ideas seem reasonable to large chunks of the population'. 'Take him out of the equation,' added Hutcheon, 'as was the case when he resigned the SNP leadership in 2000, and his party nosedives.'[3] This was a reference to the four years in which Salmond was absent from the SNP helm. The shine certainly appeared to have come off Nationalism under John Swinney's leadership, only to be restored when his predecessor returned to the fray in 2004. But Salmond, like any other politician, had strengths and weaknesses. Above all a gifted media communicator, he did not so much debate as dance on the head of a pin, often pursuing points to infinity while indulging in intellectual pirouettes. If genius was, as F. Scott Fitzgerald put it, the 'ability to hold two opposed ideas in the mind at the same time' then Salmond was a political genius with few rivals.

So he was certainly popular, but in a very particular way.

Polling in late 2012 demonstrated that in all the important measurements – such as competence, image, leadership, and 'standing up for Scotland' – Alex Salmond's party beat Labour hands down. The 2007–11 Scottish government had a stratospheric +36 per cent rating, and even though people felt their living standards were falling, they blamed the UK government rather than Holyrood. Salmond, much like Boris Johnson in London, benefited from being both in government (at Holyrood) and in opposition (to Westminster). And, like Johnson, Salmond was a shrewd populist.

But it was his prowess as a devolved leader, rather than his ability to increase support for independence, which dazzled Salmond's London audience, and they often conflated the two, writing him up as a political 'wizard' and, with more than a hint of hyperbole, as the 'most talented politician in the UK'. Doubtlessly a talented politician, Salmond was also lucky in his opponents, who not only overestimated him but depicted the SNP leader as an Arthur Daley-type figure, someone who would stop at nothing – and say anything – in order to achieve independence. 'How can this country have an honest debate about our future', asked Johann Lamont rhetorically, 'when we cannot trust a word that Alex Salmond says?' Labour's shadow Scottish Secretary Margaret Curran, meanwhile, said the Scottish government was infected with a 'culture of casual dishonesty', producing 'lies, cover-ups and an unbelievable disregard for the truth'. Towards the end of 2013, the Scottish Labour Party tried to recast the debate as 'Salmond against Scotland' rather than 'Scotland against England'. Given that polling showed Salmond to be more popular than the SNP *and* independence, the thinking behind these highly personalised attacks was clear. It was straight out of the US political play-book: define your opponent in voters' minds early on in the campaign, and not in a good way.

So although not front and central to Yes Scotland, Salmond remained – almost by default – the public face of the independence campaign, a status he acknowledged with some pre-referendum dieting (he lost more than a stone on the '5:2' diet, which involved fasting twice a week). No matter how much the SNP rationed his media appearances (his public engagements remained extensive) he still had to face MSPs every Thursday in the Scottish Parliament and, in the electorate's eyes, *was* the SNP and thus the face of independence. It was clear, meanwhile, via various slips and off-hand remarks, that Salmond regarded Yes Scotland as, at best, disappointing and, at worst, irrelevant.

Salmond was not alone, with senior Nationalists remarkably unguarded in their criticism of the formal 'yes' campaign. Some privately regretted contracting out the SNP's *raison d'être* to an umbrella group in the first place: better to do it themselves, they muttered, voters would not differentiate between the two in any case. Key figures at Yes Scotland (based, appropriately enough, on Glasgow's Hope Street) were obviously aware of these critical noises but did their best to maintain a brave face, pursuing what they frequently called the 'largest and most exciting community based campaign in Scotland's history'.

A prominent element of this was the formation of several US-style 'communities of interest' for women, carers, Christians, creatives, crofters, disabled people, farmers, new Scots (i.e. English people or immigrants), pensioners, Scots Asians, LGBT people, trade unionists, veterans, youth and students, and ecoScots (environmentalists). More prominent (although lacking many high-profile names) were Business for Scotland and two political sub-groups, Liberal Democrats for Independence (Judy, wife of the former Liberal leader David Steel, was a 'yes' voter), and Labour for Independence (LfI), headed up by the Scottish Labour member Allan Grogan. The official Scottish Labour Party was dismissive, its deputy leader, Anas Sarwar, condemning LfI as 'nothing more than a sham and a SNP front'. Yes

Scotland drew the line at a group for Conservatives although there were at least two pro-independence Tories in the public eye: the historian and journalist Michael Fry (whose Scotfree2014 blog promoted independence from a libertarian perspective),[4] and the Dutch financier Peter de Vink, who was elected to Midlothian Council on a pro-independence Conservative ticket in May 2012. Apart from Business for Scotland (which had more than 300 members), however, few of these groups enjoyed significant support, for Yes Scotland (and Better Together) struggled to mobilise new activists and supporters from beyond the traditional party bases.

After its first year of campaigning Yes Scotland had hosted 1,184 events, recruited 2,671 'Yes Ambassadors', set up 173 local groups and distributed 3.2 million leaflets, not to mention attracting more than 17,000 followers on Twitter and more than 56,000 Facebook 'likes'. Figures in the Radical Independence Campaign, a group stronger on rhetoric than actually setting out 'radical' policies, were unimpressed. 'Anyone can sit at their desk pumping out infographics or playing with social media,' said one unnamed critic. 'But no matter what they say, this is not going to be won on Facebook or Twitter.' The Scottish Socialists and Scottish Greens also regularly criticised the campaign of which they were a part, usually a consequence of policy differences over the monarchy, currency and NATO membership. Even Yes Scotland's chairman, the former Labour MP Dennis Canavan, indirectly criticised SNP policy in calling a hereditary monarch 'an affront to democracy and a complete anachronism in a modern 21st-century democracy'.

After the first year of activity, even mainstream Nationalist critics of the 'yes' campaign began to surface. In an open letter to Alex Salmond, the former SNP candidate and commentator George Kerevan said 'yes-leaning' voters were 'dispirited' and 'downright de-motivated' by a 'boring' campaign that 'lacks passion' and 'sets no agendas'. Former

SNP leader Gordon Wilson, meanwhile, attacked a 'sterile' sort of Nationalism which had been 'diluted beyond trace' and a 'yes' campaign that delivered its arguments 'with all the excitement of a robot'. A more considered critique came from the Scottish Independence Convention (SIC), which existed to promote Scottish independence 'outside the party boundaries' (its convener was the actress Elaine C. Smith, who had been present at the launch of Yes Scotland). An SIC paper criticised the SNP's 'nervous, cautious and conservative' approach to the referendum and its tendency to compromise on certain policies, raising 'questions as to why bother with independence at all'. It continued:

> The independence movement is being split by commitments being given without proper consideration of the big picture. U-turns are making the campaign look weak and are not resolving the problem anyway … On no occasion so far has the outcome been a strengthened case for independence in the public debate. This is unsurprising since the strategy has been developed by the No campaign to have this outcome – to create a sense of disruption with no benefit.

Instead the SIC urged the pro-independence camp to shift from an 'answers-based' approach to a 'resolution-based' one, focusing on negotiations with the rest of the UK, the drafting of a constitution and then debate. The Scottish government, it reasoned, should steer clear – certainly prior to the referendum – of making 'commitments to public policy which are rightly the subject of future democratic elections'.

The SNP affected to be relaxed about this, for it reminded voters that Yes Scotland was a broad church (though a less credible one than Better Together) which, as Nicola Sturgeon conceded, would 'not agree on everything'. 'That is healthy,' she added. 'Indeed, it is confirmation of the vibrant democracy that an independent Scotland would be.' But the

SIC had a point. The SNP's overarching ambition was to achieve independence, but since 2007 it had concentrated on the business of government rather than pursuing its ultimate aim. And once in the business of government, it found breaking free of a policy/answers-based approach difficult.

So while Yes Scotland insisted a 'yes' vote had little to do with Alex Salmond or his party, the SNP muddied the waters by conflating public policy with the referendum via its promised 'independence prospectus' and a written constitution. As a UK government adviser put it:

> They can't decide if they need a vision or not. On the one hand they say it's not about them; 'this isn't up to us, it's for the first government elected in an independent Scotland to decide what to do in policy terms' and so on ... but at the same time they feel pressurised into giving lots of detail which people then swarm all over and eat them alive.[5]

In a carefully timed intervention on 18 September 2013, a reverse anniversary which prompted a flurry of commentary and debate, Alex Bell, the Scottish government's former senior policy adviser, touched on this in criticising the pro-independence campaign's 'temptation to focus on old songs and tired policies'.

> The campaigns to date have been a tedious parade of union flags versus saltires, of pop identity about caring Scots versus heartless Tories. By insisting on something particular to Scotland and contrasting it to the UK, Salmond has denied a crucial truth about the debate: Scotland's problems are common to the developed world, and the questions for him are the same as those for David Cameron and Ed Miliband, François Hollande and Angela Merkel. What is the relationship between citizen and state if governments are weak in the face of a financial crash? Why should the young pay the

pensions of the old if they are never going see similar rewards? What is the best balance between taxation and services? How do we tackle inequality when the coffers are empty and the electorate untrusting?[6]

The SNP, he concluded, had to decide if the point of its arguments and white paper was to give 'a tactical answer that will win hearts or a more profound assessment that will persuade minds'. This, however, was not a choice the party was willing to make a year out from polling day. The 'real battle', Alex Salmond had argued in 2011, was 'psychological', reasoning that if individual questions were combined – i.e. do you want Scotland to control troop deployment, gas revenues and renewables – 'and there's a majority for each [then] the task and challenge for the SNP is to make people generalise on independence from the particular aims and ambitions of these individual questions'. It was by no means a straightforward or simple task, he added, 'but it's certainly a doable one'.[7] He also believed the official 'no' campaign, what Salmond called an 'anti-Scottish' alliance, would eventually 'run out of steam', a 'wholly negative' campaign that, like Dracula, would 'be dragged out in the light of day and crumble'.

The best of both worlds

Better Together had at least got off to a slightly slicker start. Its name (which deliberately eschewed the words 'Union' or 'Unionist'), positive but also respectful to those who believed in independence, and messaging ('we want the best of both worlds', being Westminster and devolution) were thoughtfully contrived, even though the launch itself, at Edinburgh's Napier University a month after Yes Scotland's, was a little flat. A speech from Alistair Darling ('chairing this campaign is one of the most important things I have ever done in politics') looked better on paper than it sounded in the flesh.

'The decision we make is the most important we will make in our lifetime,' he began, a little melodramatically. 'Those of us who believe that it is best for Scotland to be part of the UK – from whatever political views – have a duty now to work in harmony to argue for the better, stronger choice.'

Thus was the rationale for the cross-party Unionist campaign, three very different parties putting differences to one side in order to campaign for greater higher purpose. 'This is a campaign that will make sure that the patriotism of the quiet majority will be heard alongside the voices of the committed few,' continued Darling, slipping into sub-Churchillian mode. 'Our case is not that Scotland cannot survive as a separate state. Of course it could. This is about what unites us, not about what divides us.' He continued:

We have achieved so much together, in times of peace and war. We created and then dismantled an empire together. We fought fascism together. We built the welfare state together. The BBC and the Bank of England were founded by Scots. The NHS was founded by a Welshman. The welfare state was founded by an Englishman.

Darling also aped Yes Scotland by linking a 'no' vote with tangible policy objectives. 'It is a big and difficult world and independence is an inadequate response,' he argued. 'And a world where the gap between rich and poor countries keeps on growing.'

These are the big challenges that we – as a strong partner in the UK – can influence ... Think of all the big questions the world is challenged by and then think – think really hard – about which of these questions is Scottish independence the answer ... We need more growth, more jobs and a more prosperous Scotland. These are the issues that Scotland should be focusing on. The last things we need are the new areas of uncertainty, instability and division that separation will involve.

Darling concluded with what was supposed to be an uplifting peroration:

> It is make your mind up time for us in Scotland. Our campaign runs across party and political borders. So, even if you've never joined a political party before, it doesn't matter. Come and join our cause. If you've never campaigned on anything before this, nothing has ever mattered as much as this. Come and get involved. If you've never even voted in an election, get registered to vote now. This isn't about voting in a government for a few years. It is about making history … So, as proud Scots who want a better future for Scotland, let's be confident in saying: Yes, we are Better Together.[8]

But then Better Together did not have to dazzle. The burden of proof lay firmly in the 'yes' camp; all that was required of the official 'no' campaign was to introduce an element of doubt, pick apart its opponents' arguments and, importantly, not screw anything up. The rather dour Alistair Darling, meanwhile, was presented as the very antithesis of Alex Salmond. Andrew Marr said it promised to be 'a contest about which of the two is the favoured caricature of modern Scottishness: the bouncy and demagogic upstart rebel or the furrow-browed man of authority'.[9] Unionists had realised early on that its campaign could not be led by a UK government minister or a Conservative; Darling, usefully, was neither.

The former Chancellor was solid rather than inspiring, while his frequent critiques of coalition economic policy made his willingness to share a platform with Conservatives and Liberal Democrats an easy target for the SNP. The former Liberal Democrat leader Charles Kennedy, whom

Nationalists feared as a genuinely popular proponent of the Union, failed to show up at the Better Together launch, while the Prime Minister caused problems of his own. Although regarded as a 'neutral figure' by Tory strategists (neither loved nor loathed in Scotland), his involvement required careful management, with Labour split when it came to campaigning alongside the Conservative leader (Jim Murphy said he would not; Johann Lamont appeared more amenable). The referendum, meanwhile, was seen by Scottish Conservative strategists as an opportunity to raise the profile of their new leader, Ruth Davidson, an eloquent defender of the Union if not a particularly effective figurehead for a party in historical decline.

Maintaining discipline also proved a challenge. No one did internecine strife quite like the Scottish Labour Party and thus Darling was seen as a figure who could, Tito-like, paper over the cracks and keep the show on the road ('We're relying on AD to hold everyone in the Labour Party together,' commented one senior Tory),[10] but even the appointment of Blair McDougall – the campaign's strategic brains – was delayed as a result of factional discontent, Johann Lamont and her adviser Paul Sinclair objecting to his close links to Jim Murphy. 'It wasn't until I got involved with this [campaign]', said one Liberal Democrat, 'that I realised how dysfunctional the Labour Party was – some of the relationships are toxic and go back generations.'[11]

Inter-party relations were rather easier. Anyone who witnessed Labour, Liberal Democrat and Tory politicians together at close quarters would have been struck by their sense of common purpose. 'We don't pretend we're all holding hands and singing Kumbaya,' joked Blair McDougall in an interview to mark the campaign's first anniversary. 'We are three parties who bitterly disagree on where Scotland and Britain should go ... we just happen to agree on this single policy.' Asked how he felt about Darling receiving an ovation at a Scottish Tory conference fringe meeting two weeks earlier, McDougall repeatedly ducked the question before offering: 'I was encouraged the parties think Alistair and the campaign are doing a good job.' The SNP dubbed him the 'Darling of the Tory conference'.

It was recognised, therefore, that each party involved with Better Together would also need to do its own thing. In March 2012 the Scottish Tories launched a 'Conservative Friends of the Union' initiative at their spring conference, and were evidently taken aback when 50,000 people donated almost £150,000, while Labour's 'no' campaign, 'United with Labour', launched the following year, betraying a certain sensitivity over SNP jibes that the party was campaigning in 'cahoots' with the Conservatives.

As Scottish Labour's deputy leader, Anas Sarwar, explained, 'Constitutional politics brings together people who wouldn't normally be on the same side ... but the Labour movement has a different view of Scotland's future from the Conservatives and Liberals.' What Sarwar meant was that affiliated trade unions had a different view. 'While I appreciate the referendum campaign has to have a formal Yes and No campaign,' said Dave Watson of Unison, 'most of us in the Labour movement have a huge difficulty with any campaign that includes the Tories.' Similarly Mary Lockhart, chair of the Labour-aligned Scottish Co-operative Party, quit after writing an article (headlined 'Socialism will work better in independent Scotland') in which she argued that it was 'insulting' and 'offensive' that Labour had joined forces with the Conservatives in the Better Together campaign. At points it also looked as if the Scottish Trades Union Congress was flirting with backing 'yes', its deputy general secretary, Dave Moxham, stressing that it was 'undecided' as late as September 2013. Most trade unions, however, understood unity was strength, with the train drivers' union ASLEF, steel worker union Community and the Union of Shop,

Distributive and Allied Workers (USDAW) all endorsing the constitutional status quo.

Meanwhile Gordon Brown – no stranger to internecine strife himself – was drafted in to head up United with Labour, a convenient way of involving the former Prime Minister without getting in Alistair Darling's way. But it also fragmented the pro-Union message. Expecting the voting public to keep track of several anti-independence campaigns – let alone one or two – was most likely asking a little too much.

The SNP exploited these internal tensions by presenting Better Together as little more than a Tory Unionist front, comprising three parties which – to varying degrees – subscribed to austerity economics, welfare cuts and generally 'anti-Scottish' policies. It also tried to throw the United Kingdom Independence Party into the mix, implying that Nigel Farage's Eurosceptic band ought to fall under the Better Together banner. The 'no' campaign, of course, gave this short shrift, also distancing itself from overtures by the Northern Irish Progressive Unionist Party (affiliated with the Ulster Volunteer Force paramilitary group), which intended to promote its own 'Maintain the Union' campaign, although presumably it meant 1800 rather than 1707.

In media terms, Better Together generally got an easier ride than Yes Scotland. Its main figures were all well known to journalists, particularly McDougall, who in a long career at Westminster (latterly with David Miliband's failed Labour leadership campaign) had impressed many with his sharp political antennae, and Rob Shorthouse (a former SNP member) who had filled a number of prominent roles in the public sector.

But one area where the 'no' campaign was weak in comparison with Yes Scotland was in terms of hand-to-hand combat, i.e. engaging with real people. Both campaigns established a series of local groups – 'Yes Dumfries' and 'Better Together Airdrie' for example – but the Unionist side often looked as if it was struggling to keep up with Yes Scotland, and even borrowed some of its techniques, Better Together setting up separate 'interest' groups such as Rural Better Together (launched at the 2013 Royal Highland Show) and Forces Together, launched, rather uncomfortably, by Alistair Darling at the Scottish Conservative conference.

Better Together was, however, rather better at recruiting high-profile non-politicians to promote its cause. Sportsmen featured prominently, Gavin Hastings (a former rugby international), Alex McLeish (former Scotland manager) and Sir Alex Ferguson (the legendary Man United manager) all joining the fray during 2013. Mostly they issued bland statements on national identity ('I am a proud Scot', said McLeish, 'but also passionate about Scotland being part of the United Kingdom'), but their involvement reflected a desire to break out of the political village. Third-party endorsements, so important to the SNP's successful election campaign in April/May 2011, were also likely to be prominent in the battle for Scotland, although Blair Jenkins mused that something about 'the etiquette of Scottish public life' prevented senior figures backing independence publicly.

Project Fear

And although the Prime Minister had promised to make a 'big optimistic case for the UK' in May 2011, Better Together faced repeated accusations – mainly from Yes Scotland – of indulging in negative campaigning and 'scaremongering'. According to one report, even those involved in the official 'no' campaign jokingly referred to themselves as 'Project Fear'. The SNP, naturally, wasted little opportunity in exploiting this – and '*Bitter* Together', a particular favourite of Salmond's – to refer to the 'anti-independence' campaign.

Preaching 'no' rather than the more upbeat 'yes' was certainly difficult to do in a positive way (a dynamic explored in the 2012 Chilean film *No*, which dramatised a

1988 plebiscite on Pinochet's rule), which was not to say negative campaigning could not be highly effective, the Alternative Vote referendum in 2011 being a good example. Some of what Better Together (or rather the UK government) produced did fall into the 'scaremongering' category, most memorably a suggestion two Chinese pandas at Edinburgh Zoo might be threatened by a 'yes' vote ('no one has fully understood the ramifications', commented a Westminster official with no obvious sarcasm, 'for the pandas of any bid for Scottish independence'), although Yes Scotland had a tendency to dismiss even legitimate points of detail in the same way.

And when, in the summer of 2013, stories surfaced about Scots facing mobile phone roaming charges (which the EU was, in any case, gradually phasing out) and charges for driving HGVs on English roads, there was a general sense the UK government was giving credence to Nationalist claims. Jackson Carlaw, the deputy leader of the Scottish Conservative Party, tweeted that the roaming charge story was 'silly', while Henry McLeish, a former Labour First Minister, even urged his party to quit Better Together to avoid becoming tainted by association. 'Next they'll be saying there will be seven years of famine in an independent Scotland', he remarked ruefully, 'and that aliens will land here.'

But Labour's instinct when up against the SNP was to indulge in 'Nat-bashing': relentlessly negative attacks on independence and its imagined consequences. This had been their stock in trade during the 1970s and again in the late 1990s, when they warned 'divorce is an expensive business' prior to the first Scottish Parliament elections. Yes Scotland – which worked hard to fashion a 'hope versus fear' narrative – unveiled a clever poster in which David Cameron was quoted saying (in April 2007) that it 'would be wrong to suggest that Scotland could not be another such successful, independent country'. So why, it added, 'is the No campaign always doing so?'

Nicola Sturgeon argued that the name 'Project Fear' 'may be new, but that approach to opposing progress for Scotland is age-old', citing similar tactics from the 1979 and 1997 devolution referendums. 'It does not want to build up – it wants to knock down,' she said. 'It does not want to inspire – it wants to scare. It has abandoned any pretence of positivity, and chooses to define itself, at least internally, as an essentially negative proposition.' Alex Salmond called them a 'parcel o' rogues'.

Embarrassed by the widespread use of 'Project Fear', Better Together attempted to moderate its tone as Holyrood and Westminster wound down for the summer of 2013. Blair McDougall acknowledged the 'no' campaign could not 'simply test the nationalist argument to destruction'. 'We need to reach both to people's heads and hearts,' he said. 'Our positive argument is that we are all stronger when we work together around shared interest.' A speech by Alistair Darling echoed this more emotional point ('Choices about nationhood are not just hard-headed calculation, they involve sentiment and belonging') and stressed that Better Together wanted 'Scots to make a positive choice to remain part of the UK, and not merely to reject the risks and uncertainties of independence'. The Prime Minister, meanwhile, said he realised the importance of 'keeping the right balance between positive and negative', particularly in his Commons exchanges with SNP MPs.

But at the same time, scaremongering was not the sole preserve of the 'no' campaign. Throughout 2013 Yes Scotland had gradually turned, almost imperceptibly, from the positive to the negative, emphasising the dangers of what might happen if Scots rejected independence in 2014. 'If they don't define what "no" means in policy terms,' explained a strategist, 'then we'll fill the gap.'[12] This included the 'uncertainty' surrounding the UK's economic performance and membership of the European Union, while Nationalists hinted darkly that not only would 'more powers' fail to materialise, but that existing ones might even be taken away. Health Secretary Alex Neil said Westminster would not miss a chance to 'kick us in the teeth' in the event of a 'no' vote, while arguing that 'Better Together' actually meant 'Poorer Together, More People Being Forced To Rely On Food Parcels Together, Unemployed Together, More Debt Together, More Unwanted Wars Together'.[13]

SNP ministers repeatedly framed the referendum as a choice between 'two futures', one good (independence), the other bad (the status quo), while flagging up points of differentiation between its devolved government (good) and the UK's (bad). In September 2013 Salmond told MSPs there was 'a heavy cost' when decisions were left 'in the hands of Westminster'. 'We get governments that we did not vote for,' he said, 'we get the bedroom tax; we get cuts to capital spending in the teeth of a recession; we get attacks on the poor and on people with disabilities; and we get weapons of mass destruction on the River Clyde.' John Swinney's 2013 'budget for independence' also compared his spending priorities with those of Chancellor George Osborne, although both omitted to mention that the apparently wicked Westminster Parliament had also devolved more power to the Scottish Parliament (via the 2012 Scotland Act), legislated for same-sex marriage (before Holyrood) and maintained the world's second largest international aid budget.

Nevertheless Stephen Noon, Yes Scotland's chief strategist, remained confident that a positive (or more accurately 'optimistic') campaign would always trump the negative. He explained:

If the battle is between two negatives, then the most negative will win. If it is between a negative and a mixed (part positive, part negative), the negative will win. But if a wholly positive faces a negative or mixed, then the positive will come out victorious. There is a great deal of misunderstanding about what a positive campaign can or cannot do. It doesn't mean you can't highlight a problem or a concern, but rather, the problem has to be balanced with offering a solution.[14]

Tellingly, however, Noon's rulebook did not cover a scenario in which both campaigns were 'mixed', which was arguably the case when it came to Better Together and Yes Scotland. The 'yes' campaign also had to be careful not to overdo its rose-tinted vision of an independent Scotland as a Nordic (and very wealthy) nirvana. Relentless optimism only worked if it was believable, and claims Scotland would enjoy unparalleled living standards while eliminating poverty often stretched credibility to breaking point. It was, of course, possible to be *too* positive as well as overly negative.

'A sh*t storm of aggression'

Character assassination, meanwhile, was a notable – and generally unwelcome – by-product of the referendum debate, much of which manifested itself online. When the Olympic cyclist Sir Chris Hoy expressed concern Scottish athletes might find it harder to compete on the world stage should Scotland become independent he was branded a 'bigoted anti-Scot', a 'creep' and an 'imbecile' on Twitter, even though the six-time gold medallist explicitly refused to reveal how he planned to vote.

The comedian Susan Calman (whose father, Sir Kenneth, had chaired a commission on more powers for the Scottish Parliament in 2007/08) came in for similar treatment following an appearance on BBC Radio 4's *News Quiz*. Again, she diligently avoided taking sides, but in poking fun at the SNP's currency policy she unleashed what she later called 'a sh*t storm of aggression', online accusations of 'betraying my country, of being racist towards my own people' and even death threats.[15] And when the actor Ray Winstone joked on *Have I Got News for You* that Scotland's main exports were 'oil, whisky, tartan and tramps', it prompted around 100 complaints. Humour and the independence debate seemed not to mix.

But although online abuse was nothing new (the Labour peer Lord Foulkes dubbed pro-independence practitioners 'CyberNats', who responded by referring to their opponents as 'BritNats'), the Calman incident seemed to provide something of a tipping point. Former First Minister Lord McConnell called for a 'grown-up' pact between Yes Scotland and Better Together to refrain from 'personal abuse and threats', while the Culture Secretary, Fiona Hyslop, said Scotland was 'big enough to embrace all different arguments and to do so in a responsible and tolerant way'. Yes Scotland, meanwhile, said the treatment of Calman had been 'utterly disgraceful'.

In a thoughtful Judith Hart Memorial Lecture, Labour's shadow Foreign Secretary, Douglas Alexander, warned the referendum campaign could descend into a 'battle for standing', as one side attempted to knock down their opponents' case by questioning their right to be heard. 'It seems to me the real debate we need is not who we are, but how we are,' he said. 'We need vision, not viciousness, as we make our choice.'[16] The SNP said it agreed, reminding Alexander that Nicola Sturgeon had been sent death threats on Twitter. 'A posting on the No campaign's Facebook page talked about firing bullets into SNP leaders,' it added, '[and] appalling remarks about Alex Salmond's dad were made on a Labour Party website.' 'All of it must stop,' added a spokesman decisively.

Better Together, however, was in no mood to forgive and forget, posting a slightly over-the-top blog on its website claiming its supporters had 'faced personal attack, hate mail and boycotts, all because they dared to oppose the break-up of the UK'. It went further in alleging this was 'part of a co-ordinated pattern of behaviour by the independence campaign'. Not only were critical journalists attacked on Twitter (Unionists had long implied some of this was orchestrated by SNP HQ), business leaders apparently felt intimidated into not speaking out (by people, claimed Alistair Darling, 'representing the Scottish government'). 'Why are they doing all this?' concluded the Better Together blog. 'Because they know the vast majority of Scots disagree with them and to win the referendum they need to silence the voices of the majority.'[17] In August 2013, meanwhile, Yes Scotland locked down its IT system after it appeared a hacker had gained access to its emails. Blair Jenkins spoke ominously of his campaign being 'under attack' from 'forces unknown'.

Twitter debate (usually under the hashtag #indyref), however, acted as an echo chamber rather than an effective means by which to spread the pro- or anti-independence gospel. As the 2011 Holyrood campaign had demonstrated, online tools worked better in terms of augmenting, rather than constituting, a campaign.

And it was not just online that referendum-related abuse manifested itself. When the UKIP leader, Nigel Farage, visited Edinburgh in mid-2013 he was barracked by around fifty students from the Radical Independence Campaign, including unintentionally ironic cries of 'we don't want racists here, go back to England'. 'If this is the face of Scottish Nationalism, it's a pretty ugly picture,' responded an obviously rattled Farage. 'I have heard before that there are some parts of Scottish Nationalism that are akin to fascism. Yesterday I saw it face to face.' Alex Salmond dismissed this, saying the incident had to be kept in context. 'A student demonstration', he added, 'ain't the Dreyfus trial.' Michael Moore, meanwhile, likened the SNP to UKIP, while other senior Unionists likened Scottish Nationalism to 'a cancer' (Lord Strathclyde) or 'a virus' (Johann Lamont).

Reports even suggested there were concerns for the First Minister's safety as the referendum approached. Stuart Crawford, an Army officer, said it was possible the risk to Salmond domestically and publicly 'could increase as the independence debate becomes increasingly heated', while a senior policeman was appointed to strengthen security at his Edinburgh residence and Aberdeenshire home. One poll showed a majority of Scots believed the independence debate was creating new tension and antagonism among families, friends and Scottish society in general, while in September 2013 an eighty-year-old 'yes' campaigner was apparently assaulted for wielding a pro-independence banner on Edinburgh's Royal Mile. The atmosphere even concerned the normally upbeat Stephen Noon. Scotland, he blogged, would 'not vote Yes in a mood of acrimony or in an atmosphere dominated by anxiety'.[18] The debate, agreed the political scientist James Mitchell, had managed to be both 'arid and acrimonious'.

Campaign finance
There was inevitable tension over campaign funding. In January 2013 the Electoral Commission published its advice on spending limits for the referendum campaign, allowing designated 'lead campaigners' (i.e. Yes Scotland and Better Together) to spend £1,500,000 and political parties represented in the Scottish Parliament varying amounts depending upon their strength (the SNP was allowed £1,344,000, Labour £834,000, the Conservatives £396,000, the Liberal Democrats £201,000, and the Greens £150,000). Other registered campaigners were told they could spend £150,000, although the commission made clear it had strict guidelines to prevent these (or individual donations of more than £10,000) being exploited by both sides as 'dummy' outfits.

These rules, however, only covered the 'restricted' sixteen-week campaigning period prior to 18 September 2014; until that point registered parties could spend as much as they wished. Particularly controversial was a £500,000 contribution from a Scots oil trader called Ian Taylor, whom a pro-independence website linked (via Taylor's company Vitol) to unsavoury characters in the Balkans. The SNP – including Alex Salmond – piled on the pressure for Better Together to return the donation, but it held firm, defending Taylor as a 'respected' international figure with 'a long history of philanthropy', including the revival of the Harris Tweed industry. If the SNP wanted it to return Taylor's donation to the 'no' campaign, ran the argument, then why not the money he had invested in an historic Scottish textile company?

Yes Scotland, which tried not to get drawn into the Taylor controversy, said donations from foreign (or non-Scotland-based) donors should be limited to £500, a clearly self-serving argument that would have severely restricted Better Together's fund-raising efforts. But disclosure of the Taylor donation did increase pressure on the 'yes' campaign to release its list of donors, which it did in April 2013. It was well known the SNP had received two separate donations of £1 million from lottery winners Colin and Christine Weir and the late Scottish Makar (poet or bard) Edwin Morgan, but instead of handing this 'independence war chest' to Yes Scotland, the Weirs instead donated an additional £1 million, the brunt of the £1.7 million raised since May 2012.

By contrast Better Together had received donations of £1.1 million since launching in June the year before, almost half of which had come from Ian Taylor. The 'no' campaign said Yes Scotland's failure to name a single non-SNP donor provided 'inescapable evidence' it was 'simply an SNP front'. Better Together boasted that it had not received 'a penny from any political party' and had received 'far more' small donations from grassroots supporters than Yes Scotland. It was all rather petty. Both sides, meanwhile, predicted 'a bit of an arms race' between the end of 2013 and late May 2014, when the formal hostilities were due to begin.

Climbing mountains

Viewed from London, one might have thought support for independence had risen inexorably over the previous decade. In fact it had stayed much the same, wavering at around a third of those consulted by opinion pollsters; it had not even changed very much as a consequence of the SNP becoming a party of government. By the autumn of 2013, sixteen different polls had asked the ballot paper question on independence and found that, on average, 33 per cent agreed that Scotland should be independent, with an average 'no' vote of 48 per cent and a little under a fifth claiming to be undecided. Although this seemed clear-cut, as the US polling guru Nate Silver explored in his 2012 bestseller *The Signal and the Noise: The Art and Science of Prediction*, distinguishing between the noise and clutter surrounding major issues like independence and the true signals as to what was actually going on was, in short, incredibly difficult.

Nevertheless, 'big data', or opinion polling, was significant for both sides in the referendum debate with new technology offering a more sophisticated picture of individuals and their voting habits, allowing campaigners to deliver customised messages as well as predict outcomes. The May 2011 Holyrood election had been a case in point, and a particularly painful one for Labour. Both sides, however, frequently pointed out that however static polls had been in the past, this might change as referendum day approached. But while constant media exposure gave the impression the issue was one of high priority for the Scottish electorate, studies showed the vast majority ranked the economy, jobs and the cost of living far above constitutional reform. One poll found that 28 per cent of Scots felt 'engaged' by the referendum debate, 20 per cent saying they felt 'bored', while polling by Lord Ashcroft found that 61 per cent of Scots thought the Scottish government had the wrong 'priority', i.e. pursuing independence.[19]

The Scottish Centre for Social Research (ScotCen) and its whatscotlandthinks.org website was the one-stop shop for up-to-speed information on Scots' referendum-related thinking. The ubiquitous psephologist Professor John Curtice posited that the SNP had become a victim of its own success. The more successful the SNP, it seemed, then the more satisfied Scots were with the devolution settlement and therefore less likely to support independence. Voters, in short, enjoyed being able to have their cake and eat it, a devolved administration that 'stood up for Scotland' and a Westminster government that footed the bill. Thus no matter how well the SNP did when it came to voting intentions (48 per cent according to one 2013 poll), Salmond et al. struggled to leverage consistently high public support for their Scottish government into support for independence.

Voters generally divided along gender lines. The Scottish Social Attitudes Survey (SSAS) data showed women were significantly less likely to back independence, only 20 per cent planning to vote 'yes', down from 29 per cent the previous year, while 29 per cent of men supported independence, down from 36 per cent. ScotCen reckoned this was not because female voters disliked Salmond (his approval ratings among women had always been lower), but because they were generally more practical, less prepared to imagine a different future under independence. The SNP leader attempted to rectify this gender gap by talking about childcare (at the 2012 SNP conference), being less combative (deploying what Johann Lamont called his 'wee quiet voice' at First Minister's Questions) and standing up for women's rights (boycotting, rather inconsistently, male-only golf clubs). Blair Jenkins joked that while Yes Scotland might have difficulty attracting female voters, equally that meant Better Together had a 'men problem'.

In June 2013 Yes Scotland claimed private polling showed rising support for independence among women, 16–24-year-olds and parents with young children, although revealingly, when challenged by Better Together to publish the full figures (as required under British Polling Council rules), it refused. Blair Jenkins also told journalists that Yes Scotland's internal polling was closer to one survey that showed 36 per cent planning to vote 'yes'. That was as may be, but most polls showed support at least a few points lower than that. 'I'm in no doubt', predicted Jenkins, 'that polls will move our way as we move deeper into the campaign.' At risk of sounding patronising, he also insisted that the better informed people felt, then the more likely they were to support independence.

Nicola Sturgeon argued that despite the polling, there existed a 'natural majority' in Scotland for independence, in other words a majority of persuadable voters, while Yes Scotland (and, indeed, Better Together) deployed sliding scales to gauge how strongly voters felt about constitutional change, '1' representing definite support for independence and '10' similarly strong backing for the status quo. The majority of voters sat between 3 and 8, desiring neither full autonomy nor an unreconstructed UK, but then the same had been true since the 1970s. 'They might not be ready to vote "yes" yet,' commented one Yes Scotland strategist in early 2012, 'but we have an understanding of what we have to do to turn that desire into a "yes" vote. The ground is the most fertile that I've ever encountered.'[20]

'I see the numbers,' insisted Yes Scotland's chief strategist, Stephen Noon, in August 2013:

People are moving up the support scale, including in key groups that we need to attract to win. Those campaigners on the doorstep know exactly what I am talking about. Numerous people have told me that they sense a shift, they feel the movement in our favour … the centre of gravity of the debate has shifted. The true power of those ranged against us has waned. They can't see it, but they are no longer the centre of the political universe.[21]

Strategists divided the 'yes' campaign into four distinct phases: 'Think About It', 'Tell Me More', 'Everyone's Voting Yes', and finally 'Vote Yes'. One insider drew a direct parallel with the SNP's 2007 and 2011 election wins. 'In 2007 very few people of my acquaintance (non-political) admitted that they were going to vote SNP (even though many went on to do it),' he remembered, 'whereas in 2011 most people who subsequently voted SNP said that they were going to do it … we must make voting "Yes" the norm.'[22]

Yes Scotland also took solace in survey data that showed support for independence, as with devolution, cut across traditional party lines. Support came from Unionists, most notably Labour voters (an Ipsos MORI poll suggested 13 per cent might vote 'yes'), just as the SNP counted many ardent 'no' voters among its supporters at election time. Veteran pollster Peter Kellner of YouGov concluded Scots were generally 'pro-Salmond, [but] anti-independence'. He argued (convincingly) that Yes Scotland had an even tougher task than the polls suggested. In referendums used to resolve national divisions (for example Europe in 1975) the status quo tended to prevail, the only exceptions (Scotland in 1997) being when a clear consensus for change had existed. The 'yes' campaign, therefore, could not be content going into the formal campaigning period in the summer of 2014 with a narrow lead over Better Together. In order to stand any chance of victory, it would need to be ahead by almost two-to-one in advance of polling day, and even if the number of undecided and 'yes' voters in most polls were added together, it did not produce a majority in favour. Nevertheless, noted Kellner of Alex Salmond, if 'anyone is able to climb the mountain and deliver a "yes" majority, it is he'.[23] Yes Scotland chairman Dennis Canavan got a cheer at the 2013 SNP spring conference when he quipped: 'I'm often told we've got a mountain to climb – well I like climbing mountains!'

The economist John Kay likened the situation to that facing David Cameron over the UK's membership of the EU. 'Britain in Europe, like Scotland in the UK, is a known quantity: the alternative is not,' he mused in the *Financial Times*. '"*Always keep a hold of nurse, for fear of finding something worse*"', wrote [the Anglo-French writer] Hilaire Belloc. It is not a bad maxim: and an influential one when voters consider constitutional issues.'[24] But, as Alex Salmond observed a year out from the referendum, 'an uncomfortable truth' for those in politics (and those writing about it) was that 'most people don't engage in the political process until the point they have to'. In other words, the situation could change – as it had in the closing weeks of the 2011 Holyrood election campaign, and indeed during the 1995 Quebec referendum – at the very last moment.

Electoral franchise

So exactly who would be considering Scotland's constitutional future on 18 September 2014? The electoral franchise for the referendum had, of course, been one of the major negotiating points prior to the signing of the Edinburgh Agreement in October 2012, and indeed who controlled it. The franchise in Scotland, as throughout the UK, was a matter reserved to Westminster; but since the Edinburgh Agreement (temporarily) granted the Scottish Parliament the power to hold a legal (if not legally binding) referendum, then it also (temporarily) devolved control of the referendum franchise.

Ministers opted to base this on the existing electoral roll for Scottish Parliament and local government elections, so all those resident in Scotland by the relevant registration date would be eligible to vote, meaning a franchise of more than four million voters. Reaching them all presented a massive logistical challenge for both Yes Scotland and Better Together. Although most parties had their own electoral databases, not least the SNP's groundbreaking 'Activate' system (which had played a vital role in the 2007 and 2011 election campaigns), they were acknowledged as insufficient for the referendum and, in any case, could not be used by the 'yes' or 'no' campaigns. Better Together set itself a target of reaching one million registered voters a year using its 'Patriot' software (developed by Blue State Digital of Obama campaign fame), while Yes Scotland planned to send a personal newsletter to every single home in the country.

The franchise would, of course, be *slightly* bigger given the UK government had sanctioned the inclusion of sixteen- and seventeen-year-olds, something London-based ministers made clear would not be extended to other UK elections. It was expected to cost the taxpayer an extra £358,000 (the total cost of the referendum was expected to be £1.3 million, roughly the same as 2011's AV ballot). The SNP, often accused of cynical gerrymandering, had actually been admirably consistent in this respect: it had lowered the voting age for elections to the Crofting Commission and in trial elections to some Scottish health boards, while votes at sixteen had featured in the party's 2002 constitution. Within the British Isles, the Channel Islands and Isle of Man had all pioneered votes at 16–18 in various reforms adopted since 2006, although their experience suggested that giving younger people the vote did not necessarily mean they chose to exercise it. Indeed, in the 2010 health board elections in Dumfries and Fife, sixteen- and seventeen-year-olds were only half as likely to vote as those aged eighteen and older, while according to the SSAS much the same had been true of 18–24-year-olds at the 2011 Holyrood election.

Opponents assumed the Scottish government believed

this age group would be more likely to vote 'yes', but the polling, as mentioned above, indicated that would not necessarily be the case. On that basis the UK government was relaxed about conceding the point, also churlishly assuming that handling such a change to the electoral register would be more trouble than it was worth. There were indeed complications. A House of Lords committee flagged up issues over data protection (the law prohibited making available information about juveniles), while it also seemed unlikely *all* eligible sixteen-year-olds would be able to vote given the required cut-off date for registration. The Scottish government, however, was confident it had dealt with all this, also announcing that only the official 'yes' and 'no' campaigns would be given access to the final merged list of all eligible voters. The First Minister's official spokesman explained it was striking 'a balance between putting young voters on an equal footing with other voters and a desire to ensure that their data is treated sensitively and responsibly'. Nevertheless, Better Together and Yes Scotland clashed over the former's plan to distribute teaching material to every secondary school in the country. 'Our children's education is too important', said a 'yes' campaigner, 'to be politicised in this way'; although it too intended to provide a 'schools pack', it planned to do so via 'young supporters in each school' rather than teachers.

A major Economic and Social Research Council-organised poll published in June 2013 confirmed what most already suspected, that there was less support for independence among that age group than among Scots generally, with 60 per cent of 14–17-year-olds intending to vote 'no' and only 21 per cent 'yes' (19 per cent were undecided, from a sample of more than 1,000 teenagers). The only glimmer of comfort for Yes Scotland was the desire of more than two thirds of those surveyed for 'more information'. Campus ballots at Glasgow and Napier universities revealed comfortable margins against independence (on typically low turnouts), while a mock referendum of more than 11,000 schoolchildren in Aberdeenshire (a strong SNP area) found only 24.5 per cent intending to vote 'yes'. Explaining this youthful preference for the status quo was difficult, although the journalist Peter Jones concluded that 'much of the lives of today's 16- to 24-year-olds is spent in a space where nations and governments are completely unimportant – the internet'.[25]

The use of existing electoral registers, meanwhile, meant all UK and EU citizens resident in Scotland would be able to vote, along with Armed Forces personnel registered at a Scottish address. The *Daily Telegraph*, however, took up the cause of Scottish soldiers who would be based outside the country come referendum day (including, according to the newspaper, two out of Scotland's five Royal Regiment of Scotland battalions). Labour's shadow Defence Secretary, Jim Murphy, was critical, as was Major General Andrew Mackay, a retired General Officer Commanding Scotland. 'It seems incongruous', he commented, 'that as a born and bred Scot you can serve your country yet be denied a vote.' Although the anomaly meant only a few thousand soldiers would be excluded, critics made the reasonable point that if it was possible to include sixteen- and seventeen-year-olds, then why not overseas military personnel.

There was another inconsistency when it came to Scotland's 8,100 prison inmates, all of whom were technically registered at 'a Scottish address'. In successive rulings the European Court of Human Rights had decided the UK's blanket ban on prisoners having the vote contravened the European Convention on Human Rights. The Scottish government, however, argued that only applied to general and local elections rather than referendums. A June 2013 ruling on a prisoner unable to vote in the 2011 AV referendum appeared to back them up on this point, although the human rights lawyer Tony Kelly (who had represented al-Megrahi) agreed to help a group of prisoners formally challenge the relevant regulations. Most likely ministers at Holyrood – as at Westminster – were alive to the political consequences of granting convicted prisoners a vote. Questioned by the Scottish Parliament's Referendum Bill Committee, Nicola Sturgeon said there would be no U-turn and that the legal position was 'perfectly clear'.

Also perfectly clear was the virtual impossibility that Scots living in other parts of the UK – and indeed across the globe – would be able to cast a vote, an issue that had also surfaced during the devolution referendums of 1979 and 1997. But since 1973 there had been a clear precedent that referendums on constitutional change – be they in Northern Ireland, Wales, Scotland, London or the north-east of England – should only cover those resident in each nation or region. Only the European referendum of 1975 and that on electoral reform in 2011 had consulted voters in every part of the UK.

This clearly angered many of the 800,000 Scots resident in other parts of the UK. In Corby, a Northamptonshire town with a 12,000-strong 'Little Scotland' (a distinct community comprising steel workers who had moved south for work), a campaign sprang up to formally request a vote from the Scottish government. The outgoing Manchester United manager, Sir Alex Ferguson, also criticised the disenfranchisement of Scots, like him, who lived and worked outside Scotland. 'You may not have a vote in the referendum, but you do have a voice,' Alistair Darling told London-based Scots in June 2013. 'You have a right to have your opinion heard and you have a right to play your part in keeping Scotland in the UK.' While it was perfectly possible to extend the franchise to voters beyond Scottish electoral territory – France's National Assembly even elected MPs representing overseas constituencies – the Scottish government was reluctant to play ball, perhaps conscious most expat Scots would not be well disposed towards independence, not to mention the logistical challenges.

Many Scots, of course, were not registered despite having lived in Scotland for decades. This was partly historical (the introduction of the poll tax in the late 1980s had led to a discernible reduction in the electoral roll) but also demographic: the lower a person's socio-economic group then the less likely he or she was to be registered, and even if they were on the roll, he or she was less likely to be a regular voter. This phenomenon was most evident in deprived parts of Glasgow, where the turnout in some constituencies averaged around 35 per cent. Yes Scotland strategists referred to this as the 'missing million', and much of the campaign's focus on welfare cuts had these voters in mind, driven by a belief that benefit reforms (i.e. cuts) could motivate the disenfranchised into not only voting for the first time but voting 'yes' to the prospect of a brighter future under independence.

This owed more than a little to SNP class consciousness. In the 1979 referendum on devolution, for example, 57 per cent of working-class Scots had voted for a Scottish Assembly, whereas 60 per cent of middle-class Scots had voted against.[26] In 1997, meanwhile, 91 per cent of working-class voters had backed the creation of a Scottish Parliament compared with 69 per cent of middle-class voters.[27] Similarly, a January 2013 Ipsos MORI poll showed support for independence was much higher among Scots living in deprived areas (58 per cent) than it was among those living in affluent areas (27 per cent).

All of which raised the question of referendum turnout. It was generally assumed this would be high (Nicola Sturgeon predicted it would be at least 70 per cent) although it was of course difficult to predict a precise figure. In the Quebec referendums of 1980 and 1995 turnout had been, respectively, 85.6 and 93.5 per cent of a similar-sized electorate, but few expected Scotland to match that in September 2014.

Voter engagement had generally been falling, with only 50 per cent bothering to vote in the 2011 Holyrood election despite a high-profile campaign, and a slightly higher turn-out of 63.8 per cent at the 2010 general election. Exactly the same percentage had voted in the 1979 devolution referendum, and fewer (60.4 per cent) in 1997, despite decades of campaigning for a Scottish Parliament. Nevertheless it was reasonable to conclude that a referendum on *independence*, ostensibly a more radical constitutional proposition, would attract greater interest; but perhaps not that much more.

'Winning conditions'

Alistair Darling was quite clear the 'no' campaign not only had to win but 'win well', reflecting concerns within Better Together that a turnout both low (say 60 per cent) and differential (i.e. a more motivated 'yes' vote) would produce a narrow 'yes' vote. The Prime Minister, however, made it known that in his opinion even a marginal victory would settle the matter 'for a long time', while Chief Secretary to the Treasury, Danny Alexander, cited the Canadian experience of a 'neverendum' in Quebec. 'I want this debate to settle this question for a generation in Scotland,' he said. 'We shouldn't have to keep coming back to this year after year after year.'

The most recent referendum in Quebec had, of course, produced a knife-edge vote. Indeed, the Canadian experience was much in Unionist minds throughout the referendum campaign; there were striking parallels between the 'yes' and 'no' campaigns in 1995 and those in 2012–14.[28] The rapid erosion of the federalist lead in the weeks immediately before Quebeckers cast their vote weighed particularly heavily. As a result, 'we're confident but not complacent' became almost a mantra in Better Together circles, but given the number of different parties involved in the 'no' campaign, keeping everyone on message was not always possible. 'We have won the argument on independence,' a UK government minister told *The Herald* in the summer of 2013. 'Ordinary people on the doorsteps have made their mind up about this issue. But they may vote Yes next September for other reasons. We are now fighting to ensure we've got a big enough majority to determine what happens after the referendum.' Better Together called the briefing 'unhelpful', adding emphatically, 'This is not in the bag.'

The first edition of the (Scottish) *Sun on Sunday* had revealed 18 October 2014 as Scotland's 'date with destiny', but it seemed ministers had second thoughts about holding it during a two-week school holiday in the second half of the month and only a week before the clocks went back on the twenty-seventh. Another consideration was probably extensive television coverage of the UK party conferences in late September and early October, which would inevitably have become pro-Union jamborees (the Liberal Democrats decided to hold both their 2013 and 2014 conferences in Glasgow, although the latter was moved to October in order to avoid clashing with the week of the referendum).

'Most people now recognise the timing was correct,' reflected a Yes Scotland adviser in July 2013. 'If we'd held it this year we would have been in deep trouble – we'd have been looking at 30 per cent of the vote.'[29] And while the date had of course been conceded in the Edinburgh Agreement, the Prime Minister remained impatient, telling journalists he wished it 'could be tomorrow'. Alistair Carmichael's appointment as Scottish Secretary in October 2013 also betrayed an upping of the ante in terms of dealing with the SNP.

Privately, Alex Salmond set Yes Scotland a polling target of 40/60 (yes/no) by the end of 2013, once the Referendum Bill (expected to pass its Stage 3 reading in November) was out of the way and the white paper on independence in the public domain. By that point, pro-independence strategists hoped seemingly interminable debates over process and policy detail would have been laid to rest, enabling them to gear up for what the First Minister called 'an incredibly busy year on the international stage'.

Unveiling his 2013–14 Programme for Government in September 2013, Salmond directly mentioned the Commonwealth Games, the Ryder Cup and the 'Homecoming' event, all of which would, he observed, allow the world to see a country with a 'growing confidence and sense of itself'. He and other pro-independence supporters hoped, as the journalist Eddie Barnes put it, that the 'yes' campaign could 'surf on that wave of positivity next year and drown out people's inner doubts'. It was all about creating what the Quebecker politician Lucien Bouchard had once called 'winning conditions'.

The summer of 2014 was due to begin early on 22 May when it looked likely the SNP and UKIP would capture the most votes (in Scotland and England respectively) in elections to the European Parliament. The SNP even had high hopes of securing a third MEP in its eightieth year, and even if it did not, the electoral contrast would play to one of its central narratives about northern and southern Britain moving in different directions. Conveniently, the formal sixteen-week referendum campaign was due to begin exactly a week later, at which point Scottish and UK government activity would relinquish most of the heavy lifting to Yes Scotland and Better Together, as well as individual party campaigns, perhaps including an SNP 'yes' movement led by Alex Salmond.

Throughout that summer Homecoming, an extensive programme designed to showcase the 'very best of Scotland's past, present and future', would appeal to Scotland's 'diaspora', while events in late June would commemorate the 700th anniversary of the Battle of Bannockburn (the SNP had been less enthusiastic about marking the 500th anniversary of Flodden in 2013). Between 23 July and 3 August, meanwhile, the Scottish government hoped the 'eyes of the world' would be on Scotland's largest city for the 2014 Commonwealth Games in which, usefully (and unlike the 2012 Olympics), Scotland would field its own team. Belatedly, the UK government attempted to take ownership of the Games, stressing its role in delivering the international sporting event, although that did not involve Olympic-level spending. Finally, the Edinburgh festivals would showcase a nation on the cusp of deciding its constitutional future, although Sir Jonathan Mills, the outgoing director of the Edinburgh International Festival, made it clear the 2014 programme would remain 'a politically neutral space for artists', with a focus on the Commonwealth Games and centenary of the First World War rather than the independence referendum. Nick Barley of the Edinburgh International Book Festival, on the other hand, said the literary event had an 'absolutely crucial' role to play in the debate while the massive Fringe festival, which had touched on the debate in August 2013, looked likely to pay closer attention in 2014.

On 21 August a period of 'purdah' would kick in, restricting (more in theory than practice) major spending or policy announcements from the UK and Scottish governments. A 13 September 'Rally for Scottish Independence', the last of three annual marches organised by the 'Independence for Scotland' group (not part of Yes Scotland), was also likely to be a major pre-referendum event. The first, in September 2012, had seen up to 10,000 people march from the Meadows to Edinburgh's Princes Street Gardens, although it was dwarfed by a similar event in Barcelona, which some claimed had been attended by up to a million Catalans. The Last Night of the Proms was also due to take place the same day, with its Union flags and gusty renditions of 'Rule, Britannia!' (written by a Scot) and 'Jerusalem' likely to provide a Unionist counterpoint in the Royal Albert Hall. Finally, the Ryder Cup was actually due to begin at Gleneagles five days after

Scots went to the polls, although the First Minister, a golfing fanatic, was likely to exploit the build-up.

Not to be outdone by what the media called a 'summer of Scottishness', there were also convenient hooks for celebrations of Britishness. Largely focused on the twentieth century's two world wars, Unionists hoped to use the seventieth anniversary of the D-Day landings on 6 June and the seventy-fifth anniversary of the UK's declaration of war on Nazi Germany to remember Britain's 'finest hour' when Scots, English, Welsh and Northern Irish soldiers helped liberate continental Europe. The centenary of the outbreak of the First World War and the first day of conflict on 28 July and 4 August, meanwhile, would likely be more sombre. In that regard, the Scottish government planned to stage its own events, including ceremonies to mark the battles at Loos and Arras, where Scottish battalions suffered a high number of casualties, and domestic incidents such as the loss of HMS *Iolaire*. Conveniently, meanwhile, the 2014 Armed Forces Day was due to take place in Stirling on 28 June.

Playing on this theme, the 'English' Education Secretary, Michael Gove (a product, ironically, of a Scottish education), said 2014 would be a 'great battle of Britain', in which Alex Salmond would cynically channel historical sentiment in order to get his way. He continued:

He thinks somehow that that 700-year-old anniversary will stir Scottish hearts. But next year is the anniversary of so much more. Next year is also the anniversary of the First World War when English, Scottish, Irish and Welsh soldiers stood together. And next year of course will also be the seventieth anniversary of D Day. When this country liberated Europe from totalitarianism it was the skirl of the pipes that was heard as the first troops went ashore in Normandy; Scottish, British, Irish, united under the United Kingdom flag, determined to hold off tyranny, determined to stand up for

liberty. That is woven into who I am. Alex Salmond wants to
rip that out. Let's not let him.

But while Better Together planned to make more of an
'emotional case' by emphasising common 'British' bonds,
Yes Scotland planned to do the same with Scottishness ('it
will be talked up next year,' predicted a strategist, 'there's no
doubt about it'). But flag-waving – by either side – seemed
unlikely to succeed. Not only had 2012's 'Jubilympics' failed
to produce any discernible 'British bounce', but brandishing
Saltires (as demonstrated by Alex Salmond at Wimbledon
in 2013) could also backfire. Flag-waving, after all, was
often taken to be the raw essence of identity politics. The
summer of 2014 risked becoming a battle between two
different nationalisms, what Stephen Noon characterised
as 'Scotland's brand of civic nationalism' and 'the British
nationalist variant', the latter relying on 'an increasingly
outdated and anachronistic view of the all-powerful state'.[30]

The SNP (supported by the Greens and Independent MSPs)
even recast MSPs' summer holidays to give them more time
to fight for (or indeed against) independence, not by granting
extra leave but by sitting for three weeks in August – tradi-
tionally part of the summer recess – and thereby enjoying
two breaks, one in July and another in the twenty-eight days
before polling day. The three Unionist parties called it an
'affront to democracy', although they were probably rather
relieved; it hardly benefited one side more than the other.
The 18 September vote, meanwhile, would be counted overnight, ensuring some traditional drama, while the Scottish
government's Referendum Act allowed for local results to be
declared before the national result.

And while the Scottish parties would undoubtedly be
focused on the big day, the Westminster political classes
looked likely to be preoccupied with not only the inevitable
fallout from another UKIP surge at the European elections

in May, but preparations for the 2015 general election and, of course, the UK's own 'independence' referendum due to take place by the end of 2017. This had occurred to Yes Scotland, which spoke of several different 'spinning plates' influencing the political climate at that point. 'One of those is the European elections,' explained a strategist, 'another is what happens in terms of the three Unionist parties offering more powers, and finally how the progressive middle class reacts to the UK government's welfare changes.'[31] The last of those seemed unlikely given the similarity of public opinion north and south of the border (Salmond claimed the bedroom tax would be 'one of the key spurs to independence'), although polling had indicated that more Scots would vote 'yes' in response to increasing Euroscepticism in rUK and the prospect of another Conservative-led government at the 2015 general election (although the latter factor had only a marginal impact).

Much of the intervening period had been, as Salmond put it in a June 2013 interview with the *New Statesman*, a 'phoney war'. 'This is not the campaign,' he said. 'The real game hasn't even started. We are just clearing the ground.' Clearing the ground was important in itself. As one senior Nationalist put it towards the end of 2011, 'if we haven't done what we need to do by the end of 2013 then we won't have done it'.[32] Those on the ostensibly winning side were also prone to bouts of self-doubt. 'I think there's a credible chance we'll lose,' one Westminster adviser reflected in April 2012. 'It's an understatement to say I'm not taking this for granted: we really might lose this.'[33]

The First Minister said in 2007 that an independence referendum would be 'a once in a generation thing', and it bore repeating that he had not really wanted a vote in 2014, or indeed anytime soon. The arch-gradualist had been compelled by his own electoral success to take the final step on the path to independence earlier than he might have

wished. Thus in addition to making the best of a bad situation, Alex Salmond also had to plan for devolved elections in
May 2016, a contest he – assuming he was still at the helm
– and his party had a realistic chance of winning. So while
the SNP leader had a relatively low profile during 2012 and
2013, the plan was to bring him out, as one former adviser
put it, with 'all guns blazing' in 2014, as the party had done
in 2011. There was even under-the-radar speculation (from
those on the inside) that Salmond might relinquish office in
order to run the 'yes' campaign full time, allowing Nicola
Sturgeon to become Scotland's first female First Minister.

After all, Salmond was something of a Nationalist veteran,
having led his party (with a four-year hiatus) since 1990,
political longevity unheard of in post-war British politics.
'The SNP looks and hopefully behaves … like the party
… Scotland would like to be governed by,' he reflected in
October 2012.

> [But] the SNP of course mustn't get complacent … every
> party has support by consent, if people think your heart's in
> the right place, you know what you're doing; you've got the
> right people they'll forgive you a great deal. If they believe
> your heart's in the wrong place, and you've not got the right
> people, they won't forgive you anything.

Salmond was acutely aware of the need to maintain
momentum; like Lyndon Johnson, he did not believe it was
'a mysterious mistress' but a 'controllable fact of political
life'.[34] Thus sustaining the popularity of the SNP was a crucial
factor in the onward march of Nationalism. 'Our polling is
very clear that as soon as we lose trust on the basics,' said a
former adviser, 'then we don't have a chance of winning the
main prize.'[35]

At the same time Salmond realised that winning in 2016
was not contingent upon victory in 2014, the referendum

having long separated the two contests in the minds of voters, who were well able to distinguish the man from what Labour characterised as his political 'obsession'. The case of Quebec in 1980 and 1995 demonstrated that nationalists could lose two referendums and still form a government. And when, for example, the legendary Irish nationalist Éamon de Valera stood in the presidential election of 1959, he simultaneously held a referendum to change Ireland's voting system, fully expecting his popularity to carry the day. Voters, however, had other ideas, re-electing de Valera but rejecting his new voting system.

When the Irish Free State had seceded from the UK in 1922 there had been no question 'independence' enjoyed majority public support, unlike Scotland in 2014 when some 'yes' campaigners gave the impression of being content with the idea of just scraping home. 'It would of course be a legitimate victory,' judged an insider, 'but one which left a gaping wound to be healed',[36] not least among the 49 per cent or so who had voted no. Former Scottish civil service chief Sir John Elvidge warned that a 'Scotland in which everyone was defined by which side they were on a particular day' would not be 'anyone's definition of a healthy, modern society'. 'Each of us will have argued our case strongly and passionately,' predicted Nicola Sturgeon in stateswoman mode. 'But when the people have spoken, we will emerge from it as one united nation. We will be Team Scotland.' Similarly, President Clinton predicted Scotland would emerge from the referendum 'better, regardless, if you go about it in the right way'.

Alex Salmond was above all a realist, something he disguised with relentless optimism. 'You have to put the accent on the positive, and you have to absolutely believe it with every fibre of your being,' he told Russia Today. 'And that way of thinking, of looking at the world, of approaching the people, I'll take into the referendum campaign.'[37] But in a more reflective mood the Grand Old Man of Scottish politics – Salmond would turn sixty a few months after the referendum – conceded it was possible to 'not believe in independence and still believe passionately in Scotland'.

> I mean if I didn't believe in independence I would still want to see Scotland do well; I would want Scots to have the confidence to say 'no' to independence for the right reasons as opposed to being dragooned into some fear-laden doom-ridden atmosphere of 'they didn't think they could'... but you see things in my view have gone beyond that: I think a lot of folk in Scotland have passed that psychological tipping point where they're not prepared to accept this nonsense any more, and a lot more are getting there.

Therefore, he concluded, there remained – whatever the opinion polls showed – a momentum 'leading in a certain direction'. 'I can't claim to know what the timetable is, *even now*,' Salmond added revealingly, 'but I'm pretty certain the destination is set.'[38]

CHAPTER 9

LOOKING BACK: SCOTLAND VOTES 'NO'

On 18 September 2014 a decisive majority of Scots voted 'no' to independence. A decade later, calls for a second referendum are growing louder...

What do we get from leaving our powers in the control of others? A high-risk economy and an eroding social fabric.

And let us be clear – to vote no in 2014 consigns us to that path.

A deeply indebted state spending money on Trident weapons of mass destruction while cutting welfare.

A state adrift from Europe and increasingly isolated on the wider stage.

And to those who say that the answer is to change the occupant of No. 10 and the colour of the UK government, I say we have been there and done that and the challenges we face remain undiminished.

Nicola Sturgeon, University of Strathclyde (2012)

It would have been rather odd to mark a decade since Scotland's independence referendum on 18 September 2024, particularly considering it had produced a fairly decisive 'no' vote. The Scottish and UK governments thought about it, of course, but given both administrations were controlled by the Labour Party their respective advisers decided it might look churlish and instead opted to let sleeping dogs lie. Nevertheless the digital media (printed newspapers were by then rare) was full of blogs and articles reflecting on what might have been.

The SNP, now in opposition at Holyrood following an unbroken run of devolved government between 2007 and 2021, attempted to capitalise by announcing a renewed push for independence. If the party managed to oust the Scottish Labour Party – and First Minister Jenny Marra – at the next election in 2026, Humza Yousaf pledged, an SNP administration would negotiate another Section 30 Order from the UK government and hold a second referendum within the lifetime of that five-year Holyrood parliament.

A few years before, such a pledge might have appeared self-indulgent, a reawakening of fears that defeat in 2014 would result in a 'neverendum', with SNP governments rerunning the vote – like Ireland on the Lisbon Treaty – again and again until they achieved their desired result. Alex Salmond and others had promised, after all, that the first vote would be a 'once in a generation' opportunity to secure independence. But then a second referendum might not take place until around 2030 which, at a push, could be considered a generation after the first, roughly the period of time between the first and second sovereignty votes in Quebec.

It demonstrated that, as many had foreseen, even a decisive 'win' in 2014 had not been enough to settle the Scottish Question once and for all. While the polls had narrowed in the months before Scots went to the polls – Better Together's 'scaremongering' having annoyed a lot of undecided voters – Yes Scotland and the SNP had never really sealed the deal on independence. Neither the alleged problem nor the proposed solution had appeared sufficiently compelling, although by polling day the pro-independence vote had been higher than anticipated at 40 per cent of those voting (turnout had been a lower than expected 68 per cent).

The Prime Minister hailed the result as a decisive vindication not only of the UK, but his government's strategy of giving the

SNP, as some had seen it, 'just enough rope to hang themselves'. As Yes Scotland's chief strategist, Stephen Noon, had blogged in advance of polling day, 'as soon as the votes are counted there would be only one person in the No victory spotlight'.

> Peer into that future and what do you see? It's David Cameron, UK PM, alone on the winner's podium. Ed Miliband and Johann Lamont, thank you, your job is done. I bet the Tories are rubbing their hands in anticipation at the fillip a Scottish No would give them as they enter their pre-election Conference. They would hail the PM as the man who saved their 'nation'. Success breeds success. And no one does flag waving better than the Tories. If you thought John Major was saved by his soapbox campaign to save the Union in 1992, well you ain't seen nothing yet.[1]

Although certainly buoyed by the result, what had actually secured David Cameron his second term in Downing Street was the economy. This had steadily improved throughout 2014, moving (in the Chancellor's words) from 'rescue to recovery', demonstrating to voters that four years of austerity had been worth it to get the country back on track. Given that both Labour's and the SNP's tactics were based on the economy getting worse, it had proved almost impossible for the former to craft an election-winning narrative and the latter to argue that only independence could secure Scotland a bright future.

Westminster advisers, meanwhile, had studied Canada's experience with Quebec in 1995 and were therefore well prepared to win the peace in the aftermath of the referendum, killing 'Home Rule with kindness' as a Tory grandee had once put it. Although the trio of Unionist parties had not collectively committed to any coherent package of further powers prior to polling day, all three had moved quickly to make public the relevant sections of their respective manifestos for the 2015 general election. There was a general consensus on devolving all of income tax, along with air passenger duty (long demanded by the SNP), vehicle excise duty and a range of other more modest fiscal levers.

Naturally, there were critical voices, some Labour MPs arguing that nothing more should be done to 'appease' the Nationalists now their independence project had been roundly defeated. But cooler heads prevailed, and the UK government also announced plans for a UK-wide constitutional convention to consider institutional reform in a more holistic way. Labour's Douglas Alexander, meanwhile, also revisited his idea of convening a 'Scotland 2025' convention, something that gathered momentum as a memorable year drew to a close.

Citing Australia, where Prime Minister Kevin Rudd had brought together more than 1,000 leading figures to debate and develop long-term options for the nation, Alexander had envisaged a Scottish 'National Convention' looking 'beyond an agenda of constitutional change'. He explained:

> For Scotland, a national convention could be a gathering that embedded itself into and enriched our civic life as a cornerstone of public debate and reflection, shaping the very framing of how we engage in dialogue and discussion. From how to raise our economic productivity, to the needs of our rural and island communities, from the challenge of sustainability, to harnessing the full potential of Scotland's creative industries, it could draw on the talents, ideas and energy of Scotland's many communities.

And rather than pretending politicians had all the answers, Alexander continued, 'it could engage the people of Scotland in deliberating together a new vision for an old nation'.

It could create a space for a new kind of politics. It could help change the way power is distributed and shared. It could change the way we made sense of the ideal of the people being sovereign. And it could genuinely help put people in charge of writing the next chapter of Scotland's story. It could make sure that the debate of the last four years is not lost. It could exemplify the value that we are better when we share together what we have, and care about our neighbour.

'And it could turn a referendum lost by those who want to walk away', he concluded, 'into an opportunity for us all to walk forward together, no matter where our cross went on the ballot paper.'[2]

For once, the SNP agreed to take part, having remained aloof from the Scottish Constitutional Convention (which helped draw up the blueprint for a Scottish Parliament in the late 1980s and early 1990s) and the cross-party Calman Commission in the wake of its 2007 election victory. Conscious of looking like bad losers, the party swallowed its pride and nominated Nicola Sturgeon as the Scottish government's representative at the convention.

Otherwise the SNP had not, as some predicted, torn itself apart having failed to achieve its eighty-year-old *raison d'être*. Instead the iron discipline instilled by Alex Salmond as leader stood the party in good stead. Rather than scape-goat Sturgeon, who had nominally been the so-called 'yes minister', the umbrella group Yes Scotland got most of the blame for having run a lacklustre and often confused pro-independence campaign.

The focus also turned to the First Minister, who had, after all, driven the independence agenda for much of the last decade. 'Leave politics?' the journalist Iain Macwhirter had asked rhetorically. 'They'd have to drag him out of Bute House with wild horses.' And so it proved; not only had Salmond initiated the refurbishment of the old governor's mansion next to St Andrew's House to serve as his official residence – a pretty clear indication he intended to remain in post – but he presented the 40 per cent 'yes' vote as significant progress (most polls had shown support at around a third) and believed (privately) that he was still needed to 'stand up for Scotland'.

And so he remained, nearly sixty years old but still energetic, articulate and above all popular. Although the 2015 general election proved disappointing – the SNP polling its usual 20 per cent of the vote – the 2016 Holyrood campaign represented a third triumph for Salmond and his party, easily beating Labour, whose leader, Johann Lamont, had neglected the domestic front as a result of the referendum. And while the SNP no longer enjoyed an overall majority the Scottish Liberal Democrats, who had enjoyed a modest revival, agreed to form a coalition with the SNP now the independence issue had been laid to rest for the foreseeable future.

It was at that point, after a year or so of rather unimaginative domestic government, Salmond chose to bow out. His health was a factor, while retirement gave him an opportunity to make some serious money as an adviser (after becoming Sir Alex Salmond KT) to various energy companies. Nicola Sturgeon faced no serious opposition to succeed him, and took forward her predecessor's strategy of pushing for 'devo-max' while preaching social justice. After all, by 2020 the Scottish Parliament would have much wider powers over taxation and thus the ability to make a tangible impact on inequality. As the closest thing to a genuine social democrat in the SNP, the new First Minister was in her element.

Meanwhile at Westminster David Cameron had to grasp another referendum nettle, his promised in/out ballot on the UK's membership of the European Union. The debate echoed, in many ways, that experienced by Scotland a few years before, with advocates of 'British independence', chiefly the United Kingdom Independence Party (which had won the European Parliament elections in 2014 but failed to break through at Westminster in 2015), arguing the UK would be better off trying to become the 'Hong Kong of Europe', and others, led by the Prime Minister and new Labour leader Yvette Cooper, urging voters to accept a predictably underwhelming renegotiated settlement. Realistically, the UK government was never going to get much, but its beefed-up rebate and opt-outs on certain criminal justice regulations was just enough to make the pitch seem credible.

In the autumn of 2017, therefore, the UK voted to remain in the EU by a margin of 60/40, an exact replay of the Scottish independence referendum three years before. Although politically vindicated, Cameron faced a split party, around a third of his MPs having been completely unconvinced by what was known as the 'Brussels Agreement'. Just as the 1975 European referendum had eventually split the Labour Party, history repeated itself with the Conservatives.

All of which derailed David Cameron's government in the middle of his second term (he had formed a second coalition with the Liberal Democrats in 2015), allowing a reinvigorated – and more unified – Labour Party to return to office in 2020 with Cooper becoming the UK's second female Prime Minister. A year later Jenny Marra, long considered the bright young hope of the Scottish Labour Party, also succeeded Nicola Sturgeon as First Minister, meaning that both Scotland and the UK were under the same political stewardship for the first time since 2007. And with the Queen in the sixty-ninth year of her long reign, the UK had become a very matriarchal democracy.

Sturgeon, though capable and genuinely radical in some policy areas, had never quite sustained the Salmond stardust and, with her campaign for devo-max having failed to capture the imagination of activists – not to mention voters – the SNP lost the drive and discipline it had once enjoyed. And although the UK-wide Constitutional Convention convened in 2015 had, as Harold Wilson once remarked, taken minutes and wasted years, Labour, both in London and Edinburgh, finally decided to make a concerted push for a more coherent constitutional settlement for the whole of the United Kingdom.

As the Scottish Conservative leader, Ruth Davidson, had put it back in March 2013:

> We must find a means whereby we do not lurch from one commission to another, year after year; where the constitutional and commercial certainty we all crave is never reached. Where devolution is not viewed as a bilateral arrangement between Holyrood and Westminster, Cardiff Bay and Westminster or Stormont and Westminster. But a mechanism which reviews devolution across – and within – our whole United Kingdom.

Davidson had also described the 'much-derided and little-understood Barnett Formula' as, at that point, already being in 'its death-throes', and indeed by 2020 it had suffered death by a thousand cuts. When the Scottish Parliament gained the power to set its own 'Scottish rate' of tax in 2016 the block grant had been cut significantly, and again a few years later when complete control of income tax was devolved to Holyrood.

Following the UK government's belated response to the Silk Commission on the powers of the Senedd (or National Assembly for Wales) in 2014, Wales was set to receive similar powers, which made the case for extending control of income tax to the Northern Ireland Assembly unanswerable. By the 2020 general election, therefore, the Barnett Formula had become an indefensible relic of the *ancien régime*. A Conservative victory in 2015 had also given David Cameron a mandate to finally implement 'English Votes for English Laws', creating a 'fourth reading' for legislation judged by the Speaker to affect only the UK's largest component 'nation'.

Although this went some way to satisfying backbench

Tory MPs, it had done little to appease a growing sense of national identity (related in many ways to the growth of Euroscepticism) among the English. It also created two classes of MP, which ironically weakened the United Kingdom Parliament rather than strengthening it. And while demand for an English parliament had historically been low, by the time Yvette Cooper entered Downing Street she – and almost everybody else with political influence – realised something had to give.

Federalism had long been talked of as a logical answer to the Scottish Question, and indeed growing nationalist sentiment in other parts of the UK including, most recently, England. The 2015–17 Constitutional Convention, which reported shortly before the in/out referendum on the EU, had recommended a quasi-federal settlement for the UK, and it was this Cooper and Marra used as their proposed blueprint, calculating that the political climate post-2020 was as conducive to federalism as the 1997–98 period had been to devolution. It was all the more attractive because it enabled the political establishment to kill several birds with one stone, the House of Lords having stalled (yet again) during David Cameron's second term.

The journey towards a codified federal constitution would be controversial and slow, but the process had begun. David Melding, Presiding Officer of the Welsh Assembly since 2016, had first sketched out how a federal UK might work back in 2009, documents now regarded as a British version of *The Federalist Papers*. 'Federalism works', he had argued in 2012, 'because it is a *bargain*.'

No constitution is free of significant dissonance (and certainly not our present half-unitary, half-federal hybrid) and an imaginative leap is required where we concentrate more on the desired end rather than the intricate physics involved in jumping. If the abandonment of absolute parliamentary sovereignty is necessary to save the Union, then the simple question is whether Britain is worth the price. Happily, within wider British political experience, there is a latent, federal alternative that can accommodate this fundamental shift in constitutional thought. That alternative is parliamentary federalism. Most states that dissolve do so because the original organising ideal loses its efficacy and fails to strike an alternative bargain to rejuvenate the Union. We are fortunate indeed to have at hand a solution to our most urgent constitutional challenges.[3]

In 2020 the political classes, if not the electorate, decided it did want a new federal Union and, having finally abandoned its piecemeal approach to constitutional change, the unwritten British constitution was about to renew itself in a way many observers – not least Scottish Nationalists – had considered inconceivable just a decade before. As the Scottish commentator Bruce Anderson had once written, in politics 'fundamental changes occur far less often than excitable headline writers would have us believe'. 'Sometimes, however, there is a basic realignment. Often, the early stages are imperceptible. Then everyone realises that events have spun out of the politicians' control. The eventual outcome may not what be anyone would have wished, but nothing can be done. History has altered course.'[4]

By 2024, as the 'New Union' took shape, the SNP was relaxed about being on this side of history. It, like its sister party Plaid Cymru, had become increasingly attracted by the idea of federalism, especially the sort that combined, as David Melding had advocated, the best features of Unionism and Nationalism, which, after all, much of Alex Salmond's constitutional triangulation had leaned towards. At the same time it remained committed to what it still called 'independence', regarding federalism as simply another step along the gradualist route to that long-standing goal. First Minister

Jenny Marra, however, saw things very differently. 'I do not see a tide of nationalism sweeping this country,' was her judgement as she launched her Union reboot. 'We are not all nationalists now.'

The intervening years had also brought some clarity to all the usual arguments over the likely costs and benefits of independence. Having found itself on the back foot for much of 2012–14, particularly when questioned on points of detail, the SNP now believed itself to be much better prepared. Humza Yousaf often harked back to 1979 (although he had not been born until 1985), when Scotland voted for a Scottish Assembly but was robbed of devolution due to a spurious electoral threshold. And while the Unionist parties had taken the wind out of the SNP's sails by actually delivering more devolution in the wake of the 2014 referendum defeat, Yousaf nevertheless detected regret among a sizeable minority of Scots, a lingering guilt that they had rejected the opportunity of independence ten years before.

As Stephen Noon had written in June 2013, the 'no' campaign 'thinks its biggest strength is fear. However, its biggest weakness is an equally powerful emotion: regret.' He continued:

> Just think how we will feel if there is a 'no' vote; if in 2015 we get another government we didn't vote for; if in 2016 we're taken out of the European Union against our own expressed wishes; if in 2017 there are new welfare changes that introduce a lower rate of payment for people in Scotland; or if in 2018 we are still wasting £250 million a year on nuclear weapons. We'll regret the lost opportunity that was a Yes in 2014, with an intensity that will be brought to mind again and again. The pain of what could have been will go on.[5]

The SNP, therefore, regarded 2014 as 'unfinished business', an old song still very much in need of a new arrangement.

And Yousaf believed the political momentum was on his side, with Scotland about to become one of the new UK Federation's four 'Home Nations', a relatively buoyant economy and opinion polls showing consistent support for independence of about 40 per cent, rather than the 30–33 per cent of a decade before. Independence, he felt, was finally within touching distance.

He began his referendum push with a speech, a memorable address delivered by Yousaf on the tenth anniversary of the first referendum. 'Scotland has been on an incredible journey,' he began, 'particularly over the past ten years.'

We have been treading a vastly different path from the rest of the UK. Whether with the previous SNP–Lib Dem coalition's introduction of a North Sea oil fund or the current Scottish government's introduction of a living wage, we have managed to entrench social welfare and egalitarianism with the powers that we have. That is in complete contrast to the political landscape of the UK, where the NHS is slowly being privatised, even greater financial barriers to education are being erected and our civil liberties are being steadily eroded.

The evident truth is that we do things differently here in Scotland. Think what we could achieve if we had control over our entire economy, foreign affairs and defence. No longer would we have to spend hundreds of billions of pounds on pointless wars and weapons. Imagine how we could unleash in full that entrepreneurial thirst and egalitarian spirit. That is not to say that we are better than our neighbours. It is simply about being true to our traditional social democratic values.

Yousaf ended on a more ecumenical note. 'The debate about Scotland's future is much bigger than any political party or individual in this chamber or any other,' he said. 'It is about the people. It is about their hopes, their dreams, their ambitions and the chance to hand over a better nation to our children. I hope that we do not waste it.'[6] The second battle for Scotland – and indeed Britain – was about to begin.

CHAPTER 10

LOOKING BACK: SCOTLAND VOTES 'YES'

It is 2024 and Scotland is marking ten years since a slim majority of Scots voted 'yes' to independence in an historic referendum...

The relationship between our two countries has never been stronger or more settled, as complex or as important, as it is today.

Our citizens, uniquely linked by geography and history, are connected today as never before through business, politics, culture and sport, travel and technology, and of course family ties.

These vital human links are nowhere more evident than in the presence of a large, confident, valued and integrated Scottish community in Britain and in the increasing number of British people who now live and work in Scotland.

Our two economies benefit from a flow of people, goods, investment, capital and ideas on a scale that is rare even in this era of global economic integration.

We are partners in the European Union and firm supporters of the Single Market.

2024 also marks the beginning of a year of commemorations of the referendum in 2014 that helped shape our political destinies. This series of events offers us an opportunity to explore and reflect on key episodes of our past. We will do so in a spirit of historical accuracy, mutual respect, inclusiveness and reconciliation.

But we want to ensure that this is a decade not only of

remembering but also of looking forward; a decade of renewed and strengthened co-operation between our two countries.[1]
Joint statement by the UK Prime Minister, Michael Gove, and the Scottish Prime Minister, Nicola Sturgeon, 18 September 2024

The year is 2024, and Sir Alex Salmond is preparing to attend a series of celebrations to mark a decade since he led Scotland to independence. Also in attendance will be Queen Elizabeth, now in the seventy-second year of her record-breaking reign, who had not exactly been thrilled about the break-up of Great Britain, one half of her (formerly) United Kingdom. But then, she was a pragmatist who had witnessed dozens of former British colonies make the transition to self-government in the early years of her reign. As a gesture of goodwill – and in tacit recognition of the former First Minister's efforts to ensure she remained head of state in an independent Scotland – the Queen had invited him to join the Order of the Thistle in 2016.

As a staunch royalist and keen student of history, this honour had tickled Salmond, who in 2024 was approaching his seventieth birthday. He had presented it as proof that the 'social union' – pan-UK bonds of history, family and culture – would, as he had always predicted, endure even after Scotland became independent. Indeed, looking back to the independence referendum, as many did that day, it was striking how straightforward Scotland's departure from the Unions of 1707 and 1800 had been. Of course the negotiations had been arduous and often bad tempered, but nevertheless they had concluded by 31 March 2016 when, as planned, the Union flag had been swapped for a Saltire in a special midnight ceremony at Edinburgh Castle.

In a reprise of the 2011 Scottish Parliament election, the opinion polls had shifted dramatically in the few weeks before referendum day on 18 September 2014, reminding many of the 1995 Quebec sovereignty referendum when a consistent federalist lead had been whittled away to almost nothing by polling day, only in Scotland the number of 'yes' voters had been big enough to cross the winning line. But it had nevertheless been close. Contrary to expectations turn-out had only been 65 per cent despite a high-profile (and very long) referendum campaign, and with 50.5 per cent of those who turned out voting 'yes', that meant independence had been secured by just 32.8 per cent of the total electorate.

Better Together, the cross-party 'no' campaign led by the former Labour Chancellor Alistair (now Lord) Darling, had started well but lost ground (and credibility) with increasingly silly attacks on the possible consequences of independence during late 2013 and 2014, usually dismissed as 'scaremongering' by the SNP. Meanwhile Yes Scotland, aided by a summer of high-profile events – including a memorable Commonwealth Games in Glasgow – had stead-ily eroded its opponents' hitherto solid lead. By polling day 'yes' and 'no' were neck and neck.

The count at Edinburgh's Meadowbank Stadium had been nail-bitingly close and immediately controversial. In the City – again in an echo of the Quebec experience – the stock market took a tumble, sterling came under severe pressure and capital flight, caused by customers transfer-ring their savings from north to south, had increased from a pre-referendum trickle to a post-polling day flood. Several Labour MPs immediately challenged the validity of the result, arguing that barely a third of Scottish voters should not have been able to 'tear' Scotland out of the United Kingdom. There was even talk of the Labour Party fighting the 2015 general election on the basis of reversing the 2014 vote. As the former Canadian Prime Minister Jean Chrétien had put it, 'I *lose* my country because somebody loses *their glasses* on polling day? I have a problem with that.'

But such speculation had not lasted long. The Electoral

Commission, which had overseen the referendum process since October 2012, when Alex Salmond and David Cameron signed the Edinburgh Agreement, deemed the result free and fair, as had the usual team of international observers. The UK government also accepted, as the Agreement had stipulated, that it constituted 'a decisive expression of the views of people in Scotland' and agreed to start immediate negotiations with a diplomatically non-jubilant Scottish government. The First Minister had taken care to remind the Prime Minister of the Agreement's Paragraph 30, which had committed the two governments to continuing 'to work together constructively in the light of the outcome, whatever it is, in the best interests of the people of Scotland and of the rest of the United Kingdom'.

Although this had been deliberately vague, it had of course been in the interests of both Scotland and the rest of the UK to keep financial and political disruption to a minimum. The SNP's policy on retaining sterling was well known, and the UK government swiftly conceded the need for a formal currency union between the two countries, similar to those governing the Isle of Man and Channel Islands. And despite speculation that the Bank of England would impose strict fiscal conditions, not least on the Scottish government's plan to lower corporation tax, the expected 'fiscal sustainability' agreement had actually turned out to be reasonably flexible, although there was a *quid pro quo* in terms of public spending and a population share of the UK's ever-increasing debt pile.

This, which meant by mutual consent both the rest of the UK (rUK) *and* Scotland became successor states, also helped clear up the long-running dispute as to the latter's membership of the European Union. Brussels pragmatism had kicked in as soon as the outcome of the referendum became clear, with the European Commission hinting that parallel negotiations on the terms and conditions of Scotland's membership could begin from 'within' the United Kingdom. As with the currency union, this helped appease the financial markets, which, although nervous about Scottish independence right up until March 2016, more or less bounced back from their initial referendum day crisis.

The negotiations had been surprisingly amicable. As Sir Neil MacCormick had foreseen in 2001, the key was 'good will' on both sides:

> Why should England treat Scotland well if Scotland is in the process of departing from a union of three hundred years? If there were no other answer, such as English decency and a sense of fair play, the answer 'common self-interest' is a very obvious one. Any suggestion of a turbulent or resisted move to independence, or indeed any prolonged period of uncertainty about the stability and permanency of governments, is likely to cause severe loss of confidence internally to these islands and also overseas. That would be deeply damaging to everyone, as damaging in the City of London as in Glasgow or Edinburgh.[2]

A geographical share of North Sea oil, quickly conceded under scrutiny from the international community, provided the new state with a comfortable beginning, while a transitional period for the payment of benefits and pensions was agreed to minimise disruption to both Scottish and rUK claimants. Defence – never the SNP's strong point – proved more complicated. The Armed Forces did not take lightly the loss of billions of pounds' worth of hardware when Scotland gained a population share of its UK assets, and did its best to disrupt attempts at shared arrangements post-2016. NATO membership, meanwhile, proved a formality, although the Scottish government was forced to compromise on removal of Trident. Under huge international pressure, not least from the United States, it agreed to retain the present nuclear deterrent until 2035. It took all Salmond's powers of persuasion to avoid a split in his party, although Westminster's decision to foot the bill gave him useful wriggle room.

There was also the parallel business of writing a new constitution, a novelty for a country that, as part of the UK, had always muddled through on the basis of convention and precedent. This, as Deputy First Minister Nicola Sturgeon had promised before the referendum, had been 'a thoroughly inclusive process', as were the independence negotiations themselves, the Scottish government having included representatives from the Conservatives, Liberal Democrats and Labour Party in what was dubbed 'Team Scotland'. In a remarkable moment for hitherto tribal Scottish politicians, all of them had put their differences to one side and got down to the demanding task of securing the best deal for Scotland.

Queen Elizabeth, or as the SNP restyled her, 'Elizabeth, Queen of Scots', was of course a feature of that constitution, something that caused a degree of unhappiness among more republican Nationalists. But both countries viewed Her Majesty as a crucial source of continuity and, fulfilling her constitutional duty, she remained aloof from the proceedings. Of more direct concern had been her precise status in a newly independent Scotland. Although the Scottish government tried to argue the Presiding Officer of the Scottish Parliament should represent the Queen during her long absences from Scotland, Buckingham Palace had insisted upon appointing a governor general, citing decades of precedence around the world. Although Scotland was neither a dominion nor a former colony, the Queen acknowledged its special status by appointing as governor her daughter Princess Anne, a figure who met with broad approval from across Scottish society. The Queen, however, made a point of personally opening the first session of Scotland's newly independent Parliament in the summer of 2016.

But while the monarch continued her reign in two nations rather than one, the Prime Minister, who had until 2014 looked certain to beat Labour's Ed Miliband, never quite recovered from the loss of Scotland. Although English identity had been rising for the previous decade, public opinion also enjoyed residual feelings of Britishness and, combined with persistent discontent over the UK's membership of the European Union, began to turn against the Conservative Party, even though there were steady signs of economic recovery throughout 2014.

In the midst of the independence negotiations, therefore, Labour became the largest party in another hung Parliament when rUK went to the polls in 2015 (an election Scotland's fifty-nine MPs chose not to contest) and formed a 'partnership' with the Liberal Democrats, by then led by Vince Cable. The Labour–Lib Dem coalition had a slim overall majority but was ideologically more coherent than the previous administration. Europe, however, remained a boil in urgent need of lancing and, having belatedly committed to an in/out referendum before the general election, Labour stuck to the Conservatives' timetable of a ballot by the end of 2017.

By that point, Scotland had become the EU's twenty-ninth member state shortly after its formal declaration of independence in March 2016. Scottish independence, however, had led to an existential crisis in the rest of the UK, particularly England, further fuelling Euroscepticism. So by the time of the referendum – which reminded many commentators of the debate over Scottish independence – those wanting to reassert British 'independence' enjoyed a significant lead. Again it was close, and while the new Prime Minister tried hard to present the UK's 'renegotiated' settlement as a 'good deal for Britain' (as had another Labour leader, Harold Wilson, in 1975), voters were unconvinced and voted by a narrow margin to come out.

This provoked a constitutional crisis, not least in Wales

where a majority of voters had voted 'yes'. Indeed, the constitutional response to Scottish secession in 2016 – as in the case of the Irish Free State in 1922 – had been incremental and very slow. Reluctant to embark on an expensive rebranding of the country he governed, David Cameron simply kept its name and flag, although the United Kingdom's subheading (as in 1927) was eventually changed to 'of England, Wales and Northern Ireland'. Support for Welsh independence had increased slightly after Scotland left (though not by much), while Sinn Fein tried (unsuccessfully) to stage a reunification poll to coincide with the centenary of Ireland's Easter Rising.

Meanwhile Scotland adjusted to the realities – often uncomfortable – of being an independent country, even one with strong links to the rest of the UK and the European Union. In a speech following the referendum result Alex Salmond had tried to prepare Scots psychologically by stressing the bigger picture:

> This is a great opportunity; an historic opportunity. Having voted for independence we have a platform to mobilise our natural and human resources to build a very special society here in Scotland. Will everything be flowing with whisky and oil and will everything be perfect? No, it won't all be perfect; I dare say we'll make a few mistakes along the way. But that combination of these natural resources and the human talent and ingenuity of our people should give people confidence that they and their families will be better off.[3]

And while a second oil boom – as predicted by Salmond before the referendum – helped avert an economic crisis it did not mean, as the First Minister put it, that everything flowed with whisky and oil. The new Scottish Treasury still found financing its population share of the UK's national debt a huge burden, while demographic changes – regularly flagged up by Unionists in 2013/14 – also began to bite. John

Swinney, who remained Scotland's Finance Secretary after independence (the title 'Chancellor' was considered a pompous relic of the *ancien régime*), did his best to meet expectations but also had to make a series of difficult – and therefore unpopular – decisions. A North Sea oil fund, meanwhile, *was* established in order to fulfil a key pre-referendum pledge, but investment was painfully slow, a problem compounded by the rising cost of decommissioning after 2015/16.

Of course the SNP – which comfortably secured victory at the first independent Scottish elections in May 2016 – now controlled all significant tax-raising powers in Scotland, although that power often appeared more theoretical than real. Income tax, for example, generally stayed in line with the rest of the UK, although the SNP's flagship corporation tax cut enjoyed modest success. Swinney, meanwhile, used independence as an opportunity to simplify Scotland's tax collection and regulatory arrangements. Although initially costly, it eventually resulted in significant savings.

The UK economy had also bounced back (finally) from its prolonged post-2008 recession, which – given how integrated the Scottish economy remained with the rest of the British Isles – naturally benefited Scotland too. Anticipating rUK's withdrawal from the EU, meanwhile, the Scottish government had finally announced plans to create its own currency (to be called, all in the name of continuity, the Scottish pound), thus avoiding the obvious difficulties associated with being tied to the monetary policy of a country now firmly on the EU exit route. Again this was not easy but, having demonstrated fiscal probity in the first few years of independence, the international markets (largely unimpressed at the UK's impending departure from the EU) looked more kindly on Scotland's plans.

Domestic politics, meanwhile, shaped up to become – like Ireland post-1922 – a prolonged battle between two competing records of nationalism resulting from the sides taken in the independence referendum of 2014. Labour was inevitably cast as the 'anti-independence' party (despite its significant role in delivering a Scottish Parliament) while the SNP saw themselves as de Valera-style Soldiers of Destiny. Brian Wilson, the former Labour MP and minister (and thorn in the side of Nationalists), called it 'de-politicised politics',

> a squabble over votes between two conservative parties, whose support has always been tribal, rather than based on any more creative social dynamic ... The SNP is Scotland's Fianna Fail. Big tent, non-ideological, populist, everything to be resolved through constitutional change, unembarrassed by where its money comes from since Scottish millionaires are, by definition, part of the same big happy family as the rest of us. And what better-equipped Soldier of Destiny to lead this regiment of Jock Tamson's Bairns than General Salmond?[4]

A few years into the independence project, however, Sir Alex Salmond was no longer as well equipped as he had been in his prime. Prevailed upon by the 'men in grey kilts' (as the SNP minister Mike Russell had once called them) to retire before he became unpopular and unwell, he made way for his heir apparent, Nicola Sturgeon, amid generous tributes and scholarly assessments of his life and legacy.

Radical policy-making, never of much interest to a born tactician like Salmond, had naturally played second fiddle to keeping the 'new' Scotland financially sound. A Scottish Cabinet paper leaked in advance of the referendum had warned of a climate of austerity as Scotland got to grips with its new-found autonomy, while an authoritative paper prepared by the Scottish government's Fiscal Commission Working Group had also hinted at further pressure on public spending.

All that had come to pass, and of course it took many Scots – indeed the majority of the country who had either voted 'no' or not at all – time to reconcile themselves to an often harsh new constitutional reality. As the authors of a 2013 book on the referendum had predicted, the 'most significant effects would be psychological and cultural and might take years to become clear'.[5]

None of this made Sturgeon's premiership easy. Although capable and probably more in tune with mainstream Scottish opinion than her predecessor, she lacked Sir Alex's panache and had the misfortune to take over the governor's mansion (converted into a First Ministerial residence by Salmond) just as public opinion had grown tired of the party and its leadership. They had, after all, been around for a very long time. Familiarity had bred not exactly contempt, but low-level apathy.

When Holyrood went to the polls in 2021, therefore, Labour's Jenny Marra looked fresh and new, relaxed about Scotland's new status but not as prone to blaming London for perceived interference in Edinburgh's tax and spending plans (the currency union had recently come under repeated strain, particularly after the Scottish government announced plans to quit sterling). Labour set out to restore relations with Michael Gove's government at Westminster, something made slightly easier by the Prime Minister's Aberdonian roots.

Nevertheless, Sturgeon was still present at the banquet on 18 September 2024, and delivered a memorable speech that won plaudits for its eloquence and historical sweep:

As a nation, we have done a lot of exploring – we were a sovereign, independent country, and then gave our independence away. We helped to build an empire, and saw it decay. We transformed a rural economy into the workshop of the world – and then watched as the work left. We discovered oil and stood by as the revenues were spent by others ... Politically, we have been a Liberal stronghold. We have voted Tory in huge numbers – hard though it is to believe that now. We have been a bastion for the Labour Party. We have argued over our best form of government for centuries and after three hundred years without it now have our own parliament. A parliament that was intended to kill demand for independence stone dead, but ended up governed by a pro-independence majority. And in 2014 a nation many believed would never leave the United Kingdom voted to do precisely that.[6]

Indeed, Scotland, much like Ireland in 1922, had demonstrated that the secession of one part of a modern, successful welfare state – unprecedented in the modern era – was achievable. Nevertheless it was not always easy. The 2016 independence 'settlement' had left control of Scotland's monetary policy and energy market in the hands of a government no longer directly answerable to Scottish voters, while the new country's defence capability, banking system and trade regime were, more than ever before, heavily guided by NATO and the European Union. But, again like Ireland, few seriously sought to reverse Scotland's 'sovereignty' now it had been secured – no matter how often the reality of self-determination departed from the theory.

CONCLUSION

STANDS SCOTLAND WHERE IT DID?

Writing shortly before another Scottish referendum in 1979, William McIlvanney looked back on four years of debate about devolution, 'where every quibble was a Russian doll of other quibbles'. 'Passion', he judged, 'was neutered by boredom.' The novelist also highlighted the contradictions in both Scotland ('a country nominally Socialist and blatantly conservative') and the SNP ('recognisable features but no coherent identity'), although he argued that whatever 'mists' obscured the party's 'essential position in the political spectrum', the choice at hand remained 'separable from them'.

He could have been describing the remarkably similar debate that gripped Scottish (and to a lesser extent UK) politics between May 2011 and September 2014; indeed the journalist Neal Ascherson said the independence referendum was 'little more than the third putting of the same question'.[1] But in 1979 it was not to be. With SNP support having peaked in 1978, those backing that choice – a devolved Scottish Assembly – fell short of the necessary 40 per cent of the electorate as stipulated by the 1978 Scotland Act. McIlvanney had feared such an outcome. 'I think', he had written, 'a lot of us are feart.' After the result the *Glasgow Herald* ran a cartoon of the Scottish lion, no longer rampant but cringing in a corner; the caption read simply: 'I'm feart.'

McIlvanney revisited this motif a few days later in a poem

called 'The Cowardly Lion', imagining its keepers dreaming up ways to prevent it escaping. 'It wanted freedom,' wrote McIlvanney. 'Why not give it some, extend its compound but still keep it trapped?' So its compound was extended, every stone of which was 'argued over fiercely'. And when the day of 'freedom' came, the lion's keepers watched as it emerged, 'its snout raised to the wind':

> It smelt the terrible distances of freedom,
> It felt the risk of being not confined,
> It knew the pain of hunger unassuaged,
> It sensed the emptiness where self is found,
> It heard the bitterness where life is waged.
> Slowly the keepers relaxed into a smile
> And giggled and nodded again, were winking while
> Those who loved the lion had nothing to say.
> For the lion had turned to its cage and slunk away
> And lives still among stinking straw today.[2]

Such bleak imagery reflected the genuine disappointment felt by many at the failure to secure devolution in 1979, a feeling that Scots had been presented with an opportunity for self-advancement but somehow bottled it. Although this was exaggerated – the sense of loss being more acute among the chattering classes than the population at large – it nevertheless shaped Scottish politics for the next thirty-five years; a mood so potent that even after a Scottish Parliament was finally established in 1999 (and endowed with greater powers in 2012) proponents of full independence still harked back to that day in 1979 when, as they argued, Westminster, the Labour government or even the Union – the guilty party had many guises – had *let Scotland down*.

The creation of a Scottish Parliament twenty years later was supposed to provide some historical closure. In another poem for the *Herald*, McIlvanney said the Scottish lion was a 'kittlin' (kitten) again:

> It micht grow tae be mauchty an gurly
> An staun as a stell o the guid
> But juist noo it needs nae hurly-burly
> For it's feart and its wee een are hid
> An its roar's like a wean cryin oot for its ain
> For the lion's a kittlin again.[3]

But even now the Scottish lion's cage had been extended, support for independence did not significantly increase. The desire for more powers did, but then that had been the direction of travel since the 1970s. For the majority of Scots, who wanted neither independence nor the status quo, devolution was the obvious path to take, and once that had been delivered, they wanted more of it. Scotland was caught in a sort of constitutional limbo.

Instead, Nationalists and Unionists increasingly fought over this middle ground, the former restyling themselves nationalist Unionists, who spoke of more devolution, and the latter unionist Nationalists, increasingly inclined towards confederalism. Both accepted the UK would best function with some powers shared and others devolved; the only disagreement was over the extent of each. Indeed, at points Alex Salmond appeared to be arguing *against* independence: when it came to currency, monarchy and energy he claimed Scotland and the UK were Better Together, only he did not use that language. Rather, both sides spoke of Scotland having 'the best of both worlds'.

In reality the best of both worlds was actually something neither side wanted: an SNP-controlled Scottish government operating within a UK led by its Unionist opponents, be they red, yellow or blue. This, as the 2011 election demonstrated, suited most Scots, who wanted a team of competent ministers to 'stand up for Scotland', but within the constitutional status quo. As the journalist Ian Bell put it, 'Dissatisfaction with the Union is evident; enthusiasm for the alternative offered is muted.'

Thus in the best of both worlds, Unionists had to accommodate Nationalism and vice versa, although it was Nationalists – particularly populist Nationalists – who thrived most in the halfway house of devolution, claiming credit for policy successes and pinning any failures on the *ancien régime*. This phenomenon cut across party lines, practitioners including not just Alex Salmond but Carwyn Jones in Wales and Boris Johnson in London, Labour and Conservative small 'n' nationalists who stood up for the interests of their fiefdoms, often in opposition to their own parties and, naturally enough, Westminster.

Scotland, via the old Scottish Office, was a veteran practitioner of this constitutional game, successive Scottish Secretaries having wielded the threat of Nationalism, exerting pressure from within to gain greater expenditure and political representation. After 2007, when the SNP penetrated the citadels of hitherto Liberal-, Conservative- and Labour-dominated Scottish politics, the concessions continued to flow: more powers, less punitive (relatively speaking) spending cuts and, above all, political attention, thus the historian Peter Hennessy's belief that Scotland would continue to 'be to the UK what Quebec is to Canada and the UK is to the European Union, the awkward one spewing out a constant drizzle of complaint but never pushing it to the point of rupture'.[4]

And the SNP, a much more subtle movement than its opponents often gave it credit for, had long ago reconciled itself to the fact that political 'sovereignty' was limited and the likely enthusiasm of electors muted.[5] Initially it acknowledged this by lobbying for dominion status within the British Empire, a proposition that owed something to the 'Imperial

Federation' of which Joseph Chamberlain (and others) had dreamed in the early twentieth century, while in 1956 a joint SNP, Plaid Cymru and Common Wealth Party publication advocated what it called 'Confraternity', an association of free and equal nations within a wider Commonwealth.[6]

By the 1970s the SNP, electorally successful for the first time, began fashioning a 'Council of the Isles' to manage this co-operative relationship, while its Westminster leader, Donald Stewart, went so far as to say Nationalists had no intention of seeking the 'Break-up of the United Kingdom'.[7] In the late 1980s the party – later than most – embraced the European Union, though preferring to emphasise its confederal elements rather than its commitment to 'ever closer union'. So political Nationalism in Scotland, setting aside its most hardline fringe elements, had always acknowledged the need for a supra-national security blanket. Thus Alex Salmond's concept of Scotland's 'six unions', five of which he wished to retain, was but the natural extension of eighty years of SNP thinking, although one that presented supporters of independence with a strategic challenge: having framed the debate on its opponents' terms, it seemed unlikely that Nationalists would ever out-unionist Unionists, just as no one under the Better Together umbrella could ever hope to out-nationalist seasoned pros like Salmond, no matter how much they emphasised their 'Scottishness' and 'patriotism'.

But if Unionists caricatured Nationalists as inflexible fundamentalists, then the reverse was also true, with supporters of independence depicting their opponents as closet abolitionists, intent on clawing back power at every opportunity. Yet any reading of twentieth-century Scottish politics showed the reverse to be true: not only had the Conservatives been instrumental in gradually devolving administrative power to Scotland after 1885, but Labour had tried (and failed) to deliver devolution in 1979 and tried again (successfully) in 1997. And far from clinging fiercely to its sovereignty, Parliament had ceded it repeatedly, most notably to Ireland (in 1922), Brussels (in 1973) and even Canada (in 1982). The use of referendums to decide constitutional issues had also recognised, for more than forty years, that people in various parts of the UK were sovereign rather than the Westminster parliament.

Similarly, Westminster had always – albeit reluctantly – acknowledged the right of different parts of the (much misunderstood) United Kingdom to secede. In 1922 the Irish Free State's secession was negotiated, surprisingly amicably after much bloodshed (and with more to follow), while in 1973 the then novel use of a referendum in the six counties of Ulster acknowledged that the province could follow suit if a majority so desired, a concession reiterated in the 1993 Downing Street Declaration and 1998 Good Friday Agreement. In that context the Edinburgh Agreement of October 2012 was not a novelty, but very much in the British constitutional tradition.

The crucial issue was public support. In 1922 it was obvious which route southern Ireland wished to take, just as it was in British colonies after the Second World War. As the Anglo-Scottish Conservative Prime Minister Harold Macmillan acknowledged in the context of Africa, 'the growth of national consciousness is a political fact', although in Scotland it was never that clear-cut: support for devolution was not the same as a desire for independence (although they were often conflated). 'For separation to succeed', observed the 1973 Royal Commission on the Constitution, 'it must command the general support of the people concerned. If it is not widely supported it is a complete non-starter; if it has that support, then even the most serious economic obstacles will not be allowed to stand in its way.'[8] If a nation, in other words, truly coveted independence, then details – even important economic ones – ought to present no barrier.

Seldom had opinion polls, or indeed election results,

demonstrated anything approaching majority support for independence in Scotland, a rather important fact often overlooked by proponents and commentators, who also missed many of the nuances when it came to dealing with the Scottish Question. In 2011–14 all the talk was of Unionists and Nationalists advocating, respectively, 'the Union' and 'independence', when in reality the meaning of both those constitutional options had changed almost beyond recognition. So the question to be put on 18 September 2014 – 'Should Scotland be an independent country?' – looked a little odd, particularly in the absence of any qualification. It was actually a straight choice between two constitutional visions that contained multitudes, glorious contradictions.

Both sides ended up attempting to escape from this political straitjacket. Unionists, conscious that the events of 1979 still cast a long, bitter shadow, emphasised that voting 'no' did not mean 'no change', while Nationalists, equally conscious that public opinion still was not on side, presented 'independence' as a Middle Way between full sovereignty and the 1997 devolution settlement. Thus the 2012–14 referendum campaign involved an exceedingly rich and complex array of discourse, a 21st-century echo of the 'pamphlet wars' that preceded the 1707 Act of Union. The Scottish Green MSP Patrick Harvie referred to voters being bombarded with a 'blizzard of factoids', although there was often more heat than light.

There was also a quixotic desire for 'neutral information', although as the journalist Peter Geoghegan pointed out, differences of politics and economics, of competing social visions, could not be 'solved' like a scientific problem. 'It is possible that atomic theory could be demonstrated to be false,' he wrote, 'it is not possible to show empirically that Scotland would be a happier/fairer/richer/safer country (delete as appropriate) with or without independence.'[9]

At points the respective campaigns appeared to be travelling around the country, as Willie Whitelaw once said of

Harold Wilson, stirring up apathy. A big part of the problem was engaging voters so far ahead of the actual vote. Better Together and Yes Scotland were launched in the summer of 2012, more than two years before decision day in the autumn of 2014. For strategists used to the strictures of a four- or five-week election campaign, this proved problematic, and often they indulged in vague generalities, dancing on pinheads and scraping rhetorical barrels, often (one suspected) to fill time.

Yes Scotland took its cue from Voltaire, generating the impression that independence offered the best of all possible worlds, with only fleeting acknowledgement of the potential downsides, while Better Together preferred to cultivate its garden, eschewing optimistic visions and gloomily observing that while independence was possible it would not necessarily be desirable. But if Unionists were too negative, then Nationalists were overly positive, often retreating into hyperbole – mainly concerning the riches that might befall ordinary Scots – inviting easy derision and most likely incredulity from voters already suspicious of 'jam tomorrow' pledges (Better Together claimed that SNP spending promises since 2012 totalled at least £32 billion).

A tired old fixture of Scottish politics, the conflation of policy goals with constitutional change, also dominated much of the debate, with the SNP frequently soft-soaping the electorate, particularly those on the left, by arguing that a 'yes' vote was simply a means to an end, and that once independence had been secured 'the Scottish people', rather than an independent Scottish government, would decide what policies they wished to pursue.

That argument, however, could not easily be squared with a constant enunciation of policies – on everything from the monarchy to consumer regulation – which culminated with a white paper, the 'independence prospectus', in the autumn of 2013, which specifically referred to a post-referendum scenario. On the one hand voters were told independence was the *only way* to banish Trident, preserve the welfare state and avoid a Tory government, while on the other they were informed that in 2016, when the first elections to an independent Scottish Parliament took place, every outcome – which presumably included retaining Trident, cutting welfare and electing a Tory government – would be up for grabs. Both Yes Scotland and the SNP struggled to separate the *principle* of independence from the *practice*.

There were similar contradictions among those making the contrary case. The UK government's impressively thorough 'Scotland Analysis' series was undoubtedly a comprehensive survey of the Union and its benefits, although of course it could not guarantee that future Westminster governments would necessarily preserve all it described. It also did not constitute a *philosophical* defence of political and economic union per se; rather it was an excessively utilitarian approach which was often just as easily picked apart as the SNP's wilder claims. The redistributionist, pan-UK welfare state was posited as an argument for the Union, yet at the same time a Conservative–Liberal Democrat coalition and its Labour opposition were generally agreed that benefits had to be reformed, cut, refashioned and so on. In that context, Nationalists could legitimately argue, were Scotland and the UK really 'Better Together'?

The constant claims and counterclaims of government publications also masked the dearth of new policy ideas that generally afflicted both Scottish and UK politics. Yes Scotland and the Scottish government pitched things in general terms, promising a better welfare state or economic strategy, for example, but falling short when it came to high-lighting specific proposals. There was endless talk of 'social democracy', a term rendered meaningless by political parties – both Nationalist and Unionist – who defined it along low-tax and high-spend lines. It did not help that the Scottish government often faced in two directions at once, on welfare (anti-bedroom tax but pro-benefit cap), on defence (anti-Trident but pro-nuclear-powered submarines), hereditary privilege (anti-House of Lords but pro-monarchy) and the economy (anti-inequality but pro-neo-liberal economics). As Patrick Harvie put it, 'People used to accuse the Liberal Democrats of being all things to all people, but they were never as good at it as the SNP are.'[10]

At times Salmond's Scotland looked suspiciously like a Little Britain: low tax, 'business-friendly', entrepreneurial, dedicated to keeping everything fundamentally the same but tweaking it round the edges, in other words nothing close to the 'comprehensive assault' on the neo-liberal status quo urged by the First Minister's own economic adviser Joseph Stiglitz. As Gregor Gall argued, even with the most radical will in the world (and the SNP often claimed to be 'radical'), there were 'distinct limits' to the extent to which 'Scottish solutions' could solve problems in Scotland – Scottish or otherwise – largely because the Scottish economy was 'very much part of a capitalist world economy and subject to the same dynamics and ebbs and flows as other parts of the global economy'.[11]

And often there was a feeling of déjà vu, a rerun of the arguments deployed in favour of devolution in the late 1970s and again in the 1990s. Paradoxically, it was essentially a conservative pitch: just as it had been suggested devolution would protect Scots from Thatcherite change in the 1980s, independence was presented as the means by which to protect the sons and daughters of Thatcher from neo-liberal orthodoxy in the early twenty-first century. And, as in the 1970s and 1990s, it was all too tempting for advocates of independence or greater devolution to pose as political visionaries, as if constitutional change was a substitute for detailed policy-making.

As Nye Bevan once thundered, implying that engrained

economic problems could be solved through constitutional change was 'not socialism', it was 'escapism', a means by which a politician or political party could avoid tackling much bigger and infinitely more challenging problems. Indeed, it was telling that in the midst of the referendum debate, a compelling and original vision of a post-2008 Scotland (or indeed UK) failed to emerge, both sides simply reheating orthodox economic and social arguments.

The First Minister made strenuous efforts to separate policy and process, arguing that independence was not an end in itself, but a means to an end. But if 'independence' was somehow incidental to the SNP's aims, then why not advocate independence for the northern half of the UK rather than just Scotland, or for the western part of Scotland from the east? After all, arguments based on economics and equality applied as much to Shetland or Glasgow as they did to Scotland in general. There was no reason why a utilitarian argument for independence ought to stop at Berwick-upon-Tweed.

So, buried beneath arguments that self-consciously rejected Nationalism were, in essence, rather old-fashioned *Nationalist* arguments, only these took different forms. Fundamentally, argued Salmond, the Scottish economy would be 'run better by people who live in Scotland than those who don't',[12] a statement which suggested a rather touching faith in innate Scottish good sense that flew in the face of experience both historic (the disastrous Darien scheme, for example) and contemporary (RBS). It could not be assumed that a Scottish Treasury would necessarily be cleverer and wiser than an English one, while as D. I. MacKay concluded in a 1977 book about the economics of independence, 'in the long run economic growth is never a function of a particular constitutional arrangement, but the product of the temper of a people and the policies they pursue'.[13]

Depictions of Scots (from both sides) as desiccated calculating machines, liable to ditch support for the Union or acquire a longing for independence on the basis of £500 or projected oil revenues, were neither convincing nor particularly edifying. Such arguments also contradicted the widespread acceptance (by both Nationalists and Unionists) that there existed an identifiable set of 'Scottish values', which of course implied superiority – often stated in moral terms – over English, Welsh and Northern Irish 'values'. But then it was easy to push this point given that Scotland had diverged from England politically and electorally since the 1970s, while at the same time converging with the rest of the UK in economic and social terms. It also suited the SNP to present Scottish 'problems' as homogeneous, the same from the oil-rich north-east to post-industrial Clydeside, something that made as much sense as arguing that all parts of England – whether north or south, rural or urban – shared the same political sympathies and economic characteristics.

In truth, no one could emerge victorious from a battle over statistics and hypothetical scenarios. But what the referendum microscope exposed were weaknesses in the philosophies of both Nationalism *and* Unionism. With September 2014 looming, both sides were compelled to justify their *raisons d'être* as never before. This was more pronounced on the Unionist side, an ideology (such as it was) unused to defending itself and no longer, as Iain McLean and Alistair McMillan argued, 'masked by its usefulness to politicians and its popular appeal'.[14]

Steadily weakened by the loss of Ireland in 1922 (a major body-blow to 'Unionism', as defined in 1886) and most of the British Empire in the decades that followed, by the 1970s 'Unionism', by virtue of events in Northern Ireland, had acquired negative, even violent connotations. Thereafter it lapsed into what Richard Rose called 'unthinking Unionism', a corollary of Michael Billig's 'banal nationalism'. 'Political authority is not to be won once and for all, like a victory in some distant battle of the past,' judged Rose. 'Instead, it must be reaffirmed every day.'[15]

Ernst Renan called this a 'daily referendum', rather than the once-in-a-generation vote (to use Salmond's chronology) planned for September 2014. While Unionism still lived and breathed in certain areas, most visibly in the redistributive (and inherently left-wing) welfare state, it still lacked an overarching narrative. Although David Cameron, leader of the Conservative *and Unionist* Party, made a better fist than most of articulating modern Unionism, it was undermined by his government's all-too-typical *ad hoc* approach to constitutional policy, proceeding at different speeds in Wales, Northern Ireland, Scotland and above all England – where the pace was glacial.

This vacuum was – paradoxically – filled by Nationalists, increasingly keen to locate their independence project in the context of wider structures. Indeed an intriguing sub-narrative of the referendum debate was the tendency by some pro-independence campaigners to reject 'Nationalism' altogether, stressing practical rather than less tangible motivations, while the SNP zealously rejected dictionary definitions of 'separatism'. Equally, however, Unionist attacks on 'Nationalism' as a political creed were hypocritical given that Unionism was itself a form of nationalism, asserting the primacy of the British (rather than Scottish) state, a feature – as the political scientist Michael Keating argued – that became more obvious when 'faced with challenges from within (from Scottish nationalism) and without (from European integration)'.[16]

But if Nationalism was an ideology (and this was a moot point among those who dwelled on such things) it remained essentially an opportunistic one – often a solution in search of a problem. Inevitably, that problem (or issue) changed from decade to decade. In the 1970s it was North Sea oil, in the 1980s Margaret Thatcher, in the 1990s a booming economy, in the 2000s opposition to 'illegal wars' in Iraq and, by the 2010s, a combination of all those things. In historical context, therefore, it became hard to pinpoint the rationale for independence between 1934, when the SNP had been founded, and, say, 1967, when Winnie Ewing captured Hamilton in a by-election. The point was that Nationalists had campaigned for 'independence' long before the Iraq War, the discovery of North Sea oil and Thatcherism, so the desire for change went much deeper than transient policy objectives or objectionable Prime Ministers.

Scottish Nationalism also lacked a convincing precedent for dismantling a modern, democratic welfare state free of religious, political or economic repression. As Alex Salmond stated in the foreword to the Scottish government consultation paper *Your Scotland, Your Referendum*, 'Scotland is not oppressed and we have no need to be liberated'. But if that was true, what then was the compelling case for independence? As the former *Economist* editor Bill Emmott argued, the SNP leader often failed to define 'the problem to which independence is the solution'.[17]

Talk of 'sovereignty', meanwhile, only took advocates of independence so far, for in practical terms the economic crisis of 2007–08 had rendered such abstract concepts virtually meaningless. Would an independent Scotland (and, for that matter, Ireland or the UK) within the European Union be truly sovereign? Would an independent Scotland in a currency union with the rest of the UK possess full 'self-determination'? Perhaps in an academic sense it might, but politics was of course about the art of the possible, not the art of the *theoretically* possible.

Arguing that independence was 'inevitable', meanwhile, made as much sense as claiming the United Kingdom would last forever. As the historian J. G. A. Pocock observed, future historians might 'find themselves writing of a "Unionist" or even a "British" period' in history, located 'between a date in the thirteenth, the seventeenth or the nineteenth century, and a date in the twentieth or the twenty-first'.[18] Multinational states came and went, just as small independent nations might opt to join larger political units.

Curiously, both campaigners and commentators seemed keen to play down the role of *emotion* in such debates, although it seemed clear that *sentiment* was as important to many voters as their bank balances. As the urban activist Jane Jacobs observed of Canada and Quebec in 1980, 'emotions are deeply felt by separatists, and they are felt equally deeply by those who ardently oppose separatists'. 'The conflicts are not between different kinds of emotions,' she added. 'Rather, they are conflicts between different ways of identifying the nation, different choices as to what the nation is.'[19]

Instinct was also important. 'To its adherents the nationalist goal is a self-evident moral truth', wrote the playwright Kevin Toolis, 'that reaches far beyond rational argument, personal ambitions or petty quibbles about economics', while Iain McLean and Alistair McMillan argued that Unionism 'may be either primordial or instrumental'. 'A Unionist … is primordial if he/she/it regards the Union as a value in and of itself,' they wrote. 'A Unionist is instrumental if he/she regards the Union as good because it has good consequences.'[20]

In truth, both proponents and opponents of independence were driven by a combination of what Sir Neil MacCormick called 'existential' and 'utilitarian' concerns, just as, in a UK context, were those who advocated British 'independence' from the European Union. Perhaps surprisingly, it was David Cameron who proved willing to concede that the argument, and its eventual solution, would rest upon issues of both 'head and heart'. The Scottish lion, after all, was an emotional as well as an intelligent creature.

Jane Jacobs's observation underlined another important, although seldom acknowledged, point, that the Scottish constitutional question did not exist in isolation. As Karl Marx had observed in 1852, both sides conjured 'up the spirits of the past to their service and borrow from them names, battle cries and costumes in order to present the new scene of world history in this time-honoured disguise and this borrowed language'.[21] Other western nations – most notably Canada and Spain – had experienced similar debates within the last forty years. Although naturally the detail and geography differed, there were nevertheless parallels in terms of how 'independence' within each of those states had been conceived and presented to their respective electorates. The Quebec experience informed both Yes Scotland and Better Together. Nationalists essentially combined Parti Québécois strategy from the 1980 and 1995 referendums: a redefined notion of 'sovereignty', an emphasis on shared links with the rest of the UK and 'democracy'. The Unionists, meanwhile, took a leaf out of the federalist playbook, attacking the concept of 'independence' on offer as fraudulent and potentially damaging while promising more powers, something only conceded at the last moment in the second Quebec referendum.

Canada offered Scottish Nationalists much food for thought, for crucial in the narrowing of polls prior to the 1995 referendum had been the gradual persuasion of public opinion that continued partnership with the rest of Canada after 'separation' was both plausible and practical. If Yes Scotland and the SNP were able to convince Scots that a continued regal, currency and social union was realistic in the event of a 'yes' vote, then they would be on to something – although for the same reason, the UK government (just like Canadian federalists) was equally keen to emphasise that such an approach assumed too much. The 1995 referendum, of course, had not been won and thereafter Quebec separatism had gone into retreat (polling between 30 and 32 per cent, rather than its pre-1995 level of 45 per cent). As the former Liberal leader Michael Ignatieff reflected, after 1995 'Canadians were able to joke that what Quebeckers really wanted was an independent Quebec inside a united Canada'. 'I suspect a majority of Scots want something similar,' he added, 'independence plus the pound, a "social union" in place of a political union; sovereignty, in other words, without its economic or psychological costs.'[22]

Quebec also offered pointers for likely SNP strategy post-2014. A 'yes' vote would obviously look after itself, with the National Movement the inevitable benefactors, but even in the event of a 'no' vote Alex Salmond – like the Parti Québécois' Louis Bouchard – could probably rise above a referendum defeat and continue to govern Scotland at a devolved level. As the journalist Eddie Barnes speculated, 'The day after, far from engaging in in-fighting, the SNP accepts the verdict with good grace and pledges to get back to work, focusing in the short-term on the gradual extension of powers for Scottish ministers.'[23]

In that context, the dream of certain Labour Unionists that Scottish politics would somehow revert to a mythical 'norm' following a 'no' vote was fanciful. The divergence of Scottish electoral politics was already half a century old and looked set to continue, accompanied by a general Northern Irish (Sinn Fein), Welsh (Plaid Cymru) and English (UKIP) trend towards electoral support for anyone but the established parties. So continued electoral success at a devolved level was the SNP's medium-term goal, with another referendum, timed at a propitious moment à la Quebec, undoubtedly a long-term aspiration. In summer 2013 the US polling guru Nate Silver stated the then orthodox view that the 'yes' campaign had 'virtually no chance' of victory, making the reasonable point that support for a change proposition usually retreated in advance of polling day (Quebec in 1995 confirmed rather than contradicted this rule).

Of course, that might change. But Silver suggested only

a 'major crisis', most likely originating in England, could conceivably alter that dynamic prior to September 2014. Looking ahead, it was difficult to envisage any disruptive events, but then that was the nature of political prediction, which, as Silver wrote elsewhere, was as unreliable as it was extensive. The magic figure for 'yes' campaigners was around 33 per cent, that being the figure generally accepted as representing support for independence, so in order to demonstrate progress, Nationalists needed to get above that figure. A 40 per cent 'yes' vote would be good for the Scottish government, roughly what the Parti Québécois managed in 1980. Although still a decisive defeat, it could easily be explained away on the basis of a relentlessly negative 'no' campaign and the full might of the British state.

But even an emphatic Unionist majority would represent a reprieve rather than a victory. Anti-separatists in Canada had the relative flexibility of a properly federal state and well-developed pan-Canadian ideology; their UK counterparts were unlikely to enjoy that luxury in their attempts to win the peace in the closing months of 2014. What then of the solution? Although formal federalism (or perhaps confederalism) was often dismissed as a Liberal pipedream (as if full 'independence' was tidier and more achievable), it struck many protagonists and commentators as a sensible compromise, the logical conclusion of both nationalist Unionism and unionist Nationalism. 'Does the UK become a federal state, or does it break up?' David Marquand asked in mid-2013. 'It would be nice to think we shall do better than our great-grandparents did.'[24]

It was hardly an original idea, as Marquand suggested, owing much to the 'Home Rule all Round' as envisaged by Liberals (and many Conservatives) a century earlier. England was of course the elephant in the room, although not an immovable one.[25] After all, English 'regions' clearly existed when it came to the Barnett Formula, in terms of regional development and so on, just not as strongly in the public consciousness. England, meanwhile, was no longer as dominant as it had been in the unreformed, pre-1999 UK.

Whatever the problems, a more holistic approach to constitutional reform in the UK was long overdue, a point acknowledged among the independence debate's more thoughtful protagonists. Whether the UK political classes possessed the imagination, and indeed willingness, to invest the necessary political capital in such a scheme was another matter, although it could be presented as in keeping with the British constitutional tradition. The creation of northern and southern Irish parliaments in 1920, for example, had been federal in nature, while the British–Irish Council, however much of a talking shop, demonstrated that co-operation between the British Isles' eight governments was feasible.

And while the Good Friday Agreement of 1998 had been forged in a very different context, it offered a template that could be extended across the UK: an acknowledged right to secede and cross-border consultation all underpinned by a spirit of goodwill. These were positives that had arisen from a decades-old negative. More to the point, federalism might give moribund Unionist ideology a *raison d'être* fit for the twenty-first century, a rationale capable of matching Nationalism in terms of spiritual appeal, proactively arguing for a new Act of Union that clearly codified the relationship between central, devolved and local government. 'It is more important to promote a new Union', argued the Welsh Tory Unionist thinker David Melding, 'rather than obdurately defend the old.'[26]

The other alternatives had obvious flaws. 'Devo-max' was the biggest red herring, presented as unilateral federalism by some and a fiscally neutral option by others, when in reality it was ill defined and in any case rendered unworkable by a Nationalist emphasis on Trident and 'illegal' wars, both of which would remain the preserve of Westminster under such a settlement. That or devo+, devo-more or whatever, meanwhile, would simply exacerbate all the existing unevenness of the status quo, producing dozens more West Lothian Questions in the process, as indeed would an 'independence' qualified by a currency union, UK-wide energy market and 'transitionary' welfare state. Independent or not, the Scottish lion would doubtless find itself, as Pierre Trudeau memorably put it, in bed with an English elephant. No matter how friendly and even-tempered the beast, a sovereign Scotland, as in Ireland for much of the twentieth century, would be affected by every twitch and grunt.

It became almost a cliché of the referendum debate that regardless of the outcome, the status quo would no longer be an option. But then the status quo was already in flux, with more powers heading north in 2015–16 via the Scotland Act and demands for parity emanating from Wales and Northern Ireland, the latter forever in a special category of its own. Constitutional reform in the UK generally moved extremely slowly, as repeated attempts to nudge the House of Lords into the twenty-first century demonstrated. As Iain McLean and Alistair McMillan predicted in 2005, it seemed likely the 'union state' would 'lumber on, anomalies and all, for at least a few decades more. A union state without unionism can survive for a long time. But not, perhaps, forever.'[27] In broader terms the lesson of recent years was that when UK politics promised 'never to be the same again', the same again was precisely what it turned out to be.

But it remained the case that independence – however defined – was now a serious proposition, a *political fact* whether Unionists liked it or not, and one that would have seemed incomprehensible to a 1960s audience still grappling with the wind of change blowing across Africa. In one sense it could even be said the theoretical argument for independence had already been won, for few with a stake in the debate seriously disputed its legality or practicality, while the economic case, readily dismissed even at the height of the North Sea oil boom, also enjoyed general acceptance (something that could not be said in the context of Northern Ireland or Wales). The contemporary debate turned instead on its desirability, which was much narrower – and potentially more winnable – territory.

In 2014, as in 1979, there were what William McIlvanney recognised as doubts or reservations, seemingly interminable debates in which 'every quibble was a Russian doll of other quibbles', while any passion in the long road to the referendum was once again 'neutered by boredom'. The events of 2011–14 begged an inquiry after the health and status of his Scottish lion. Although a little older it was relatively content with its halfway house but keen to explore the limits of its 'freedom', and perhaps push them a little further. No longer feart, the lion was confident yet apprehensive – would not life beyond its extended compound offer more challenges than opportunities? Again, tentatively at first, it raised its snout to the wind and pondered at length the possibilities; the possibilities that a new, much larger cage might bring.

ENDNOTES

Introduction

1   Tom Nairn, *The Break-Up of Britain: Crisis and Neo-Nationalism* (London, 1981), pp. 74, 77, 91.
2   Eric Hobsbawm, 'Some Reflections on "The Break-Up of Britain"', *New Left Review* I/105, September–October 1977, pp. 8–9, 14.
3   *The Times*, 9 May 2011.
4   Gregor Gall (ed.), *Scotland's Road to Socialism: Time to Choose* (Edinburgh, 2013), p. 170.

Chapter 1

1   The only alternative in terms of backdrop was a print of the Declaration of Arbroath, which did not strike UK government officials as wise.
2   Alex Salmond was filmed reading the following passage: 'We're going on a bear hunt / We're gonna catch a big one / What a beautiful day / We're not scared.'
3   Interview, 4 March 2013.
4   Private information.
5   The Anglo-Irish Treaty of 1921 (despite its name) and the Belfast Agreement of 1998 had been similarly lacking in any formal legal status.
6   http://www.scotland.gov.uk/About/Government/concordats/Referendum-on-independence
7   http://www.scotland.gov.uk/Resource/0040/00404789.pdf
8   Also present were the UK and Scottish governments' lead negotiators, respectively Ciaran Martin and Ken Thomson.
9   Correspondence, 8 July 2013.
10   *The Scotsman*, 16 October 2012.
11   Christopher Carman, Robert Johns & James Mitchell, *More Scottish than British: The 2011 Scottish Parliament Election* (Basingstoke, 2013).
12   http://www.scotland.gov.uk/Resource/Doc/194791/0052321.pdf
13   http://votesnp.com/campaigns/SNP_Manifesto_2011_lowRes.pdf
14   There was some evidence that a sizeable minority of Scots agreed, a poll for the *Scottish Daily Mail* finding 41 per cent believed Scotland would be independent by 2070.
15   *Holyrood Magazine*, 13 May 2011.
16   Interview, 23 November 2011.
17   Interview, 14 February 2012.
18   Interview, 8 November 2011.
19   In an intriguing what-if, senior figures from the Scottish Labour Party had attempted to persuade the then Prime Minister, James Callaghan, to

include a second question on independence in the 1979 Scottish devolution referendum, the aim being to shoot the Nationalist fox (see *The Herald*, 30 December 2008).

20 Dr Matt Qvortrup, *Nationalism, Referendums and Democracy: Voting on Ethnic Issues and Independence* (London, 2013).
21 http://www.publications.parliament.uk/pa/ld200910/ldselect/ldconst/99/99.pdf
22 Interview, 23 November 2011.
23 Interview, 9 July 2013.
24 Correspondence, 8 July 2013.
25 Interview, 9 July 2013.
26 Interview, 23 March 2013.
27 http://stephennoon.blogspot.co.uk/2012/01/thank-you-mr-cameron.html
28 Interview, 23 June 2012.
29 Interview, 21 February 2012.
30 Interview, 23 February 2012.
31 http://www.bbc.co.uk/news/uk-scotland-16502955
32 Interview, 16 September 2012.
33 Interview, 23 February 2012.
34 http://www.scotland.gov.uk/Resource/0038/00386122.pdf
35 http://news.bbc.co.uk/1/hi/programmes/andrew_marr_show/9689183.stm
36 Interview, 21 February 2012.
37 Interview, 17 April 2012.
38 Interview, 4 April 2012.
39 Back in April 1999 Alex Salmond had supported 'a straight question' – 'Do you want to see Scotland become an independent country?'
40 Interview, 17 October 2012.
41 Correspondence, 8 July 2013.
42 Interview, 9 July 2013.
43 Interview, 23 March 2013.

Chapter 2
1 http://www.royal.gov.uk/LatestNewsandDiary/Speechesandarticles/2011/TheQueensspeechattheIrishStateDinner18May2011.aspx
2 http://www.scotland.gov.uk/News/Speeches/scotparlopngJuly1-2011
3 Norman Davies, *Vanished Kingdoms: The History of Half-Forgotten Europe* (London, 2011), pp. 6, 680.
4 http://bettertogether.net/blog/entry/the-union-is-a-scottish-invention
5 Christopher A. Whatley, *The Scots and the Union: Then and Now* (Edinburgh, 2014).
6 *Daily Record*, 6 March 2012.
7 Alvin Jackson, *The Two Unions: Ireland, Scotland, and the Survival of the United Kingdom, 1707–2007* (Oxford, 2012).
8 House of Commons Debates 7 June 1886 vol. 306 c. 1223.
9 See S. Rosenbaum (ed.), *Against Home Rule: The Case for the Union* (London, 1912) for a comprehensive summary of the arguments against Irish Home Rule.
10 *The Scotsman*, 14 January 2012.
11 http://www.scotland.gov.uk/Resource/Doc/194791/0052321.pdf
12 http://www.legislation.gov.uk/ukpga/Geo6/12-13-14/41
13 Davies, *Vanished Kingdoms*, p. 681.
14 *The Scotsman*, 26 June 2013.

15   http://web.archive.org/web/20110827065548/http://www.cooper.edu/
     humanities/core/hss3/e_renan.html
16   https://www.gov.uk/government/uploads/system/uploads/attachment_data/
     file/79417/Scotland_analysis_Devolution_and_the_implications_of_Scottish_
     Independan...__1_.pdf
17   https://www.gov.uk/government/uploads/system/uploads/attachment_data/
     file/79417/Scotland_analysis_Devolution_and_the_implications_of_Scottish_
     Independan...__1_.pdf
18   http://www.scotland.gov.uk/Resource/0041/00413757.pdf
19   http://www.scotreferendum.com/2013/02/11/uk-governments-legal-opinion/
20   *The Scotsman*, 3 September 2013.
21   *Portillo on Salmond* (BBC Scotland), 15 May 2011.
22   For example *Scotland's Parliament*, the white paper that set out plans for
     devolution in 1997, asserted: 'The United Kingdom is and will remain
     sovereign in all matters.'
23   *The Scotsman*, 16 May 2011.
24   *The Scotsman*, 17 May 2013.
25   James Mitchell et al., *The Scottish National Party: Transition to Power*
     (Oxford, 2011), p. 88.
26   Interview, 23 February 2012.
27   Jo Eric Murkens et al., *Scottish Independence: A Practical Guide* (Edinburgh,
     2002), p. 50.
28   http://www.lrb.co.uk/v20/n05/hcg-matthew/the-british-way
29   For the sake of completeness, powers over railways were transferred to
     the then Scottish Executive from the Department for Transport in 2005,
     while three years later so was responsibility for all planning and nature
     conservation matters at sea up to 200 miles from the Scottish coast.
30   https://www.gov.uk/government/uploads/system/uploads/attachment_data/
     file/79417/Scotland_analysis_Devolution_and_the_implications_of_Scottish_
     Independan...__1_.pdf
31   http://www.snp.org/blog/post/2012/jan/
     hugo-young-lecture-scotlands-place-world
32   http://blogs.spectator.co.uk/alex-massie/2011/08/
     nationalist-measures-for-unionist-aims/
33   *The Herald*, 8 December 2011.
34   http://www.ukpolitics.org.uk/node/2823
35   http://news.scotland.gov.uk/News/Democracy-at-heart-of-independence-case-
     for-fundamental-change-to-political-and-economic-union-266.aspx
36   *The Scotsman*, 27 July 2013.
37   Davies, *Vanished Kingdoms*, p. 680.
38   http://www.yesscotland.net/declaration
39   http://www.bbc.co.uk/news/uk-scotland-18225861
40   The phrase 'a more perfect union', for example, drew inspiration from Queen
     Anne's 1706 letter to the Scottish Parliament, which spoke of 'an entire and
     perfect union' (Akhil Reed Amar, *America's Constitution: A Biography* (New
     York, 2005), p. 36).
41   Neil MacCormick, 'A Constitution for Scotland', *Edinburgh Essays in Public
     Law* (Edinburgh, 1991), p. 122.
42   http://devolutionmatters.files.wordpress.com/2013/01/snp_2002_text-1.
     pdf Dr W. Elliot Bulmer also published *A Model Constitution for Scotland:
     Making Democracy Work in an Independent State* in 2011.

43   *MacCormick v Lord Advocate* 1953 SC 396, 1953 SLT 255.
44   Margaret Thatcher, *The Downing Street Years* (London, 1993), p. 624.
45   The Scottish Office, *Scotland in the Union: A Partnership for Good* (London, 1993), p. 5.
46   http://www.bbc.co.uk/news/uk-21752581
47   http://www.scotland.gov.uk/Resource/0041/00413757.pdf
48   https://www.gov.uk/government/speeches/setting-the-scene-for-2013
49   See Kenny MacAskill, *Building A Nation: Post Devolution Nationalism in Scotland* (Edinburgh, 2004).
50   http://b.3cdn.net/better/c1d14076ee08022eec_u9m6vd74f.pdf
51   For a full account of the Irish peers, see: http://archive.is/Kt260
52   http://www.constitutionalcommission.org/production/byre/images/assets/file/Resources%20Folder/citizens%20not%20subjects.pdf
53   http://www.royal.gov.uk/ImagesandBroadcasts/Historic%20speeches%20and%20broadcasts/SilverJubileeaddresstoParliament4May1977.aspx
54   There was no suggestion, meanwhile, that an independent Scotland might revert to the Stuart monarchy, the rightful heir to which was Franz, HRH the Duke of Bavaria. But, as Jacobites do not recognise the Act of Union, the Duke styles himself 'HM King Francis II of England, Scotland, France and Ireland' (http://jacobite.ca/kings/index.htm).
55   Murkens, *Scottish Independence*, p. 109.
56   *Financial Times*, 30 October 2012.
57   http://www.yesscotland.net/nicola_sturgeons_speech_in_full_may_13_2013
58   Interview, 7 March 2013. The answer, for the uninitiated, is 42.

Chapter 3

1   Robert A. Young, 'How Do Peaceful Secessions Happen?', *Canadian Journal of Political Science / Revue canadienne de science politique* vol. 27, no. 4 (December 1994), pp. 773–92.
2   Margaret Thatcher, who died two days after Salmond's speech, made a similar point in a US speech she gave as Leader of the Opposition in 1977.
3   http://www.scotland.gov.uk/News/Speeches/PrincetonUniversity2013
4   *Scotland Tonight* (STV), 30 January 2012.
5   Mike Russell and Dennis MacLeod, *Grasping the Thistle: How Scotland Must React to the Three Key Challenges of the Twenty First Century* (Argyll, 2006).
6   http://b.3cdn.net/better/c1d14076ee08022eec_u9m6vd74f.pdf
7   Andrew Goudie (ed.), *Scotland's Future: The Economics of Constitutional Change* (Dundee, 2013), p. 130.
8   http://www.parliament.uk/briefing-papers/SN06292
9   Goudie, *Scotland's Future*, pp. 24–25.
10   http://emergenteconomics.com/2013/05/24/the-economic-case-for-scottish-independence/
11   http://b.3cdn.net/better/c1d14076ee08022eec_u9m6vd74f.pdf
12   Goudie, *Scotland's Future*, p. 173.
13   http://www.scotland.gov.uk/Publications/2013/05/4084/downloads
14   Goudie, *Scotland's Future*, p. 69.
15   The FCWG included two Nobel Prize-winning economists, Joseph Stiglitz and Sir Jim Mirrlees, as well as the Scottish economist Andrew Hughes-Hallett and Frances Ruane, an expert in public finance from the Republic of Ireland.
16   This was despite having argued in 2008 that the 'financial incompetence of

UK authorities' was 'a strong argument for independence, not an argument for the continuation of London mismanagement'.

17   http://www.scotland.gov.uk/Resource/0041/00414291.pdf

18   http://www.snp.org/blog/post/2013/mar/scotland-wealthy-country

19   *The Scotsman*, 15 February 2013.

20   http://www.scotland.gov.uk/Resource/Doc/919/0120770.pdf

21   Gregor Gall (ed.), *Scotland's Road to Socialism: Time to Choose* (Edinburgh, 2013), p. 115–16.

22   http://b.3cdn.net/better/c1d14076ee08022eec_u9m6vd74f.pdf

23   http://www.totalpolitics.com/print/383/in-conversation-with-alex-salmond.thtml

24   http://www.scotland.gov.uk/News/Speeches/better-nation-031212

25   http://www.ifs.org.uk/bns/bn140.pdf

26   http://www.scotland.gov.uk/Resource/0041/00415875.pdf

27   Goudie, *Scotland's Future*, p. 73.

28   http://www.gla.ac.uk/media/media_275906_en.pdf

29   Iain McLean, et al, *Scotland's Choices: The Referendum and What Happens Afterwards* (Edinburgh, 2013), p. 150.

30   http://www.oilofscotland.org/mccronereport.pdf

31   This was *de rigueur*, although the SNP has made great play of the document being kept 'secret', as if confidential civil service advice was habitually published for general consumption.

32   http://stephennoon.blogspot.co.uk/2013/03/weve-heard-it-all-before.html for a comprehensive list of quotes.

33   *Scotland on Sunday*, 22 September 2013.

34   http://stephennoon.blogspot.co.uk/2012/01/fair-shares.html

35   Gavin McCrone, *Scottish Independence: Weighing Up the Economics* (Edinburgh, 2013), p. 101.

36   See http://www.scotland.gov.uk/Resource/Doc/280368/0084457.pdf

37   http://www.scotland.gov.uk/News/Speeches/scotlandandunion

38   Graham Stewart, *Bang! A History of Britain in the 1980s* (London, 2013), p. 282.

39   Goudie, *Scotland's Future*, p. 248.

40   http://www.scotland.gov.uk/Resource/0042/00428074.pdf

41   https://www.gov.uk/government/uploads/system/uploads/attachment_data/file/236579/scotland_analysis_macroeconomic_and_fiscal_performance.pdf

42   *The Scotsman*, 12 July 2011.

43   http://www.bbc.co.uk/news/uk-scotland-scotland-politics-23428903

44   The SNP paper 'Raise the Standard' said: 'The currency shall continue to be sterling until such time as Parliament decides to change that position.'

45   http://www.optionsforscotland.com/wp-content/uploads/sites/4/2013/09/independent-scotland-policy-options.pdf

46   Goudie, *Scotland's Future*, p. 105.

47   https://www.gov.uk/government/publications/scotland-analysis-currency-and-monetary-policy

48   http://bettertogether.net/blog/entry/why-let-salmond-gamble-with-your-money

49   http://www.consoc.org.uk/wp-content/uploads/2013/08/APPG-Scotland_SirJohn.mp3

50   http://www.official-documents.gov.uk/document/cm70/7022/7022.pdf

51   Lord Heseltine issued a similar warning to those (in UKIP and his own party) who wanted to take the UK out of the European Union. 'The alternative to EU membership … is not independence,' he said. 'It is being told by the

EU what conditions it will accept for us to trade in that vast area with little recourse for us to appeal their decisions.'

52   *The Scotsman*, 13 March 2013.
53   McLean, *Scotland's Choices*, pp. 94–95.
54   Brian Quinn, *Hume Occasional Paper No 99 – Scottish Independence: Issues and Questions Regulation, Supervision, Lender of Last Resort and Crisis Management* (Edinburgh, 2013).
55   http://www.scottish.parliament.uk/parliamentarybusiness/28862.aspx?r=8026&mode=html
56   http://blogs.ft.com/the-a-list/2013/05/01/#axzz2Y6iNXiFt
57   Interview, 7 March 2013.
58   http://stephennoon.blogspot.co.uk/2011/07/emerging-truth-about-bank-bailout.html
59   http://www.bettertogether.net/press/entry/full-transcript-of-the-launch-event-speech-by-alistair-darling
60   Gavin McCrone, *Scottish Independence*, pp. 83–84.
61   https://www.gov.uk/government/uploads/system/uploads/attachment_data/file/200491/scotland_analysis_financial_services_and_banking_200513.pdf
62   http://www.scotland.gov.uk/Resource/0043/00430128.pdf
63   http://www.scotland.gov.uk/Resource/0042/00422987.pdf
64   http://www.scotland.gov.uk/Resource/0042/00422011.pdf
65   http://stucbetterway.blogspot.co.uk/2013/05/scottish-government-banking-strategy.html 66   https://www.gov.uk/government/uploads/system/uploads/attachment_data/file/236579/scotland_analysis_macroeconomic_and_fiscal_performance.pdf
67   *The Scotsman*, 12 June 2013.
68   https://www.prospectmagazine.co.uk/magazine/to-the-brink-no-further-snp-independence-referendum/#.UiTTPBbpxFI
69   http://www.johnkay.com/2013/02/21/the-economic-challenges-facing-an-independent-scotland
70   *The Scotsman*, 22 May 2013.

Chapter 4

1   *Foreign Affairs*, September/October 2012.
2   http://www.nytimes.com/2013/03/28/opinion/a-vote-on-scottish-independence.html?_r=0
3   http://www.bbc.co.uk/news/uk-scotland-scotland-politics-21535425
4   *The Herald*, 12 November 2012.
5   http://articles.washingtonpost.com/2012-12-07/opinions/35701290_1_scottish-national-party-scotland-independent-nation
6   Interview, 14 April 2013.
7   *The Scotsman*, 10 April 2013.
8   Robert A. Young, 'The Political Economy of Secession: The Case of Quebec', *Constitutional Political Economy* (1994) vol. 5, no. 2.
9   http://www.english.rfi.fr/asia-pacific/20130727-french-pm-promises-new-caledonia-referendum-and-return-rebel-chiefs-head
10   http://www.scotland.gov.uk/News/Releases/2012/02/international18022012
11   Rebecca Johnson and Angie Zelter (eds), *Trident and International Law: Scotland's Obligations* (Edinburgh, 2011), p. 31.
12   https://www.gov.uk/government/speeches/transcript-pm-scotland-speech
13   *The Scotsman*, 29 November 2011.

14 http://www.publications.parliament.uk/pa/cm201213/cmselect/
cmfaff/643/643.pdf

15 http://www.scotland.gov.uk/News/Speeches/scotland-global-citzen

16 *The Irish Times*, 15 June 2013.

17 http://www.scotland.gov.uk/Resource/0040/00409256.pdf

18 http://www.globaltimes.cn/content/762781.shtml

19 http://www.scotland.gov.uk/Resource/Doc/285018/0086543.pdf

20 https://www.snp.org/media-centre/news/2006/may/
snp-take-economic-case-across-scotland

21 http://wingsoverscotland.com/without-frontiers/

22 https://www.gov.uk/government/news/
foreign-secretary-speech-on-the-united-kingdom-stronger-together

23 http://www.yesscotland.net/some_news_for_william_hague

24 http://www.theguardian.com/politics/scottish-independence-blog/2013/
feb/08/alexsalmond-quebec-canada

25 Interview, 8 March 2013.

26 Liz Castro (ed.), *What's Up with Catalonia?* (Barcelona, 2013), p. 168.

27 Gordon Wilson, *SNP, the Turbulent Years 1960–1990* (Stirling, 2009), p. 69.

28 David Torrance, *Salmond: Against the Odds* (Edinburgh, 2011), p. 78.

29 The split produced the 'Scottish Sovereignty Movement', which was
reconvened in the summer of 2013 to campaign for 'restoration of 100 per
cent ... Scottish National Sovereignty by and for the Scottish People' (https://
www.facebook.com/pages/Scottish-Sovereignty-Movement/55457544122200
7?id=554575441222007&sk=info)

30 http://www.bloomberg.com/video/u-k-s-cameron-speaks-on-eu-membership-
08Cf4wISTy2QiBHrIpPGWA.html

31 http://blogs.lse.ac.uk/europpblog/2013/02/04/scotland-uk-referendums/

32 Jo Eric Murkens et al., *Scottish Independence: A Practical Guide* (Edinburgh,
2002), p. 45.

33 *The Scotsman*, 17 May 2013.

34 Emile Noel, Lord Mackenzie-Stuart and Eamonn Gallagher had given their
opinions between 1989 and 1992, before Maastricht, the single currency and
a host of other major reforms, not least the Lisbon Treaty. And far from being
'eminent legal authorities', as Sturgeon called them, only Mackenzie-Stuart
had been a lawyer; the others were bureaucrats (*Sunday Herald*, 4 November
2012).

35 Interview, 23 March 2013.

36 *Independent on Sunday*, 28 October 2012.

37 http://www.parliament.uk/documents/lords-committees/economic-affairs/
ScottishIndependence/EA68_Scotland_and_the_EU_Barroso's_reply_to_
Lord_Tugendhat_101212.pdf

38 'Europe is not going to throw Scotland out,' the former Foreign Secretary
Robin Cook said in 2000. 'It's in the nature of the European Union, it
welcomes all-comers and Scotland would be a member.'

39 http://www.britac.ac.uk/policy/Scotland-and-the-UK.cfm

40 *Sunday Herald*, 16 December 2012.

41 Gregor Gall (ed.), *Scotland's Road to Socialism: Time to Choose* (Edinburgh,
2013), p. 45.

42 http://www.publications.parliament.uk/pa/cm201213/cmselect/cmfaff/
writev/643/m05.htm

43 http://www.scottishconstitutionalfutures.org/OpinionandAnalysis/

ViewBlogPost/tabid/1767/articleType/ArticleView/articleId/852/David-Edward-Scotland-and-the-European-Union.aspx

44 http://www.bbc.co.uk/iplayer/episode/b01p8v08/
HARDtalk_Jose_Manuel_Barroso_President_of_the_European_Commission/

45 Murkens, *Scottish Independence*, p. 46.

46 Andrew Goudie (ed.), *Scotland's Future: The Economics of Constitutional Change* (Dundee, 2013), pp. 57–58.

47 http://futureukandscotland.ac.uk/blog/what-future-scottish-eu-relationship

48 Interview, 9 June 2013.

49 Interview, 6 July 2013.

50 SNP, *Your Scotland, Your Future* (Edinburgh, 2011).

51 *The Guardian*, 14 May 2011.

52 http://stephennoon.blogspot.co.uk/2011/07/founding-father.html

53 http://www.angusrobertson.org/policies.php

54 http://www.publications.parliament.uk/pa/cm201213/cmselect/
cmscotaf/139/120523.htm

55 http://henryjacksonsociety.org/wp-content/uploads/2013/07/HJS-In-Scotlands-Defence-Report-LOW-RES.pdf

56 *Sunday Post*, 9 September 2013.

57 https://www.gov.uk/government/
speeches/2013-03-14-stronger-and-safer-together

58 http://www.publications.parliament.uk/pa/cm201314/cmselect/
cmdfence/198/198.pdf

59 *The Scotsman*, 7 June 2013.

60 http://www.iiea.com/blogosphere/
reflections-on-defending-an-independent-scotland-a-view-from-ireland

61 *Sunday Herald*, 9 June 2013.

62 http://www.scotlandinstitute.com/wp-content/uploads/2013/06/Defence_
Report_-_Scot_Inst.pdf

63 *Sunday Herald*, 14 October 2012.

64 Interview, 16 April 2012.

65 http://articles.chicagotribune.com/2013-04-04/news/sns-rt-us-scotland-salmondbre93400t-20130404_1_independent-scotland-scottish-national-party-alex-salmond

66 https://www.gov.uk/government/news/moore-scottish-government-u-turn-on-nato-shows-their-claims-have-no-foundation

67 *The Guardian*, 15 August 2013.

68 *The Scotsman*, 8 January 2012.

69 Johnson and Zelter, *Trident and International Law*, p. 29.

70 Tony Blair, *A Journey* (London, 2010), p. 636.

71 http://lordashcroftpolls.com/wp-content/uploads/2013/05/Trident-Poll-Summary.pdf

72 http://www.guardian.co.uk/uk-news/2013/jul/10/
mod-trident-scotland-independence

Chapter 5

1 http://www.snp.org/blog/post/2013/mar/
snp-spring-conference-address-nicola-sturgeon

2 http://www.scotland.gov.uk/News/Speeches/better-nation-031212

3 http://www.snp.org/blog/post/2013/mar/
snp-spring-conference-address-nicola-sturgeon

4 The journalist Alf Young carefully filleted these statistics in *The Scotsman*

(6 April 2013), concluding that only Gordon Brown-style double, triple and quadruple accounting could possibly arrive at a figure of £4.5 billion.

5   http://www.ifs.org.uk/bns/bn139.pdf
6   http://www.scotland.gov.uk/Resource/Doc/293639/0090721.pdf
7   SNP, *Your Scotland, Your Future* (Edinburgh, 2011).
8   http://www.scotland.gov.uk/News/Releases/2013/01/welfare06012013
9   Gregor Gall, *Scotland the Brave? Independence and Radical Social Change* (Glasgow, 2013).
10 http://www.scotland.gov.uk/Resource/0042/00424088.pdf
11 https://www.gov.uk/government/news/leaving-the-uk-and-keeping-uk-welfare-doesnt-add-up
12 http://www.scotland.gov.uk/News/Speeches/jimmy-reid-lecture-29012013
13 http://www.bbc.co.uk/news/uk-scotland-scotland-politics-19711805
14 http://www.snp.org/blog/post/2012/jan/hugo-young-lecture-scotlands-place-world
15 http://www.scottishlabour.org.uk/campaigns/entry/devolution-commission
16 http://www.scotland.gov.uk/Resource/0041/00414291.pdf
17 Interview, 7 March 2013.
18 *Sunday Herald*, 2 August 2009.
19 *Scotland on Sunday*, 14 August 2011.
20 http://www.yesscotland.net/yes_to_a_just_scotland_response_to_stuc_report?agreed=Agreed
21 http://www.ifs.org.uk/bns/bn139.pdf
22 *The Scotsman*, 18 August 2013.
23 Andrew Goudie (ed.), *Scotland's Future: The Economics of Constitutional Change* (Dundee, 2013), p. 292.
24 Gavin McCrone, *Scottish Independence: Weighing Up the Economics* (Edinburgh, 2013), p. 24.
25 *Scotland on Sunday*, 3 March 2013.
26 *The Scotsman*, 19 April 2013.
27 http://www.commissiononscottishdevolution.org.uk/uploads/2009-06-12-csd-final-report-2009fbookmarked.pdf
28 http://esrcscotecon.files.wordpress.com/2013/05/social-protection-and-social-benefits-in-scotland-5.pdf
29 http://www.scotland.gov.uk/Resource/Doc/352649/0118638.pdf
30 http://b.3cdn.net/better/c1d14076ee08022eec_u9m6vd74f.pdf
31 *Scottish Daily Mail*, 2 March 2013.
32 http://icas.org.uk/News/ScotlandsPensionsFutureNewsrelease/
33 http://www.scotland.gov.uk/News/Releases/2013/06/pensions18062013
34 http://www.scotland.gov.uk/Resource/0043/00434502.pdf
35 Stephen Maxwell, *Arguing for Independence: Evidence, Risks and the Wicked Issues* (Edinburgh, 2012), p. 108.

Chapter 6

1   https://www.gov.uk/government/speeches/transcript-pm-scotland-speech
    Cameron's father had been born at Blairmore, an Aberdeenshire country house built by his great-great-grandfather, Alexander Geddes, who had made a fortune in the Chicago grain trade.
2   http://www.conservatives.com/News/Speeches/2012/03/David_Cameron_Scottish_Party_Conference.aspx
3   Interview, 29 March 2012.
4   Tony Judt, *Postwar: A History of Europe Since 1945* (London, 2005), p. 706.

5   http://www.ons.gov.uk/ons/dcp171776_290558.pdf

6   Interview, 2 July 2013.

7   Interview, 8 March 2013.

8   http://www.sfu.ca/~aheard/bill1.html

9   *The Scotsman*, 5 December 2012.

10   http://www.snp.org/blog/post/2012/dec/building-better-nation

11   James Mitchell et al., *The Scottish National Party: Transition to Power* (Oxford, 2011), p. 88.

12   'A Union for the Next Generation', Scottish Conservative press release, 30 August 2013.

13   *The Scotsman*, 2 February 2012.

14   Interview, 23 March 2013.

15   I. Urwin and D. W. Budge, *Scottish Political Behaviour* (London, 1966).

16   Dennis Kavanagh and Anthony Seldon (eds), *The Thatcher Effect: A Decade of Change* (Oxford, 1989), p. 259.

17   http://www.scotland.gov.uk/News/Speeches/better-nation-031212

18   Lesley Riddoch, *Blossom: What Scotland Needs to Flourish* (Edinburgh 2013), p. 297.

19   http://www.newstatesman.com/politics/2013/03/douglas-alexanders-speech-scotland-full-text

20   http://whitehall1212.blogspot.co.uk/2012_08_01_archive.html

21   http://www.snp.org/blog/post/2012/dec/building-better-nation

22   *The Observer*, 28 August 2011.

23   http://www.snp.org/media-centre/news/2013/jul/yes-independence-only-vote-more-powers

24   Andrew Marr, *The Battle for Scotland* (London, 2013), p. xxv.

25   *The Herald*, 20 February 2013.

26   http://nationalcollective.com/2012/08/30/50-artists-creatives-who-support-scottish-independence/ In a bizarre Twitter attack the Scottish composer James MacMillan said NC had 'a creepy, fascistic mob mentality'. 'Scottish artists of individual integrity', he added, 'should avoid them.'

27   In fact Gray had paraphrased the line from a poem called 'Civil Elegies' by the Canadian poet Dennis Lee.

28   *The Observer*, 28 August 2011.

29   http://www.scotland.gov.uk/News/Speeches/Culture-Heritage05062013

30   http://www.scottishreview.net/TheCafe33b.shtml

31   *The Observer*, 28 August 2011.

32   C. J. Sansom, *Dominion* (London, 2012), p. 345.

33   http://www.thinkscotland.org/thinkculture/articles.html?read_full=12364&article=www.thinkscotland.org

34   Interview, 18 June 2012.

35   *Scotland on Sunday*, 29 July 2012.

36   James G. Kellas, *The Scottish Political System* (Cambridge, 1984), p. 2.

37   See Donald Smith, *Freedom and Faith: A Scottish Question* (Edinburgh, forthcoming) for an examination of the independence debate's spiritual dimension.

38   http://www.thetablet.co.uk/latest-news/5217

39   http://blogs.lse.ac.uk/politicsandpolicy/archives/35369

40   Here I must declare an interest, for I am an associate director of Five Million Questions.

41   See http://fivemillionquestions.org, http://ukchangingunion.org.uk, http://

britac.ac.uk/policy/Enlightening_Constitutional_Debate.cfm and http://futureukandscotland.ac.uk

42   Tom Nairn, 'The Three Dreams of Scottish Nationalism', *New Left Review* I/49, May–June 1968.

43   Marr, *The Battle for Scotland*, p. xxviii.

44   The short-lived *Scottish Daily News* in the 1970s had advocated 'independence or nothing at all. There's no halfway house', while Sir Hugh Fraser, proprietor of the then *Glasgow Herald*, was a high-profile convert to the independence cause.

45   http://www.scotland.gov.uk/News/Releases/2012/08/failed-by-westminster24082012

46   *The Scotsman*, 29 August 2012.

47   Iain Macwhirter, *Road to Referendum* (Edinburgh, 2013), p. 232.

Chapter 7

1   Interview, 23 February 2012.

2   Interview, 5 March 2013.

3   Interview, 23 February 2012.

4   http://www.scotland.gov.uk/Resource/Doc/293639/0090721.pdf

5   Iain McLean et al.., *Scotland's Choices: The Referendum and What Happens Afterwards* (Edinburgh, 2013), p. 96.

6   *Royal Commission on the Constitution 1969–73 v 2 Report* (London, 1973), p. 235.

7   *Prospect*, June 2011.

8   *The Guardian*, 25 April 2013.

9   http://www.commissiononscottishdevolution.org.uk/uploads/2009-06-12-csd-final-report-2009fbookmarked.pdf

10   http://www.legislation.gov.uk/ukpga/2012/11/contents/enacted

11   http://www.scottishconservatives.com/2013/03/strengthening-devolution-taking-scotland-forward/

12   http://scotlibdems.org.uk/homerule

13   Eric Hobsbawm, 'Some Reflections on "The Break-up of Britain"', *New Left Review* I/105, September–October 1977, p. 13.

14   http://news.scotland.gov.uk/News/Lerwick-Declaration-2a7.aspx

15   http://www.institute-of-governance.org/news-events/news/2007/wendy_alexander_presents_a_new_agenda_for_scotland

16   http://www.lrb.co.uk/v33/n15/david-runciman/socialism-in-one-county

17   http://www.scottishlabour.org.uk/campaigns/entry/devolution-commission

18   For a fuller analysis of each party's referendum strategy see Peter Lynch (ed.), *Parties and the Referendum* (Cardiff, forthcoming).

19   Interview, 2 July 2013.

20   http://www.scottishconservatives.com/2013/03/strengthening-devolution-taking-scotland-forward/

21   Interview, 21 February 2012.

22   *The Scotsman*, 8 August 2013.

23   Gavin McCrone, *Scottish Independence: Weighing Up the Economics* (Edinburgh, 2013), p. 150.

24   *The Scotsman*, 4 September 2013.

25   http://www.theguardian.com/politics/scottish-independence-essential-guide

26   http://www.ippr.org/publication/55/10210/funding-devo-more-fiscal-options-for-strengthening-the-union

27 McCrone, *Scottish Independence*, pp. 33–34.
28 Gregor Gall (ed.), *Scotland's Road to Socialism: Time to Choose* (Edinburgh, 2013), p. 89.
29 http://scottishcommonweal.org/what-is-common-weal/
30 Interview, 23 February 2012.
31 David Melding, *The Reformed Union: The UK as a Federation* (Cardiff, 2013).
32 *The Scotsman*, 10 September 2013.
33 *The Scotsman*, 3 September 2013.
34 *The Herald*, 18 September 2013.
35 Richard Wyn Jones and Roger Scully, *Wales Says Yes: Devolution and the 2011 Welsh Referendum* (Cardiff, 2012).
36 https://www.gov.uk/government/uploads/system/uploads/attachment_data/file/32080/11-1338-rebalancing-britain-liverpool-city-region.pdf
37 Michael Keating, *The Independence of Scotland* (Edinburgh, 2009), p. 162.
38 *Financial Times*, 16 May 2013. See also http://www.london.gov.uk/sites/default/files/Raising%20the%20capital.pdf
39 Stephen Maxwell, *Arguing for Independence: Evidence, Risks and the Wicked Issues* (Edinburgh, 2012), p. 49.
40 http://www.northumbria.ac.uk/sd/academic/sass/events/sassnews/acex
41 http://www.northeastcouncils.gov.uk/curo/downloaddoc.asp?id=589
42 http://www.ippr.org/images/media/files/publication/2012/02/dog-that-finally-barked_englishness_Jan2012_8542.pdf
43 http://webarchive.nationalarchives.gov.uk/20130403030652/http://tmc.independent.gov.uk/wp-content/uploads/2013/03/The-McKay-Commission_Main-Report_25-March-20131.pdf
44 *The Independent*, 10 July 2013.
45 http://www.thecep.org.uk
46 http://www.ippr.org/images/media/files/publication/2013/07/england-two-unions_Jul2013_11003.pdf
47 *The Guardian*, 8 July 2013.
48 Maxwell, *Arguing for Independence*, p. 181.
49 Keating, *The Independence of Scotland*, p. 179.

Chapter 8
1 John Kay, *Obliquity: Why Our Goals Are Best Achieved Indirectly* (London, 2011), p. 6.
2 See http://scot.gr/w/GreenHolyrood2011.pdf and http://www.scottishsocialistparty.org/policies/
3 *Sunday Herald*, 2 August 2009.
4 http://scotfree2014.blogspot.co.uk
5 Interview, 3 July 2013.
6 http://www.theguardian.com/commentisfree/2013/sep/17/scottish-independence-after-the-flag-waving
7 *Beyond Westminster* (BBC Radio 4), 4 June 2011.
8 http://www.bettertogether.net/press/entry/full-transcript-of-the-launch-event-speech-by-alistair-darling
9 Andrew Marr, *The Battle for Scotland* (London, 2013), p. xx.
10 Interview, 18 June 2012.
11 Interview, 11 May 2011.
12 Interview, 5 July 2013.
13 http://www.snp.org/blog/post/2012/oct/snp-conference-address-alex-neil-msp

14 http://stephennoon.blogspot.co.uk/2013/05/keep-it-calm-your-country-needs-you.html
15 *The Scotsman*, 2 May 2013.
16 http://www.labourhame.com/archives/3604
17 http://www.bettertogether.net/blog/entry/smear-and-fear
18 http://nationalcollective.com/2013/05/04/keep-it-calm-your-country-needs-you/
19 http://lordashcroftpolls.com/wp-content/uploads/2013/09/Lord-Ashcroft-Scottish-Political-Attitudes-poll1.pdf
20 Interview, 23 February 2012.
21 http://stephennoon.blogspot.co.uk/2013/08/onslaught.html?m=1
22 Correspondence, 15 July 2013.
23 http://yougov.co.uk/news/2012/05/28/independence-salmonds-mountain/
24 *Financial Times*, 29 January 2013.
25 *The Scotsman*, 17 September 2013.
26 John Bochel et al. (eds), *The Referendum Experience: Scotland, 1979* (Aberdeen, 1981).
27 Hugh Bochel et al., *Scotland Decides: The Devolution Issue and the 1997 Referendum* (London, 2000).
28 http://www.parliament.uk/briefing-papers/RP13-47
29 Interview, 6 July 2013.
30 *The Scotsman*, 3 September 2013.
31 Interview, 2 July 2013.
32 Interview, 8 November 2011.
33 Interview, 19 April 2012.
34 Robert A. Caro, *The Years of Lyndon Johnson: The Passage of Power* (London, 2012), p. 601.
35 Interview, 23 February 2012.
36 Interview, 31 August 2012.
37 http://rt.com/shows/sophieco/independence-policy-england-scotland-723/
38 *The Cause* part 5 (BBC Radio Scotland), 22 October 2012.

Chapter 9
1 http://stephennoon.blogspot.co.uk/2013/03/who-would-benefit-from-no.html?m=1
2 http://www.newstatesman.com/politics/2013/03/douglas-alexanders-speech-scotland-full-text (with minor changes)
3 http://www.clickonwales.org/2012/02/the-reformed-union-a-british-federation/#melchap3
4 http://conservativehome.blogs.com/thecolumnists/2012/11/bruce-anderson-cameron-should-tell-merkel-that-quitting-the-eu-is-an-option-not-a-nightmare.html
5 *The Scotsman*, 25 June 2013.
6 Based on Humza Yousaf's 31 May 2012 speech in the Scottish Parliament: http://www.scottish.parliament.uk/parliamentarybusiness/28862.aspx?r=7221&mode=pdf

Chapter 10
1 Based on a joint statement by David Cameron and Taoiseach Enda Kenny from March 2012: https://www.gov.uk/government/news/british-irish-relations-the-next-decade

2 Neil MacCormick, *Questioning Sovereignty: Law, State, and Practical Reason* (Oxford, 2001), p. 203.
3 From a (slightly altered) interview with Alex Salmond in *Road to Referendum* III (STV), 18 June 2013.
4 *The Scotsman*, 2 March 2011.
5 Iain McLean et al., *Scotland's Choices: The Referendum and What Happens Afterwards* (Edinburgh, 2013), p. 205.
6 http://www.snp.org/blog/post/2012/dec/building-better-nation (with certain changes)

Conclusion
1 *Sunday Herald*, 15 September 2013.
2 William McIlvanney, *Surviving the Shipwreck* (Edinburgh, 1991), pp. 12–25.
3 *The Herald*, 8 May 1999 (with thanks to the Scottish Poetry Library). 'Mauchty' means strong, 'gurly' is fierce and 'stell' translates from Scots as 'prop'.
4 http://www.qmul.ac.uk/media/qmnews/items/48980.html
5 Peter Lynch, *SNP: The History of the Scottish National Party* (Cardiff, 2013).
6 *Our Three Nations* (Tonypandy, 1956).
7 M. G. Clarke and H. M. Drucker, *Our Changing Scotland: A Yearbook of Scottish Government 1976–77* (Edinburgh, 1976), p. 67.
8 *Royal Commission on the Constitution 1969–73 v 2 Report* (London, 1973), p. 151. A survey conducted for the Royal Commission found that 23 per cent of Scots supported independence in 1970.
9 *The Scotsman*, 5 September 2013.
10 *Holyrood*, 27 February 2012.
11 Gregor Gall, *Scotland the Brave? Independence and Radical Social Change* (Glasgow, 2013).
12 *Frost All over the World* (Al Jazeera), 18 February 2012.
13 D. I. MacKay (ed.), *Scotland 1980: The Economics of Self-government* (Edinburgh, 1977), p. 17.
14 Iain McLean and Alistair McMillan, *State of the Union* (Oxford, 2005), p. 239.
15 Richard Rose, *Understanding the United Kingdom: The Territorial Dimension in Government* (London, 1982) p. 223.
16 Michael Keating, *The Independence of Scotland* (Oxford, 2009), p. 38.
17 http://www.billemmott.com/article.php?id=314
18 J. G. A. Pocock, 'British History: A Plea for a New Subject', *Journal of Modern History* vol. 47, no. 4 (1975), p. 603.
19 Jane Jacobs, *The Question of Separatism: Quebec and the Struggle over Sovereignty* (Montreal, 2012), p. 5.
20 McLean and McMillan, *State of the Union*, p. 135.
21 Karl Marx, *The Eighteenth Brumaire of Louis Bonaparte* (London, 1852).
22 *Financial Times*, 18 January 2012.
23 *The Scotsman*, 30 July 2013.
24 *New Statesman*, 19–25 July 2013.
25 See David Melding, *Will Britain Survive Beyond 2020?* (Cardiff, 2009), p. 196.
26 David Melding, *The Reformed Union: The UK as a Federation* (Cardiff, 2013), p. 111.
27 McLean and McMillan, *State of the Union*, p. 256.

BIBLIOGRAPHY

Published works

Akhil Reed Amar, *America's Constitution: A Biography* (New York, 2005)

Tony Blair, *A Journey* (London, 2010)

John Bochel, David Denver and Allan Macartney, *The Referendum Experience: Scotland, 1979* (Aberdeen, 1981)

Hugh Bochel, David Denver, James Mitchell and Charles Pattie, *Scotland Decides: The Devolution Issue and the 1997 Referendum* (London, 2000)

British Academy/Royal Society of Edinburgh, *Scotland and the United Kingdom: A Conference Report written by Beth Foley* (Edinburgh, 2012)

Pauline Bryan and Tommy Kane (eds), *Class, Nation and Socialism: The Red Paper on Scotland 2014* (Glasgow, 2013)

W. Elliot Bulmer, *A Model Constitution for Scotland: Making Democracy Work in an Independent State* (Edinburgh, 2011)

Christopher Carman, Robert Johns and James Mitchell, *More Scottish than British: The 2011 Scottish Parliament Election* (Basingstoke, 2013)

Robert A. Caro, *The Years of Lyndon Johnson: The Passage of Power* (London, 2012)

Liz Castro (ed.), *What's up with Catalonia?* (Barcelona, 2013)

M. G. Clarke and H. M. Drucker, *Our Changing Scotland: A Yearbook of Scottish Government 1976–77* (Edinburgh, 1976)

Linda Colley, *Britons: Forging the Nation 1707–1837* (London, 1992)

Commission on Scottish Devolution, *Serving Scotland Better: Scotland and the United Kingdom in the 21st Century* (Edinburgh, 2009)

Jim and Margaret Cuthbert, *Economic Policy Options for an Independent Scotland* (Edinburgh, 2013)

Norman Davies, *Vanished Kingdoms: The History of Half-Forgotten Europe* (London, 2011)

Devo+, *A New Union: Third Report of the Devo Plus Group* (Edinburgh, 2012)

Devo+, *A Stronger Scotland Within the UK: First report of the Devo Plus Group* (Edinburgh, 2012)

Gwynfor Evans, *Our Three Nations* (Tonypandy, 1956)

Gregor Gall, *Scotland the Brave? Independence and Radical Social Change* (Glasgow, 2013)

Gregor Gall (ed.), *Scotland's Road to Socialism: Time to Choose* (Edinburgh, 2013)

Andrew Goudie (ed.), *Scotland's Future: The Economics of Constitutional Change* (Dundee, 2013)

George Grant, *In Scotland's Defence? An Assessment of SNP Defence Strategy* (London, 2013)

Alasdair Gray, *Why Scots Should Rule Scotland* (Edinburgh, 1992)

James Hallwood (ed.), *If Scotland Says 'No': What Next for the Union?* (London, 2013)

Scott Hames (ed.), *Unstated: Writers on Scottish Independence* (Edinburgh, 2012)

Simon Heffer, *Nor Shall My Sword: The Reinvention of England* (London, 2000)

Eric Hobsbawm, 'Some Reflections on "The Break-up of Britain"', *New Left Review* I/105 (September–October 1977)

HM Government, *The National Asset Register* (London, 2007)

HM Government, *Royal Commission on the Constitution 1969–73 v 2 Report* (London, 1973)

HM Government, *Scotland Analysis: Business and Microeconomic Framework* (London, 2013)

HM Government, *Scotland Analysis: Currency and Monetary Policy* (London, 2013)

HM Government, *Scotland Analysis: Devolution and the Implications of Scottish Independence* (London, 2013)

HM Government, *Scotland Analysis: Financial Services and Banking* (London, 2013)

HM Government, *Scotland Analysis: Macroeconomic and Fiscal Performance* (London, 2013)

HM Government, *Scotland in the Union: A Partnership for Good* (London, 1993)

HM Government, *Scotland's Parliament* (London, 1997)

Lord Heseltine and Sir Terry Leahy, *Rebalancing Britain: Policy or Slogan? Liverpool City Region – Building on its strengths: An independent report* (London, 2011)

House of Commons Foreign Affairs Committee, *Foreign Policy Considerations for the UK and Scotland in the Event of Scotland Becoming an Independent Country* (HC 643) (London, 2013)

House of Commons Library, *The Quebec Referendums* (Research Paper 13/47) (London, 2013)

House of Commons Library, *Scotland's Economy: Current Situation and Issues Related to Independence* (London, 2012)

House of Commons Scottish Affairs Committee, *The Referendum on Separation for Scotland: How Would Separation Affect Jobs in the Scottish Defence Industry?: Government Response to the Committee's Eighth Report of Session 2012–13* (HC 257) (London, 2013)

House of Lords Select Committee on the Constitution, *Referendums in the United Kingdom* (HL Paper 99) (London, 2010)

IPPR, *The Dog That Finally Barked: England as an Emerging Political Community* (London, 2012)

IPPR, *England and its Two Unions: The Anatomy of a Nation and its Discontents* (London, 2013)

IPPR North, *Funding Devo More: Fiscal Options for Strengthening the Union* (Newcastle, 2013)

Alvin Jackson, *The Two Unions: Ireland, Scotland, and the Survival of the United Kingdom, 1707–2007* (Oxford, 2012)

Jane Jacobs, *The Question of Separatism: Quebec and the Struggle over Sovereignty* (Montreal, 2012)

Rebecca Johnson and Angie Zelter (eds), *Trident and International Law: Scotland's Obligations* (Edinburgh, 2011)

Tony Judt, *Postwar: A History of Europe since 1945* (London, 2010)

Dennis Kavanagh and Anthony Seldon (eds), *The Thatcher Effect: A Decade of Change* (Oxford, 1989)

John Kay, *Obliquity: Why Our Goals Are Best Achieved Indirectly* (London, 2011)

Michael Keating, *The Independence of Scotland* (Oxford, 2009)

James G. Kellas, *The Scottish Political System* (Cambridge, 1984)

Colin Kidd, *Union and Unionisms: Political Thought in Scotland 1500–2000* (Cambridge, 2008)

Colonel Dorcha Lee, *Reflections on Defending an Independent Scotland: A View from Ireland* (Dublin, 2013)

London Finance Commission, *Raising the Capital* (London, 2013)

Peter Lynch, *SNP: The History of the Scottish National Party* (Cardiff, 2013)

Peter Lynch and Kevin Adamson (eds), *Parties and the Referendum* (Cardiff, forthcoming)

Kenny MacAskill, *Building a Nation: Post Devolution Nationalism in Scotland* (Edinburgh, 2004)

Neil MacCormick, 'A Constitution for Scotland' in Wilson Finnie et al. (eds), *Edinburgh Essays in Public Law* (Edinburgh, 1991)

Neil MacCormick, *Questioning Sovereignty: Law, State, and Practical Reason* (Oxford, 2001)

Gavin McCrone, *Scottish Independence: Weighing Up the Economics* (Edinburgh, 2013)

William McIlvanney, *Surviving the Shipwreck* (Edinburgh, 1991)

The McKay Commission, *Report of the Commission on the Consequences of Devolution for the House of Commons* (London, 2013)

D. I. MacKay (ed.), *Scotland 1980: The Economics of Self-government* (Edinburgh, 1977)

Iain McLean and Alistair McMillan, *State of the Union* (Oxford, 2005)

Iain McLean, Guy Lodge and Jim Gallagher, *Scotland's Choices: The Referendum and What Happens Afterwards* (Edinburgh, 2013)

Iain Macwhirter, *Road to Referendum* (Edinburgh, 2013)

Andrew Marr, *The Battle for Scotland* (London, 2013)

Karl Marx, *The Eighteenth Brumaire of Louis Bonaparte* (London, 1852)

Stephen Maxwell, *Arguing for Independence: Evidence, Risks and the Wicked Issues* (Edinburgh, 2012)

David Melding, *The Reformed Union: The UK as a Federation* (Cardiff, 2013)

David Melding, *Will Britain Survive Beyond 2020?* (Cardiff, 2009)

James Mitchell, Lynn Bennie and Rob Johns, *The Scottish National Party: Transition to Power* (Oxford, 2011)

Jo Eric Murkens, Peter Jones and Michael Keating, *Scottish Independence: A Practical Guide* (Edinburgh, 2002)

Tom Nairn, *The Break-Up of Britain: Crisis and Neo-Nationalism* (London, 1981)

Tom Nairn, 'The Three Dreams of Scottish Nationalism', *New Left Review* I/49, May–June 1968

David Phillips, *Government Spending on Benefits and State Pensions in Scotland: Current Patterns and Future Issues* (IFS Briefing Note BN139) (London, 2013)

David Phillips and Ben Deaner, *Government Spending on Public Services in Scotland: Current Patterns and Future Issues* (IFS Briefing Note BN140) (London, 2013)

J. G. A. Pocock, 'British History: A Plea for a New Subject', *Journal of Modern History* vol. 47, no. 4 (1975)

Brian Quinn, *Hume Occasional Paper No 99 – Scottish Independence: Issues and Questions – Regulation, Supervision, Lender of Last Resort and Crisis Management* (Edinburgh, 2013)

Matt Qvortrup, *Nationalism, Referendums and Democracy: Voting on Ethnic Issues and Independence* (London, 2013).

Lesley Riddoch, *Blossom: What Scotland Needs to Flourish* (Edinburgh, 2013)

James Robertson, *And the Land Lay Still* (London, 2010)

Richard Rose, *Understanding the United Kingdom: The Territorial Dimension in Government* (London, 1982)

Simon Rosenbaum (ed.), *Against Home Rule: The Case for the Union* (London, 1912)

Mike Russell and Dennis MacLeod, *Grasping the Thistle: How Scotland Must React to the Three Key Challenges of the Twenty First Century* (Argyll, 2006)

C. J. Sansom, *Dominion* (London, 2012)

The Scotland Institute, *Defence and Security in an Independent Scotland* (Glasgow, 2013)

Scottish Government, *An Oil Fund for Scotland: Taking Forward Our National Conversation* (Edinburgh, 2009)

Scottish Government, *Choosing Scotland's Future: A National Conversation* (Edinburgh, 2007)

Scottish Government, *Commission on the Future Delivery of Public Services* (Edinburgh, 2011)

Scottish Government, *Consumer Protection and Representation in an Independent Scotland: Options* (Edinburgh, 2013)

Scottish Government, *Devolving Corporation Tax in the Scotland Bill* (Edinburgh, 2011)

Scottish Government, *Europe and Foreign Affairs: Taking Forward Our National Conversation* (Edinburgh, 2009)

Scottish Government, *The Expert Working Group on Welfare* (Edinburgh, 2013)

Scottish Government, *Fiscal Commission Working Group First Report: Macroeconomic Framework* (Edinburgh, 2013)

Scottish Government, *Government Expenditure & Revenue Scotland 2011–2012* (Edinburgh, 2013)

Scottish Government, *Maximising the Return from Oil and Gas in an Independent Scotland* (Edinburgh, 2013)

Scottish Government, *Pensions in an Independent Scotland* (Edinburgh, 2013)

Scottish Government, *Scotland's Economy: The Case for Independence* (Edinburgh, 2013)

Scottish Government, *Scotland's Future: From the Referendum to Independence and a Written Constitution* (Edinburgh, 2013)

Scottish Government, *Sustainable Responsible Banking: A Strategy for Scotland* (Edinburgh, 2013)

Scottish Government, *Working with China: A Five Year Strategy for Engagement Between Scotland and the People's Republic of China* (Edinburgh, 2012)

Scottish Government, *Your Scotland, Your Voice: A National Conversation* (Edinburgh, 2009)

Scottish Labour Devolution Commission, *Powers for a Purpose – Strengthening Devolution: Interim Report* (Glasgow, 2013)

Scottish Liberal Democrats, *Federalism: The Best Future for Scotland* (Home Rule and Community Rule Commission report) (Edinburgh, 2012)

Scottish National Party, *The Parliament and Constitution of an Independent Scotland* (Edinburgh, 1997)

Scottish National Party, *Re-Elect: A Scottish Government Working for Scotland* (Edinburgh, 2011)

Scottish National Party, *Your Scotland, Your Future* (Edinburgh, 2011)

Donald Smith, *Freedom and Faith: A Scottish Question* (Edinburgh, forthcoming)

Graham Stewart, *Bang! A History of Britain in the 1980s* (London, 2013)

Joseph E. Stiglitz, *The Price of Inequality* (London, 2013)

Margaret Thatcher, *The Downing Street Years* (London, 1993)

David Torrance, *Salmond: Against the Odds* (Edinburgh, 2011)

I. Urwin and D. W. Budge, *Scottish Political Behaviour* (London, 1966)

Murray Watson, *Being English in Scotland* (Edinburgh, 2003)

Christopher A. Whatley, *The Scots and the Union: Then and Now* (Edinburgh, forthcoming)

Richard Wilkinson and Kate Pickett, *The Spirit Level: Why Equality is Better for Everyone* (London, 2010)

Gordon Wilson, *SNP: The Turbulent Years 1960–1990* (Stirling, 2009)

Richard Wyn Jones and Roger Scully, *Wales Says Yes: Devolution and the 2011 Welsh Referendum* (Cardiff, 2012)

Yes Scotland, *Yes to a Just Scotland: Response to the STUC's Interim Report* (Glasgow, 2013)

Robert A. Young, 'How Do Peaceful Secessions Happen?', *Canadian Journal of Political Science / Revue canadienne de science politique* vol. 27, no. 4 (December 1994)

Robert A. Young, 'The Political Economy of Secession: The Case of Quebec', *Constitutional Political Economy* vol. 5, no. 2 (1994)

Broadcasts

The Andrew Marr Show (BBC1), 29 January 2012

Beyond Westminster (BBC Radio 4), 4 June 2011

The Cause part 5 (BBC Radio Scotland), 22 October 2012

Frost All over the World (Al Jazeera), 18 February 2012

HARDtalk (BBC News Channel), 10 December 2012

Portillo on Salmond (BBC Scotland), 15 May 2011

Road to Referendum part 3 (STV), 18 June 2013

Scotland Tonight (STV), 30 January 2012

INDEX

Act of Union (1707) 38, 39, 40, 59, 65, 204, 221, 244, 311, 328
Act of Union (1801) 40, 64, 244, 311
Adams, Gerry 34
Albright, Madeleine 112
Alexander, Danny 14, 36, 98, 102, 183, 242, 287
Alexander, Douglas 26, 71, 191, 273, 300–301
Alexander, Wendy 11, 230
Allan, Dr Alasdair 207
And the Land Lay Still 198
Anderson, Bruce 306
Andrew, Hugh 200
Anglo-Irish Treaty 41, 64
Anne, Princess 315
Archer, Janet 196
Archers, The 200
Arguing for Independence 154
Ascherson, Neal 322
Ashcroft, Lord 151, 278
ASLEF 266
Attlee, Clement 170
Avery, Graham 133, 134

Bagehot, Walter 36, 67
Bailes, Alyson 142
Balls, Ed 161
Bank of England 46, 52, 79, 80, 96, 100, 101, 102, 104, 106, 263
Banks, Iain (M.) 198–9
Barley, Nick 290
Barnes, Eddie 289, 338
Barnett Formula 86, 169, 234, 304, 339
Barosso, José Manuel 131, 133–4, 137
BBC Scotland 212–16
'bedroom tax' 85, 158
Being English in Scotland 193
Bell, Alex 261–2

Bell, Ian 256, 325
Belloc, Hilaire 281
Benedetti, Nicola 108
Benedict, Pope 205
Benn, Tony 256
Better Together 27, 31, 80, 88, 108, 170, 175, 182, 210, 233, 251, 259, 260, 262–72, 298, 312, 324, 326, 329, 337
Bevan, Nye 169, 192, 331–2
Beveridge, Crawford 79
Beveridge, Sir William 169, 175
Billig, Michael 333
Blackley, Stan 254
Blair, Tony 73, 138, 150, 189, 208, 243
Blanchflower, David 102
Blick, Dr Andrew 49–50
Blue State Digital 282
Bogdanor, Vernon 65, 66, 248
Bond, James 180–81
Borgen 216
Bouchard, Lucien 187, 289, 338
Boyd, Stephen 81, 85, 106
Boyle, Alan 45–7, 49
Boyle, Danny 202
Braveheart 37
Break-Up of Britain: Crisis and Neo-Nationalism, The ix–x, 111, 178
Brennan, Tommy 252
British Academy 208
British–Irish Council 220, 241, 243, 340
British Library 62
Britons: Forging the Nation 1707–1837 180
Brown, Gordon 11, 162, 191, 230, 242, 267
Browne, Lord 149, 150
Burns, Robert 57, 197, 206
Burnside, John 199

Bush, President George W. 148
Business for Independence 258, 259

Cable, Vince 316
Caldwell, Jacqueline 255
Calman Commission 170, 221, 224, 237, 301
Calman, Sir Kenneth 272
Calman, Susan 272–3
Cameron, David 14, 23, 26, 60, 82–3, 94, 140, 168, 181, 192, 211, 227, 261, 269–70, 281, 287, 299, 302, 303, 304, 313, 317, 334, 336
  and Alex Salmond 1–6, 8, 20, 24, 28, 30, 216
  and more powers 15, 25–6
  and referendum announcement 18–19
  and speech in Edinburgh 25–6, 116, 178–80, 225
  Europe 125, 126, 127, 316
Campaign for an English Parliament 247
Campbell, Sir Menzies 227, 228
Canavan, Dennis 104, 239, 253, 259, 281
Candide 111
Capaldi, Peter 215
Cardiff University 208
Carlaw, Jackson 269
Carmichael, Alistair 228, 288
Carnegie, Andrew 114
Chamberlain, Joseph 326
Charles II, King 39
Child Poverty Action Group 158
Choosing Scotland's Future 42
Chrétien, Jean 187, 312
Christie Commission 172
Church of Scotland 204–5, 208
Claim of Right 61
Class, Nation and Socialism: The Red Paper on Scotland 2014 242
Clegg, Nick 14, 23, 36, 229
Clements, Alan 149
Clinton, President Bill 113, 186, 295
Cochrane, Alan 237
Colley, Linda 180
Collins, Michael 58
Common Travel Area 120, 133
Common Weal 238–40
Common Wealth Party 326
Commonwealth Games 289, 312

Community 266
Connery, Sir Sean 252
Connolly, Billy 201
Conservative Friends of the Union 266
Cook, Robin 115
Cooper, Yvette 303, 305
Cornish, Professor Paul 145
corporation tax 82–3
Cox, Brian 252
Crawford, Bruce xii–xiii, 28
Crawford, James 45–7, 48, 49
Crawford, Stuart 115
Crawford, Stuart (Army officer) 275
Creative Scotland 196–7
Crofting Commission 282
Cromwell, Oliver 39
Cumming, Alan 252
Cuomo, Mario 250
Curran, Margaret 257
currency 96–104
Curtice, Professor John 127, 182, 245–6, 278
Cuthbert, Jim 96, 132
Cuthbert, Margaret 96, 132

Dalyell, Tam 220, 234–5
Darling, Alistair 22–3, 24, 25, 80, 92, 100, 105, 116, 182, 192, 213, 232–3, 262–4, 265–6, 267, 268, 270, 274, 285, 287, 312
Davey, Ed 95–6
Davies, Norman 35, 36, 43, 58
Davies, Ron 229
Davidson, Ian 214
Davidson, Ruth 187, 225, 226, 233, 265, 304
Davison, David 174
Declaration of Arbroath 61
defence 138–53, 284, 314
devo-max 22, 24, 217–20, 340
devo-more 236–7, 341
devo-plus (or devo+) 15–16, 25, 235–6, 341
Dewar, Donald 11, 57–8, 220, 229, 230
Dimbleby, David 214
Disraeli, Benjamin 244–5
Ditchley Foundation 118
Dixon, Andrew 196
Doctor Who 215
Dominion 199
Dommett, Ian 255

Dowler, Milly 211
Downing Street Declaration 327
Dryden, John 10
Duncan Smith, Iain 158, 168
Dundee University 208
DVLA 63

EastEnders 213
Eden, Anthony 189
Edinburgh Agreement 1–8, 16, 28, 29,
    31, 227, 281, 288, 313, 327
Edinburgh, Duke of 33
Edward, Sir David 133
Edwards, Jonathan 240
Electoral Commission 4, 20, 30, 31,
    48–9, 275, 312–13
Elis-Thomas, Dafydd 241
Elizabeth II, Queen 33–4, 65, 66–7,
    303, 311, 315
Elliot, Alison 25
Elvidge, Sir John 100, 295
Emmott, Bill xii, 335
England and its Two Unions: The
    Anatomy of a Nation and its
    Discontents 248
English Constitution, The 36
European Union 46, 48, 54, 59, 123,
    124–38, 281, 313, 316, 317, 326
Ewing, Fergus 93
Ewing, Winnie 115, 335
Expert Working Group on Welfare
    156–9

Farage, Nigel 126, 214, 241, 242, 267,
    273
Farquharson, Kenny 164
Featherstone, Vicky 195–6
federalism 52, 225, 226, 227, 241–3,
    246, 340, 305–6
Federalism: the best future for Scotland
    227, 228
Federalist Papers, The 305
Ferguson, Sir Alex 201, 268, 285
Fergusson, Alex 25
Field, Frank 247
Financial Services Compensation
    Scheme 175
Finnie, John 147
First World War 290, 291
Fiscal Commission Working Group
    (FCWG) 70, 71–2, 78–80, 98, 99,
    100, 101, 103, 163, 173, 319

Fitzgerald, F. Scott 256
Five Million Questions 208
Forces Together 268
Forsyth, Lord 15, 26, 77
Foulkes, Lord 15, 234, 273
Fox, Colin 238, 252, 255
Fox, Liam 140
Franklin, Benjamin 251
Fraser, Douglas 59
Fraser, Murdo 225
Frost, Sir David 115, 185
Fry, Michael 259
Funding devo more: Fiscal options for
    strengthening the union 236–7
Future of Scotland 25, 27

Gall, Gregor 158, 331
Gallagher, Jim 242–3
Galloway, George 214
García-Margallo, José Manuel 123
Gay, Dan 76
Geoghegan, Peter 109, 328
George V, King 33, 41
Gethins, Stephen 135
Giddens, Anthony 73
Gieve, Sir John 106
Gillespie, Paul 118
Gladstone, W. E. 40–41, 226
Glover, Julian 26
Glyndŵr, Owain 37
Goldie, Annabel 225
Good Friday Agreement xi, 23, 31, 34,
    327, 340
Good Morning Scotland 215
Goodwin, Fred 104
Goudie, Andrew 75–6, 78, 88, 136
Gove, Michael 26, 291–2, 311, 320
Government Expenditure and Revenue
    Scotland (GERS) 86, 87, 88, 91
Government of Ireland Act (1920) 41,
    65
Government of Wales Act (2006) 55
Grasping the Thistle 73
Gray, Alasdair 195–6
Great Don't Know Show, The 196
Greenstock, Sir Jeremy 115
Greig, David 8, 193–4, 196
Grogan, Allan 258

Hague, William 96, 121, 122, 136
Hall, Tony 215
Hammond, Philip 140, 142, 150

Hardie, Keir 179
Harvie, Christopher 139, 204
Harvie, Patrick 253, 254, 328, 331
Hastings, Gavin 268
Have I Got News for You 273
HBOS 105
Healey, Denis 89, 148
Heath, Edward 57, 188, 224
Heffer, Simon 247
Hennessy, Peter 325
Henry VIII, King 39
Henry Jackson Society 142
Heseltine, Lord 244
Hobsbawm, Eric ix, x, 228
Hollande, François 261
Home, Lord 27
House of Lords 64, 305, 331, 341
Howell, Claire 255
Hoy, Sir Chris 6, 202–3, 272
Hunt, Jeremy 49
Hutcheon, Paul 57, 164, 256
Hyslop, Fiona 114, 187, 197, 216, 273

Ignatieff, Michael 338
Iolaire, HMS 291
Independence Declaration 59, 252,
    253–4
Ingram, Paul 142
Institute of Chartered Accountants of
    Scotland (ICAS) 174, 175
Irish Free State 36, 41, 50, 64, 295,
    317, 327
Irvine, Derry 246
Isle of Man 65, 99, 101, 203, 219, 282,
    313

Jack, Ian 139, 185
Jackson, Alvin 40
Jacobs, Jane 336, 337
James VI, King 37
Javid, Sajid 105
Jeffreys-Jomes, Rhodri 121
Jenkins, Blair 88, 165, 254, 268, 274,
    278, 279
Jimmy Reid Foundation 104, 240
John Paul, Pope 205
Johnson, Boris 202, 244, 257, 325
Johnson, Lyndon 294
Jones, Carwyn 98, 169, 241, 325
Jones, Peter 125–6, 129
Judt, Tony 74, 181
Julius, DeAnne 103

Kane, Pat 200, 255
Kay, John 68–9, 95, 97, 103, 109–10,
    133, 136, 220, 251, 281
Keating, Michael 74, 249, 334
Kellas, James 204
Kellner, Peter 280–81
Kelly, Michael 187, 234–5
Kelly, Tony 285
Kemp, Alex 89, 93, 94
Kennedy, Charles xiii, 264–5
Kerevan, George 52–3, 259
Kettle, Martin 221
Keynes, John Maynard 169
Kidd, Colin 38, 56, 72, 180
Kilmorey, Earl of 64
King, Charles 112
King, Lord 150–51
King, Sir Mervyn 102
Kukan, Eduard 123
Kvist, Jon 160

Labour for Independence 258
Lamont, Johann 25, 26, 100, 161, 172,
    230, 232, 257, 265, 274, 278, 299,
    302
de Lampedusa, Tomasi 54
Lane, Robert 68
Lang, Ian 86
Leahy, Sir Terry 244
Leask, David 113
Lee, Colonel Dorcha 144
Lenin ix
Lennox, Annie 200
Letwin, Oliver 247
Leveson Inquiry 211–12
Leveson, Lord Justice 36
Lincoln, Abraham 115
Livingstone, Ken 244
Lloyd George, David 169
Local Government Association 248
Lochhead, Liz 252
Lockhart, Mary 266
Logie Baird, John 213
London Finance Commission 244
Louis Stevenson, Robert 250

McAleese, Mary 34
McAllion, John 82
McAlpine, Joan 38–9, 210
MacAskill, Kenny 63, 193
McCluskey, Lord 212
McColl, Jim 108, 220

McConnell, Jack 116, 273
MacCormick, Sir Neil 59, 128, 184, 314, 336
McCrone, Dr Gavin 89, 91, 105, 169, 235, 237
MacDiarmid, Hugh 193
MacDonald, Ramsay 40
McDougall, Blair 265–6, 267, 270
McGrath, Harry 122
MacGregor, Ewan 200–201
MacGregor, Sir Neil 195
McGuinness, Martin 23
McGuire, Eddie 195
Machiavelli, Nicoló 250
McIlvanney, William 178, 199, 322–4, 342
Macintosh, Ken 88
Mackay, Major-General Andrew 145, 284
Mackay, Derek 147
MacKay, D. I. 71, 332
Mackay, Shena 195
McKay, Sir William 246–7
McKenna, Kevin 210
Mackintosh, John P. 180
McLaren, John 107
MacLean, Dougie 252
McLean, Iain 333, 336, 341
McLeish, Alex 268
McLeish, Henry 269
MacLennan, David 196
MacLeod, Dennis 73
McMillan, Alistair 333, 336, 341
Macmillan, Harold 169, 327
McNeil, Duncan 25
MacPherson, Sir Nicholas 70
Macwhirter, Iain 43, 73, 205, 216, 301
Mair of Haddington, John 38
Major, Sir John 34, 60, 219, 299
Mallon, Seamus 42
Mandelson, Peter 57, 84
Marois, Pauline 122
Marquand, David 339
Marr, Andrew 24, 34, 194, 209, 264
Marra, Jenny 298, 303, 305, 306–7, 320
Martin, Ciaran 16
Martin, David 128, 130
Marwick, Tricia 66
Marx, Karl 337
Mary Queen of Scots Got Her Head Chopped Off 252

Massie, Alex 57, 199
Massie, Allan 199
Mathews, Vice Admiral Andrew 143
Mathewson, Sir George 252
Matthew, H. C. G. 55
Maxwell, Stephen 154, 177, 244, 248
May, Theresa 120
media 208–16
al-Megrahi, Abdelbaset 112, 204, 284–5
Melding, David 217, 241, 242, 305–6, 340
Merkel, Angela 261
Miliband, David 267
Miliband, Ed 23, 161, 230, 247, 261, 299, 316
Miller, Maria 197
Mills, Sir Jonathan 290
Mitchell, Professor James 14, 51–2, 53, 275
Mone, Michelle 108
Montesquieu 50
Moore, Michael 5, 14, 15, 16, 18, 20, 21, 22, 30, 57, 62, 105, 137, 159, 235, 274
Morgan, Edwin 276
Morgan, Rhodri 241
Morrison, Herbert 53
Moving to Federalism: A New Settlement for Scotland 227
Moxham, Dave 266
Mullin, John 215
Mundell, David 15, 28, 120, 226, 233
Murdoch, Rupert 210–11
Murkens, Jo 54, 125–6, 129, 135
Murphy, Jim 265, 284
Murray, Andy 6, 28, 203
Murray, Craig 214

Nairn, Tom ix–xi, 111, 178, 208
National Collective 194–5
National Health Service (Scotland) Act (1947) 169
national identity 182–94
National Theatre of Scotland 195
National Union of Journalists 63
NATO 48, 52, 53, 54, 113, 116, 145–9, 314
Naughtie, James 22, 215
Neil, Alex 49, 156, 183, 271
Neil, Andrew 128
Nesbitt, Rab C. 253

newsnetscotland.com 209
Newsnight Scotland 214
No 268–9
Noon, Stephen 7, 21, 51, 90, 105, 108, 121, 140, 235, 243, 271–2, 275, 279–80, 292, 299, 307
Nor Shall My Sword: The Reinvention of England 247
North Sea oil 75, 79, 82, 88–94, 99, 228, 235, 308, 318, 335, 342
Nyborg, Birgitte 216

Obama, President Barack 113, 282
O'Brien, Cardinal Keith 165, 205–6
O'Brien, Phillips 141, 143, 144–5
O'Donnell, Sir Gus xiii, 74, 100–101
Omand, Sir David 121
Orkney 228–9
Osborne, George 14, 26, 98–9, 107, 271
Outlander 216

Parizeau, Jacques 122
Parti Québécois 54, 96, 122, 187, 337, 338, 339
Partnership for Peace 146
Patten, Lord xiii, 214, 215
Peerage Act (1963) 64
Pennington, Professor Hugh 207
Pension Protection Fund 175
pensions 171–6
Pensions Regulator 175
Pickett, Kate 163
Plaid Cymru 240, 248, 255, 326, 338, 306
Pocock, J. G. A. 335–6
Post Office 62
Powell, Enoch 256
Powers for a purpose – strengthening devolution 231–2
Price, Adam 240
Price of Inequality, The 163
Pringle, Kevin 190–91, 255
Progressive Unionist Party 267
Public Health England 62

Question Time 214
Quinn, Professor Brian 102
Qvortrup, Dr Matt 17, 110, 187

Radical Independence Conference/ Campaign 259, 273

Raich, Alan 194
Rankin, Ian 198
Reader, Eddi 200
Rebalancing Britain: policy or slogan 244
Rees-Mogg, Jacob 247
Reform Scotland 15, 235
Reformed Union: the UK as a Federation, The 242
Reith, Lord 213
Renan, Ernst 44, 334
Rennie, Willie 227
Revenue Scotland 84, 223–4
Riddoch, Lesley 191, 214
Rifkind, Sir Malcolm 148, 150
Road to Referendum 43, 212
Robertson, Angus 19, 117–18, 142, 143, 145, 146, 147, 148, 150, 151, 214
Robertson, George 58, 148, 183
Robertson, James 198, 199
Robinson, Nick 6
Robinson, Peter 23, 243–4
Robison, Shona 202
Rogue Nation 149
Roman Catholic Church in Scotland 205–6
Rose, Richard 37, 188, 333
Rowling, J. K. 199
Royal Bank of Scotland 72, 104, 105
Royal Commission on the Constitution 220, 327
Royal Mail 62
Royal Regiment of Scotland 141
Royal Society of Edinburgh 208
Rudd, Kevin 300
Runciman, David 230
Rural Better Together 268
Russell, Mike 73, 319
Russell, Sally 170

St Andrews University 207
Salmond, Alex 21–2, 23, 30, 41–2, 43, 58, 61, 81, 85, 108, 160, 172, 174, 195, 202, 203, 207, 210, 223, 229, 230, 238, 241, 244, 252, 253, 255, 259, 261, 262, 297, 301–2, 306, 311, 313, 317, 320, 324, 326, 331, 332, 335, 338
and David Cameron 1–6, 8, 20, 24, 26–7, 30, 116, 216, 227

Salmond, Alex *cont.*
  welfare 7, 159–61, 161–2, 164–5
  and 2011 election 8–9
  and referendum policy 9–10, 11–13, 31
  and definition of 'independence'/devo-max 13–14, 15–16, 28, 50–51, 53, 218, 220, 226–7, 243
  and the monarchy 34, 42–3, 54, 67
  civic nationalism 44
  economics 71–3, 75, 79, 83, 87, 89, 91–2, 104, 107
  renewables 94–5
  currency 96–104
  and the USA 111–14
  foreign affairs 117–19
  Europe 124–5, 126, 127–8, 129, 136, 138
  defence 138, 140
  NATO 145–6, 148, 149, 152
  national identity 182–3, 185–6, 188, 193, 197
  religion 204–5
  Rupert Murdoch 210–11
  media 210–12
  broadcasting 213, 214, 215, 216
  referendum campaign 255–8, 264, 268, 270, 271, 273, 274, 281, 288, 289, 291–2, 293–6
Salmond, Moira 147
Sansom, C. J. 199
Sansom, Laurie 196, 197
Sarwar, Anas 258, 266
Scheffer, Professor David 49
Scotland Act (1998) 11
Scotland Bill/Act (2012) 55, 221–4, 237, 271, 341
Scotland's Choices 88, 101, 170, 219
Scotland's Economy: the case for independence 84–5
Scotland's Future 168
Scotland Tonight 214
Scott, Tavish 25, 228, 229
Scott, Sir Walter 57, 197
Scottish Campaign on Welfare Reform 158
Scottish Centre for Social Research 278
Scottish Control of Scottish Affairs 57
Scottish Council for Voluntary Organisations 25
Scottish Development International 120

Scottish Football Association 204
Scottish Green Party 253
Scottish Home Rule Association 40
Scottish Independence Convention 260–61
Scottish Independence: Weighing Up the Economics 237
Scottish Office 55, 72, 325
Scottish Socialist Party 252
Scottish Trades Union Congress (STUC) 81, 82, 106, 162, 266
Sharma, Kamalesh 66
Shaw, Professor Keith 245
Shelley, Percy Bysshe 199
Shetland 228–9
Shorthouse, Rob 267
Signal and the Noise: The Art and Science of Prediction, The 277
Silk Commission 243, 304
Sillars, Jim 134, 204
Silver, Nate 277, 338–9
Sinclair, Paul 265
Singh Kohli, Hardeep 201
Sinn Fein 244
Skyfall 180–81
Smart, Ian 193
Smith, Adam 72–3, 179
Smith, Alyn 129, 130
Smith, Elaine C. 253, 256, 260
Smith, John 189, 205
Snow, Jon 165
Soames, Rupert 107–8
Somerville, Shirley-Anne 255
Sorel, Albert 50
Souter, Sir Brian 165
Spirit Level: Why Equality is Better for Everyone, The 163
Spiteri, Sharleen 200
Steel, Judy 258
Steel, Lord 65, 227, 258
Stewart, Graham 93
Stiglitz, Joseph 82, 103, 163, 164, 331
Strachan, Professor Hew 143–4, 153
Strathclyde, Lord 225–6, 274
Sturgeon, Nicola 5, 6, 19, 28–9, 30–31, 38, 49, 50, 66, 69, 70, 81, 85, 101–2, 108, 120–21, 129, 130–33, 134, 143, 154–6, 158, 159–60, 165, 169, 171, 184–5, 190, 192, 195, 201, 215–16, 217–18, 234, 239, 255–6, 260, 270, 273, 279, 285, 286, 294, 295, 297, 301, 303, 311, 315, 319, 320–21

Susman, Louis 113
Sustainable, Responsible Banking 106
Swinney, John 63, 79, 80, 81–2, 84, 87, 99, 102, 106, 108, 133, 141, 147, 172, 174, 182, 200, 218, 223, 244, 256, 271, 317–18

Taylor, Ian 276
Thatcher, Margaret 60, 136, 138, 168, 188, 224, 331, 334
Theory of Moral Sentiments, The 72
Thick of It, The 215
Tomkins, Adam 47
Toolis, Kevin 336
Top Gear 213
Trainspotting 200
Tranter, Nigel 185
Travers, Tony 244
Trench, Alan 236, 237
Trident 63, 139, 144, 145, 149–53, 219, 330, 331, 340, 297, 314
Trudeau, Pierre 341
Tusa, Francis 141

Union and Unionisms: Political Thought in Scotland 1500–2000 56
United Kingdom Independence Party (UKIP) 125, 126–7, 190–91, 214, 241, 274, 289, 292–3, 302–3, 338
United Nations 90, 114, 115, 142, 146
United with Labour 266, 267
Unstated: Writers on Scottish Independence 195
Urquhart, Jean 147
USDAW 266–7

de Valera, Eamon 295, 319
Vanished Kingdoms: The History of Half-Forgotten Europe 35
Vidal-Quadras, Alejo 123
de Vink, Peter 259
Visit Britain 62
Volker, Kurt 148
Voltaire 111

Walker, David 38
Walker, Professor William 149–50
Wallace of Tankerness, Lord 14, 17–18
Watson, Dave 266
Watson, Murray 193
Wealth of Nations, The 72
Webb, Steve 173

Weir, Christine 276
Weir, Colin 276
welfare 154–71, 263, 293, 297
Wellington, Sheena 200
Welsh, Irvine 199
West Lothian Question 246–7, 341
Whatley, Christopher 38
Whitelaw, Willie 328–9
Why Scots Should Rule Scotland 196
Wilkinson, Richard 163
Willetts, David 207
Williamson, Kevin 196
Wilson, Brian 43–4, 95, 184, 213, 319
Wilson, Gordon 124, 193, 235, 260
Wilson, Harold 89, 125, 328–9, 303–4, 316
wingsoverscotland.com 209
Winstone, Ray 273
Wishart, Pete 53, 67, 120, 182–3, 201, 247
Wishart, Ruth 212
Wolfe, Billy 205
Wood, Sir Ian 94
Wood, Leanne 240, 248
written constitution 47, 59–62
Wyn Jones, Richard 240

Yes Scotland 27, 31, 51, 63, 87, 88, 104, 108, 121, 164, 165–6, 171–2, 182, 200, 210, 235, 238, 239, 243, 251, 252–62, 263, 267–8, 269, 270–71, 272, 273, 274, 275, 278, 279, 280, 283, 286, 288, 292, 298, 299, 301, 312, 329, 330, 337
Yes to a Just Scotland 165–6
Young, Alf 58
Young, Professor Robert A. 72, 114–15, 217
Your Scotland, Your Future 156
Your Scotland, Your Referendum 335
Your Scotland, Your Voice 155–6, 219
Yousaf, Humza 117, 298, 307, 308–9

Zuleeg, Dr Fabian 137